Irish Americans
in the Confederate Army

Irish Americans in the Confederate Army

SEAN MICHAEL O'BRIEN

Foreword by
Kelly J. O'Grady

McFarland & Company, Inc., Publishers
Jefferson, North Carolina, and London

LIBRARY OF CONGRESS CATALOGUING-IN-PUBLICATION DATA

O'Brien, Sean Michael, 1944–
Irish Americans in the Confederate Army /
Sean Michael O'Brien ; foreword by Kelly J. O'Grady.
p.   cm.
Includes bibliographical references and index.

ISBN-13: 978-0-7864-2998-1
Illustrated case binding : 50# alkaline paper ∞

1. United States—History—Civil War, 1861–1865—Participation, Irish American.
2. Irish American soldiers—Confederate States of America—History.
3. Confederate States of America. Army—History.
4. United States—History—Civil War, 1861–1865—Campaigns.
5 Irish Americans—Southern States—History—19th century.
6. Immigrants—Southern States—History—19th century.
7. Irish Americans—Southern States—Social conditions—19th century.
I. Title.

E585.I75O27   2007   973.7'420899162—dc22   2007012669

British Library cataloguing data are available

On the cover: *Noble Band of Brothers*
by Rick Reeves, oldgloryprints.com

Manufactured in the United States of America

*McFarland & Company, Inc., Publishers
Box 611, Jefferson, North Carolina 28640
www.mcfarlandpub.com*

Contents

List of Maps

Foreword

Some aspects of history will never be fully understood. Sometimes the passage of time so distorts the true nature and meaning of events that no one, even with the best of intentions, can decipher the facts of the matter. Throw in the vagaries of human nature—self-delusion, bald-faced deception, or the love of myth and legend—and the best we can hope for is an understanding based on a consensus of academics and politicians. Consensus, which eventually becomes conventional wisdom, has been known to mold historical understanding to fit political whim, social acceptance or economic theory. Consensus can be unreliable; conventional wisdom sometimes is simply wrong.

A little more than ten years ago, a few scholars began to explore the topic of the Irish who fought for the Confederacy. Much of this work was met with disinterest or disdain. Those who pursued it were told they didn't have a good understanding of Ireland or Irish history—that all the "true" Irish fought for "freedom" and a place in American society as Federal soldiers. It was apostasy to write that the Irish fought for the South. There were no Irish in the American South, they said; or, if there were, how could an Irishman fight for slavery? (Here again, the conventional wisdom stepped in, with the usual assumptions about the cause of the war.) Did those soldiers in gray have Irish surnames? Well, perhaps they were not really Irish.

Nevertheless, the facts have disproved the nay-sayers. Numerous books, including my own, now recount what damn good Confederate rebels the Irish in the South made.

Now out of Alabama comes Sean Michael O'Brien with a workhorse of a book which will solidify the facts about the Irish in the Confederate armies. *Irish Americans in the Confederate Army* is a military book, with battle narratives, background and context. But it is so much more than battles and blood. To date it is the most comprehensive look at Irish leaders and units in the Confederate forces. O'Brien's workhorse compiles virtually all that is known about the topic of the Irish in southern forces and neatly packs its burden in one handy volume.

Perhaps best of all, O'Brien's writing is plain and simple—the simple truth—devoid of political slant and social cant. It is a fact-filled tome that guilelessly lays out the facts mined from a mountain of primary and secondary sources. O'Brien relentlessly chronicles the Irish in the war from Belmont to Bentonville, from the Army of Northern Virginia to the forces in the west, both Catholic and Protestant, famine and fortuitous, Irish lace and Irish lackey.

Along the way, O'Brien never misses an opportunity for background and biography. Indeed his command of biographical fact is the strongest part of the book. Even those with a passing interest in the war will find much use in his chapters on immigration, the character of the Irish soldier in the South, and the Irish on the southern home-front. More serious historians will covet this book for the hardy sheaf of reference material found in the appendices which catalogue Irish commands and leaders in the Confederate armies. Eighteen battle maps nicely complement the battle narratives.

Some aspects of history may never be fully understood, 'tis true. But with the publication of Sean Michael O'Brien's book, *Irish Americans in the Confederate Army*, readers can rest assured that the consensus on the Irish in our War of Rebellion will reflect the truth on the subject.

Kelly O'Grady
King George, Virginia

Kelly J. O'Grady has worked as an educator and as a National Park Service historian at Fredericksburg and Spotsylvania National Military Park. He is the author of the groundbreaking study Clear the Confederate Way! The Irish in the Army of Northern Virginia.

Preface

In her exceptional study of immigrants in the Confederate military, *Foreigners in the Confederacy*, historian Ella Lonn cited a Rebel general who, when asked to reflect on the soldiers he regarded the most, replied in this way:

> If tomorrow I wanted to win a reputation, I would have Irish soldiers in preference to any other; and I'll tell you why. First, they have more dash, more *élan* than any other troops that I know of; then they are more cheerful and enduring—nothing can depress them. Next, they are more cleanly. The Irishman never failed to wash himself and his clothes. Not only were they cheerful, but they were submissive to discipline when once broken in—and where they had good officers that was easily done; but once they had confidence in their officers their attachment to them was unbounded. And confidence was established the moment they saw their general in the fight with them.... I repeat, if I had to take from one to 10,000 men to make a reputation with, I'd take the same men as I had in the war—Irishmen from the city, the levees, the river, the railroads, the canals, or from ditching and fencing on the plantations. They make the finest soldiers that ever shouldered a musket.[1]

And another old story of post–Civil War America recounts the meeting of two Irish veterans, one who fought for the Union and one who fought for the Confederacy. Swapping old war stories, the two veterans speculate on why the North won the war. "The only reason the North won," the Rebel Irishman growls, "is they had more of us fightin' on their side."

These two anecdotes illustrate the legendary fighting reputation of the Irish. They also allude to the important contribution that the Irish made to the manpower of both sides in the American Civil War. Of the thousands of recently-arrived immigrants to America who served with distinction in the Civil War, no group gave more in courage and tenacity than the Irish. But while the Army of the Potomac's famous Irish Brigade has achieved near legendary status in the historiography of the war, the contributions of the thousands of Irish who fought in the Confederate Army have been largely ignored.

At least 40,000 Irish soldiers served in the Confederate armies. Although the South's Irish population was much smaller than the North's, Irish Confederate soldiers played a major part in the fighting, far disproportionate to their numbers. They served in every major Confederate army and in every major military theater of the war, and the combat death rate among Irish Confederate units was consistently among the highest in the Rebel army.[2]

A thoughtful addressing of the Irish contribution to the Confederate war effort is long overdue. Recent scholars have shown the way. Kelly O'Grady in *Clear the Confederate Way!: The Irish in the Army of Northern Virginia* (2000) chronicles the story of the Irish in the Confederacy's foremost army in the East. Ed Gleeson's *Rebel Sons of Erin: A Civil War Unit History of the Tenth Tennessee Infantry Regiment (Irish) Confederate States Volunteers* (1993) recounts the history of one regiment of Irishmen in the Army of Tennessee. Terry L. Jones in *Lee's Tigers: The Louisiana Infantry in the Army of Northern Virginia* (1987) throws the spotlight on the Irish composition of many Louisiana commands. Phillip Thomas Tucker in *Westerners in Gray: The Men and Missions of the Elite Fifth Missouri Infantry Regiment* (1995) sheds new light on the forgotten Irish immigrants who served in one of the South's best combat units from west of the Mississippi. The career of the most outstanding Irish Confederate officer, Patrick R. Cleburne, has been studied in *A Meteor Shining Brightly: Essays on the Life and Career of Major General Patrick R. Cleburne* (2000), edited by Mauriel Phillips Joslyn. The purpose of this study is to recognize the vital input that the Irish gave to the South's military struggle and to present the first comprehensive history of the Irish in the Confederate army.

It is appropriate to reflect on why the Irish came to the South, how they assimilated into Southern society, and why they chose to fight for the Confederacy. In the South, the Irish made their homes in seaports like Charleston, New Orleans, Savannah, and Mobile; in river towns like Memphis, Nashville, and St. Louis; and in rail and industrial centers like Atlanta, Richmond, and Montgomery. They tended to settle in the poorest sections of these cities. No account of the Irish in the Civil War would be complete without mention of the communities that the Irish immigrants carved out for themselves—vibrant, growing neighborhoods that today are largely swallowed up by the urban metropolis.

One cannot consider Irish Confederate soldiers as standing alone. There were wives and children, fathers and mothers, who remained at home. They too played a role in supporting the war and in sustaining their loved ones on the battlefield. Another staunch backer of the Rebel war effort was the Catholic Church in the South, an institution that represented an important factor in mobilizing and maintaining Irish willingness to fight.

Part I of the following study considers these factors, provides an overview of Irish Americans in the South and their experience as immigrants, examines the character of the Irish Confederate soldier and the community he came from, and explains how Irish families, neighborhoods, and the Catholic Church in the South supported the war. Subsequent parts look at how the Irish Confederates performed on the battlefield and cover their contributions to Confederate armies in four major combat theaters: Part II follows the participation of Irish-American units in the Army of Northern Virginia. Part III similarly considers the role of the Irish in the Army of Tennessee. Parts IV and V highlight the contributions of Irish Confederates to the campaigns waged on the Atlantic and Gulf Coasts, the Mississippi, and in the Trans-Mississippi.

I have chosen not to make a firm distinction regarding the religious affinity or economic status of Irish Confederates. Irish Catholics formed the bulk of many distinctly Irish companies, but there were also Irish Presbyterians (or Scotch-Irish) who dominated other units. There were many second or third generation Irish-Americans whose families had long since assimilated into the South's culture. Whatever their origins or religious affiliation, their heritage was Irish. In their new homeland, they hailed from busy seaports, from small farms in the interior, and from the isolated mountains of Appalachia. While enlisted ranks were filled with laborers or poor farmers, officers generally were planters, professionals, or merchants. This was typical of the Confederate army as a whole. All fought for the Confederacy for their own individual reasons.

My focus is on the military actions in which Irish-American Confederate soldiers were present in significant numbers or influenced their course or outcome. A few events are included because key commanders were Irish Americans. It will be seen that Irish-American Southerners played a significant role in nearly every major battle and campaign of the war.

Three resources that have proved invaluable in this study are U. S. census records, the surviving muster rolls of Confederate military companies, and the battle reports in the massive *War of the Rebellion* series. Census records help to identify Irish communities (many of which no longer exist) in Southern cities, and they often are the only clue that we have to learning more about individual Irish-American soldiers and their families. An examination of the Confederate muster rolls often reveals the now-forgotten Gaelic presence in many Confederate commands. One readily discovers that many Confederate companies that did not identify themselves by familiar Celtic names (such as Emerald Guards or Irish Volunteers) nevertheless had substantial numbers of soldiers with Irish surnames. I have cited extensively from the *War of the Rebellion*, and as will be seen, this very useful reference is fairly peppered with references to Irish Confederates and their units.

Prologue: Celtic War Cry

The exhilarating spring of 1861—when young men from the North and the South marched enthusiastically off to what they expected would be a short and glorious war—witnessed thousands of willing recruits joining up to fight for their country. Some of the most eager volunteers came from the ranks of America's most recent immigrants, young men who wanted to demonstrate their loyalty to their new homeland. In the fledgling Confederacy, by far the largest bulk of this immigrant military manpower came from the Emerald Isle.

As the conflict's first major clash began to take shape along an obscure stream called Bull Run, twenty miles south of the city of Washington, a Rebel infantry brigade guarded an important crossing at Blackburn's Ford. On July 18, when leading elements of the blue-coated Federal army began probing the Rebel defenses there, soldiers from Colonel Patrick T. Moore's 1st Virginia Infantry Regiment quickly deployed for battle. Moore raised his sword and bellowed a distinctive command: *"Faugh a ballagh* and charge!"[1]

Two hours of skirmishing followed in which Moore fell victim to a serious head wound—never to fight again. Finally, the bluecoats—discouraged by the surprisingly stiff Confederate resistance—withdrew, and the Rebels secured the ford. The 1st Virginia's stubborn defense dealt a psychological blow to the enemy and helped set the stage for the Confederate victory at Bull Run (or Manassas) three days later on July 21. The regiment lost 13 men killed and 27 wounded in the clash at Blackburn's Ford, with a disproportionate number of casualties borne by Moore's old company from Richmond, the Montgomery Guard.[2]

As an Irish immigrant, when Moore uttered the Gaelic war cry, *"Faugh a ballagh (Clear the Way!),"* he was drawing on a centuries-old

BRIGADIER GENERAL PATRICK T. MOORE. An Irish immigrant and prominent merchant, Moore helped make Richmond's Montgomery Guard a reliable volunteer militia company. He led the 1st Virginia Infantry at First Manassas, where he encouraged his soldiers with the Gaelic war cry—"Faugh a Ballagh!" (National Archives)

warlike tradition from his native homeland. He was also manifesting a heartfelt pride in military service to his adopted nation. Moore's old company, the Montgomery Guard, had been a fixture among Richmond's Irish community for over a decade.

Richmond's Irish first settled in the low-lying Shockoe Creek section of the city, where many immigrants found work in tobacco warehouses and flour mills. Slaughterhouses and tanneries sprang up in Butchertown, a rough district where gangs of immigrant boys vied for territorial dominance with boys from the more prosperous Shockoe Hill. The Kanawah Canal that connected Richmond with Lynchburg in the western part of the state also attracted Irish workers. The massive Tredegar Iron Works, the largest industrial facility in the South and future arsenal for the Confederacy, also employed many Irish who made their homes in the nearby Oregon Hill neighborhood.

As in most large Southern antebellum cities, the Irish in Richmond formed a volunteer militia company, the Montgomery Guard, named for Irish-born General Richard Montgomery who died in the December 1775 American assault on Quebec during the Revolutionary War. The company became a familiar sight to Richmond citizens who came out to watch the Irish drill in their green uniforms and distinctive black dress hats with white feathers tipped green, carrying their company flag—the "stars and stripes, the first in a ground work of green surrounding the harp of Erin." Some of the early members of the Montgomery Guard were veterans of the British army who had already seen combat in the Crimean War in Russia. As captain of the Montgomeries, County Galway native (and now prominent Richmond merchant) Patrick Moore forged it into one of the most dependable companies in the pre-war 1st Virginia Infantry Regiment. Throughout the decade of the 1850s, as interest waned in other companies in the regiment, the Montgomery Guard remained active.[3]

As the secession crisis deepened, the Montgomery Guard in Richmond became ever more involved with the military preparations for war. The company was deployed to Harpers Ferry and Charlestown following abolitionist John Brown's raid in October 1859. Well-to-do Richmond businessman John Dooley, a 49-year-old immigrant from Limerick, served as captain of the company at the outbreak of the war—and would also play a conspicuous role in the Blackburn's Ford skirmish. Dooley and his wife Sarah had carved out a good life for themselves in Richmond, raising nine children, building up a prosperous business in hats and furs, and becoming eminent figures in the city's social elite.

Men like Patrick Moore, John Dooley, and other Irish immigrants saw the Civil War in America as an opportunity to give something back to their new homeland. They viewed the North-South conflict through the prism of both Ireland's experience of struggle for independence from England and America's successful Revolutionary War against the same European power.

The Irish represented the largest immigrant group in the antebellum South. Ireland's disastrous Potato Famine of the 1840s produced a wave of emigration that terminated in Southern seaports like New Orleans, Charleston, Mobile, and Savannah. There the Irish immigrants toiled to make a living. Often they did the most menial types of labor, building canals and railroads, doing the work considered too dangerous for slaves to do. But they struggled to assimilate into American society, sometimes facing violent anti-foreign opposition that peaked in the nativist "Know Nothing" political movement of the 1850s.

Although they had little in common with the South's planter aristocracy, the Irish were among the Confederacy's most enthusiastic supporters. Many of them saw the South's war for independence from the industrial North as a parallel to agrarian Ireland's long and painful struggle for freedom from industrial, imperialistic England. They viewed the prospect of slave emancipation with hostility, because free blacks represented keen competition in the scarce job market. One can argue that Southern Irishmen were actually more dedicated to their ideology than their Northern Irish brethren, many of whom were recruited into the Union army as they arrived off the immigrant ships with little notion of why they were fighting.

The Irish became some of King Cotton's most loyal and stubborn foot soldiers, taking an aggressive part in the bloodiest battles of the Civil War. In these engagements, the Irish were generally in the thick of the fighting. Irish officers also served in outstanding leadership positions. One of only two foreign-born officers to attain the rank of major general in the Confederate Army, County Cork's Patrick Ronayne Cleburne has been called the "Stonewall Jackson of the West." Historians generally regard his division as the shock troops of the Army of Tennessee, often present in the most decisive phases of battles.

In the Army of Northern Virginia, green flag companies—like Company K, 1st South Carolina Infantry (the Irish Volunteers from Charleston) and Company I, 8th Alabama (the Emerald Guards from Mobile)—often guarded the regimental colors. In the Army of Tennessee, Irish companies frequently were called upon to serve as skirmishers, doing hazardous duty as the advance element of the army. The 15th Arkansas's Company D (Napoleon Grays), 5th Missouri's Company F (the "Fighting Irish Company"), and Nashville's 10th Tennessee Infantry ("Sons of Erin") all performed this perilous duty on many occasions.[4]

Historian Kelly O'Grady identifies more than forty-five distinctive Irish companies in the Army of Northern Virginia. At least that many more can be found in the Army of Tennessee, where two regiments (the 10th Tennessee from Nashville and the 5th Confederate Infantry from Memphis) both were described as Irish commands. While there was never a distinctive Irish Brigade, as in the Federal army, there were two Louisiana brigades (with many Irishmen from New Orleans) in the Army of Northern Virginia and at least one in the Army of Tennessee that came close. Many individual Irishmen did not serve in distinctive Irish companies at all, but were scattered throughout the armies of the South. Even in the last diehard strongholds of Confederate arms on the Atlantic and Gulf coasts and in the Trans-Mississippi theater of the war, the Irish soldier may be found.[5]

PART I. THE IRISH EXPERIENCE IN THE SOUTH

1. The New Country: Irish Immigrants in the South

Eighteenth and nineteenth century Ireland offered only the bleakest chance for her children to better themselves. Beset by poverty and poor employment prospects, these sons and daughters of the Emerald Isle brought to America a heritage of oppression and rebellion.

In the eighteenth century, Northern Ireland (or Ulster) folk—Irish Presbyterians whose Scottish forebears were forcibly re-settled by the English in Northern Ireland—immigrated to the American colonies for religious freedom. The Anglican upper class in eighteenth-century Ireland's parliament discriminated against them—and also against Irish Catholics. Ulster Presbyterians came to America for economic opportunity as well. These middle class farmers and artisans settled much of the Southern Appalachian region. We know them today as the "Scotch-Irish"—a term that did not come into vogue until the late nineteenth and early twentieth centuries, when this early wave of "Old Irish" sought to distinguish themselves from Irish Catholic immigrants, the "New Irish." The early immigrants themselves simply described themselves as "Irish."[1]

Irish Catholics also sank roots in the American colonies in the eighteenth century, often for the same reasons as Irish Presbyterians. But many Irish Catholics were poorer and came as indentured servants. A good many wore the red coats of soldiers in Britain's army stationed in the colonies, and some even came as convicts. They often chose to migrate farther west and settle in the more isolated Appalachians, where they usually shed their Catholic faith and blended into the Ulster Presbyterian settlements.[2]

But it was in the nineteenth century that Irish Catholics flocked in large numbers to the American republic, and they came in two distinct waves—the first in the period 1815–1845, when a million Irishmen came seeking employment opportunities in canal and railroad building projects, the second in the years 1845–1854, when the Great Famine deposited close to a million and a half more. The cataclysmic potato blight that afflicted Ireland brought partial crop failure in 1845, complete failure in 1846 and 1848. Ireland, one observer wrote, is "from sea to sea one mass of unvaried rottenness and decay." Starvation claimed about as many souls as the fortunate ones who sought refuge in America, bringing with them a hatred of England and hoping as they sailed across the Atlantic in their "famine ships" that they might find a better life here.[3]

In the pre-war South, the Irish population jumped by more than 55 percent between 1850 and 1860, with dramatic increases of over 100 percent in Arkansas, Mississippi, and

IRISH EMIGRANTS LEAVING FOR AMERICA. In the mid-nineteenth century, economic hardships and political repression forced thousands of Irish to emigrate to America. The path to a better life led many of them to Southern cities. (Library of Congress)

Texas, and nearly a 400 percent increase in Tennessee. Memphis' Irish community rose from 704 people in 1850 to 4,159 in 1860, an increase of nearly 500 percent. New Orleans by 1850 ranked second only to New York City as the main entrepot for foreign immigrants. Irish immigration came at the precise time when America's early industrial revolution cried out for a laboring class. The tough pick-and-shovel work for the nation's canals and railroads was provided by Irish immigrants.[4]

The early nineteenth century was the great age of canal building in America, and Irish immigrants furnished the labor. In coastal Georgia, the Brunswick and Altamaha Canal project, begun in 1830 with slave labor and state funds, began to falter by 1834 and the state bailed out. A Boston-backed company took over the job and introduced Irish work gangs with experience in canal-building projects (like the famous Erie Canal) in the Northeast. The company finally went bankrupt in 1839. But the canal brought many Irish Catholic immigrants to Georgia, and many gravitated to Savannah, which became a depot for Irish labor in the 1840s, along the lines of Boston and New York City.[5]

New Orleans' New Basin Canal project, designed to provide a shorter channel from the Mississippi River to Lake Pontchartrain, employed thousands of Irish workers. When the job was finished in 1836, most of the Irish remained in New Orleans to find work on other projects. Like Savannah, the city became a sort of labor pool for other jobs, such as digging ditches in the nearby "sugar parishes." Many immigrants found more stable jobs in the city or on the busy wharves as stevedores, screwmen, or draymen, hauling goods from the docks to storehouses and businesses in the city.[6]

Skilled jobs brought higher wages, but the work was often dangerous. Screwmen wielded large "jackscrews" to squeeze heavy cotton bales into the smallest package, so as to fit as many as possible into a ship's hold. It was a hazardous job, in close quarters. Southern planters often hired Irish immigrants to do work considered too dangerous for slaves to do. Irish laborers were far more expendable than slaves and their lives considered cheaper.[7]

By the 1850s, the South was actually constructing railroads at a rapid rate, although lagging far behind the Northern states. For the work, railroad companies hired gangs of Irish rail hands who generally lived together in tent settlements in groups of six or more. The work was hot and rough, but they made twice the average wage of rail hands in the Northern states. Drinking was a problem, as was fighting due to rivalries among the various Irish rail gangs from different counties in the old country. The Central of Georgia from Savannah to Macon drew heavily on Irish labor, as did the Western and Atlantic that linked Chattanooga and Atlanta. Thousands of Irish immigrants were finding steady work on the new Pacific Railroad project in St. Louis, on the Opelousas Railroad in Louisiana, and on the Mobile and Ohio Railroad.[8]

Most of the Irish railroad workers settled in urban areas, although their work sometimes brought them into areas farther inland. Promoters conceived the Ocmulgee and Flint Railroad in Georgia as a means to create an inland shipping route connecting the Atlantic with the Gulf of Mexico. And, since the seventy-six miles of rail from Mobley's Bluff on the Ocmulgee to the future site of Albany on the Flint was to be built with Irish labor, the Irish were expected to settle and create a Catholic colony in south Georgia. These high hopes were dashed when the company ran low on funds and fell behind schedule. In September 1843, the rail hands—angered at not being paid—armed themselves and were on the verge of storming the company headquarters when a local militia company arrived to rescue the manager. The project never recovered; but many of the Irish workers chose to stay and make a home in their settlement of Loyola in present-day Irwin County, Georgia.[9]

Considering the propensity of the Irish laborers for drinking and fighting, employers frequently found them to be a troublesome, quarrelsome lot. Irish laborers were far from passive. In Memphis in 1844, they held a strike demanding a ten-hour work day and in 1853 won a twenty-five cent per day pay increase. The Irish organized the first labor union in New Orleans, the Screwman's Benevolent Organization.[10]

Although the majority of Irish immigrants were unskilled laborers like those who built the canals and railroads—such workers made up 57.3 percent of Irish workers in Savannah in 1860 (61.8 percent of whom were laborers and 24 percent female domestic servants)—it would be a mistake to overlook the Irish immigrant professional and middle class. Irish wit and entrepreneurship accounted for numbers of small shops, groceries, hotels, boardinghouses, and taverns in Southern cities. In 1860 there were 114 Irish white collar workers in Savannah (almost half of whom were clerks), 196 petty proprietors (including 59 grocers and 74 boardinghouse managers), and 39 merchants, hotel managers, or small business owners.[11]

Irish women found work as domestic servants, seamstresses, dressmakers, teachers, and boardinghouse managers. In 1860 Savannah, women made up 28.8 percent of Irish semiskilled workers and 37.4 percent of skilled Irish workers. In St. Louis, many Irish domestic servants attended early Sunday morning Mass at 5 a.m. so that they could return to their employers' homes in time to serve them breakfast.[12]

Irish immigrant professionals left their marks on many Southern communities. Teacher Eugene Magevney settled in Memphis, where he operated a fine private school and later helped found the city's public school system. In New Orleans many Irish residents, including some women, operated private academies and seminaries. One out of five attorneys in the Crescent City in 1855 was Irish, like Samuel O'Callaghan, whose criminal law practice was largely supported by the activities of Irish roughs who constantly got in trouble with the law. Savannah's twenty-one Irish professionals in 1860 included a druggist, an attorney, a physician, two teachers, two priests, and twelve nuns.[13]

Journalism provided a fertile field for Irish intellectuals. Hugh Kennedy was publisher and John McGinnis editor of New Orleans' *True Delta*. Irish native J. C. Prendergast published the *Orleanian*, in English and French. Charles Cassidy, who ran a gambling establishment in the Crescent City, wrote horse racing pieces for the New York sports magazine *Spirit of the Times*. Edward Carroll was part owner and associate editor of Memphis' first daily newspaper, the *Memphis Daily Eagle*. Irish expatriate John Mitchel wrote powerful editorials for the *Richmond Daily Enquirer*.[14]

The steady lure of public service also beckoned. Charleston and New Orleans had heavily Irish police departments. By 1860, the police force and most of volunteer fire companies in Savannah were also largely Irish. Irish immigrant Stephen O'Leary was appointed police chief of New Orleans, and James McDonough became police chief in St. Louis.[15]

Some Irishmen became very prosperous in America. Industrious entrepreneurs like Natchez bridge builder Patrick Murphy, New Orleans carpenter James Keating, and "boss drayman" Thomas Dunne accumulated property and in some cases slaves. Tipperary native Maunsel White made his fortune in New Orleans, serving as a captain of volunteers in the War of 1812, later becoming a commission merchant and plantation owner, and finally as one of the Crescent City's "Big Five" of wealthy Irishmen. In Richmond, Limerick native John Dooley owned a profitable hat factory. Saddle-maker and County Sligo native Michael Burns became a prominent leader in Nashville's business community, served on the board of directors for two banks and two railroads, and was elected to the state legislature.[16]

The vast majority of Irish immigrants were country tenant farmers who generally disdained city life. But the isolation of Southern farms and plantations didn't agree with them, and they preferred nearness to friends and family. It was in the Irish nature to create close-knit neighborhoods in American cities. In the South, there were large Irish communities in the seaports of Charleston, Savannah, Mobile, New Orleans, Wilmington, and Galveston. River towns along the Mississippi and Ohio—Natchez, Vicksburg, Helena, Memphis, St. Louis, and Louisville—also saw enclaves of Irish, as did the developing Southern capitals at Richmond, Columbia, Montgomery, Jackson, and Nashville.

Cosmopolitan New Orleans, the third largest city in the United States, attracted the greatest number of Irish immigrants in the Deep South, even before the Great Famine. There were 24,398 Irish living in the Crescent City in 1860, making up a fourth of the city's population. Memphis had the next biggest Irish community (with 4,159), followed by Mobile, Charleston, Savannah, and Louisville (each with over 3,000), and Richmond (with 2,294).[17]

Where the immigrant Irish settled, they usually found themselves in the very worst sections of Southern cities: in Savannah, the Yamacraw district near the railroad depot west of the city; in Memphis, the "Pinch;" in Nashville, "Black Bottom;" in Natchez,

NEW ORLEANS AS SEEN FROM ST. PATRICK'S CHURCH, 1852. More than 24,000 Irish, a quarter of the city's population, called the Crescent City home at the outbreak of the Civil War. (Library of Congress)

the "Under-the-Hill" section; in St. Louis, the shantytown known as "Kerry Patch;" in New Orleans, the slums near the wharves in the city's third district, known as the "Poor Third." Although they had different names, they suffered from a sameness: horrendous housing conditions, unsafe drinking water, sewage in the streets, infestations of rats and fleas, cholera, rampant crime and prostitution, and alcoholism. They were the first American ghettos.

The unhealthy, marshy locations of many Irish neighborhoods made them magnets for disease. The yellow fever epidemic of 1853 killed one out of every five Irish immigrants in New Orleans and then spread to Natchez, Vicksburg, Memphis, and other towns up the Mississippi. Another outbreak of the "yellow jack" took the lives of hundreds of immigrants in Savannah in 1854, one of the victims Irish-born Bishop Francis X. Gartland.[18]

Cholera claimed six thousand deaths in New Orleans in 1832, a large percentage of them Irish. Irish canal diggers immortalized the disaster in a song:

> Ten thousand Micks, they swung their picks,
> To dig the New Canal.
> But the choleray was stronger 'n they.
> An' twice it killed them awl.[19]

Despite the difficult circumstances of their new lives, many immigrants wrote glowing letters to their family members back home encouraging them to make the passage to America. They often put aside their hard-earned money for ship fare; in the period between 1848 and 1861, they were able to send some sixty million dollars in bank drafts and money orders home. The encouragement of immigrant family members, friends, or neighbors often resulted in cluster migration, with the Irish settling in the same communities in America where those tied by neighborhoods or kin had preceded them. In 1860 Savannah, most of the Irish were from six of the thirty-two Irish counties. In any event, there was little to offer the Irish but hope. "In post–Famine years," historian Lawrence J. McCaffrey observes, "Irish parents raised most of their children for export."[20]

Besides family and friends, the Irish Church served a paramount role as a community mainstay and leant comfort and support to Irish immigrants. Irish priests labored tirelessly to meet the needs of their flocks, materially as well as spiritually. They built schools and orphanages, stood up to those who sought to intimidate the immigrants, and helped create bridges to the native communities in Southern cities. Men like Father James Ignatius Mullon, who pastored St. Patrick's Church in New Orleans, Father John B. Duffy of nearby St. Alphonsus in Lafayette, Father Jeremiah O'Neill in Savannah, and many others worked as liaisons between Irish immigrants and the local communities, recruited workers for construction projects, acted as mediators in labor disputes, and tried to keep the unruly Irish laborers relatively law abiding. Father James Graham, the young Irish priest assigned to the Ocmulgee and Flint Railroad project, literally worked himself sick and into an early grave from the demands of traveling to the wilderness camps in harsh conditions, in a valiant effort to tend to the rail hands' spiritual needs. The Sisters of Charity in New Orleans and the Sisters of Mercy in Savannah staffed schools and orphanages for Catholic children.

To be sure, not all of the Irish lived in slums. Early Irish immigrants in New Orleans lived "uptown" in the "American section" (or Second Municipality) in a neighborhood known as Irish Channel (a term later used to embrace the entire Irish community of New Orleans). Residents here tended to be more middle class and more stable. The older French Quarter (First Municipality) also contained smaller concentrations of wealthier Old Irish. It was in the city's third ward (the "Poor Third") that the bulk of the famine immigrants lived.

But it was the middle class "lace curtain Irish" living near St. Patrick's Church in the Second Municipality who became the social elite of New Orleans' Irish community. Middle class Irish organized New Orleans' Hibernian Society and sponsored charitable organizations like the Shamrock Benevolent Society and St. Joseph's Charitable Society, groups that did their best both to help and to Americanize the immigrants. This pattern was followed in Savannah, Charleston, St. Louis, and other cities.[21]

The middle class Irish also took the lead in forming volunteer militia companies in Southern cities. Such companies performed regular drills, competed in marksmanship contests, sponsored dances and banquets, and held other social affairs. They paraded on specific occasions: the anniversary of Andrew Jackson's victory at New Orleans (January 8), Washington's birthday (February 22), St. Patrick's Day (March 17), May Day (May 1), and Independence Day (July 4). While they drew many members from the poorer working class of recent immigrants, many of its officers were young sons from the Irish middle and professional classes.

Military companies fostered Irish pride as well as American patriotism. The Irish were fond of green uniforms and made liberal use of Irish symbols like the harp and shamrock. As to the names of the companies, "Emerald Guards" was a favorite, as was the ubiquitous "Irish Volunteers." Members often named their companies after Irish national heroes like Daniel O'Connell, Patrick Sarsfield, Robert Emmet, and Thomas F. Meagher, as well as Andrew Jackson, who they considered the first Irish-American president.

In bigger cities, the Irish frequently organized several ethnic companies. New Orleans' Emmet Guards, formed in 1850, drew its membership from the First Municipality with many of its officers being prominent Irish politicians. The company wore bright green coats and sky blue pants with gold stripes, their headgear topped with green plumes. The Montgomery Guards (organized in 1854)—decked out in their expensive blue jackets, pants, and dress cap, trimmed with yellow—attracted prosperous young Irishmen of the city.[22]

In Mobile, Captain Theodore O'Hara organized the Alabama Light Dragoons, outfitted in a flashy uniform with a white-plumed helmet. A veteran of the Mexican War and editor-in-chief of the *Mobile Register*, O'Hara became the celebrated author of the poem "Bivouac of the Dead." O'Hara later served as a staff officer in the Confederate army and was with Albert Sidney Johnston when he died on the battlefield at Shiloh. Also an officer in the Dragoons was Irish native James Hagan, destined to become an outstanding cavalry officer.[23]

Nearly every large city had at least one Irish volunteer militia company—Savannah's Irish Jasper Greens (formed in 1842), Charleston's Irish Volunteers (dating back before 1822), Memphis' Jackson Greens, Columbia's Emmet Guards (formed in 1854), Louisville's Jackson Guards—or if not a predominant Irish unit, one in which a significant number of Irish were members. Many Mobile Irish enlisted in the Alabama State

IRELAND'S HISTORICAL EMBLEMS. The Irish in America cherished traditional symbols that reminded them of the Emerald Isle. Gaelic slogans, the shamrock, and the harp were liberally employed in the green flags of Irish Confederate military companies. (Library of Congress)

Artillery Company (formed in 1836), an outfit that would see action at Shiloh. In Jackson, quite a few Irish joined the green-coated Mississippi Rifles, formed from a local fire company in 1858; this unit escorted Jefferson Davis through Jackson on the way to his inauguration as Confederate president in Montgomery, carrying the flag of Davis' old Mississippi Rifles Regiment of the Mexican War. One can spot a number of Irish names in South Carolina's elite Columbia Flying Artillery, formed in 1854.

Besides the duty of defending America in the event of war, volunteer militia companies performed three important functions in Southern cities: to assume police duties if needed (especially in the dreaded event of a slave uprising), to serve on patriotic occasions, and to provide a social outlet for the members. The opportunity to serve in these companies had a special meaning for Irish Americans, who had been forbidden even to own firearms in the old country. Hibernians in Savannah fancied this St. Patrick's Day toast: "America as she is, and Ireland as she ought to be—free and independent."[24]

The Irish retained close ties to their homeland. They maintained a steady interest in the cause of Irish independence and extended a warm welcome to Irish patriots like John Mitchel, the fiery revolutionary leader of the Young Ireland movement of 1848 who was first exiled to Tasmania and later escaped to America. When Irish political reformer Daniel O'Connell launched his Repeal Association in the 1840s, chapters of the movement sprang up in Southern cities like Milledgeville and Savannah. Whenever uprisings reared their heads in Ireland, the immigrant community in America was quick to lend its support with donations. But the Irish as a whole never showed an inclination to go back to their old homeland.[25]

In fact, although they cherished their attachment to Ireland, the Irish in the South actively sought to fit into American society, choosing not to be culturally separate. Their cheerful and enthusiastic participation in the South's economic life, military affairs, and politics (especially through the dominant Democratic Party organization), won them acceptance from the local community and ensured them a place in Southern society. All of this happened at the same time that Southerners themselves were seeking their own identity as separate and distinct from the North.[26]

It was in the rough-and-tumble world of Southern politics that the Irish excelled. Irish immigrants John Park and John Loague became mayors of Memphis, and Eugene Magevney served as an alderman there. George Maguire and Bryan Mullanphy were mayors in St. Louis in the 1840s. Matthew Hall McAllister was mayor of Savannah, and the Irish Jasper Greens' John McMahon served seven terms on the city council. And in 1858, with the help of Irish voters, a red-haired young Scotch-Irishman, Randal McGavock, captured the mayor's office in Nashville.

But not everyone was keen to embrace the Irish immigrants. The biggest challenge to the Irish in America came in the 1850s with the Know-Nothing movement (or American Party). The Know-Nothings (so called because members refused to make public the secret details of their movement) capitalized on a backlash among many native born Americans who resented Irish and German immigrant competition for jobs. Anti-Catholic and anti-immigrant, the Know-Nothings were stronger in the North, but Irish Southerners still felt the recoil from nativist hostility and violence.

The ugliest and bloodiest incidents occurred in 1855 in Louisville, where Irish and Germans made up a third of the city's population. A bitterly contested mayoral contest between Whigs and Know-Nothings created an explosive situation that was fueled by inflammatory newspaper rhetoric. One nativist editor wrote sarcastically of "those dear exotics with the perfume of the faderland and the bog mud of the 'ould counthry' lingering about them." On August 6, "Bloody Monday," election day for state officials and Congress, the Know-Nothings took control of the polling places and began intimidating naturalized voters. In the sweltering summer heat, fights at the polls broke out and quickly escalated. Mobs of Know-Nothing thugs took to the streets that night and descended upon the Irish neighborhood west of the downtown section. They beat residents, looted shops, and set fire to homes. The worst of the violence took place at Quinn's Row, a row of rental houses. The mob set fire to the dwellings, prevented firefighters from extinguishing the blaze, and shot and killed several Irish residents as they attempted to escape. The death toll of the night's violence was at least twenty-two.[27]

Turbulent times came to other river towns. In St. Louis, Know-Nothing ruffians trashed shops and homes in the older downtown Irish neighborhoods. Rioting broke out in the city on election day August 7, 1852, after someone was knifed at one of the polling places, and troops had to restore order.[28]

In 1854, anti-immigrant thugs in New Orleans scuffled frequently with Irish policemen and election officials. In one incident, toughs killed two policemen and attacked and injured Irish police chief Stephen O'Leary. The Know-Nothings swept city offices in the election (all but the mayor's and three judges). Rumors circulated that the Know-Nothings planned an attack on St. Patrick's Church. The Irish armed themselves and took to the streets, met the nativist gang in a bloody street fight near the church on Camp Street, resulting in injuries to both sides.[29]

Four years later, during the 1858 city elections, New Orleans nearly exploded as Know-Nothings and the Irish "Vigilance Committee" faced off again. Some 500 armed Irishmen seized the state arsenal and occupied Jackson Square in the French Quarter. The Know-Nothings occupied Lafayette Square in the American section. This dangerous situation passed without any bloodletting as more sensible voices on both sides made themselves heard. The American mayor reined in his hotheads, and a period of more peaceful co-existence emerged.[30]

Savannah proved to be more tolerant of immigrants than in the North (or for that matter in more blue-blooded Charleston), and the Irish vote helped to swing the crucial 1856 mayoral election in Savannah for the Democrats. In Charleston, the Democratic candidate for mayor owed his victory to the support of the Irish on the city's police force, as well as the endorsement of Bishop Patrick Lynch.[31]

The Know-Nothing phenomenon passed and faded from the American scene as quickly as it had emerged. The nativists failed in their efforts to elect a U. S. president, and their party split up over the slavery issue. In many ways, Irish communities actually grew stronger as a result of the nativist threat. They overcame the prejudice and the violence of this period, and it was largely their community solidarity, the support of their Church, and their ties with the Democratic Party that allowed them to endure.[32]

In fact, the Irish in the South considered themselves loyal Southerners. They had prospered in this new country, and with sectional warfare looming they now felt compelled to defend their homes from invasion. County Tyrone native John McFarland, who had settled in Yazoo City, Mississippi, wrote in 1860, "My affections, my family, my home are all here and whatever the fortunes of my adopted country mine rises or falls with it." Although many Irish had supported the federal union, they quickly became champions of the Confederacy once it became clear that the South was about to be invaded in 1861. Most of the New Orleans Irish voted for Northern Democratic candidate Stephen Douglas—and against secession—in November 1860. But after the election of Republican Abraham Lincoln, Irish opinion there shifted radically in favor of secession.[33]

In Helena, Arkansas, 33-year-old attorney Patrick Ronayne Cleburne summed up his feelings in this manner:

> I have never owned a Negro and care nothing for them, but these people have been my friends and have stood up to me on all occasions. In addition to this, I believe the North is about to wage a brutal and unholy war on a people who have done them no wrong, in violation of the constitution and the fundamental principals of the government.... We propose no invasion of the North, no attack on them, and only ask to be let alone.[34]

While many Irish Americans opposed slavery in the early 1800s—two respectable Irishman were vice-presidents of the American Colonization Society in Louisiana—by mid-century, Irish opinion had turned against abolition. Some prosperous Irish merchants owned slaves themselves. Irish Catholics were quick to note that Northern abolitionists, while passionate to condemn the Southern planters' treatment of slaves, were totally silent about Northern factory owners' mistreatment of their Irish immigrant workers.[35]

The Irish also remembered that abolitionist leaders like Reverend Lyman Beecher had been caught up in the anti–Catholic sentiment of the Know-Nothing movement. Many Know-Nothings had also filtered into the new Republican Party. The Irish in the South came to defend slavery almost as much as the planter class. When Irish reformer Daniel O'Connell adopted an anti-slavery stand, it cost him some support in the Irish community in America.

Working-class Irish had little sympathy for slaves in the South. "[T]he slave in Virginia is better fed and clothed than the poor Irish farmers," Pat Kennedy, an immigrant railroad worker in Virginia, wrote. "[O]h, it would be well for the Irish labourer if he was half as well fed and taken care off [sic] as the slaves.... [T]here may be a few bad masters, but compare the conduct of bad masters with the conduct of Irish Land Lords who will drive out [their] Tenant[s] on the road side to starve."[36]

As for the free blacks, the Irish regarded them as competitors for scarce jobs. Rivalry over work often broke out into fist fights on the New Orleans docks. By 1860 the Irish had largely squeezed African Americans out of many service and transportation jobs in the city—draymen, hackmen, and hotel servants—and this left much bitterness between the two groups. There was hostility too between Irish and black domestic workers in the Crescent City. "It's a fine city in troth it is," an Irish maid remarked, "Barrin the nagurs."[37]

Many African Americans seemed to have an equal disdain for the Irish. Writing in his diary, Natchez black barber William Johnson described a wild drunken brawl involving a group of "wild Irishmen fighting all among One another It was realy Laughable indeed." "Just like such people," Johnson concluded.[38]

Being able to vote as naturalized citizens, the Irish had an advantage that free blacks couldn't acquire in the South, and they intended to keep things that way. Irish members of the Savannah Fire Company protested the city's 1850 decision to authorize uniforms for black firefighters. They regarded this as a symbolic granting of equality to blacks, something they refused to accept.[39]

But there was much more than blind racism, economic wants, and loyalty to their adopted homeland that spurred the Irish in the South to support the Confederacy in 1861. Irish immigrants and even second-or-third-generation Irish in the South nursed bitter memories of Britain's oppression of Ireland. It took no great leap of logic for them to transfer that animosity to the case of the North's domination of the South. Inherently distrustful of a powerful central government, the Irish saw the South's war for independence from the industrial North as a parallel to agrarian Ireland's long struggle for freedom from industrial, imperialistic England.

For John Mitchel, an ardent Irish nationalist and one of the South's staunchest idealists, Ireland's struggle was indelibly intertwined with that of the South. The fiery revolutionary could not comprehend how his Irish countrymen in the North could be willing to keep the Southern states in the federal union by force, while Ireland agonized from a similar union with England, writing that they were badly misguided to suppose that "the repeal of one union in Europe depends on the enforcement of another union in America."[40]

Irish Catholic Church leaders in the South also supported the Confederacy, and their opinions carried much weight with their constituencies. Bishop Patrick N. Lynch of Charleston bitterly blamed the crisis between the North and the South on Northern anti-slavery fanatics. "Taking up antislavery," he wrote, "making it a religious dogma, and carrying it into politics, they have broken up the Union." In Mobile, Bishop John Quinlan also spoke out. "We must cut adrift from the North," he announced, "we of the South have been too long on leading strings." Taking his place at Savannah's secession meeting in December 1860, Father Jeremiah O'Neill declared that he was "*ra*publican and *sa*cessionist and *sa*tizen of Georgia; and in case there should be war, he would be the first to *lade* them into battle."[41]

The euphoria of secession captivated the Irish as much as it did other Southerners. Harry McCarthy was a popular Irish comedian who found himself on tour in Jackson when Mississippi became the second Southern state to secede from the union in January 1861. McCarthy was so caught up in the emotion of the moment that he scratched off the first few verses to a new song, "The Bonnie Blue Flag," which became a popular war anthem for the Confederate army. It was another Irish immigrant, John Logan Power, who first published the new song in the *Jackson Mississippian*.[42]

In South Carolina, Bishop Lynch blamed Northern Republicans for starting the war. Charleston's Irish Volunteers were eager to attack Federal-held Fort Sumter. And when Irish patriot Thomas Francis Meagher made it known that he intended to fight for the Union, Charleston Hibernians unanimously struck his name from the Society's honorary membership, and members of a new Irish volunteer company, the Meagher Guards, quickly changed their name to the Emerald Light Infantry.[43]

After the fall of Fort Sumter, Lincoln issued his call for 75,000 volunteers to crush the rebellion, and war now was inevitable. Irish Southerners flocked to the Confederate banner. There were far less Irish in the South than in the North, but their presence in the Confederate army was proportionally much higher. At least 40,000 men—an astounding 90 percent of the able-bodied Irish population in the South—fought for the Confederacy, and this despite the fact that no one compelled them to fight. As non-citizens were exempt from military service, Irish immigrants could have elected not to serve. If we factor in second or third-generation Irish Americans and Southerners of Scotch-Irish descent, the Irish contribution to the Confederate army becomes even greater. Also, because a large number of Irish were experienced sailors, both in the navy and on commercial boats, they provided valuable service to the infant Confederate navy.[44]

Irish volunteer militia companies rushed to offer their services to the Confederacy. In New Orleans, Father John Duffy blessed the flag of the Montgomery Guards, and old volunteer companies as well as new—like Steve O'Leary's Southern Celts and Rob Wheat's Louisiana Tigers—began to sign up to fight. In the new Confederate capital at Richmond, Captain John Dooley's Montgomery Guard received the blessing of Bishop John J. McGill, and other Irish companies began to fill up.

In Nashville, Randal W. McGavock organized an Irish company, the Sons of Erin, from the same voting constituency that had elected him mayor in 1858. The Sons of Erin later expanded into an Irish regiment, the 10th Tennessee. And from Memphis' Pinch district, another solidly Irish regiment, Colonel Knox Walker's 2nd Tennessee, mustered in at the Ancient Order of the Druid Hall. Whole regiments of Irish from Louisiana were on their way to serve in Virginia.

In Helena, Pat Cleburne joined "a splendid company of Riflemen," the Yell Rifles. Cleburne's earlier experience in the British Army proved to be a plus, and the members of the company quickly chose him as their captain. Later, when the Yell Rifles became part of the 15th Arkansas Infantry Regiment, Cleburne was elected colonel. "This is a fearfully responsible position," he wrote, "and I dread the honor but intend to turn my whole attention to it and do the best I can for the cause I am embarked in." For Cleburne, an Irish immigrant who had made good in America, the moment of destiny had arrived. "I am with the South," he wrote his brother, "in life or in death, in victory or defeat." Pat Cleburne would come to be regarded as one of the Confederacy's most able and admired commanders.[45]

Irish Southerners served in all theaters of the war, winning glory in the Army of Northern Virginia, the Army of Tennessee, and the Trans-Mississippi army. But their thoughts were never far from Ireland. By 1864, John Mitchel's son John Jr., was an artillery officer in command of Fort Sumter, where he was fatally wounded on July 20. Three hours later he spoke his last words: "I die willingly for South Carolina, but oh that it had been for Ireland!"[46]

2. Fighting Irish: The Character of the Irish Confederate Soldier

No Irish-born officer made more of an impact on the Confederate army than Patrick Ronayne Cleburne. The son of a prominent physician, Cleburne was born on St. Patrick's Day 1828 near Cork, but he was raised an Episcopalian rather than a Catholic. By the time he reached his teens, both of his parents had died. Pat would have followed in his father's footsteps, but he failed his examinations at Dublin's Trinity College (mainly because he had never really taken well to Latin and Greek). Feeling that he had let his parents down, he enlisted in the British army (the half–Irish 41st Regiment of Foot), served for more than three years in Ireland, and came out of the army as a corporal at the age of 21. He was a good marksman and an avid chess player.

Part of the vast surge of Irish immigrants who came to America in 1849, Cleburne made his way first to New Orleans and then to Cincinnati, where his experience as an apothecary's apprentice in Ireland landed him a job as a clerk in a drug store. In 1850 he accepted a better-paying job managing a drug store in Helena, Arkansas, and soon the shy, sensitive Irishman became a well-liked and respected member of the community in the busy river town.

During the yellow fever epi-

MAJOR GENERAL PATRICK RONAYNE CLEBURNE. The capable Irish immigrant who commanded the Army of Tennessee's best division was one of only two foreign-born officers to attain the rank of major general in the Confederate army. (Library of Congress)

demic of 1855, Cleburne risked his own health to make his rounds among the sufferers and to help bury the dead. He also felt the sting of Know-Nothingism when one of its supporters shot him in the back during a gun battle in front of his drug store as he was aiding his friend Thomas Hindman. As a result, Cleburne (like many Irish Americans) switched political parties—from the Whig Party to the Democrats. By 1860, he was a successful attorney, an active participant in local politics, and had come to know other prominent men who would become Confederate officers.

General William J. Hardee, Cleburne's corps commander and a close friend, recognized the leadership abilities of the Irishman, writing that he possessed "the rare qualities of a strict disciplinarian, a brave and skillful leader and a popular commander." Even General Braxton Bragg, the unpopular Confederate commander of the Army of Tennessee (with whom Cleburne as well as other officers had disagreements) respected his abilities, writing in 1863, "He is cool, full of resources, and ever alive to a success."[1]

In the spring of 1864, Cleburne had more reason than usual to be in an optimistic mood, because an unexpected development in his life had occurred in January. His friend, Hardee, had become engaged to 25-year-old Mary Foreman Lewis, the daughter of a well-to-do Alabama planter; and he invited Cleburne to be best man at his wedding scheduled for January 13, 1864. The shy and unassuming Irishman, who was generally something of a loner, was glad to oblige his friend and accompanied the groom to the Lewis mansion near Demopolis, Alabama. During the romantic atmosphere of the wedding service, Cleburne promptly fell for the maid of honor, 24-year-old Susan Tarleton from Mobile. It seemed a case of love at first sight. Susan was an intelligent young woman who enjoyed literature and music and shared Cleburne's love for poetry, and "Old Pat" was clearly smitten. After a whirlwind romance of six weeks the couple announced their engagement, setting the date for their wedding as sometime in October.

Although the prospect of married life had his head in the clouds, the young Irishman had more weighty problems to occupy his mind, and the one that worried him most was the Confederate army's growing manpower shortage. Cleburne gave the matter serious thought, and in January 1864 he drafted what would become the most controversial proposal ever made by any Southern fighting man. In a "memorial" or letter addressed to General Joseph E. Johnston, the newly named commander of the Army of Tennessee, Pat Cleburne endorsed the recruitment of African Americans into the Confederate army, an act that would have become the first step in ending slavery in the South.

Cleburne was an aggressive officer who pulled no punches, but he was also a compassionate man who cared about his soldiers, and the carnage that he had witnessed at Shiloh—and at subsequent bloodbaths at Murfreesboro and Chickamauga—deeply affected him. With no political ax of his own to grind, he also clearly grasped the manpower disadvantage the South had against the numerically superior North. Under Cleburne's proposal, any male slave who enlisted to fight in the Confederate army would receive his freedom. The South could recruit tens of thousands of highly motivated fighting men to bolster the army's declining numbers and perhaps turn the tide in the war with the North. The emancipation of the slaves would also win friends for the Confederacy in Europe and possibly bring badly needed military assistance from Britain or France. Cleburne's "memorial" was signed by the officers of his division, including Brigadier General Mark Lowrey, Colonel John Edward Murray, and Brigadier General John H. Kelly, a young Irish-American whom Cleburne had recommended for promotion.

As an Irish patriot, Cleburne clung staunchly to the ideal of political freedom, seeing the South's struggle against the North in the exact same light as Ireland's struggle for independence from Britain. The consequences of failure and defeat were too appalling to even consider. "[I]t means the loss of all we now hold most sacred," Cleburne declared. "It means that the history of this heroic struggle will be written by the enemy; that our youth will be trained by Northern school teachers; will learn from Northern school books their version of the war; will be impressed ... to regard our gallant dead as traitors."

For Cleburne, a non-slaveholder, the goal of Southern liberty was worth any sacrifice—even the abolition of slavery, if that was what it took. "As between the loss of independence and the loss of slavery," he wrote, "we assume that every patriot will freely give up the latter—give up the negro slave rather than be a slave himself." Sadly, his superiors did not share this belief. Cleburne's radical proposal was shot down before it could even become public. An outraged President Jefferson Davis ordered the document immediately quashed. Cleburne never received another promotion in the Army of Tennessee. More than a year later, Davis and the Confederate Congress finally reconsidered and in March 1865 approved a slave emancipation bill, but by then it was too late. Had they acted when Cleburne first proposed it, one can only wonder how it might have affected the outcome of the war.[2]

The skyrocketing battlefield losses that prompted Pat Cleburne to put forth his controversial slave emancipation proposal affected the Confederate Irish more deeply than their native Southern brethren, because they were even harder to replace. It was almost impossible to rebuild the Irish commands that were decimated in the fighting. The Federal naval blockade meant that Southern seaports were virtually closed off to Irish immigrants during the war years. As wartime attrition thinned their ranks, some Irish Confederate companies lost their Irish character.

While the blockade made it difficult for the Confederacy to recruit soldiers overseas in Ireland, the Federals were busily working to enlist as many Irish as they could. Northern recruiters were not afraid to use unscrupulous "bait and switch" tactics, promising the Irish jobs and better economic opportunities in America and then pressuring them to join the army as soon as they got off the boats. Union recruitment drives likely account for a jump in Irish emigration to the United States from 33,000 in 1862 to 94,000 in 1863. And yet in the Northern army the Irish were the most underrepresented immigrant group in relation to their population, while the Confederate Irish remained the largest immigrant group in service in proportion to their population.[3]

The Irish earned the reputation as the hardest fighting soldiers in the Confederate army. Rebel commanders regarded them as tenacious, cheerful, and even well disciplined when properly led by officers that they respected.

Even toward the end of the war in January 1865, the Confederate War Department was actively attempting to recruit volunteers from among Federal prisoners of war. "Catholic Irish be preferred," the department recommended.[4]

In the Army of Northern Virginia, it was Emerald Islanders who frequently protected the regimental colors. Examples of Irish color companies include Mobile's Emerald Guard in the 8th Alabama, the Montgomery Greys in the 6th Alabama, the Jackson Guards of the 19th Georgia, the Irish Volunteers of the 1st South Carolina, and the Virginia Hibernians of the 27th Virginia.[5]

In the Army of Tennessee, Confederate commanders often called on Irish compa-

PORT GIBSON RIFLES AT PENSACOLA, APRIL 1861. This largely Irish company became part of the 10th Mississippi Infantry, a command that saw heavy fighting in the Army of Tennessee. Irish dock hands in river towns like Port Gibson, Vicksburg, Helena, Memphis, and St. Louis were among the Confederacy's most enthusiastic recruits. (State Archives of Florida Photographic Division)

nies to perform the dangerous duty of skirmishers and rear guards, both spearheading an advance and protecting a withdrawal. According to the Irish 5th Confederate Infantry Regiment's Captain Charles W. Frazer, Cleburne himself "often went with the skirmish line." Major John E. Austin's 14th Louisiana Sharpshooters Battalion, Captain George Dixon's Napoleon Grays in the 15th Arkansas, Captain Thomas J. Fletcher's Company A (largely Irish from Memphis) of the 13th Arkansas, Captain Patrick Canniff's "Fighting Irish Company," of the 5th Missouri from St. Louis, Captain Mumford H. Dixon's 3rd Confederate regiment (with numbers of Vicksburg Irish), and the 10th Tennessee's Sons of Erin (from Nashville and nearby communities) often performed skirmisher duty. Led by crack shot Major John G. ("Gentleman Johnny") O'Neill, a detachment of sharpshooters in the 10th Tennessee performed excellent service at Chickamauga and Missionary Ridge.[6]

Early in the war the Irish earned their reputation for fearlessness in battle and eagerness to do combat. The Irish 2nd Tennessee Infantry (later to become the 5th Confederate Infantry) saw its first battle on November 7, 1861, when then Brigadier General Ulysses S. Grant—in one of his very first combat commands in the Civil War—attacked the small Rebel outpost at Belmont, Missouri. Word of the attack quickly reached the rest of General Leonidas Polk's Confederate army stationed just across the Mississippi River at Columbus, Kentucky, where the only work that the 2nd Tennessee had done so far was to construct Rebel batteries on the river. While waiting to be sent into battle, rumors they heard that the Federals had brutally bayoneted sick soldiers at Belmont. The Irish boys were so incensed that they vowed to swim the river if need be to avenge their comrades. When the regiment fell in, fourteen Irishmen were hailed from guard duty, and four eager men even piled in from the hospital, all anxious to get into the fight.

The 2nd Tennessee soon got their chance. Ferried across the river as part of a wave of fresh reinforcements, the Irishmen shouldered their flintlock muskets and helped to reverse the Rebels' fortunes in the battle, turning back Grant's attack and retaking a fallen battery to boot. "Irishmen take to this," Captain Charles Frazer wrote, "as readily as ducks to water." The fierce little engagement was a bloody one, and the Irish regiment left 18 members dead on the field and 64 more men wounded. The first of the Irish regiment to die included Patrick McGillicuddy, John Reeby, Thomas Clark, Thomas Haffey, James Tracey, E. S. Hanford, Patrick Murphy, John Mulholland, John Dempsey, Patrick Cain, John Stewart, Dennis Lynch, James Spelman, David Volmer, and Captain J. Welby Armstrong. They would not be the last.[7]

The Irish-American soldier's legendary fondness for a good fight has no better illustration than the 45th Mississippi's Corporal Joel T. McBride, a farmer who hailed from Simpson County. Part of a line of skirmishers at Murfreesboro in December 1862, he was captured in the first day's fighting after a band of bluecoats literally had to pull him off a Federal major who had struck him on the head with his saber. McBride continued to resist, kicking and swinging until his own company commander, Captain Thomas P. Conner, yelled at him to stop. Even still, McBride was so belligerent that his captors finally clapped him in irons. "Ef yer'll turn me loose," McBride vowed, "I kin lick every one uv yer, one at er time!"

McBride, Captain Conner, and several hundred other Rebel prisoners were corralled behind Federal lines and were watched by a guard of bluecoats. One of them, an Irishman, boasted that he could "lick the divil out av any bloody Confetherate from Jeff Davis down to the lowest private, be dad!" McBride's ire was raised, and he took up the challenge. Guards and prisoners proceeded to form a ring, and the two men went at it, but McBride got the worst of it and was knocked out.

But McBride still wasn't whipped. Watching groups of the bluecoats fleeing the battlefield during the day's seesaw fighting, he lashed out again. "What yer runnin' fer?," McBride taunted. "Why don't yer stand and fight like men?" "For god's sake, Joe," an exasperated Conner interjected, "don't try to rally the yankees! keep 'em on the run ... and let's make our escape." But as the day wore on, they had no chance to make a break for it. McBride was sent to Camp Douglas as a prisoner of war, and it was not until the following spring that he was exchanged. He returned to the Army of Tennessee and fought at Chickamauga, Missionary Ridge, Ringgold Gap, and throughout the Atlanta campaign in 1864 as a color-bearer. He was finally killed in the Rebel assault at Franklin, Tennessee, in November 1864.[8]

The 10th Tennessee had the "Fighting Fitzgeralds," identical twin brothers who had grown up in the rough Irish neighborhood of Nashville. Morris (Mo) and William (Willie) earned their nickname not only because they fought Yankees so hard but because they spent much of the time fighting each other as well. One evening in July 1861, while the 10th Tennessee was stationed at Fort Henry, the brothers Fitzgerald had a strong difference of opinion over a jug of whiskey they were consuming while returning by boat from Lady Peggy's Tavern, a dance hall and saloon on the other side of the Tennessee River. Willie proceeded to try to drown Mo by pushing his head under the water and holding it there. This caused the boat to capsize, and several of their friends had to pull the brothers to shore since neither could swim. According to fellow Irish soldier Jimmy

Doyle, there was one sure way to tell them apart: "Willie's long, ratty-looking brown beard was most of the time dirtier than Mo's long, ratty-looking brown beard."[9]

Whatever hardships or horrors came their way, the Confederate Irish always responded with stoic tenacity and with a dark sense of humor. At Murfreesboro, Captain Charles W. Frazer recalled his Irish lieutenant who was killed in one of the costliest charges of that day. Frazer had noticed the young man earlier that morning wearing his new uniform coat and gloves. When he questioned him about it, the lieutenant merely shrugged and replied that this was the occasion that he had saved the uniform for and that he intended "to die like a gentleman."[10]

To die alone in a new country was a sad prospect, but even here the Irish kept their sense of humor. As the New Orleans Irishmen in the 13th Louisiana were setting off for war, a big crowd gathered to give them a send-off. Mothers and sweethearts shed many tears as the soldiers loaded themselves and their gear aboard a steamer. "I wish I had a gurl to cry for me;" one Irish lad moped, "but the devil a wun cares whether I go or stay." His comrade was more indifferent. "Be me soul," he declared, "I'm glad I've no wun. If I get kilt me people will never know what became of me, and the only monument I'll get will be an entry on the Company books—Killed in battle, Mike Morrisy—and that's not me thrue name, at that."[11]

The Irish soldier's wit often manifested itself in prankish antics both on and off the battlefield. During the Gettysburg campaign, as a tattered Confederate column passed through Chambersburg, Pennsylvania, townspeople gathered to show their defiance of the Rebels by flying their Union flags and appearing in their Sunday best. One of the Mobile Irish, John Donnally of the 8th Alabama, spied one of the spectators, an elegantly decked out gentleman sitting on the sidewalk. Donnally impishly left ranks, dashed up behind the man, and snatched the man's hat off his head, replacing it with his own bullet-ridden hat before scampering away to the howls of laughter from his comrades. Donnally had deserted his company but had just returned to duty. He never made it back from Pennsylvania and died from sickness near Gettysburg.[12]

Officers of Irish companies and regiments were not always Irish themselves. Colonel Valery Sulakowski, who was born in Poland, commanded the largely Irish 14th Louisiana Infantry. The first commander of the 10th Tennessee "Sons of Erin," Colonel Adolphus Heiman, was a Prussian immigrant, whose English was poor and whose temper often flared. "Uncle Dolph," as the Irish called him, would curse at them in German, and his English was so faltering that the Irish claimed that they could only understand "Gaelic." But the Prussian soon gained both the respect and affection of the Sons of Erin.[13]

In units like the 13th Louisiana, the officers were more likely to be French Creoles. As a young lieutenant in the original 13th Louisiana, John McGrath recalled that the regiment's Creole officers gave instructions in French and that he was the only officer who did not speak it. When the word came down that officers were to begin giving orders in English, this did not set well with the Irish, who were used to being drilled in French. "Leftenant," one of the men told McGrath, "I don't know what oi'll do. You want us to drill in English, and the divil a wurd I know but French."[14]

The Irish seemed to accept battlefield injuries with indifference. The 5th Confederate's Captain Frazer remarked that he never heard one of his men cry out when wounded. Frazer remembered a soldier at Murfreesboro who lay on the ground with his leg severely smashed by a Federal musket ball. Asking to be taken to the rear, and finding no one offering to do so, he spotted a Federal prisoner nearby and with the help of another soldier he hopped on the man's back and "rode" him toward the rear. The last Frazer saw of him, he was cheerfully riding away on the back of his prisoner and was whistling the tune, "The Girl I Left Behind Me."[15]

And then there was the 10th Tennessee's Sergeant Barney McCabe at Chickamauga in September 1863. The 30-year-old County Donegal native was the regiment's commissary sergeant, and he had just forded Chickamauga Creek with his mess mules to bring rations to the men in the field. Suddenly, he was struck directly in the forehead by a Yankee bullet. As blood gushed from his head, McCabe sank down beneath a tree and began to pray to the Blessed Virgin for divine intervention. His prayers were answered, for as others gathered around him and inspected his wound, they found that the ball had not penetrated his head. It had been fired from too far away to do mortal damage. McCabe would in fact live for forty-four more years. One of only a handful of Irishmen in the 10th Tennessee to survive the war, he became a successful hotel owner in Nashville. He would always laugh about his experience at Chickamauga, joking that his head was so hard that it once stopped a Yankee bullet.[16]

Irish hard-headedness was often an asset on the battlefield, but it could cause problems when dealing with authority. As a new lieutenant, the 13th Louisiana's Captain John McGrath got some sneers from the Irish enlisted men of the newly formed regiment, many recruits already looking scruffy, some with black eyes or broken noses. "Oh, Mike, look at that new lefttenant!" one of them teased. "Don't he think he is purtty wid the new chicken guts [insignia braid] on his arms. Look at his strut!" McGrath quickly turned on the man and gave him a stern chewing out. This same soldier, Daniel Dunn, would later save McGrath's life on the battlefield, losing his own in the process.[17]

For most regimental commanders, Irish units presented a thorny problem. Major Rob Wheat's Louisiana Tigers battalion, recruited largely from New Orleans Irish dock workers, fought furiously at First Manassas but behaved like such hellions off the battlefield that no commander wanted them; they were in fact disbanded after Wheat's death at Gaines' Mill in 1862.

The 14th Louisiana, with many Irish recruits, had a terrible reputation for drunkenness, unruliness, and theft of civilian property. On the way to Virginia in 1862, the regiment made a brief stop at Grand Junction, Tennessee. Colonel Sulakowski, anticipating trouble, ordered all of the towns' liquor stores closed and posted guards to prevent his soldiers from entering them. But many of the men, after sneaking two barrels of whiskey aboard the train, were already drunk by the time they reached Grand Junction. Defying the colonel, they began breaking into stores, overpowering the handful of guards left to protect them. The melee that followed snowballed into a drunken riot. Officers drew their revolvers and used them to subdue the crowd. When it was all over, seven men were dead and nineteen wounded, and the local hotel was wrecked. Yet this same outfit raised $1,200 in the winter of 1862–1863 to help needy orphans in Richmond. Such Louisiana commands were, in the words of historian Terry L. Jones, "the Dr. Jekyll and Mr. Hyde of the Confederacy."[18]

Keeping such men in check called for strict discipline, but a commander had to balance sternness with fairness and a sense of humor. Cleburne believed in discipline, but not when carried to an extreme. His punishments took the form of extra guard duty, cleaning details, or loss of privileges, never physical abuse. Major J. C. Dickson, the division inspector general, had a reputation as a very strict drillmaster and would punish the slightest mistake with extra guard duty. Sometimes as many as four to five hundred troops would gather just to watch the drills, anticipating one of Dickson's tirades. Once Cleburne chanced to drop by when the caustic major was inspecting a picket detail— but not strictly according to regulations. "Major Dickson," the Irishman interrupted, "bring your men to order arms while you give those instructions not in a book." This produced a wild cheer from the soldiers—and afterward unmerciful ribbing for Dickson. Whenever Dickson passed a group of soldiers, one of them was bound to shout out the well remembered remark: "Who gave those instructions not in a book?" Someone else would quickly cry out, "Major Dickson."[19]

The story of the 1st Virginia Infantry Battalion, called the Irish Battalion, illustrates the dualistic nature of many Irish commands. The Irish Battalion was composed of five companies recruited in Richmond, Alexandria, Norfolk, Lynchburg, and Covington—all large Virginia cities that were either rail centers or seaports where numbers of Irish laborers had clustered to find work. The spring of 1861 found the Irish Battalion in Richmond, where drinking and brawling earned them a reputation for rowdiness. Privates William Sexton and William Looney, confined in the guardhouse for mutiny, managed to get hold of weapons and attacked the guards and Lieutenant John Heth. Other officers, sidearms drawn, managed to overpower the two prisoners, who were sentenced to three months at hard labor.

The Irish Battalion had a good record of service under Stonewall Jackson in the Shenandoah Valley in the spring of 1862, and brigade commander Charles S. Winder commended them for their "coolness, bravery, and discretion" at Gaines' Mill in June. But in August 1862, the command performed poorly at Cedar Mountain, where it fled from the battlefield. A succession of three commanders over an eighteen-month period did not help the situation. Then Major David B. Bridgford, a 30-year-old Richmond merchant and son of a British army officer, took command of the battalion. Bridgford gave stability to the little battalion.

The Irish Battalion finally found its niche when it became the provost guard for the Army of Northern Virginia. As such, its job was to protect rail stations and crossroads, guard prisoners, and arrest stragglers. The battalion did its job as military police so well that it earned a new reputation—that of the "Irish cops" of the Confederacy.[20]

Drinking was a continual problem in Irish units, just as it was in Confederate units in general. In the Irish 2nd Tennessee, the regiment's chaplain, Father Daly, was rumored to spend his afternoons serving Mass and his evenings in breaking up the drunken altercations among his flock. In spite of the best efforts of commanders to curtail drinking, the soldiers always managed to get their hands on liquor. One soldier in the 2nd Tennessee even had whiskey hidden in the barrel of his musket! And it was not only enlisted men who had a problem with liquor. Officers were prone to drink too. It was hard drinking that ended the military career of Cleburne's friend and fellow Irish immigrant John H. Calvert, a regular army veteran who helped Old Pat organize the Yell Rifles and who later became captain of the Helena battery of artillery. Calvert turned in his resignation after repeated episodes of drunkenness rendered him unfit for command, and Thomas J. Key took over the Helena battery.[21]

"The heavy drinking reported about the Tenth Tennessee," historian Ed Gleeson writes, "is not an Irish stereotype; it was the reality." When Colonel Heiman forbade his Irish soldiers from visiting Peggy's Tavern, many soldiers simply disregarded the order. To prevent them from crossing the river to the popular drinking place, Colonel

Heiman had the skiffs broken up—all but one rowboat that the lads had squirreled away for such an occasion. The Sons of Erin drew lots for the task of rowing across. In August 1861 Patrick Sullivan and Timothy Tansey, two farm boys from Pulaski's Company I, were making the return trip with four jugs of whiskey in tow when an unexpected storm threatened to upset the boat, and the two boys became convinced that the end was near for them. "Bejabbers, Paddy," cried Tim, "and the boat will be overturned and we will lose our whiskey." "We sure and we won't," Patrick replied, "We will drink it and save it." And so it was, the two soldiers hastily consuming the whiskey until they managed to reach shore.[22]

Frank Richardson of the 13th Louisiana recalled one Irish soldier in the regiment who became so drunk that he turned belligerent and uncontrollable, burst into the officers' dining room, slammed Captain Steve O'Leary into a window sash, destroying it, and had to subdued by sheer weight of numbers and clapped in irons. This same man, Richardson testified, became a good soldier who fought well in many battles. But the lesson of this episode was not lost on the regiment's officers. "The liquor shops," Richardson recorded, "were all very carefully closed thereafter on the approach of the 13th Louisiana."[23]

In spite of their fondness for drinking and their often unruly behavior, most of the Irish became excellent soldiers. "They were simply young and wild and were going to war, probably never to return," John McGrath wrote, "and when the clash of battle came none were braver, none more loyal to the cause, and none more easily handled in fight or controlled in quarters. There were bad men among them, but good soldiers predominated." Just as they had done in civilian life, the Irish turned to alcohol for relief from the monotony of the soldiers' routine—digging trenches and doing sentry duty—and from the frightful sights and experiences of combat. Other consolations were the treasured letters from home—and religion. Attending Mass and receiving the Blessed Sacrament were very meaningful to the Irish soldier. The same Sons of Erin in the 10th Tennessee who had caroused the night before were found in sober attendance at Mass before the Federal assault on Fort Henry in 1862.[24]

By the spring of 1864, Pat Cleburne's division was widely regarded as the best in the Army of Tennessee. Cleburne's division could not really be considered an Irish division, because Irish Confederate soldiers were scattered throughout the Rebel armies in Virginia, in Tennessee, and in the Trans-Mississippi. They never were consolidated together into a single ethnic unit the size of a division. But there were enough Irish-dominated companies and regiments in Cleburne's division to give it a decided Irish flavor. Prominent in it were the Irish 5th Confederate Infantry from Memphis, the 3rd Confederate Infantry (with a large number of Irish from Vicksburg), Cleburne's own 15th Arkansas (with complements of Irish from Helena and other river towns), and the 1st Arkansas Infantry, with a quantity of Irish from Little Rock, Pine Bluff, and El Dorado.

Cleburne credited the bravery of his soldiers to something that he himself had set in motion: the military order of the Comrades of the Southern Cross. Part fraternal, part charitable, the order encouraged members to become good soldiers. Members took an oath to stand by each other, to never leave any comrades behind, and to never desert their country. Cleburne placed great stock in this society and insisted that the Confederate army would have been unbeatable had the order been instituted throughout the service.[25]

BRIGADIER GENERAL JAMES HAGAN, AN IRISH-AMERICAN CAVALRY OFFICER. A native of County Tyrone, Hagan commanded the 3rd Alabama Cavalry, later led a calvalry brigade, and was wounded several times during the war. (Library of Congress)

Cleburne also was a practical and innovative commander. In the spring of 1864 he organized the Whitworth Sharpshooters, an elite company of first-class marksmen drawn from the very best shots in each regiment of the division. Accountable directly to Cleburne, the sharpshooters made their camp next to his headquarters. Their weapon was the deadly Whitworth rifle imported from England. In Virginia, the Whitworth rifle was responsible for the death of Federal General John Sedgwick, who boasted to his men that the Rebels "couldn't hit an elephant at this distance," just before being killed instantly by a shot to the head. One member recalled that, "The Whitworth rifles had telescopic sights on them, and after a fight those who used them had black eyes, as the end of the tube rested against the eye while taking aim, and the 'kick,' being pretty hard, bruised the eye." Cleburne's sharpshooters began operating during the Georgia campaign in the spring of 1864, and they soon won a reputation for outstanding work, rated the equal of a light battery in their effectiveness. The sharpshooters could silence an enemy battery from as far away as 800 yards and could wreak havoc with enemy skirmish lines. Despite heavy casualties among these men—as high as 60 percent during the 1864 Georgia campaign—there was always a waiting list of men eager to join.[26]

Outstanding officers like Pat Cleburne and the tough veterans he commanded helped to cement the Irish Confederates' reputation as the South's most aggressive and dependable soldiers. Whether in Virginia or in the western theater, they performed some of the hardest combat and sustained some of the highest losses. After the war, there would be few left who would even remember them, the unsung heroes of the Confederacy.

3. Home Front: The Irish Family, Community, and Church in War

In many ways, the story of how Irish Confederate women supported their men in military service was no different from that of Southern women as a whole. Never ones to shy away from hard work, Irish women embraced the Confederate war effort enthusiastically early in the conflict. In Natchez, Irish women sent their men off to war with clothing and religious articles. In the little south Mississippi town of Paulding, they prepared a huge send-off dinner for the lads, and they remained close to each other and to the Protestant women of the town as well, comforting each other in sorrows as the casualty lists mounted. Many women served on the nursing staffs of hospitals. Some went with the troops, like Mobile's Nora McCosker and Mary McGowan, doing the laundry for the Emmet Guards, an Irish company in the 24th Alabama Infantry Regiment.[1]

Irish-born Mary Hill became known as the "Florence Nightingale of the Army of Northern Virginia." With a brother in Captain William Monaghan's company in the 6th Louisiana Infantry, she followed the New Orleans troops to Virginia to be near to him. During the Seven Days Battles near Richmond in the summer of 1862, Mary served as a matron in charge of the Louisiana troops' hospital. But that is not all she did. Back in the occupied city of New Orleans, she risked her own freedom to slip through the Federal lines and carry letters from family members to their loved ones serving in the Confederate army. Mary was arrested and was imprisoned in the Julia Street Prison. Claiming the protection of the British consul on the grounds that she was in fact a British subject, she won her release from prison. When she died in 1902, she was buried in New Orleans with military honors.[2]

There were many young Southern women like Seraphine Deery McGavock, the wife of Colonel Randal McGavock of the 10th Tennessee. A Scotch-Irish Presbyterian like her husband, "Seph," as she was called, was beautiful and bright, a vivacious lass with light brown hair. A great asset to McGavock in his political life, she worked with him in his Nashville mayoral election campaign. It was Seph who organized the wives of the Sons of Erin into the Ladies Soldiers' Friend Society. The ladies designed and sewed the company's green flag. Seph's sister-in-law, Sarah McGavock, worked as a nurse to Confederate prisoners in the hospital in Nashville where her husband, Dr. J. Berrien Lindsley, was a surgeon.[3]

Like many young women in Memphis, 24-year-old Letitia Austin gave of her time to the Ladies' Aid Society and Southern Mothers' Association to sew uniforms for the soldiers. The Scotch-Irish Letitia married Captain Charles W. Frazer of the 5th Confederate Infantry in 1862, accompanying the young officer to camp in the early days of their marriage. But in September 1863, Charles was taken prisoner and was sent to Johnson's Island near Sandusky, Ohio, on Lake Erie. Letitia located a family of Confederate sympathizers in Sandusky and moved in with them in the hopes of visiting her husband. When she learned that Charles had fallen ill, she made the long journey to Washington and secured an interview with President Lincoln and a pass for permission to visit her husband and brought him medicine and clothing with the aid of a priest.

The young bride almost was caught up in a plot to free the prisoners at Johnson's Island. Rebel agents in Canada concocted a plan to carry out a bold raid to liberate the captives. The first step was to create a diversion by firing on the gunboat *Michigan* which guarded the island, and the conspirators asked Letitia to help them by giving a signal from the Sandusky side. But Charles, who was aware of the plot, made Letitia promise not to get involved. Frazer was not released until after the end of the war in June 1865.[4]

Throughout the war, the Irish women in Savannah did what they could to keep up the spirits of the troops, and they often gave parties to boost morale. While stationed in the Savannah area in 1863, Captain William Dixon of the 1st Georgia Volunteers wrote of attending parties given by two young Irish women—21-year-old Annie Doyle, who lived with her immigrant father and family, and 24-year-old Ann McCall, who worked as a domestic servant in the household of a family with members in the Republican Blues, Dixon's company which contained many Irish or Scotch-Irish members.[5]

Irish Confederate women faced the hardships that the war brought and made painful sacrifices to support the Southern cause. In many cases, the sacrifices were deep and devastating, like those of Catherine Culhane, the owner of a Natchez tavern whose three sons died in the fighting in Virginia—one at Second Manassas, one at Fredericksburg, and one at Gettysburg.[6]

In other cases, the decision by Irish women to support the Confederacy cost them their own freedom. In Federal-occupied St. Louis, large numbers of Irish-American civilians, many of them women, were jailed as suspected Confederate sympathizers, some for doing nothing more than trying to send clothing or food to their loved ones serving in the Rebel army. For the Confederates, St. Louis came to resemble a police state. Individuals could be imprisoned merely for criticizing the U. S. government or for trying to dissuade young men from enlisting in the Federal army.

Federal military authorities exiled several women from St. Louis, and the wife of Daniel M. Frost (former captain of the Irish Washington Guards militia company) fled with her family to Canada. Even with the Irish nuns of St. Louis, Federal troops were wary. "We were looked upon as spies," wrote Sister Mary Louise Lynch, "Soldiers in uniform came hurriedly through the [railroad] car, opened our trunks and our baggage, and even examined our lunch basket."[7]

With roads into St. Louis guarded by blue-coated troops and Unionist informants ready to turn in enemy collaborators, Rebel families were completely cut off from their loved ones serving in the Confederate army on battlefields in Tennessee, Mississippi, and Georgia. Even communication by mail was difficult and dangerous, but the wives of Missouri soldiers set up a regular underground mail service and maintained a correspondence with their loved ones at considerable personal risk. They were aided by colorful characters like Absalom Grimes, a former steamboat pilot who acted as a mail runner for the Missouri brigade, slipping back and forth through the Federal gunboat blockade on the Mississippi River to bring letters from home.[8]

A steady accumulation of bitter hardships during four years of war—loss of the family's head of the household through death or capture, economic shortages caused by the Federal naval blockade, and occupation of Southern cities by Northern troops—gradually led to civilian disillusionment and loss of the will to fight. When food became scarce, Irish women took part in the "bread riot" in Richmond on April 2, 1863. A similar situation unfolded in Mobile just five months later. On September 4, a crowd of several hundred poor women of the city (many of them doubtless Irish) grabbed up brooms, hammers, hatchets, or whatever else was handy and marched down Dauphin Street to protest food shortages. The march started peacefully enough but soon got out of hand as the women broke ranks and began to loot stores in the downtown area, parceling out food items and clothing among themselves—to the sympathetic cheers of curious onlookers. When soldiers arrived to deal with the rioters, they refused to confront the "Amazonian phalanx," as one spectator called them. The mayor met with the women, who agreed to go home only after he promised to make food available and to set up a special relief committee to oversee the distribution of food and clothing to the poor of the city.

But despite the best efforts of Southern authorities, the tightening Federal blockade meant that prices would remain high for products that became harder and harder to obtain. In Mobile early in 1865, long lines formed to buy scarce goods, and fights broke out among women over scarce items like cornmeal, wheat, flour, sugar, and coffee. Mary Conley was fined $25 in the mayor's court for disorderly conduct and was said to be "good with her fists as well as her tongue, and made free use of both."[9]

Support from their family members and neighbors was very important to Irish soldiers. It helped Irish Confederates maintain their spirits on the battlefield, but when civilian support for the war declined it led to many desertions among the Irish. By the end of 1862, most of the large centers of Irish population in the South—St. Louis, Louisville, New Orleans and Memphis—were under Federal military control. Richmond, Charleston, Savannah, and Mobile remained in Rebel hands. The overriding reason for most of the desertions in the Rebel army during the war was the concern of the soldiers for their families.

And so it was that disillusionment set in quickly when the 1st Georgia Volunteers left Savannah in 1864. The city's biggest Irish military company, the Irish Jasper Greens, had been relatively content when they were close to their homes and families, but all this changed when they were shipped out to join the Army of Tennessee defending Atlanta. Before the company left Savannah, seven members had already deserted. The hardships and dangers of the Atlanta campaign continued to take a toll from June through September 1864. Of the fifty or so Irish Jaspers reported missing or captured during this period, many of them appear to have had a change of heart about service for the Confederacy. About fifteen of them became deserters and took an oath of allegiance to the United States, and about half of this number later turned up in U. S. military service (Three of the latter enlisted in U. S. regiments slated for service on the western frontier.) In another Irish company in the 1st Georgia, the Irish Volunteers, about half of the dozen or so members listed as captured during this same period also deserted to the enemy.

As the 1st Georgia marched back through their home state in late January 1865 on their way to join General Joseph Johnston in the Carolinas (with the remnant of the

Army of Tennessee left from the disastrous engagements at Franklin and Nashville in December 1864), a number of them deserted to return home to their families in Savannah, and their former commander Colonel Charles Olmstead wrote, "who can blame them for doing so?" When Savannah's Irish community celebrated St. Patrick's Day on March 17, with the city under Federal occupation, a number of the Irish Jaspers showed up marching in the parade.[10]

But earlier in the war, when the Southern cause looked much brighter, Irish communities had been a bulwark of support for the Confederacy. In the summer of 1861, an Irish crowd in Charleston attacked a group of Irish Federal prisoners captured at Manassas. Confederate troops had to protect the prisoners from the wrath of the mob who regarded these Irishmen as traitors and pelted them with rocks. In St. Louis, the whole staff of Dr. Joseph McDowell's Missouri Medical College volunteered to serve as hospital staff with the Confederate army. And throughout the war, the various Hibernian societies in Savannah, Charleston, and Mobile—who had always aided the Irish immigrants and raised funds to help orphans and widows—worked to help the families of soldiers wounded or killed in battle.[11]

Many wealthier Irish civilians felt an obligation to give something back to the communities that had given them the chance to prosper in this new land. John McFarland of Yazoo City, Mississippi, had done well in the cotton business since immigrating from Ireland's County Tyrone in 1839, and he saw his future as entwined with that of his adopted land. "[I]n the South," he wrote, "I have made the money that I am ready to offer up as well as my own arms to defend her honor and her rights." Like Pat Cleburne, McFarland drew a distinct parallel between the South's struggle for independence and Ireland's plight under British rule. With his own money, McFarland financed the Yazoo Rifles (Company K, 10th Mississippi), who expressed their gratitude by renaming themselves the McFarland Rifles. McFarland's wife sewed the company's flag, and McFarland provided uniforms and money for other expenses. He also defended the Confederate cause in correspondence with his British customers in Liverpool.[12]

Irish immigrant Thomas McGuill struggled to build up a small trading post at Blanconia in southeastern Texas, but he volunteered to work as a tailor for the Confederate army while his wife and family members remained home to manage the business. Through the activities of his associate, a hard-bitten frontier woman named Sally Scull, the McGuills obtained scarce goods in spite of the Federal blockade. Sally Scull, said to be a "merciless killer when aroused" and "possessor of a vocabulary that would put a trooper to shame," wore men's clothes, was a crack shot with rifle and pistol, and rode herd over a band of Mexican cowhands who smuggled Southern cotton across the Rio Grande into Mexico and returned with ammunition for the Rebel army.[13]

True, there were profiteers and price-gougers, but there were many other Irish merchants who made selfless acts on behalf of the Confederacy. Natchez druggist P. H. McGraw may have been too old to shoulder a musket, but he risked his life many times smuggling morphine, chloroform, and quinine through the Federal lines. Armagh native John Knox of Charleston sank thousands of his own dollars into blockade running, even late in the war, to carry Southern cotton to the Bahamas and to bring back European manufactured goods such as guns, clothing, shoes, blankets, lead, and saltpeter. William "Black Bill" Wilson, a native of Dublin, became the best known blockade runner in Mobile Bay. After he was captured and imprisoned in New York, he reportedly turned down an offer of $50,000 to pilot Federal ships into Mobile Bay.[14]

While Irish Confederates were away fighting in the Confederate army, their families and neighbors often lived under Federal occupation. When Federal troops marched into Memphis in June 1862, members of the Irish community hoped the presence of Union forces would bring stability and help restore the economy. John Park, the city's Irish mayor, retained his office largely because of his cooperation with General William T. Sherman, the military commander at the time, and what resulted was a relatively even-handed treatment of the city's civilians. On the other hand, the Federals strongly suspected many of the city's women (doubtless some Irish among them) of smuggling supplies to the Rebel guerrillas nearby. Military authorities arrested Kate Galloway, wife of pro–Confederate newspaper editor Matthew Galloway (who was already serving with Rebel partisans in the area) and removed her from the city.

But Irish city leaders did not simply become puppets of the occupation forces. Many Unionists in Memphis suspected Park of remaining a Confederate supporter. Despite his cooperation with Federal military authorities, Park never went out of his way to take part in pro–Union demonstrations while the war continued. Unionists accused Park and his police of turning a blind eye to pro–Rebel Memphis civilians who still cursed the Union and cheered the Confederacy. Still the voters reelected Park in the 1863 and 1864 mayoral elections, despite the opposition of Radical Republican newspapers. Memphis was under martial law until the end of the war, and in June 1865 the voters again reelected Park, who hired returning veterans of the old Irish regiment, the 5th Confederate Infantry, to the city's police force.[15]

The Federal blockade hit New Orleans particularly hard, because the Crescent City's economy was dependent on trade with the Midwest and Europe, and the city's Irish poor suffered the most. John McGinnis, editor of the *True Delta*, had given lukewarm support to the Confederacy, and now he became a staunch Unionist because he felt Federal military occupation offered the best chance to preserve order and to breathe life into the city's economy. He encouraged civilians to take the oath of allegiance to the Union—and not be "hanging about in bar-rooms listening to wild rumors"—so that civil government could return as soon as possible. But like Park in Memphis, McGinnis was no lap-dog for Federal occupation forces, and his criticism of the bluecoats finally raised the ire of General Benjamin Butler, the Crescent City's military governor.[16]

The presence of occupation troops in Southern cities was disturbingly familiar to Irish Southerners with fresh memories of British soldiers in Ireland. Of all the unpleasant aspects of the Confederacy's defeat, the Northern military's enforcement of Radical Reconstruction irked them the most. Radical Reconstruction disfranchised many ex-Confederates and was another bitter reminder of the Irish experience under British rule. In Savannah, Irish Jasper veteran James McGowan, who had lost an arm in the Atlanta campaign, was elected tax collector after the war. The former orderly sergeant remained an unreconstructed Rebel. When the city came under military rule as Radical Reconstruction went into effect, Federal authorities ordered McGowan to turn over tax money that he had collected. McGowan refused, and instead he sent the money to the banking firm of Eugene Kelly and Company in New York to be held in trust until the return of civil government in Savannah. He was sentenced to several months in jail, but the tax payers of Savannah refused to cooperate with Federal authorities, and the court of the ordinary declared the office of tax collector vacant and appointed McGowan to serve out his term. McGowan retained his office for many years.[17]

In the South, the Catholic Church's full support of the Confederacy went a long way toward encouraging Irish soldiers in the army and in keeping up their morale. From the beginning of the conflict, Irish Catholic bishops and priests—like Bishop John McGill of Richmond, Bishop Patrick N. Lynch of Charleston, Bishop John Quinlan of Mobile, Father James Ignatius J. Mullen in New Orleans, and Father Jeremiah O'Neill in Savannah—championed the rightness of the Southern cause, and the opinions of these men had great influence among the Irish. After the battle of Shiloh in April 1862, Bishop Quinlan personally traveled with a relief party and ministered to wounded soldiers in the field. The Bishop of Savannah, Augustin Verot, supplied priests to serve as chaplains in the army and nuns to serve as nurses in military hospitals. Verot weighed the idea that a commission of Catholic bishops going to Washington might be able to influence Lincoln to end the war, and Father Joseph P. O'Connell of Columbia, South Carolina, offered a similar plan. "[I]f both Governments appointed a half dozen Catholic priests," O'Connell wrote, "and empowered them to devise an end to this conflict, before one week they would settle the whole difficulty."[18]

Father O'Neill, who many in Savannah called "Old Hickory" because they thought he looked like Andrew Jackson, contributed money to the Confederate treasury, and congregations in Savannah's Catholic churches sang *Te Deum*s in gratitude for Confederate victories in 1862. Church-supported institutions continued to operate in Savannah throughout the war. The Academy of St. Vincent de Paul, run by the Sisters of Mercy, had been started by Father O'Neill and was the first Roman Catholic academy in Georgia. Winnie Davis, daughter of President Jefferson Davis, attended the school during the war.[19]

Catholic nuns were trained as nurses, and their skills became invaluable. In St. Louis, the Daughters of Charity and Sisters of Mercy helped care for the sick and wounded. It mattered not whether the soldiers were Federals or Confederates. The Sisters once took two children to the military prison so that they could visit their fathers there. When thirty-six railroad cars packed with 1,300 Rebel prisoners rolled into St. Louis in December 1861, Federal authorities installed the graycoats in the military prison. It was three of the Daughters of Charity who took on the burden of nursing the sick and wounded among these soldiers. After Shiloh, the Daughters of Charity rode with the wounded on transports to St. Louis and cared for them at the city's military hospital.[20]

Throughout the war-torn South, in hospitals both in cities and on the battlefield, Catholic nuns—many of them Irish—served as nurses. Many a forlorn soldier learned to recognize with gratitude the blue habits and white coronets of the Sisters of Charity. When Confederate forces evacuated Mobile in April 1865, they left many of their wounded in their care of the Sisters at the city hospital. The Sisters in Natchez served on the staff at a military hospital in Monroe, Louisiana. In Columbia, South Carolina, the Irish Ursulines became beloved for their selfless work in hospitals.

Any Irish priest who served as a chaplain in the Confederate army was something of a two-edged sword, because his authority helped to keep some of the unruly Irishmen in line, as well as to lift their morale with spiritual reinforcement. Men like Father Daly, who worked among the Memphis Irish in the 2nd Tennessee, had a sobering influence on the soldiers. In Cleburne's division, Captain Thomas Key of the Helena battery wrote, "It was indeed novel to see candles burning in daylight in the wild forest, while the worshippers bowed before God and reverently crossed themselves."[21]

Many of the Irish chaplains made great sacrifices and experienced painful personal

SISTERS OF CHARITY. Irish women in the South supported the war effort by sewing soldiers' uniforms, doing the work of laundresses, and serving as nurses on the battlefield. Irish nuns of the Sisters of Charity came to be recognized for their work in caring for sick and wounded soldiers. (Library of Congress)

losses. Stung by the death of his brother in the 8th Kentucky Cavalry, Father Abram J. Ryan took up a position with the Army of Tennessee at Missionary Ridge. Known as the "Poet-Priest of the Confederacy," Ryan served as a parish priest in Mobile for many years, and after the war his poems that exalted the Southern cause—poems like "The Sword of Robert E. Lee" and "The Conquered Banner"—brought him lasting fame.

The Army of Northern Virginia was home to several notable Irish chaplains during the war. Father John Teeling, the former chaplain of Richmond's Montgomery Guard, performed the same duty for Colonel Patrick Moore's 1st Virginia Regiment, even though most of the regiment's soldiers were Protestant. Hard-hitting Father Matthew O'Keefe, who once got the drop on Know-Nothing assassins by pulling twin revolvers on them, was the chaplain to William Mahone's brigade—and came close upon one occasion to leading Confederate troops in combat. A close friend of both Jefferson Davis and Robert E. Lee, O'Keefe was among a vocal minority of advisers that counseled the Confederate president to accept Pat Cleburne's proposal to free the slaves.[22]

All of these men were fervent supporters of the Confederacy, and one of the most zealous was Father James B. Sheeran, born in County Longford. Father Sheeran was chaplain to the Louisiana regiments in the Army of Northern Virginia, especially the hellions in the 14th Louisiana, and he also spent much of his time with the Emerald Guards of the 8th Alabama. Whenever he came into contact with Yankee soldiers, particularly Irish Federals, the staunch Father Sheeran tried to persuade them of the rightness of the Southern cause. In August 1862, Sheeran spoke with a Federal officer, who declared that he had come South to fight for the Union and to put down the rebellion. "I told him plainly that such talk was mere nonsense," Sheeran declared, "there was *No Union* to fight for, nor was there a rebellion to put down, for the people of the South were merely defending their national and constitutional rights."

On another occasion, Father Sheeran confronted an Irish soldier of the 73rd New York, wounded in the fighting at Cedar Mountain in August 1862. He recorded the following conversation in his journal.

"What's your name?" Sheeran asked the young man.

"P. Sullivan," the prisoner answered.

"Are you a Catholic?"

"Yes, I am."

"Pat, what brought you here?"

The prisoner simply hung his head. "O!," he replied, "Misfortune."

Father Sheeran also shared the not-so-uncommon fate of some of his fellow pro–Confederate priests during the war—capture and confinement in a Federal prison. From a jail cell in Baltimore, the feisty chaplain chided Federal General Philip Sheridan for "throwing a Catholic priest into a dirty prison to be the companion of drunken and disorderly soldiers, and this, too, when some of his own Catholic soldiers are dying without the sacraments."[23]

It was not an Irishman but a German-born priest who became the first American Catholic military chaplain ever to be killed in combat and the only Catholic chaplain to be killed in the war on either side. Father Emmeran Bliemel, called by the Irish "Father Emery," was the chaplain to the 10th Tennessee Sons of Erin, and also to the Kentucky Orphan Brigade. The 32-year-old Bavarian immigrant ministered not only to Catholics, but to Presbyterians, Baptists and Methodists as well. Bliemel aided the doctors, served as a litter-bearer, and prayed over the wounded. In August 1864, he was

BISHOP JOHN McGILL. Like many Roman Catholic clerics in the South, Richmond's Bishop McGill was an enthusiastic supporter of the Confederacy. The Church's sanction of the Rebel war effort was an important factor in motivating Irish Confederate soldiers. (Library of Congress)

administering last rites to the 10th Tennessee's Colonel William Grace, killed in action south of Atlanta, when he was decapitated by a Yankee cannonball.[24]

But the man who had the most colorful career as a Confederate army chaplain was Father John B. Bannon, a native of Dublin, known as the "Fighting Chaplain" of the

Confederate Missouri brigade. Father Bannon provided inspiration and guidance to Protestants and Catholics alike, but he particularly had a warm spot in his heart for the St. Louis Irish lads, because many of them had attended his own church there. A huge man at six-foot-four, the bearded "soldier-priest" had a good sense of humor and was very popular with the soldiers, laughing and kidding with them in camp, marching with them, safeguarding their army pay, and even lending a hand in battle from time to time. Bannon prayed with many a dying soldier on the field of combat.

Father Bannon shared Cleburne's view of the Confederacy's war for independence as an analogy to Ireland's struggle for freedom from Britain, and he worked for the Confederacy at the expense of his own career. He was so outspoken in support of the Confederacy that his superiors hesitated to name him to a higher post lest it bring Union reprisals. So Bannon served right alongside the soldiers in his "parish," the men of the Missouri brigade. He was with them at Pea Ridge, at Corinth, and at Vicksburg. When the Mississippi city fell in July 1863, he became a prisoner. Once paroled, he made his way to Richmond to meet with Bishop John McGill and President Jefferson Davis.

President Davis dispatched Father Bannon to Europe on a delicate and important mission—to discourage Union efforts to enlist new recruits from Irish immigrants to the United States. During the war, Irish immigrants were often victims of unscrupulous recruiting agents who used the $500 enlistment bounty and the promise of employment to entice Irish lads to America officially as "laborers" but in reality as Federal army recruits.

Father Bannon ran the blockade out of Wilmington, North Carolina, and soon made his way to Liverpool. He arrived in Ireland with high hopes but soon found his mission a daunting one. The economic situation in Ireland was so bleak that many young men found the American offer one that they could ill afford to turn down. But Bannon managed to put a dent in the Federal recruitment program anyway. Through an enthusiastic public relations effort, he launched a spirited defense of the Confederacy, taking to the speaking circuit, writing pieces in Irish newspapers, and posting bills in Dublin churches cautioning young men against risking their lives by enlisting in the Federal army.

The second part of Father Bannon's mission in Europe was even more intriguing—an audience with Pope Pius IX, who leaned favorably toward extending recognition to the fledgling Southern republic. Such a move by the Pope would have meant much to the Confederacy and might have led to the recognition—and possible military aid—from Britain and France that had so far eluded the South. But it was too late in the game, and such actions were very unlikely after Gettysburg, Vicksburg, and Chattanooga. Although he was sympathetic, Pius in the end decided to withhold recognition. Father Bannon sat out the rest of the war in Ireland, where he spent the remainder of his life.[25]

PART II. THE IRISH IN THE ARMY OF NORTHERN VIRGINIA

4. Green Flag Unfurled: Manassas and the Valley Campaign

The late morning sun blazed overhead, as the little battalion of mostly Irishmen—only some 400 strong—moved out, the first Confederate unit to be engaged in the first major battle of the war at Bull Run, just twenty miles south of Washington, on July 21, 1861. Long itching to see action, these former roustabouts and deck hands from the tough New Orleans waterfront were a colorful outfit to see, many of them wearing the dashing *zouave* costume—red fezes, dark blue or faded brown jackets, red shirts, and baggy blue and white striped trousers—inspired by the popular North African troops of the French army. Others simply wore red shirts, trousers of various hues, and wide-brimmed hats decorated with defiant slogans: "Lincoln's Life or a Tiger's Death" or "Tiger in Search of Abe." They were armed with Model 1841 "Mississippi rifles" and large wicked-looking Bowie knives. They were the famed "Louisiana Tigers," a unit that existed for only a little over a year but left an indelible mark on the literature of the American Civil War. They were led by 35-year-old Chatham Roberdeau Wheat, attorney at law, veteran of the Mexican War, and former soldier of fortune who had seen service as a *filibustero* in Nicaragua and as one of Garibaldi's revolutionary "Red Shirts" in Italy. "His men loved him," one soldier remembered, "and they feared him."[1]

The 1st Louisiana Special Battalion, better known as Wheat's Tigers, was recruited from the toughest Irish dock workers in the Crescent City. The Tigers earned a reputation as tenacious fighters, but they also were feared as undisciplined roughnecks, prone to drunkenness, thefts, and assaults. "So villainous was the reputation of this battalion," their soon-to-be brigade leader General Richard Taylor wrote, "that every commander desired to be rid of it." "I was actually afraid of them," a Louisiana soldier confessed, "afraid I would meet them somewhere and that they would do me like they did Tom Lane of my company; knock me down and stamp me half to death."[2]

The Tigers quickly came under fire from swarms of Federal troops who had crossed Bull Run on the lightly guarded Confederate left flank. "The balls came as thick as hail," one Tiger wrote, "[and] grape, bomb and canister would sweep our ranks every minute." Adding to the confusion of battlefield chaos, supporting troops from the 4th South Carolina Infantry mistook Wheat's Tigers for the enemy and let loose a volley that tore into their ranks. The Tigers returned fire, thinking that they had been fired on by the Yankees.

Overwhelming numbers began to push Wheat's little command back. Wheat

LOUISIANA TIGER ZOUAVES. Major C. Roberdeau Wheat recruited heavily among New Orleans' Irish for his Louisiana zouave battalion, shown here in a sketch near Manassas, Virginia. (*Harper's Weekly*, September 28, 1861)

attempted to rally his troops to make a stand in a nearby hayfield. Leaping from his horse, he unsheathed his sword and audaciously waved it over his head before a Federal musket ball found its mark. Wheat was struck in the chest, shot through both lungs. Several of the Tigers improvised a litter from one of the soldiers' blankets and began hauling the burly six-foot-four Wheat to the rear. Two of them fell wounded, and Wheat hit the ground. "Lay me down, boys," he told them, "you must save yourselves." They refused, and soon they had carried him out of harm's way.

After Wheat fell, other battalion officers attempted to rally the Tigers. Although struck in the thigh and lying on the ground, Lieutenant Thomas W. Adrian painfully implored his comrades not to run away. "Tigers, go in once more," he cried. "Go in, my sons, I'll be great gloriously God damn if the sons of bitches can ever whip the Tigers!" Much fight still remained in these outnumbered but stubborn Rebels. "Our blood was on fire," wrote Sergeant Robert Ritchie. "Life was valueless. The boys fired one volley, then rushed upon the foe with clubbed rifles beating down their guard; then they closed upon them with their knives."[3]

But although courage was not lacking, the Tigers were badly outnumbered and were gradually being pushed back by the bluecoats. They were left without a leader after Wheat was removed from the field, and any sense of order quickly evaporated. The Tigers broke up into smaller groups, some fighting on or joining in with other regiments as the battle went on. They left eight men dead and 38 wounded on the field.[4]

As for the charismatic Wheat, he was taken to a field hospital in the rear, where the surgeons examined his wound. Wheat asked about his chances. The surgeon was pessimistic. "Major," he replied, shaking his head, "I will answer you candidly that you can't live 'til day."

Wheat calmly responded, "I don't feel like dying yet." Wheat did indeed recover and lived to lead his battalion again the following year.[5]

Several days of probing and maneuvering had heralded a major action at Bull Run. The 1st Virginia's bold defense of Blackburn's Ford on July 18 blunted Federal commander General Irwin McDowell's reconnaissance in force there, and it was obvious that the Rebels were too strong on their right flank. The skirmish in which Richmond's Montgomery Guard had played such a key part led McDowell to fine tune his plans and to throw his forces into a major assault on the lightly-defended Rebel left. But Irish Confederate defenders were there too.

The opening of the first major battle of the war (to be known as First Bull Run in the North and First Manassas in the South) began on the morning of July 21, when McDowell sent two blue-coated divisions, with Colonel Ambrose E. Burnside's largely Rhode Island brigade in the lead, splashing across Bull Run at Sudley Ford in an attempt to turn the Confederate left. Colonel Nathan "Shanks" Evans' lone brigade of two regiments (Sloan's 4th South Carolina and Wheat's 1st Louisiana Special Battalion) swung into action to stop them. Already the morning was hot, the Federal attack two hours behind schedule.

The Rebels fought a determined holding action on Matthews Hill, just north of the Warrenton Turnpike that crossed Bull Run to the east. Evans stubbornly held on, and eventually two more Rebel brigades led by Brigadier General Barnard E. Bee and Colonel Francis S. Bartow moved up on his right to reinforce him. Piecemeal Federal attacks gradually drove the Confederate defenders from the hill. But the bulldog Rebel defense delayed the Federal advance for about two more hours, and by the time the three battered brigades were forced to give ground, Confederate commander General P. G. T. Beauregard was scrambling to bolster his crumbling left flank with more reinforcements.

The second phase of the battle unfolded in the afternoon, when Confederate troops drew up a new defensive line along the slopes of Henry House Hill, south of the Warrenton Turnpike. The Federal attackers massed for a major push, with Brigadier General Daniel Tyler's division in the lead. Prominent among the bluecoats was Colonel William Tecumseh Sherman's brigade, spearheaded by Colonel Michael Corcoran's 69th New York, the Irish "Fighting Sixty-ninth" from New York City. In the fighting near Henry House Hill, Corcoran was wounded and was taken prisoner by the Confederates. A "Louisiana zouave," probably one of Wheat's Tigers falling back from Matthews Hill, turned and fired a shot that killed Lieutenant Colonel James Haggerty, the 69th New York's second in command.[6]

The Rebel defense was primarily held by Thomas J. Jackson's Virginia brigade, which stood "like a stone wall." Two of Jackson's regiments, the 27th and 33rd Virginia, contained Irish companies from the western part of the state.

Mountainous Alleghany County was the home of the Virginia Hibernians (Company B), the color company of the 27th Virginia. The Irish company was led by Captain Henry H. Robertson, a 34-year-old attorney. There were also some 25 Irish or Scotch-Irish names on the rolls of Company A (Captain Thompson McAllister's Alleghany Roughs), Company C (the Alleghany Rifles), and Company H (the Rockbridge Rifles from Rockbridge County). The 33rd Virginia had Captain Marion M. Sib-

REBEL RESISTANCE AT MANASSAS, JULY 21, 1861. Rob Wheat's "Louisiana Tigers" in Nathan Evans' brigade hindered the Federal attack on the Confederate left flank at Manassas. Here General Joseph E. Johnston rallies the brigades of Evans, Bee, and Bartow as they reform for battle. (*Battles and Leaders of the Civil War*, 1887)

ert's Emerald Guard (Company E) from New Market in Shenandoah County. Sibert was a 34-year-old merchant from Harrisonburg. Recruits for this company included Irish rail workers who had come into the area seeking work with the Manassas Gap Railroad.

Besides the pure Irish companies, there was a strong leavening of Scotch-Irish throughout the regiments of Jackson's brigade. Every company in the brigade had large numbers of these mountain folk, many of them second or third generation Scotch-Irish whose fathers and grandfathers had emigrated and settled in the Appalachians. As many a Yankee had learned, they made tenacious fighters for the Confederacy. A staunch Presbyterian, Jackson was himself the great grandson of Irish immigrants.[7]

As the Rebels were driven back from their earlier delaying action on Matthews Hill at about 2 p.m., Jackson's brigade was drawn up in two lines of battle, each two ranks deep, amid the pines along the southeastern slope of Henry House Hill. "We were required to lie down as close to the ground as we could get, and on our arms, with heads to the enemy," wrote Sergeant William McAllister of the 27th Virginia's Company A. "We remained in this position for something like two hours."[8]

Soon the broken troops of Evans, Bee, and Bartow began streaming back from Matthews Hill. Bee galloped up to Jackson. "General!" he cried. "They are beating us back!" Jackson replied coolly: "Then, sir, we will give them the bayonet." Bee rushed away to rally his disorganized brigade. "Look!" he pointed to Jackson's brigade. "There is Jackson standing like a stone wall! Rally behind the Virginians!" Shortly afterward, a Federal musket ball claimed Bee's life.[9]

The onrushing Federals, savoring their triumph, began surging toward Henry House Hill. The bluecoats were able to place two batteries of artillery, eleven guns commanded by Captain Charles Griffin and Captain James B. Ricketts, on the slope. The Federal

FIRST MANASSAS
July 21, 1861

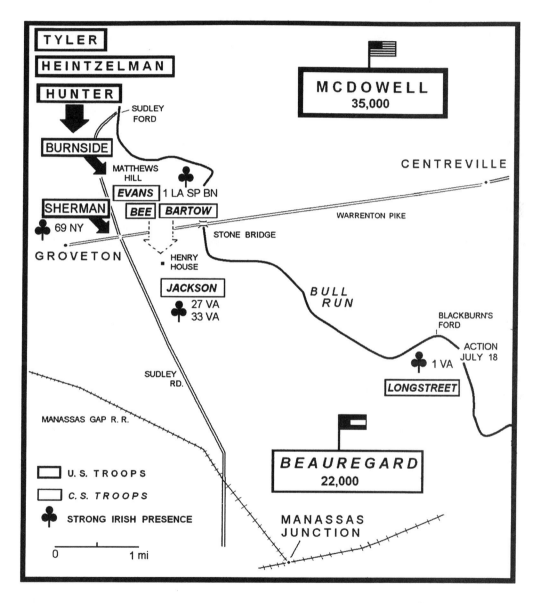

artillery began pounding Jackson's left flank, occupied by Colonel Arthur Cummings' 33rd Virginia.

The critical moment in the battle took place around 2:30 p.m., when the 33rd Virginia—tired of remaining as sitting ducks while the Federal guns banged away at them—made a surprise rush at the Federal artillery, who delayed firing on the Rebel troops in the smoke of battle because they thought they might be Federal reinforcements. The

33rd Virginia was already upon them before they realized that they were not. The Virginians swept aside a battalion of U. S. Marines and the 11th New York and overran the batteries, but enemy fire finally drove them back, pursued by the New Yorkers.[10]

Jackson turned to the officers of the 4th and 27th Virginia regiments. "Order the men to stand up," he told them. "We'll charge them now and drive them to Washington." Then he addressed the troops: "Reserve your fire until they come within fifty yards, then fire and give them the bayonet; and, when you charge, yell like furies!"[11]

Colonel Patrick Moore had raised the Gaelic war cry at Blackburn's Ford, and now a new battle cry rent the afternoon air. The Confederates seized the momentum and attacked all along the line at Henry House Hill. "[A]t a given signal," the 27th Virginia's Sergeant William McAllister wrote, "we rushed forward and charged like 'wild men,' giving the 'Rebel Yell' with a will as we hastily moved forward, firing and reloading as we went." The timely arrival of fresh Confederate reinforcements provided the coup de grace. The Rebels threw themselves at the Federal flank, which finally fell apart. The Union line cracked, and McDowell's army fell back, at first in some order and then in total confusion, back across Bull Run and all the way to Washington.[12]

The casualties of the 27th Virginia and 33rd Virginia were among the highest that day: 19 killed and 122 wounded for 27th, 45 killed and 101 wounded for the 33rd. The Emerald Guard lost 15 men, including most of its officers and NCOs. Captain Sibert, Lieutenant Thomas C. Fitzgerald (a veteran of the British army during the Crimean War), 2nd Lieutenant John Ireland, and Sergeant Michael Gavagan were wounded. Corporal John O. Sullivan was killed.[13]

Manassas was a military triumph for the South, but not a decisive one because the exhausted and disorganized Rebel army was unable to exploit its victory and push on to Washington. But Jackson earned his famous nickname, as well as greater command responsibilities, and his "Stonewall Brigade"—with its Irish companies—gained an enviable reputation as some of the toughest soldiers in the Army of Northern Virginia. Jackson wrote to his wife: "God made my brigade more instrumental than any other in repulsing the main attack."[14]

The largest armies ever seen in North America had fought each other to a standstill at Manassas, but neither side had been able to deliver the expected blow that would end the military conflict. Both sides settled in for a protracted struggle. The remainder of 1861 brought little activity to either of the opposing armies in Virginia, but by the spring of 1862 a new Federal commander, Major General George B. McClellan, was marshalling a formidable army for a second campaign against Richmond. To siphon numbers of this grand military colossus away from their proposed objective—and to protect the Confederate army's granary in the Shenandoah Valley—Stonewall Jackson was sent to western Virginia. Jackson's masterful diversionary campaign that unfolded in the spring of 1862 made his army an even greater legend to the South—and a source of anxiety in the North.

Jackson was confronted with two Federal armies in the Shenandoah Valley: General Nathaniel P. Banks with 23,000 troops advancing south into the Valley from Winchester and General John C. Fremont with 15,000 more marching from West Virginia. The campaign got under way on March 23, when Jackson's 3,000-man army boldly attacked Irish-born Brigadier General James Shields' much larger 9,000-man force south of Winchester at Kernstown. The Federals won the day after a hard-fought battle that cost the 27th Virginia 2 killed and 20 wounded and the 33rd Virginia 18 killed and 27 wounded. But the Rebels put up such a good fight that Lincoln began to consider Jackson a serious threat to the national capital, which was within striking distance of the Valley.[15]

One Rebel command that saw its first combat action at Kernstown was the 1st Virginia Infantry Battalion, better known as the Irish Battalion. The battalion's Irish recruits—former railway laborers and dockyard workers in Richmond, Alexandria, Norfolk, Covington, and Lynchburg—found themselves facing the enemy at about twenty yards distance. Out of 187 men engaged at Kernstown, the Irish Battalion lost 6 killed, 20 wounded, and 21 missing. "The firing was general and continuous along both lines," Major David B. Bridgford reported. "The ground we occupied was soon dotted with dead and wounded men. The fire of the enemy was exceedingly severe."

"The men, especially the non-commissioned officers," Bridgford continued, "acted with great courage." Captain Benjamin Watkins Leigh directed the placing of the Irish Battalion colors "and never left it except to bring up his men to the crest of the ridge and point out to them where to aim their fire. He was perfectly cool and collected, and encouraged his men to fight bravely and effectively by example and direction." Leigh later commanded the battalion at Gaines' Mill and Malvern Hill and took command of the 42nd Virginia Infantry at the end of the year. He was killed at Gettysburg in July 1863. Captain J. Pembroke Thom was wounded in the fighting at Kernstown, and Acting Sergeant Major Duggan was struck in the face while taking aim at the bluecoats.[16]

MAJOR DAVID B. BRIDGFORD, COMMANDER OF THE VIRGINIA IRISH BATTALION. **The young Irish-American merchant from Richmond did much to shape an otherwise troublesome outfit into the Army of Northern Virginia's provost guard. (Library of Congress)**

On May 8, Jackson stunned the Federals by marching his army nearly a hundred miles south and striking Fremont's advance guard at the town of McDowell so forcefully that Fremont brought his army to a halt. Jackson then turned his attention back to the Valley, where Banks still represented a danger. Lincoln now did just what Jackson hoped he would do—reroute considerable numbers of troops to the Valley to deal with Stonewall, troops that had been slated to go to McClellan's army moving on Richmond.

By mid–May, fresh reinforcements had strengthened Stonewall's army in the Valley to 16,000 men, and welcome indeed was the largely Irish brigade of Louisiana soldiers led by Brigadier General Richard Taylor. Historian Kelly O'Grady estimates some 2,000 Irish troops comprised part of Jackson's army in the Valley. The 6th Louisiana, which Taylor called his "Irish regiment," often performed rear guard duty on Jackson's many marches and counter-marches in the Valley. Taylor developed a fondness for his Irish soldiers. They were "as steady as clocks and chirpy as crickets," he recalled, "indulging in many a jest whenever the attentions of our friends in the rear were slackened." Major Rob Wheat's Tigers, now assigned to Taylor, were "sturdy marchers."[17]

Jackson's little army moved swiftly, taking advantage of their knowledge of the mountain terrain and roads, to attack where they were least expected. Stonewall's "foot cavalry" often covered 35 miles a day. On May 23, Jackson routed the Federal garrison at Front Royal. Although the old Stonewall Brigade with its Irish companies did not reach the battlefield in time to take part in the fighting at Front Royal, Taylor's Louisiana brigade played a major part in this victory, driving the bluecoats from the town. Wheat's battalion lost 1 killed and 6 wounded in the action, and Taylor reported that "Major Wheat [fully recovered from his wound at First Manassas] performed his part in gallant style." Two Irish companies in the 6th Louisiana captured two enemy flags on May 24. The tables were turned now, and Jackson now posed a threat to Banks, who withdrew northward to Winchester.[18]

Jackson dealt another blow to Banks at Winchester on May 25. On Jackson's right, the old Stonewall Brigade, now commanded by Charles Winder, was the first unit to engage the Federals, racing uphill to attack, but were soon stalled and under fire from blue-coated troops occupying a nearby hill. Taylor's Louisiana brigade launched an attack on the left, and more Rebel troops attacked on the right, forcing the bluecoats out of Winchester. Major Rob Wheat and his Tigers, Taylor reported, "rendered valuable service in assisting to repel the attempt of the enemy's cavalry to charge our line." Casualties for three days of fighting were 1 killed and 6 wounded for Wheat's battalion, 5 killed and 12 wounded for the largely Irish 7th Louisiana, and 5 killed and 42 wounded in the 6th Louisiana, where Lieutenant Colonel Joseph Hanlon was wounded.[19]

The Federals abandoned Winchester and withdrew across the Potomac. An alarmed Lincoln, concerned about the security of Washington, ordered 10,000 additional troops under Shields to move westward to attack Jackson. Stonewall now faced three Union armies in the Valley. Shields' division contained many Irishmen as well.

Taylor's veterans were not worried. "Expressing a belief that my 'boys' could match Shields's any day," Taylor wrote, "I received loud assurances from half a hundred Tipperary throats: 'You may bet your life on that, sor.... We are the boys to see it out.' ... [M]y heart has warmed to an Irishman since that night." But the fight against Shields was not to be an easy one.[20]

The crowning victory of the Valley campaign unfolded at Port Republic, strategically located at the forks of the Shenandoah River in the southern part of the Valley. Its connections with the Virginia Central Railroad made Port Republic the key to control of the southern Valley. Jackson sent General Richard Ewell's division to throw back an attack by Fremont at Cross Keys on June 8. One of the most hotly engaged Confederate regiments in this action was the 16th Mississippi Infantry, with a considerable number of Irish soldiers in companies from Natchez and the small town of Paulding in the southern part of the state. The 16th Mississippi lost 6 killed and 27 wounded.[21]

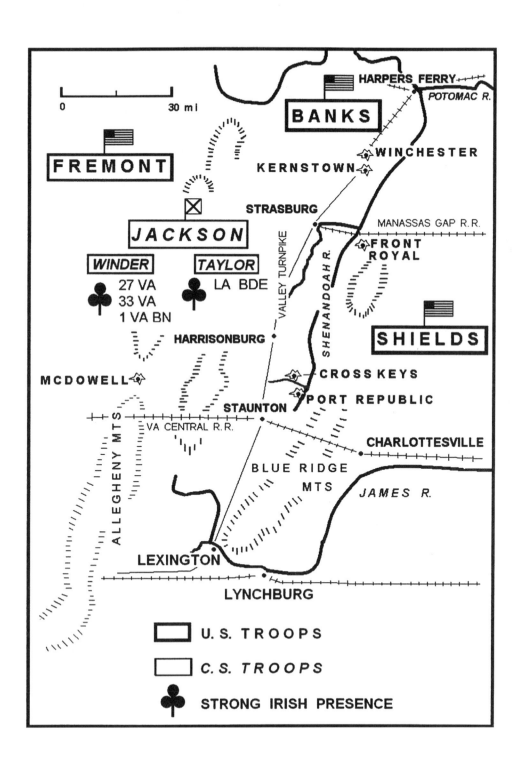

Stonewall attacked Shields at Port Republic on June 9, 1862. Crashing through rough brush-covered terrain on the Federal left flank, Taylor's brigade made the decisive action of the day by capturing a 6-gun battery that had held the Stonewall Brigade at bay. The bluecoats first opened fire on the Louisiana troops, and the 8th Louisiana's Colonel Henry B. Kelly described what followed: "With one volley in reply, and a Confederate yell heard far over the field, the Louisianans rushed down the rough declivity and across the ravine, and carried the batteries like a flash." The Rebels were forced to retreat when fresh enemy troops came up, but after two more charges they finally secured the guns. "I thought the men would go mad with cheering," Taylor remembered, "especially the Irishmen."[22]

The 7th Louisiana had the highest Rebel casualties at Port Republic—10 killed, 122 wounded—while the 6th Louisiana lost 11 killed and 55 wounded. Wheat's battalion lost 2 killed and 19 wounded, and the 27th Virginia's casualties were 8 killed, 28 wounded, and 11 missing. The hopes of the Confederacy were rising, and Irish blood had helped secure these early victories for the South.[23]

5. Defending Richmond: The Seven Days, June 1862

The cradle of Southern secession was home to a splendid group of Irish warriors, praised by the *Charleston Mercury* as "among the most efficient of our companies." As the momentous year of 1861 opened, their eagerness for an attack on Federal-held Fort Sumter could scarcely be contained. Part of a failed attempt to form a five-company Irish battalion, they were Charleston's Irish Volunteers.[1]

The Confederate bombardment and subsequent occupation of Fort Sumter furnished the fuse that touched off armed conflict between the North and South. The Irish Volunteers were the first company in South Carolina to enlist "for the war." They formed the core of Colonel Maxey Gregg's 1st South Carolina Infantry Regiment, and soon afterward they headed for Virginia.

They were a proud band. An Irish Volunteers company had existed in Charleston's volunteer militia establishment since the 1780s. Bishop Patrick Lynch blessed the flag of the Old Irish Volunteers, the senior Irish company in Charleston. The green flag—made by the Sisters of Our Lady of Mercy of Charleston and their young students—displayed the Irish harp wreathed with shamrocks on one side and on the other the South Carolina palmetto and crescent moon. "Peace is a blessing," the bishop told them, "a blessing for which we all pray to Heaven. Yet it is not always granted." The bishop went on to extol the men of the Irish Volunteers. "You come of a race," he told them, "that has ever made brave, valiant and chivalrous soldiers.... To you, then, I commit this banner. In your hands I know it will never be stained by cowardice or by any act that will disgrace you as a body of gallant Christian soldiery. Receive it, then; rally around it. Let it teach you of God, of Erin, of Carolina." Captain Edward Magrath, a 38-year-old Charleston attorney and a second-generation Irish American, replied: "[W]hen the conflict shall be over, we will come back with this banner either in honor and in glory, or, sir, we come not at all."[2]

In Virginia the Irish Volunteers soon defended yet another banner, for they became the color company for the 1st South Carolina. To the Irish Volunteers fell the honor and responsibility of protecting these colors and the regiment's color guard in battle. It was an important duty, since the colors—a blue flag with a palmetto on one side and "1st Regt S. C. Volunteers" in white lettering on the other—marked the point at which the regiment must form in battle and was the most visible emblem, bound to draw the most fire from the enemy.[3]

There were many Irish in Charleston, an old Southern city with a long tradition of immigration. Beloved by South Carolinians was the late U. S. Senator John C. Calhoun, fiery advocate of states rights—and the son of an Irish immigrant. Charlestonians remembered the intense 1832 political stand-off between Calhoun and then–President Andrew Jackson, also a Carolinian of Irish heritage. These two national leaders seemed to represent the two poles of loyalty in America, secession and union, that pulled Southern and Northern Irishmen in opposite directions in 1861.

The soldiers who shouldered the muskets in the Irish Volunteers were laborers, shoemakers, dock workers, many of them only recently arrived from the Emerald Isle. The leaders of the company were a product of Charleston's Irish community. They were young men in their twenties, friends and neighbors who had talked among themselves about secession and war for a long time—and had decided to throw in their lot with that of the Confederacy. Edward McCrady, Jr., a 28-year-old Charleston-born lawyer, became the captain of the Irish Volunteers. He was a partner in his father's law firm, along with his older brother John. McCrady's younger brother Thomas, 18, came on board with the Irish Volunteers as a brevet 2nd lieutenant in January 1862.

Michael P. Parker, a 22-year-old carpenter who lived with a fellow Irish immigrant and his family, became McCrady's 1st lieutenant. James Armstrong, Jr., a second-generation Irish American born in Philadelphia, was a 20-year-old clerk living with his parents, two brothers, a female domestic, and three Irish laborers who boarded with them. James' father was born in Ireland and was now a Charleston merchant. James became a 2nd lieutenant in the Irish Volunteers. John Sweeney, living with his wife and three children, was a 27-year-old Charleston policeman. He became the company's 1st sergeant.

Four grinding years of war was destined to take its toll on the leadership of the Irish Volunteers. Ed McCrady was promoted to major and later to lieutenant colonel, but he did not finish the war with the 1st South Carolina. He was wounded at 2nd Manassas in August 1862, and wartime injuries finally forced him out of the army. Promoted to captain in January 1862, Mike Parker was seriously wounded at Sharpsburg in September 1862, spent much of 1863 recovering, and retired from the service in the summer of 1864. 2nd Lieutenant Thomas P. Ryan left the company by the beginning of 1862, transferring to the 23rd South Carolina. Thomas McCrady was wounded at 2nd Manassas and at Fredericksburg and retired in November 1864.

John Sweeney was promoted to lieutenant in January 1862. Wounded at Chancellorsville in May 1863, Sweeney was absent for the rest of the year and was dropped from the company rolls in October 1864. Sergeant Alexander V. O'Donnell, a 23-year-old teamster, succeeded him as 1st sergeant, but fatal illness claimed him in October 1863. John J. Carroll, a 27-year-old bricklayer with a wife and a 2-year-old son, became 1st sergeant early in 1864. But Carroll was wounded in July 1864 and was absent for the rest of the year.

James Armstrong stayed with the company to the end, though. After Sharpsburg he became acting captain at the young age of 21. Armstrong was wounded four times during the war—at Sharpsburg, Fredericksburg, Gettysburg, and Spotsylvania. Promoted to captain in June 1864, he was the company's last commander and endured to the end of the war. He would be one of the few left to tell the story of the Irish Volunteers.

There were other Irishmen in the 1st South Carolina. Sixteen-year-old Daniel

Quinn was an Irish lad from Charleston, where he had lived since arriving in America with his parents in 1849. In Charleston, he served as one of the pages at the Democratic National Convention in 1860, and the passionate speeches still echoed in his mind. Daniel became one of many young men caught up in the national issues of secession, slavery, and patriotism. As a result, he signed up as a soldier in Company I of the 1st South Carolina, the Richardson Guards of Charleston, a company with some 20 Irish names on its rolls. Daniel had learned to shoot while hunting rabbits and squirrels in the woods and swamps near Charleston, and his hunting trips made him an expert marksman. Soon he was promoted to sergeant. He would be called "fearless in battle."[4]

Working-class Irishmen, many of them recent immigrants, also inhabited Alabama's busy port city of Mobile. When the Irish members of the Mechanics Fire Company met there to form a volunteer military company in the spring of 1861, it was only natural that they should give it an Irish name—the Emerald Guards. On one side of their green flag was a harp encircled with a wreath of shamrocks and the Celtic war cries "Faugh A Ballagh" (Clear the Way) and "Erin Go Bragh" (Ireland Forever); on the other was the first national flag of the Confederacy with a full-length figure of George Washington in the center. When the Emerald Guards chose a uniform, it was dark green, although Confederate gray soon became standard when active campaigning commenced. The company entered the 8th Alabama Infantry Regiment, the first in the state to enlist "for the war," and left for service in Virginia. There—like the Irish Volunteers in the 1st South Carolina—the Emerald Guards became the color company, with the honor of protecting the 8th Alabama's regimental colors.[5]

A large Irish community existed in Mobile. Irish immigrants found work on the lively docks where ships came and went each day. Irish baymen manned the commercial vessels that traversed Mobile Bay; many took jobs on steamboats along the busy Alabama, Tombigbee, and Mobile Rivers that empty into that bay. In Mobile there was employment to be had as carpenters, blacksmiths, brick masons, shoemakers, draymen, and teamsters. Mobile's celebrated Battle House Inn employed a host of young Irish men and women who worked as waiters and maids and who lived on the premises. The Emerald Guards was not the only Irish company from the Gulf City. In the 8th Alabama, a scattering of Irish also carried muskets in Companies C, E, and H from Mobile.

The captain of the Emerald Guards was Patrick Loughry, a 45-year-old Mobile merchant born in County Mayo, Ireland. Big C. P. Branagan, a six-foot-tall 23-year-old Irish store clerk, became Loughry's 1st lieutenant. One of the company's older members, Michael Nugent, was named 1st sergeant and was soon promoted to lieutenant. John McGrath, who enlisted as a private, also made lieutenant before the end of the year.

The story of this Irish company paralleled that of Charleston's Irish Volunteers. None of the original leaders of the Emerald Guards finished out the war. Two 2nd lieutenants, John T. Halpin and James Flanagan, resigned before the end of 1861. In Virginia, Pat Loughry died in a hail of gunfire at Seven Pines in 1862. Crippling rheumatism compelled Michael Nugent to resign in January 1863. Branagan was killed at Gettysburg, and McGrath was wounded three times before he was forced to retire in December 1864.

Andrew Quinn, who enlisted as a private, ultimately commanded the Emerald Guards. Taken prisoner at Seven Pines, he was confined at Fort Delaware Prison, was exchanged in August 1862, and was promoted to lieutenant in November 1862. By the end of 1864—with Loughry, Branagan, and McGrath all dead or out of action—Quinn became captain of the company. And James Killion—who also enlisted as a private, was wounded at 2nd Manassas in August 1862, and was promoted to lieutenant—lived to see Appomattox as well.

Like all too many companies of Confederate Irishmen, the Irish Volunteers and the Emerald Guards would be devastated by death, wounds, and disease during the next four years of war. And very few of them would be left to tell the story of their experiences.

The wharves and loading docks of busy Southern seaports were familiar places to the rank and file of Charleston's Irish Volunteers and Mobile's Emerald Guards. But in Mississippi, the Jasper Grays called a different place home, a place not usually associated with Irish immigrants—the piney woods of south central Mississippi and the prosperous little town of Paulding in Jasper County. Attracted by the rich soil, Irish immigrants had been filtering into the area since the late 1830s, setting down roots in the community called Rose Hill, or "Irishtown." These sons of the Emerald Isle were farmers, creating their own small Catholic refuge in this sleepy south Mississippi county. St. Michael's Cemetery in Paulding contained many Irish names like Finnegan, Brogan, Dolan, and McDevitt.

James J. Shannon, the 36-year-old editor of the Paulding *Eastern Clarion,* was the son of Irish immigrants. The tall, lanky Shannon was also an attorney and was described as "a typical piney woods country lawyer" by a Mississippi soldier. He was also a compassionate man. On a trip to New Orleans, Shannon and his wife came across a young Irish girl staying in a convent. They learned that she had been separated from her father, who had sent her money for passage from Ireland to Washington, D. C. Instead the child wound up in the Crescent City. The Shannons offered to take the "lost Irish girl" with them to Paulding. She never located her father, but she found a new home in Paulding, where she eventually married a local Irish lad.[6]

When war threatened Shannon's home and his Irish community, he organized a volunteer company, the Jasper Grays, with many of his Irish neighbors who had no intention of sitting still while their way of life was jeopardized. The Jasper Grays became Company F of the 16th Mississippi Infantry. The Irish company was destined to serve under Stonewall Jackson in Virginia's Shenandoah Valley in the sole Mississippi regiment in his command. The 16th Mississippi had 40 or so Irish names on the rolls of the Jasper Grays, but there were nearly as many Irishmen in Company D, the Adams Light Guards, from Natchez. Twenty or so more Irish names appeared on the rolls of Company A, the Summit Rifles, from Pike County.

The Jasper Grays included brothers James and Thomas Lawless, second-generation Irish Americans who lived on their parents' farm with four sisters and a younger brother. James was a 21-year-old day laborer, while Thomas was an 18-year-old student. Twenty-one-year-old John A. McDavitt lived with his parents, two younger brothers, and two younger sisters. His Irish-born father taught in a local school. Michael O'Brien, a 46-year-old mechanic from Ireland, lived with his wife and three children. Timothy O'Flinn, a 42-year-old farmer born in Ireland, had a wife and seven children. Also accompanying the Grays was Father Boneim, a local Catholic chaplain, who related well with the Protestant soldiers in the company as well as the Catholic Irish. The elderly Boneim would not last out the first year of campaigning.

The Jasper Grays' first stop after leaving Paulding was the north Mississippi town of Corinth, where they spent three months training. The Irishmen learned that they were to be lodged temporarily in the county jailhouse, since better accommodations were not available. Shannon was outraged. "We have started off to battle," he complained, "and it will commence right here if we are not removed from this place." The Grays soon exchanged their jail quarters for more respectable ones in a local church. And then it was on to Virginia.[7]

The spring of 1862 brought the reality of war home to the Confederacy in the east. Marching northwestward along the Virginia peninsula separating the York and James Rivers, Federal commander George B. McClellan's army of 100,000 men was poised to strike the Confederate capital at Richmond, defended by Robert E. Lee's army of 60,000—and to end the Southern rebellion once and for all. But the new commander of the Army of Northern Virginia had other ideas, and Marse Robert aggressively confronted the Northern host in a series of bloody engagements in June known as the Seven Days Battles.

Lee intended to isolate and destroy Brigadier General Fitz-John Porter's Federal corps north of the Chickahominy River and cut McClellan's entire Union army off from its supply base on the York River. The plan called for simultaneous June 26 attacks on Porter by Rebel generals A. P. Hill and Thomas J. Jackson.

But Stonewall Jackson, whose troops were being rushed eastward from the Shenandoah Valley, was late and did not arrive until 5 p.m. Impatient, Hill initiated a premature attack at 3 p.m. against Federal troops strongly entrenched on the eastern side of Beaver Dam Creek. Thirty-six Federal field guns pounded the Rebels who were soon pinned down in the marshy terrain along the banks of the creek. There were many casualties.

During the night, Porter withdrew his troops four miles to the southeast to a new and even stronger semi-circular position along Boatswain's Creek. Again the bluecoats held the higher ground east of the creek and mustered close to eighty field guns. The Federals had designed a triple line of defenses, with rifle pits dug in the muddy creek bed itself, a line of log earthworks on the higher ground behind them, and a final line of earthworks at the top of the hill, brimming with Yankee guns. It resembled an inverted washbowl, with the Yankees entrenched on the raised surface of the bowl and in the rim, with a swamp separating them from the Rebels. To approach these defenses, the graycoats would have to slog through a marsh clogged with downed trees and tangled underbrush, while being pounded by Federal artillery and musket fire. The Confederate assault here would be a costly one.

Lee felt that he must try. On June 27, the Rebels attacked, Jackson from the north, A. P. Hill and James Longstreet from the south.

Hill's division struck first, brushing away the Federal rear guard at a large grist works, Gaines' Mill. By 4 p.m. Hill's vanguard, Maxey Gregg's South Carolina brigade, threw itself against the bluecoats' new defenses at Boatswain's Creek. Charleston's Irish Volunteers, with the color guard and the regimental colors, were in the center of the 1st South Carolina's battle line. It was "the handsomest charge in line I have seen during the war," Hill remarked.[8]

But the result was a repeat of the previous day's fighting. Stumbling through pine thickets and swampy terrain in the intense June heat, the Confederate formations quickly dissolved in the smoke and confusion. As the Carolinians struggled to pick their way

WHITE OAK SWAMP. Rebel troops struggled through swampy terrain like this to attack strong Federal defenses at Gaines' Mill in June 1862. Confederate Irish companies like Charleston's Irish Volunteers, Mobile's Emerald Guards, and Mississippi's Jasper Grays paid a heavy price in killed and wounded. (Library of Congress)

through the twisted briar-studded undergrowth, they came within range of the triple line of Federal infantry drawn up and waiting on the opposite heights of Boatswain's Creek. The bluecoats opened fire with all they had. The noise was "deafening," wrote Major Edward McCrady, and everything was instantly drowned out in "one continuous roar of the deadly fire of small arms."

The first volley reaped a wicked harvest. "[T]he whole color guard went down," McCrady wrote. Color Sergeant Jimmy Taylor was cut down instantly, but two other Carolinians quickly grabbed up the flag and bore it for a few more paces before being struck down themselves. Finally Private Dominick Spellman of the Irish Volunteers snatched up the banner and carried it throughout the remainder of the battle. Spellman would be the color sergeant for the regiment from then on.

GAINES' MILL
June 27, 1862

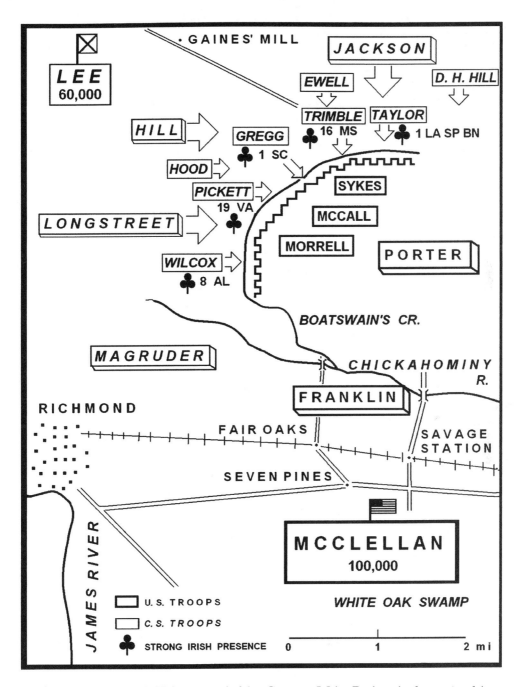

GAINES' MILL

LEE
60,000

JACKSON

EWELL

D. H. HILL

HILL

TRIMBLE

TAYLOR

GREGG
1 SC

16 MS

1 LA SP BN

HOOD

PICKETT
19 VA

SYKES

MCCALL

LONGSTREET

MORRELL

WILCOX
8 AL

PORTER

BOATSWAIN'S CR.

MAGRUDER

CHICKAHOMINY
R.

FRANKLIN

RICHMOND

FAIR OAKS

SAVAGE
STATION

SEVEN PINES

JAMES RIVER

MCCLELLAN
100,000

WHITE OAK SWAMP

☐ U.S. TROOPS
☐ C.S. TROOPS
♣ STRONG IRISH PRESENCE

0   1   2 mi

Although the Irish Volunteers, led by Captain Mike Parker, had sustained heavy losses in the previous day's engagement with Porter, they showed determination this day. The 1st South Carolina charged across open fields for several hundred yards as a frightful fire from Yankee cannon and muskets tore huge gaps in their ranks. But worse was to come. A swarm of blue-coated, red-legged Zouaves of the 5th New York, one of the best regiments in the Union army, came pouring out of the Federal works for a closer stab at the Rebels. Both sides gave as good as they got, though. "Watch me take a shot," Daniel Quinn declared. The Irish youngster coolly took aim, and his musket spoke as a Federal soldier toppled over. Lieutenant Colonel Hiram Duryea of the 5th New York said of the Rebels, "They fought bravely and contested the ground with great stubbornness."[9]

But the Carolinians' courage failed to bring them victory, for they were being cut to pieces, and the Federals still retained the works along Boatswain's Creek. The graycoats could only take shelter now in the ravines west of there and hope for relief as other Confederate units came up. The 1st South Carolina suffered 99 casualties—20 men killed and 79 wounded. In the Irish Volunteers, the dead included Thomas Gaskins, Thomas Hagerty, and John O'Rourke. Henry Donohue was wounded.[10]

Hill's attack was played out, and what was to have been a coordinated assault misfired again. Longstreet's troops were up now, on Hill's right, but Jackson again was untypically late, not arriving until 4:30 to begin the attack on Hill's left. Stonewall's divisions began to assail the northern edge of the Federal defenses. Soon heavy casualties began to mount in the same area where A. P. Hill's troops had been decimated earlier.

In Isaac Trimble's brigade, the 16th Mississippi Infantry—with the Irish volunteers from Paulding and Natchez—followed their commander into battle and ran into Rebel soldiers from Gregg's brigade falling back in disorder. "You need not go in;" they shouted, "we are whipped; you can't do anything!"

"Get out of our way;" one of the Mississippians yelled, "we will show you how to do it!"

Trimble instructed his troops to go in with the bayonet—not stopping to fire or reload so as to give the bluecoats a more tempting target—and not to stop until they reached the enemy lines. The Mississippians advanced, their officers yelling, "Charge, men; charge!" They plugged ahead through the boggy ravine, all the time under heavy fire—"a perfect sheet of fire," Trimble called it—awkwardly sidestepping the felled logs and twisted branches left to trip them up, then up the hill beyond to the Federals dug in at the top. The Yankees began to fall back, and Trimble wrote that the charge of the 16th Mississippi and 21st North Carolina, his two leading regiments, "could not be surpassed for intrepid bravery and high resolve." The 16th Mississippi's intrepid bravery cost the regiment 15 men killed, 51 men wounded, and 19 men missing, for a total of 85 casualties. It only took about fifteen minutes.[11]

More of Stonewall's combat veterans from the Shenandoah Valley moved to the attack. Richard Taylor's largely Irish Louisiana brigade entered the "perfect sheet of fire" that Trimble noted. With Taylor sick and absent, Colonel Isaac Seymour led the Louisiana brigade forward and was shot dead. It was in this desperate charge that Major Rob Wheat, the charismatic commander of the Louisiana Tiger Zouaves, the fearsome outfit of cutthroats recruited from Irish dock workers in New Orleans, was cut down scarcely twenty paces from the Federal lines. This time he did not recover from his wounds.

It was now after 5 p.m., and James Longstreet's division launched its own attack on A. P. Hill's right. George E. Pickett's Virginia brigade reached within 75 yards of the triple line of Federal defenses before heavy fire forced them to halt and take cover. The Virginians returned fire and surged forward. Pickett was wounded. The 19th Virginia's Colonel John B. Strange, taking command of the brigade, cited Lieutenant James

D. McIntire of his own regiment's Company F, for "coolness and bravery never surpassed." McIntire, a 20-year-old former student at the University of Virginia, led a company of Irishmen from Charlottesville, the Montgomery Guards. The 19th Virginia lost 11 men killed, 80 men wounded, and 1 missing at Gaines' Mill, total casualties 92.[12]

Cadmus M. Wilcox's Alabama brigade—with the 8th Alabama's Emerald Guards in the center of the line and with burly C. P. Branagan shouting the orders—plunged into the swamps west of Boatswain's Creek, then crossed an open field. The bluecoats raked the field with grape and canister and infantry fire, but the Alabamians kept on. Lieutenant Colonel Robert M. Richardson of the 12th New York counted at least four Rebel assaults during the afternoon, noting that, "Brigade after brigade of fresh troops poured down upon us from the opposite hills."[13]

It was a battered 8th Alabama that pushed off to the attack that afternoon. Just a month earlier, the 8th Alabama had lost 50 percent of its men at Seven Pines, the opening engagement in the defense of Richmond. The Emerald Guards' Captain Patrick Loughry had been killed, and other sons of Ireland died with him—Thomas Brown (a 21-year-old laborer), Corporal John Burke (a 24-year-old carpenter), 1st Sergeant Patrick Burke, Michael Egan (a 34-year-old bayman), John Hamilton (a 24-year-old steamboatman), Dennis Hays (a 25-year-old laborer), William McAfee, William McCready, Patrick Murphy (a 25-year-old laborer), Timothy Noonan, musician Edward O'Donnell, William Pickett, and Bartholomew Stafford. In the same engagement, the 6th Alabama, in Robert Rodes' brigade, had lost 102 men killed and 282 wounded, for a whopping 60 percent casualty rate. Captain John B. McCarthy of the Montgomery Greys, Company H in the "Bloody Sixth," had been killed in action. It had been truly a bloodbath.

The carnage at Gaines' Mill was no different. As the hot June sun set, the 8th Alabama's officers counted 31 men killed and 132 wounded, a total of 163 casualties in just a few minutes of combat. The dead included two more company commanders, Captain Thomas Phelan of Company A from Perry County and Captain G. W. Hannon of Company K from Coosa County. "The severity of the fight at this point of the field," Wilcox observed grimly, "is evident from the loss sustained by this regiment." The 8th Alabama lost half of its 350 men engaged at Gaines' Mill.[14]

Once again losses were heavy in the Emerald Guards. Lieutenant John McGrath was wounded—as were John H. Abbott, John Canney (who lost his left arm), William Carr, Timothy Finnegan (a 25-year-old drayman), Patrick Gilday, John Golding, Pierce Kent (a 35-year-old laborer, married with a child), Thomas Langan, John Mallon, Corporal William Mathers, James Pendergast, John Regan, Dennis Sullivan (a 26-year-old hostler), and Richard Walker. Among the dead were Thomas Donegan, William Dwyer, William Hamilton (a 34-year-old master carpenter), Durham Kain (a 26-year-old clerk), and Daniel Sullivan (a 26-year-old laborer). Sergeant Michael Sexton (the color-bearer) died while carrying the regimental colors, which were then borne by Corporal Phelan Harris of Company K.[15]

Also in Wilcox's brigade was the 9th Alabama Infantry, a command raised mostly in the northern part of the state. The 9th Alabama included the Railroad Guards, Company B, recruited in the Guntersville area from Irish laborers who worked for the Tennessee and Coosa Railroad. The 9th Alabama had seen its first baptism of fire on May 5 in an engagement at Williamsburg, where the regiment lost 10 men killed and 45 wounded. Captain W. C. Murphy of Company A had been wounded in this action and taken prisoner. "He remained on the field," Wilcox reported, "and commanded his company until shot through the body and borne from the field." At Gaines' Mill, the 9th Alabama lost 34 killed and 96 wounded.[16]

The Union defenses finally were starting to crack. The Confederates mounted their final assault near nightfall, at 7 p.m. Determined to prevail, Lee now had 56,000 men against Porter's 35,000. John B. Hood's Texas brigade stubbornly went in with the bayonet and finally shattered the center of the Federal line. And in this highly regarded combat command, Irish names embellished the rolls of the 1st Texas Infantry Regiment, at least 20–25 in Company C (the Palmer Guards from Houston) and Company L (Captain Alfred C. McKean's Lone Star Rifles from Galveston). The 1st Texas lost 14 killed and 64 wounded at Gaines' Mill. In the 4th Texas Infantry, Captain Edwin D. Ryan (a 24-year-old merchant from Waco) of Company E was killed in action. And in the 5th Texas Infantry, three companies (B, F, and H) each carried 15 or so Irish or Scotch-Irish names on roll. The Texas brigade would continue to build a solid reputation as one of the toughest and most dependable units in the Army of Northern Virginia.[17]

During the night, Porter withdrew south across the Chickahominy. He escaped to join McClellan's main army, but the Rebels had succeeded in severing the Federals from their supply base on the York. McClellan scrambled to shift his base southward to the James River. Over the next few days the Union commander fought a series of running battles with Lee at Savage's Station on June 29 and farther south at Glendale (or Frayser's Farm, also known as White Oak Swamp) on June 30. In both engagements, the Rebels paid dearly in casualties. At Frayser's Farm, it was an Irish Federal outfit (probably Philadelphia Irish in John F. Reynolds' Pennsylvania brigade) that battered the 8th Alabama, down 180 men, and again this command lost half of its soldiers. In the same action, the 9th Alabama suffered 31 killed and 95 wounded. And in the end, the bluecoats slipped away.[18]

McClellan at last determined to make a stand and fight, digging his army in on July 1 at strongly defended Malvern Hill. Lee threw five divisions at the Federal position. There were 5,000 Rebel casualties in two hours of futile assaults. "It was not war," observed Rebel general D. H. Hill, "it was murder." The hill couldn't be taken, and Lee couldn't destroy McClellan's army.[19]

Still the Army of Northern Virginia had saved Richmond. McClellan soon abandoned his offensive and withdrew from the Virginia peninsula. The human cost of the Seven Days battles was enormous. Union casualties were near 16,000, but Confederate casualties were even higher, at 20,000—twice as high as Rebel losses in the bloodbath at Shiloh in western Tennessee just three months earlier. For both sides, the illusion of a quick and relatively bloodless war had evaporated in the Virginia swamps.

The Emerald Guards of Mobile began the war with 149 men. In their first two months of combat, May and June of 1862, the Irish company lost 78 men killed, wounded, or captured. Thirty were killed outright in the fighting, most of them at Seven Pines. Most of these men would never be replaced. In the four years of war, the company lost 97 men.[20]

Of the Jasper Grays, 120 young men left Paulding in April 1861. Four years later at the surrender at Appomattox, less than 20 remained. With the prospect of a dismal future staring him in the face, a non–Irish member of the company summed up their condition: "No transportation, no rations, no money, ragged and heartsick, with miles and miles between us and our homes."[21]

BLOODY FIGHTING DURING THE SEVEN DAYS, JUNE 1862. **Rebel troops attack an enemy battery at Frayser's Farm on June 30, 1862. Irish-American Confederate commands lost heavily in the Seven Days' fighting. In a clash with a Federal Irish unit at Frayser's Farm, half the 8th Alabama Infantry became casualties. (***Battles and Leaders of the Civil War***, 1887)**

A bare few of the Confederate Irish remained to tell their story. Writing in his 81st year, Charleston's James Armstrong praised the sacrifices of his Irish Volunteers: "Though foreigners by birth, they became citizens from choice. The perils they so proudly encountered, the privations they so patiently endured, the dauntless manner in which they rushed to death proved that their love for Motherland did not detract from their devotion to the country in which they lived and for which they died."[22]

6. Southern Offensive: Second Manassas and Sharpsburg, August–September 1862

Of all the Confederate Irish in the Army of Northern Virginia, the greatest number by far hailed from Louisiana. And the largest concentration of these sons of the Emerald Isle called the Crescent City home. New Orleans furnished a half dozen Irish-dominated regiments serving with distinction in Virginia and several more in the Army of Tennessee.

The Irish in New Orleans embraced the Rebel war effort wholeheartedly. Irish recruits could be found in every volunteer regiment in the city, and in some the Irish were in the majority. "As for our Irish citizens," John McGinnis' *Daily Delta* proudly boasted, "—whew! they are 'spilin' for a fight' with old Abe."

A panoramic view of the lively New Orleans skyline unfolded from the majestic tower of St. Patrick's Church, which stood like a beacon to the Irish immigrants in the busy port city. The leaders of the city's Catholic Church enthusiastically took up the Confederate war effort. Father Ignatius Mullen even offered to donate the bells at St. Patrick's to Confederate General Pierre G. T. Beauregard so that they could be melted down for lead. Beauregard declined, thanking the pastor for his kindness but saying that it was not needed. Mullen and Father John Duffy emphasized their support for their Confederate Irish soldiers by blessing the flags of the city's Irish companies.[1]

There might not have been a true "Irish brigade" in the Army of Northern Virginia (like the Army of the Potomac's famous Irish Brigade), but there were two brigades of Louisiana troops that came close to fulfilling the concept. These two brigades—each with many Irish companies—had already proven their worth in hard-fought campaigns with Stonewall Jackson in Virginia's Shenandoah Valley and in the bloody Seven Days battles near Richmond and had become some of Robert E. Lee's most reliable combat troops.

Brigadier General William E. Starke's brigade contained the 1st Louisiana Infantry, formed from working class men—farmers, laborers, and clerks—in New Orleans; 21 percent of the soldiers in this regiment were born in Ireland. Two Irish-born officers, James Nelligan and Michael Nolan, had already been promoted to field command. These two men were characteristic of the young officers in the two most prominent Irish volunteer militia companies in New Orleans.[2]

Nelligan's prestigious Emmet Guards (Company D), two-thirds Irish, had been a fixture in the Crescent City for more than a decade, drawing its membership from the more affluent young Irishmen of the First Municipality. Their dress uniform was a snappy one—bright green coats and sky blue pants with gold stripes, their headgear topped with green plumes. Nelligan, a New Orleans auctioneer before the war, became the colonel of the 1st Louisiana.

Nolan's Montgomery Guards (Company E) also boasted an impressive pre-war lineage and attracted many prosperous young Irishmen of the city. The Montgomery Guards, 77 percent Irish, experienced only a 10 percent desertion rate during the war, a rare thing for any Confederate company. Michael Nolan, born in County Tipperary, was a 39-year-old grocery store owner when the war broke out. He enlisted as a sergeant, but soon became captain of the company. By the end of the summer of 1862 he had been promoted to lieutenant colonel. Nolan was described as a "blue-eyed, light-haired Irishmen ... mild and polite and friendly in his manners" and "the best, bravest and grandest soldier." The Montgomery Guards was now led by former sergeant Thomas Rice, recently promoted to lieutenant in July 1862.[3]

The 2nd Louisiana Infantry also had an Irish company, the Moore Guards (Company B) from Alexandria in Rapides Parish. The company's Irish-born captain, 27-year-old Michael Grogan, had been appointed to field command in July 1862. A machinist in New Orleans before the war, Major Grogan would lead the 2nd Louisiana at Fredericksburg in December 1862.

Colonel Leroy A. Stafford's 9th Louisiana Infantry contained the Emerald Guards (or Milliken Bend Guards), Company E from Madison Parish. The company's captain, 42-year-old planter William R. Peck, had already been promoted to lieutenant colonel of the 9th Louisiana. Peck's successor, Captain Edward Owens, was a 34-year-old Irish immigrant who worked as a laborer before the war. Owens would be captured at Gettysburg and would not be paroled until February 1865.

Perhaps the most unique company in the largely Irish 10th Louisiana Infantry was the Shepherd Guards (Company A), whose captain was 43-year-old Jacob A. Cohen, a laborer before the war. Cohen was Jewish, but he was born in Ireland and considered the soldiers from the Emerald Isle his brethren. Lieutenant Michael Carroll, a 27-year-old Irish immigrant laborer, would resign after Fredericksburg in December 1862. About that same time two of his countrymen, 23-year-old Patrick Barron and 25-year-old Daniel Mahoney, would both make 2nd lieutenant. And in Company C, Hewitt's Guards, Captain Thomas N. Powell, a New Orleans planter, would be promoted to major by May 1864.

Rounding out Starke's brigade was the 15th Louisiana Infantry. It had no distinctly Irish company, but more than 100 men listed their place of birth as the Emerald Isle.

Brigadier General Harry T. Hays commanded the other Louisiana brigade. In Colonel Henry Forno's 5th Louisiana Infantry, the vast majority of the soldiers were common laborers. One member said that the regiment was mostly made up of "uneducated Irishmen," but there was no distinctly Irish company, and only 94 listed Ireland as their place of birth. Irish-born painter John McGurk was captain of Company B, the Chalmette Guards. And 21-year-old James Garrity, a New Orleans clerk, was captain of Company E, the Orleans Cadet Company.[4]

The 6th Louisiana Infantry was nicknamed the Irish Brigade, because two of its companies carried that title, the result of an unsuccessful attempt to form a true ethnic organization of that name. New Orleans Irish laborers comprised the bulk of the regiment. Their first brigade commander, Richard Taylor, found them to be "stout, hardy fellows, turbulent in camp and requiring a strong hand, but responding to kindness and justice, and ready to follow their officers to the death." More than 70 percent of these boisterous lads had been born in Ireland. Irish-born Colonel Henry B. Strong, a 42-year-old New Orleans clerk, was the former captain of the Calhoun Guards (Company B), almost entirely Irish immigrants. Strong's place as company commander had been taken by another former clerk, 27-year-old Thomas Redmond, also a native of Ireland.[5]

Two of the most promising of the 6th Louisiana's field officers were the former commanders of the two "Irish Brigade" companies, F and I—William Monaghan, a 46-year-old Irish immigrant who worked as a notary public before the war, and 32-year-old Joseph Hanlon, a former newspaper reporter for John McGinnis' *True Delta*. Hanlon, who shot and killed a rival reporter in a duel in 1858, would command the 6th Louisiana at Gettysburg. Monaghan would lead the Louisiana brigade at Spotsylvania and would be killed in action in August 1864. Replacing Monaghan and Hanlon as company commanders were Captain Michael O'Connor, a 37-year-old Irish-born storekeeper in New Orleans, and Captain Blayney T. Walshe, a 23-year-old clerk. A native of County Wexford in Ireland, Walshe suffered from a wound to his ankle at Gaines' Mill and was on detached duty. Harry Hays called him "a gallant and efficient officer." Walshe would survive the war, and for many years thereafter he would be a tireless writer and speaker on behalf of Confederate veterans and for his comrades in the 6th Louisiana in particular.[6]

The 7th Louisiana Infantry (sometimes called the Pelican Regiment) was composed mostly of clerks, laborers, and farmers, with a third of the regiment born in Ireland. Described as a "crack regiment" by Richard Taylor, the 7th was Harry T. Hayes' old command before his promotion to brigadier general in July 1862. The 7th contained companies like the Sarsfield Rangers (Company C), led by Captain Johnathan Moore Wilson, a 32-year-old Irish New Orleans merchant, who would command the regiment by 1864; the Virginia Guards (Company D) and Virginia Blues (Company I, 80 percent Irish) from New Orleans; and the Irish Volunteers (Company F) from Donaldsonville in Assumption Parish.[7]

Of Colonel Henry B. Kelly's 8th Louisiana Infantry, 12 percent of its soldiers were born in Ireland. The regiment contained Captain Patrick F. Keary's Cheneyville Rifles (Company H from Rapides Parish). The 14th Louisiana Infantry contained no distinctly Irish companies, but six companies had an Irish majority.[8]

No longer with the Louisiana brigades was the 1st Louisiana Special Battalion (Major Rob Wheat's already infamous Tigers), the turbulent command recruited from New Orleans' most unruly Irish dock workers. After Wheat was cut down and killed at Gaines' Mill, the battalion was disbanded in August 1862, because it was believed that no one else could control them.

It would seem that there could be no more Irishmen left in New Orleans who had not signed up to fight for the Confederacy, but in the spring of 1862 yet another Irish command was organized in the Crescent City. The Irish Regiment, formed by distinguished Irish citizens P. B. O'Brien and W. J. Castell, was made up of men recruited for service at home. With a Federal invasion of New Orleans imminent, the Irish Regiment paraded and prepared for action. But the Irish Regiment dissolved along with other home defense units when Commodore David Farragut's Federal naval squadron blasted its way past the Rebel forts defending the mouth of the Mississippi. The Federals occupied the Crescent City on April 26, 1862. The city remained in Union hands for the rest of the war.

Missouri, Kentucky, and much of Tennessee also were now under Federal control, and Union troops had occupied St. Louis, Louisville, and Memphis, cities with large Irish populations. In the summer of 1862, Confederate strategists sought to reverse this string of losses. General Robert E. Lee's Army of Northern Virginia, euphoric after a series of successes that summer, prepared to mount its first offensive into Maryland, one in which the predominantly Irish brigades from Louisiana would play a critical role. The Confederacy seemed to be on the verge of a decisive victory and the promise of foreign recognition.

Robert E. Lee's Confederates had no time to relish their successful defense of Richmond. Already in July 1862, a fresh Union army posed a new danger. Even as George McClellan's battered Army of the Potomac was making its way slowly back to Washington, Major General John Pope—who had caught Lincoln's eye after winning victories along the Mississippi—assembled a new Federal force that threatened the northern part of Virginia. Pope's command would become an even greater peril once McClellan joined with it. The combined Pope-McClellan force would number 150,000 men, while Lee's Army of Northern Virginia mustered just 55,000.

Lee had already sent Stonewall Jackson's command of 12,000 soldiers north to Gordonsville to keep Pope under observation. A. P. Hill joined Stonewall later, raising his strength to 24,000. Jackson engaged part of Pope's army on August 9 at Cedar Mountain, about twenty miles north of Gordonsville, and defeated it. Lee's plan—a daring one—was to join Jackson and crush Pope before the link-up with McClellan could take place. He ordered Jackson to move farther north and to get behind Pope's army while he, along with James Longstreet's corps, moved north from Richmond to join him. The coming battle would unfold just to the west of Manassas, where Rebel forces had scored a victory a year earlier in the first major battle of the war.

Jackson's troops struck Pope's supply base at Manassas on August 27, looting it and putting it to the torch. Then Stonewall lured Pope north to Groveton on August 28, baiting him into an attack. Meanwhile, Lee and Longstreet approached from the south with 30,000 more men.

As August 29 dawned, Jackson waited for Pope to strike. The Rebels were drawn up north of the Warrenton turnpike along an unfinished railroad grade, an excellent natural fortification. Now it was they who were waiting behind strong natural defenses, as the Yanks had been waiting at Boatswain's Creek two months earlier. The Federal army—spread out and fatigued by two days of marching in an attempt to locate Stonewall—attacked from the south in a series of fierce piecemeal assaults throughout the afternoon. The graycoats beat off each attack.

On the Confederate left flank, Maxey Gregg's South Carolina brigade withstood a half dozen Federal assaults from one-armed Major General Philip Kearny's division, trying to turn the Rebel flank. Lieutenant Colonel Edward McCrady, former captain of the Irish Volunteers of Charleston, commanded the 1st South Carolina.

McCrady and his Carolinians moved forward into the woods and underbrush in front of the railroad grade and probed for the enemy. They did not have long to wait. McCrady's men were soon falling back in confusion, under fire from both front and

SECOND MANASSAS
Aug. 29–30, 1862

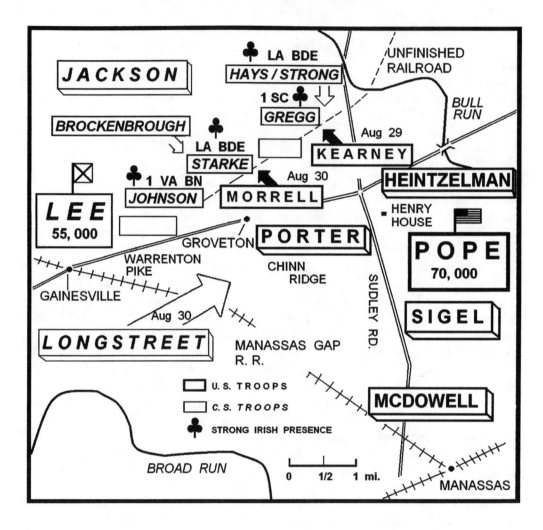

flanks. Captain Mike Parker and Lieutenant James Armstrong were able to rally Company K, the Irish Volunteers, and the rest of the regiment regrouped around the color company, Sergeant Dominick Spellman again holding the 1st South Carolina's colors aloft. But the enemy was too strong, and McCrady wrote, "it was all we could do to hold our own position." The Carolinians fell back to the railroad cut.

Waiting for another attack and low on ammunition, McCrady's men began inspecting the dead, removing cartridges that would be badly needed. Another attack soon came. Out to their front, the Carolinians could hear the snapping of bushes, tree limbs, and twigs as large numbers of unseen Federals approached in force. The Carolinians took cover and rose up to fire into the woods at the faceless enemy. Gunfire came in return. The bluecoats fell back, then returned to exchange fire again. "On they came," McCrady wrote, "The same terrific fire; the same endurance upon our part, with the same result."

The 1st South Carolina had already lost half of its officers and men, and now their ammuniton was entirely used up. At 4 p.m., the Yankees attacked in greater force. The cheers of the bluecoat soldiers and the breaking of bushes came closer. The enemy were only yards away. Quickly they plowed forward, breached the railroad embankment, and fell on the Carolinians. Mike Parker fell with a painful wound to his knee, but still managed to rally the Irish in his company, as did James Armstrong. Lieutenant Thomas McCrady, acting as officer in charge of the infirmary corps, also was wounded. The Carolinians fell back to a hillock about 300 yards to the rear of the railroad embankment and prepared to rely solely on their bayonets. It was a tense moment in the battle. The Rebels must hold or the left flank would buckle.[9]

At the last moment, help came in the form of Hays' Louisiana brigade, now led by Colonel Henry Forno. The Louisianans, along with Virginia and North Carolina regiments of A. P. Hill's reserves—many of them also without ammunition—rushed to Gregg's support and saved the day. All went in with the bayonet and pushed the bluecoats back, bringing an end to the day's fighting and securing the graycoats' flank.

A Virginia soldier, separated from his command, had fallen in with the 7th Louisiana earlier in the day. "Better stay with us, my boy," Irish-born Major Jonathan Moore Wilson had told him, "and if you do your duty I'll make it right with your company officers when the fight's over. They won't find fault with you when they know you've been in with the 'Pelicans.'" The major promptly assigned him to Company F, Captain Thomas Gibbs Morgan's Irish Volunteers from Assumption Parish. The cosmopolitan band of Irish immigrants and French Creoles—who spent much of the time in between actions in "games of 'seven up,' with a greasy, well-thumbed deck, and in smoking cigarettes, rolled with great dexterity, between the deals"—made quite an impression on the young Virginian who wrote that it "was as unlike my own as it was possible to conceive."[10]

In the fighting on the Rebels' left flank, Hays' brigade suffered a total of 135 casualties—3 officers and 34 enlisted men killed; 6 officers and 88 enlisted men wounded; 4 enlisted men missing. The 7th Louisiana "Pelicans" lost 48 of its soldiers—8 killed and 40 wounded. Forno was wounded, and command of the brigade passed to Colonel Henry B. Strong. As for the South Carolina brigade, the fight was also costly. In this "glorious but bloody day for the brigade," as the 14th South Carolina's Colonel Samuel McGowan called it, all but two of the field officers present in the brigade were killed or wounded. In the 1st South Carolina, 19 soldiers were killed and 97 wounded, for a total of 116. Irish Volunteer casualties included Privates Daniel Callaghan and Daniel Coffee killed, and Sergeant Dominick Spellman and Privates Richard Hartley, John Kiley, and Michael O'Neill wounded. McCrady was wounded in the head the next day and carried from the field, not seriously hurt.[11]

The next day, Pope remained confused about the positions and intentions of the Rebel armies. He now knew that Lee and Longstreet were just to his south, but he guessed that Lee was in retreat—a fatally wrong guess. Still obsessed with cracking the Rebel defenses along the railroad embankment, Pope again launched an assault on Jackson's corps to his north, ignorant of the fact that Lee and Longstreet were closing in for the kill.

Pope ordered Fitz-John Porter with his corps—the same bluecoats who had fought so bravely and stubbornly at Gaines' Mill—to assault the Rebel center along the railroad grade. William E. Starke's Louisiana brigade, led by Colonel Leroy A. Stafford, received the brunt of Porter's attack by the soldiers of George Morell's division. The Louisianans were posted in the right center of the Confederate line in a part of the railroad embankment called "the dump," a section that had not been filled in. Because it left a gap or opening in the line, "the dump" was a vulnerable point of attack, and the Rebels well knew it. This key sector was held by Lieutenant Colonel Michael Nolan's 1st Louisiana Infantry. Nolan's obstinate defense of this position unfolded in an extraordinary engagement known as the "battle of the rocks."

Starke had ordered the 1st Louisiana's position to be "held at all hazards." Federal attacks began early. By 8 a.m., the Louisianans could hear large numbers of bluecoats forming in the woods south of the railroad cut. Soon the Yankees attacked and kept up a series of assaults throughout the day, but the line held. The Federals suffered heavy losses. Then the Louisianans' ammunition gave out, and they seized upon the only other weapon available to them in a railroad cut—rocks of all sizes, and plenty of them. Perhaps the Irishmen had heard about the 1st South Carolina's predicament of the previous afternoon and improvised a defense to use in case they found themselves in the same boat. In any event, they quickly formed an assembly line, with part of them gathering up rocks, part handing them out, and others hurling them with all their might at the oncoming Federals.

The bluecoats hardly expected such a remarkable defense. The salvo of stones could not stop them for long, but the Irishmen were able to keep them at bay long enough for reinforcements from John Brockenbrough's brigade, posted on a hill to the rear of Nolan's position, to pour downhill into the cut and push the Federals back out.

This desperate fighting at the "dump" cost Starke's brigade 14 officers and 96 enlisted men killed, 30 officers and 239 enlisted men wounded, and 6 enlisted men missing, for a total of 385 casualties. The 2nd Louisiana suffered the most, with 36 killed and 83 wounded. Mike Nolan's 1st Louisiana lost 15 killed and 33 wounded. One of the casualties was the Jewish Irishman, Captain Jacob A. Cohen of the Shepherd Guards, 10th Louisiana. Cohen was killed in action. He is buried in the Confederate soldiers' section of Hebrew Cemetery in Richmond, the only Jewish military cemetery in the world outside of the state of Israel.[12]

Just to the right of the Louisianans, in Colonel Bradley T. Johnson's brigade, the 1st Virginia Battalion (the Irish Battalion) also resorted to some rock-throwing. These Irishmen from the Old Dominion held a section of the railroad embankment called "the deep cut." Porter's Federal troops came crashing out of the woods about 4 p.m., hurling themselves again and again at the graycoats. "The men fought until their ammunition was exhausted," Johnson reported, "and then threw stones." The Irish Battalion and the 21st Virginia counterattacked with the bayonet and threw the bluecoats back. Johnson recalled seeing Lieutenant Lewis Randolph of the Irish battalion hurl a stone at a Federal soldier. After the battle, the colonel found that same soldier with a fractured skull.[13]

By 4 p.m., the desperate resistance of the Irishmen along the railroad embankment began to pay off. Longstreet's troops were hitting the Federal army from the rear. Soon Jackson's men were scrambling out of their defenses as well and were advancing slowly toward the Federals from the north.

Federal resistance south of the turnpike focused on two critical hills that they must hold if they were to protect their route of retreat along the Warrenton turnpike and across Bull Run. By 6 p.m., the Rebels had swept the Federals from one of these, Chinn Ridge. The bluecoats drew up another defensive line on Henry House hill, the same site

HURLING ROCKS AT THE ENEMY. **Out of ammunition, William Starke's heavily Irish Louisiana brigade resorts to throwing rocks in an obstinate attempt to stem the Federal assault on the railroad grade at Second Manassas in August 1862. (Library of Congress)**

where heavy fighting had occurred a year earlier—and where Stonewall had earned his famous nickname. After a series of savage assaults failed to drive the Yankees from the hill, the Rebels broke off the attacks about 8 p.m. as a somber rain set in. The Federals retreated to Washington where the end of the line came for Pope's tenure as commander. Casualties for the 2nd Manassas were heavy—more than 14,000 for the Federals and more than 9,000 for the Confederates.

The sweeping Rebel victory at Manassas opened the door for a change in Southern military strategy. For the first time in the war, the Confederacy went on the offensive and carried the conflict into the North. The political advantage of a Southern victory on Northern soil could be enormous. Perhaps it might encourage Britain and France to recognize the Confederacy, providing the boon of badly needed foreign military assistance. At the least it could turn Northern public opinion against the Lincoln administration and force him to agree to peace with the South.

With its morale never higher, the Army of Northern Virginia pushed north across the Potomac into Maryland. But the Rebels did not get far. George McClellan, recalled to command the Army of the Potomac, moved to intercept them. Frantic maneuvering propelled the two armies into a savage collision at the small town of Sharpsburg on September 17, 1862, in what would become the bloodiest single day of the war.

Although A. P. Hill's division had not yet arrived, Lee deployed his forces—less

SHARPSBURG
Sept. 17, 1862

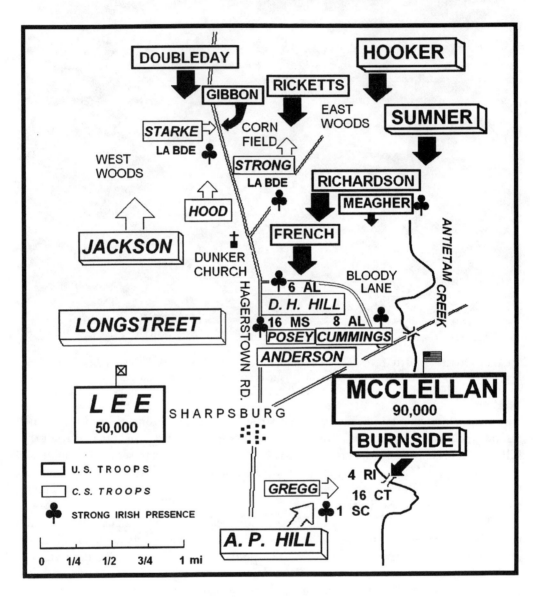

than 50,000 against McClellan's 90,000—roughly parallel to the Hagerstown pike running north to south through Sharpsburg, with Jackson in the woods north of town and Longstreet to the south closer to Antietam Creek. The Federals were poised to strike from their position east of the creek. The engagement at Sharpsburg unfolded in three phases of murderous combat rolling from north to south.

    Major General Joseph Hooker's Federal corps opened the first phase with a devastating early morning assault on the Confederate left flank in the woods north of town near the little white-sided Dunker Church. Brigadier General James B. Ricketts' division pounced on two brigades of Rebel troops posted in a field of corn northeast of town. After several savage volleys raked the cornfield, Hooker wrote, "every stalk of corn ... was cut as closely as could have been done with a knife."

Hays' Louisiana brigade occupied the woods behind the Dunker Church on the Hagerstown road. Daybreak brought the sounds of gunfire to the northeast. The Louisianans moved to assist Colonel Marcellus Douglass' Georgia brigade being mauled in the cornfield. Colonel Henry B. Strong formed his line of battle and pushed off in the direction of the firing. Soon the Louisianans came under punishing fire from Federal batteries in the woods to their right and bluecoat infantry to their front.

Hays' brigade pushed on past Douglass' ruined brigade to the edge of the cornfield, where they found themselves face to face with George Hartsuff's Federal brigade and pushed it back to the woods. Colonel Strong, mounted on his white horse, led the charge into the woods, but the Tigers only got within 250 yards of the trees before the blue-coats opened up with everything they had. The Louisiana brigade was shredded by artillery and small arms fire. "Never did I see more rebs to fire at," a Massachusetts soldier wrote, "than at that moment presented themselves." Strong was among the first to be shot down. The Louisianans held on for a few minutes longer, but Hays pulled his exhausted troops, who were nearly out of ammunition, back to the Dunker Church. The Tigers were happy to see John B. Hood's Texas brigade coming to their support. Hood's troops surged forward to the attack, throwing the Federals back, but suffering heavy losses in the process. The 1st Texas Infantry lost 45 killed and 141 wounded out of 226 men engaged—an astounding 80 percent! In the Lone Star Rifles, Company L from Galveston, Private Michael Garity was wounded and taken prisoner, and Privates James Welch and John O. Rourke were wounded, Rourke losing an arm.

In fifteen minutes, Hays' brigade was shattered, so badly cut up that they were out of action for the rest of the battle. More than 60 percent of the brigade was dead or wounded. Every regimental commander and staff officer was down. "The terrible loss among the officers," Hays wrote, "evinces with what fidelity they discharged their duties." The heaviest hit was the 8th Louisiana, with 7 killed and 96 wounded, for a total of 103 casualties. Strong's 6th Louisiana lost 11 killed and 41 wounded. Captain Michael O'Connor of Company F was wounded, as was Captain James Garrity in the 5th Louisiana. The "Pelicans" of the 7th Louisiana lost 11 killed, 56 wounded, and 2 missing.

The Tigers had inflicted heavy casualties too. The 12th Massachusetts lost 67 percent, 224 out of 334, the highest of any Federal command that day. Losses were heavy for both sides, and it is no wonder that Hooker called the cornfield a "bloody, dismal battlefield." Throughout the day, casualties would take a heavy toll of officers, shattering the command structure, with colonels commanding divisions, captains commanding regiments.[14]

On the west side of the Hagerstown road, Brigadier General Abner Doubleday's Federal division hit the Rebels hard. Starke's Louisiana brigade moved forward at 7 a.m., and at the edge of the woods they met the bluecoats in masses. Heavy fire from the front and from Federal artillery—grape and canister—from the left took its grim toll. In the 15th Louisiana, Charles Behan was killed on his eighteenth birthday when struck by an enemy shell. Brigadier General Starke was hit by three musket balls, fell and was carried away, and died an hour later. The 9th Louisiana's Colonel Leroy A. Stafford took command of the brigade. The Rebels rushed to the wooden fence along the Hagerstown road and reformed their lines there, keeping up a well-aimed fire against the Federals across the road to the east—the tough Wisconsin soldiers of John Gibbon's famed Iron Brigade, nicknamed the "Black Hats."

The graycoats and Yankees fought a see-saw struggle along the fence, alternately advancing and falling back, trading volley after volley that left the fence splintered to pieces. Amid flying wood chips and bullets, men stood up to the storm as best they could. The graycoats were raked by canister. The savage fighting left the dead in heaps all along the fence.

Commanding the 1st Louisiana, Lieutenant Colonel Michael Nolan took a bullet in the leg, but stayed at his post although in severe pain, "commanding his regiment with coolness and bravery," according to the 15th Louisiana's Colonel Edmond Pendleton, who ultimately took command of the brigade that day. Lieutenant Thomas Rice of the Montgomery Guards was wounded, as was Major Patrick R. O'Rourke, who lost his left arm. The color-bearer of the 1st Louisiana was killed, and the colors fell along the fence. A Federal sharpshooter officer who rushed forward to capture the flag quickly fell with seven bullet holes in him. But another bluecoat soldier succeeded in snatching up the banner and scurried back to his lines with it.

The Louisianans finally began to fall back, retreating to the Dunker church. As in Hays' brigade, it took only fifteen minutes to wreck Starke's brigade, with 81 killed, 189 wounded, and 17 missing, for a total of 287 casualties. The heaviest losses were in the 9th Louisiana with 25 killed and 57 wounded. Mike Nolan's 1st Louisiana lost 16 killed, 45 wounded, and 10 missing.[15]

Heavy fighting continued for the rest of the morning near the shell-pocked Dunker Church with attacks and counterattacks by both sides. Although the Federals made some gains, their assault finally sputtered to a halt and they could not break the Rebel lines that were stretched desperately thin.

Fighting now shifted farther south. Under the blue, cloudless sky of a bright mid–September day, two divisions of Major General Edwin V. Sumner's Federal corps moved forward with flags flying and struck the center of the Rebel line—D. H. Hill's division drawn up in a sunken road just to the northeast of Sharpsburg. Like the railroad grade at Manassas, the sunken road provided an excellent natural fortification for the Rebels, and from their defensive position they poured a deadly fire into the ranks of the oncoming Federals. The sunken road would become known as "Bloody Lane." Posted just to the left of a sharp inverted V or bend in the road was Colonel John B. Gordon's 6th Alabama Infantry, known as the "Bloody Sixth."

Lee himself had been in the area earlier, and Gordon, who was a distant descendant of Irish immigrants, had assured Marse Robert that he could count on his Alabamians. "These men are going to stay here, General," he had told him, "till the sun goes down or victory is won." Now, as the bluecoat masses advanced toward the sunken road, the Alabama boys were anxious to open fire. "Not yet," Gordon cautioned them. The Yankees came closer, now within range. "Wait for the order." Closer. "Fire!"[16]

The Alabamians decimated the leading Federal brigade of Brigadier General William H. French's division, Max Weber's, composed in good part of German recruits from the Northeast. Next they demolished Colonel Dwight Morris' brigade of soldiers from Connecticut, New York, and Pennsylvania. The graycoats waited for the next wave of attackers to come up.

One of the crack companies in the 6th Alabama was Company H, the Montgomery Greys. Formed in 1860, the Greys attracted a number of volunteers from the Irish community in Alabama's capital. The Irish in Mongtomery had attempted to organize their

TRAGIC DEBRIS OF WAR. **Dead soldiers of Starke's Louisiana brigade line the Hagerstown Road at Sharpsburg. Confederate losses in the bloodiest single day of the war were more than 10,000 men. (Library of Congress)**

own company, the Irish Volunteers, in February 1861. But as was the case with other Irish companies, lack of funds forced the company to disband. Instead the Irish enlisted in the Montgomery Greys. At least 30 Irish names appear on the company rolls, and the Irish residents of Montgomery raised $130 to help pay for uniforms for the company. Like their Irish compatriots from Mobile in the 8th Alabama, the Greys became the color company of the 6th Alabama. The 6th Alabama's first major combat action, the bloody engagement at Seven Pines near Richmond in June 1862, had cost the regiment dearly. Among the dead was Captain John B. McCarthy of the Montgomery Greys. By April 1865 only 11 of the Greys would be left.[17]

While the 6th Alabama and other Rebel commands fended off the Federal assault on the sunken road, Longstreet prepared a counterattack. Four fresh Rebel brigades advanced to the attack, as the bluecoats of French's shattered division began falling back. But any elation that the Rebels may have felt was short-lived, because almost immediately they encountered a second Federal division, Israel B. Richardson's, with the green flag of Colonel Thomas Francis Meagher's Irish Brigade in the lead.

"Boys," Meagher yelled, "raise the colors and follow me!" The Irish Brigade—which included the famous "Fighting 69th" regiment from New York City, as well as the 63rd New York and 88th New York Irish—surged toward the sunken road. Stationed in the eastern length of the road, George B. Anderson's North Carolina brigade replied with a blistering fire that sent the New Yorkers reeling. Captain James McGee of the 69th New York retrieved the colors from the regiment's wounded color-bearer and waved it fearlessly as the brigade suffered 60 percent casualties in a matter of minutes. Meagher took a tumble from his horse, appeared dazed, and had to be helped from the field. Some officers later charged that he was drunk. Battered and nearly out of ammunition, the Irish Brigade was forced to retreat.[18]

The Rebel counterattack fared no better. In Colonel Carnot Posey's Mississippi brigade, the 16th Mississippi—with the Irish Jasper Grays of Paulding—surged across the Bloody Lane in a furious countercharge and was badly cut up, losing 27 killed and 100 wounded. "The 16th Mississippi," a North Carolina colonel wrote, "disappeared as if it had gone into the earth."[19]

Cadmus Wilcox's Alabama brigade, led by Colonel Alfred Cummings, never even got to the road. The 8th Alabama—with Mobile's Emerald Guards—became mired in a see-saw battle in a cornfield just below the sunken road. While a dense mass of Federal infantry 120 yards to their front poured on a murderous fire, the Alabamians also suffered from artillery fire from Federal batteries across Antietam Creek to the east. Low on ammunition now as well, the Alabamians began taking cartridges from the bodies of the dead and wounded. The graycoats were gradually being pushed back into an apple orchard to their rear. A portion of the brigade, about 100 men, rallied and rushed forward but was contested by the onrushing bluecoats and finally fell back.

In the 8th Alabama, another frantic scramble played out over the regiment's colors, guarded by the Emerald Guards. Sergeant Phelan Harris, the flag-bearer, was wounded. Corporal Thomas Ryan of Company E scooped the flag up and was killed shortly afterwards. Sergeant James Castello of Company G grabbed the colors and was shot through the head. The flag then went to Major Hilary Herbert, who passed it to Sergeant G. T. L. Robinson of Company B. Robinson was quickly wounded, and Private W. G. McCloskie of Company G grabbed up the colors and carried them for the rest of the engagement.

The 8th Alabama lost 12 killed and 63 wounded out of 120 men engaged at the conflict at the sunken road. The regiment's roll of honor included John Curry of Company C, Thomas Ryan of Company E, and Private James Ryan, a wagoner of Company I, who was wounded. The 9th Alabama, with the Irish laborers in Marshall County's Railroad Guards, lost 12 killed and 42 wounded.[20]

The Rebels beat off the next assault by John C. Caldwell's Federal brigade, but now the gray line was weakening. The critical moment came when Colonel Francis C. Barlow's two New York regiments (the 61st and 64th) worked their way around to the inverted V in the sunken road and enfiladed the position of the 6th Alabama. The sunken road made a rise at the V, where the 6th Alabama was posted, making it more open to Federal fire. The Alabamians had already come under severe fire from Meagher's and French's troops.

The fresh Federal attacks finally stampeded the Rebels in the Sunken Road. The 6th Alabama had lost 52 killed and 104 wounded. Colonel Gordon was wounded for a fifth time and was out of action. Lieutenant Colonel J. H. Lightfoot, who took command of the 6th Alabama, misinterpreted an order to re-deploy from the V to a more protected position, and instead he ordered a retreat. Other regiments followed suit. The Confederates abandoned the sunken road, now clogged with bodies.[21]

After some hard-fought gains, the bluecoats now had a chance to shatter the Rebel center and push on into Sharpsburg inself, just half a mile away. With most of his troops used up, Longstreet scrambled to prevent what would have been a Federal victory. Only by scraping together all the available artillery and a few scattered troops did the Rebs offer any resistance. Finally the exhausted Yanks held up, because no fresh troops came up to back them. The ever-cautious McClellan would not risk committing his reserves and failed to exploit this opportunity.

The day's final Federal assault unfolded along Antietam Creek near one of three bridges across the stream. Major General Ambrose E. Burnside overcame Rebel resistance at the lower bridge and pushed his troops on across. The bluecoats established a beachhead in the fields south of town. But instead of Federal reinforcements, they were surprised to meet A. P. Hill's corps, arrived after a forced march from Harper's Ferry— just in time to push them back.

Hill's division, with Gregg's South Carolina brigade in the lead, stormed into an irregular rock-strewn cornfield at about 4 p.m. The Rebel attack shattered the inexperienced 16th Connecticut, drawn up at a stone wall running along the southern and western sides of the cornfield. Members of the 4th Rhode Island thought they spotted the Stars and Stripes amidst the dark swarm of troops approaching from the west, but a hail of gunfire showed them that what they had seen was the 1st South Carolina's blue flag and the accompanying Irish Volunteers of Company K. Adding to the Federals' confusion, many of Hill's soldiers were wearing captured blue clothing that they had looted from Federal stores in Harper's Ferry.

The Carolinians quickly routed the 4th Rhode Island. Soldiers of the 1st South Carolina were firing so rapidly that the rounds fouled their muskets and the Rebs had to use stones to hammer the charges down. Of the thirty men wounded in the 1st South Carolina in this battle, nine were members of the Irish Volunteers from Charleston. Captain Mike Parker was wounded again, as was Sergeant Peter McKeon, who later died. Privates James Brown, Edmund Dillon, Michael Duffy, Michael Feeney, Patrick Holloran, James Reilly, and Thomas Sullivan were also wounded.[22]

A. P. Hill's troops saved the day for the Confederates. Burnside's thrust disintegrated under the pressure of fresh Rebel troops. By 5:30 p.m., the fighting was over. Neither side had the strength to continue, and neither side had accomplished what they had set out to do. Two days later, Lee withdrew his army, re-crossed the Potomac, and headed back into Virginia. McClellan made no attempt to pursue and finish the Rebels, and an exasperated Lincoln finally removed him from command.

The appalling losses on both sides made Sharpsburg the bloodiest single day of the entire war. More than 12,000 boys in blue lay dead or wounded, a quarter of McClellan's army. But nearly a third of Lee's army was gone as well, with more than 10,000 of his gray-clad lads killed or wounded, losses the Confederacy could ill afford. Combined casualties for both armies were 22,719. The battle left the two largely Irish Louisiana brigades shattered.[23]

The horror of the slaughter was brought home to the Northern public in a way that the printed word could never describe—in the unforgettable battlefield photographs taken by Alexander Gardner and Mathew Brady—dead soldiers of Starke's Louisiana brigade strewn along the Hagerstown road and piles of mangled bodies in the Sunken Road. The battlefield dead now had a face.

The Southern offensive was over, and perhaps the Confederacy's best chance to win the war was gone. President Abraham Lincoln issued his Emancipation Proclamation on September 23, turning the war into a crusade to end slavery and effectively discouraging European support for the Confederacy.

Ironically, the prospect of slave emancipation soured Northern Irish enthusiasm for the war, and Irish support for the Union would suffer even greater setbacks in the next few months of bloody combat.[24]

7. *"With Distinguished Gallantry and Coolness": Fredericksburg, December 1862*

Along the high ground just south of the central Virginia town of Fredericksburg, about halfway between Washington and Richmond, the Federal war machine was unleashed on a frigid, sleet-bound morning of December 13, 1862. On Prospect Hill, the 19th Georgia Infantry Regiment found itself under attack from front and rear, as swarms of blue-coated troops poured through an unintentional gap in the Rebel line. Caught in the middle was the Jackson Guards from Atlanta, the color company for the 19th Georgia.

Long before it became the industrial metropolis that it is today, long before it became the state capital, Atlanta was emerging as the manufacturing center of Georgia. A thriving community of Irish immigrants soon sprang up there. As in many other Southern cities, they formed a volunteer company in June 1861, the Jackson Guards. James H. Neal, a 25-year-old Atlanta attorney, became the company's captain. He soon recruited Dennis S. Myers and Peter Fenlon as lieutenants and Timothy O'Kelly as 1st sergeant. At one of the Gate City's popular establishments, the Planters Hotel, he enlisted 23-year-old clerk John P. Keely as a lieutenant, along with 19-year-old bookkeeper Patrick Gannon. The hotel was operated by another Irishman, W. O. O'Halloran, and during the Civil War it would be used as a military hospital. More recruits from Atlanta's Irish community soon signed up, including immigrant brothers Hugh, James, and Patrick Lynch, who lived with their parents and four younger sisters; the elder Lynch was a stonemason. The Jackson Guards became Company B in the 19th Georgia Infantry. By the end of 1862, they had seen action at Gaines' Mill, Frayser's Farm, Second Manassas, and Sharpsburg.

1st Lieutenant John P. Keely commanded the Jacksons at Fredericksburg, with Neal recently promoted to major. In a letter to his parents Keely described the fight. The Federal assault hit "with the precision of a battering ram opening a breach." "On they came," Keely wrote, "in three full lines of battle, 100 yards apart, looking magnificently, every man clad precisely like his neighbor." It took only a matter of minutes for Federal troops to surround the 19th Georgia.

After putting up a stiff fight for about fifteen minutes, the 19th Georgia broke for the rear, losing 15 killed and 39 wounded. The Jackson Guards lost the 19th Georgia's colors. The flag was captured by Adjutant Evan M. Woodward of the 2nd Pennsylvania Reserves, an action that earned the Yankee officer the Congressional Medal of Honor. The 19th Georgia was the only Confederate regiment to lose its colors at Fredericksburg, and it would remain a sore point with the Jackson Guards for a long time. Lieutenant Keely, who managed to escape capture, credited the fall of the colors to Thomas Francis Meagher's Irish Brigade (nowhere near Prospect Hill on that day), but he may have been confused because the 2nd Pennsylvania Reserves did contain several Irish companies from Philadelphia.[1]

The 19th Georgia's Lieutenant Colonel A. J. Hutchins commended Corporal Daniel Rogan, a 22-year-old Irish immigrant who worked as a barkeeper before the war, as "cool and collected" while helping him to rally the men. Among the wounded in the 19th Georgia was Major James Neal. In the Irish company itself, Sergeant Thomas Ennis and Private John B. Kennedy were killed, while 2nd Lieutenant Peter Fenlon had to have his leg amputated and later died of complications from the surgery. 1st Sergeant Timothy O'Kelly and Private James W. Wilson were wounded.[2]

The bloodletting at Fredericksburg came as a new commander of the Army of the Potomac, Major General Ambrose E. Burnside, launched a fresh drive toward Richmond. The Federals mustered an awesome 120,000-man army, opposed by Lee's 78,000 rushing to block the bluecoats at Fredericksburg, a strategically located town on the Rappahannock River

On December 11, Burnside dispatched two of his three enlarged "grand divisions" across the Rappahannock via pontoon bridges that had arrived three weeks late because of bad weather and poor planning. Major General Edwin V. Sumner's division crossed the river at Fredericksburg, deserted after the Rebels had evacuated the town's civilians, and occupied it. Major General William B. Franklin's division crossed the river about a mile downstream. The Confederates were waiting for both forces and were dug in securely behind stout earthworks, James Longstreet's corps along the ridge called Marye's Heights directly west of town and Stonewall Jackson's corps along the high ground south of town.

Burnside attacked on the morning of December 13. At 8:30 a.m., Franklin's troops advanced against Jackson's position. Kept in check temporarily by Confederate artillery, they were in motion again by noon, and by 1 p.m. a serious problem loomed for the Rebels. A. P. Hill had left a gap in the Confederate line between two of his brigades, James H. Lane's and James J. Archer's. The area between the two brigades was a dense, marshy woodland that Hill considered too difficult for the Federals to penetrate. This proved to be a false assumption. Major General George G. Meade's three Pennsylvania brigades crossed the Richmond, Fredericksburg, and Potomac Railroad tracks and plunged into the undefended woods. One brigade came up against the right of Lane's brigade, the two others hit Archer's brigade from the left.

With his South Carolina brigade pulled up slightly to the rear of the gap, Maxey Gregg committed a deadly blunder when he took the advancing Federals for Confederates and ordered his men to hold their fire. Gregg was shot down, and his command was thrown into confusion. The 1st South Carolina's Colonel D. H. Hamilton took charge of the brigade.

According to Hamilton, only the 1st South Carolina and a portion of Orr's Rifle Regiment were in a position to engage the bluecoats, but, as Stonewall Jackson later reported, they "gave the enemy a warm reception." The South Carolina brigade lost 334 killed and wounded, with the 1st South Carolina accounting for 15 killed and 58 wounded. Among the Irish Volunteers of Charleston, protecting the regimental colors, Lieutenant James Armstrong (the acting captain) was wounded, as was Lieutenant Thomas McCrady. Privates Michael Nowles, Stephen O'Connell, and James Kelly were killed. In the wounded category were Privates Michael Conway, Edmund Dillon, Joseph Donnelly, Michael Farrell, Nicholas J. Kane, Patrick Kelly, Michael Mahoney, Francis Manion, and Michael Sullivan.[3]

While one Irish color company struggled to fight off the bluecoats, another was overwhelmed by the Yankees. On the left of Archer's brigade on Prospect Hill, the 19th Georgia was swallowed up in a wave of blue-coated attackers. It was in the desperate struggle to escape from this trap that the Jackson Guards lost the regimental colors.

The Confederates scrambled to seal the breach in their lines. Jackson quickly sent in two divisions to hit Meade's troops hard. The Federals could have exploited their initial breakthrough, but Franklin—like McClellan at Sharpsburg—was over-cautious and would not commit his reserves, although he had plenty of them. The graycoats pushed Meade's Federals back beyond the railroad embankment. The Confederate line was secure, and the Federals made no more attacks here. In the aftermath of the hard-fought battle, the grass around Prospect Hill caught fire, and wounded and dying soldiers fell victim to the flames. "Sickening in the extreme," Lieutenant John Keely wrote, after seeing one wounded bluecoat ripped apart after his cartridge box blew up.[4]

Burnside launched the second prong of his assault just before noon. Sumner's grand division attacked Longstreet's troops dug in along Marye's Heights. William H. French's division, with Nathan Kimball's brigade in the lead, deployed into line and advanced across the open fields west of Fredericksburg. Kimball's men were cut up by Rebel artillery as they moved forward, but when they reached within 125 yards of the stone wall, all hell really broke loose.

Dug in behind the stone wall in a sunken road—sitting and patiently waiting for the Yanks—were solid masses of graycoats from Thomas R. R. Cobb's Georgia brigade. The Georgians let loose a well-directed series of deadly volleys, and Kimball's brigade was shredded, nearly a quarter of them wiped out. Two more Union brigades would meet the same fate.

Brigadier General Cobb was killed during the first assault. Command of the brigade fell to Irish-born Colonel Robert McMillan of the 24th Georgia Infantry, posted in the center of the line at the stone wall. McMillan ordered his men to hold their fire until the second wave of bluecoats got close. The Georgians opened up on the second and third wave of Federal infantry marching up to Marye's Heights. McMillan was not a professional soldier, but he fully played the part today, inspiring his men and acting the father figure. And there he stayed throughout the afternoon and night. "In every attack," McMillan reported, "the enemy was repulsed with immense slaughter."[5]

McMillan had raised Company K, the McMillan Guards, when the war broke out. Born in County Antrim, the 61-year-old McMillan and his wife Ruth Ann had made a successful life for themselves in the mountains of Habersham County where he became a well-to-do attorney. Of the couple's six children, three of the colonel's sons were with him in the 24th Georgia. Major Robert Emmet McMillan, a 25-year-old attorney before the war, was a field officer in the 24th Georgia. Lieutenant Garnett McMillan, 20, was a student when the war started; he later became captain of Company K. And Sergeant Wofford W. McMillan was an enlisted man in the company.

FREDERICKSBURG
Dec. 13, 1862

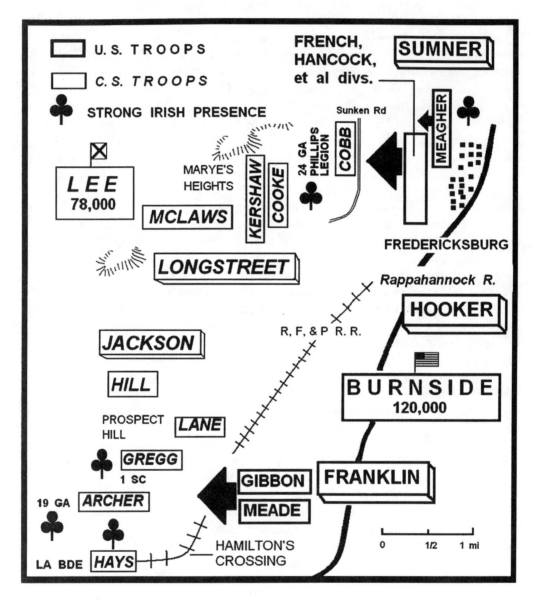

The next wave of Federals, Winfield Scott Hancock's division, had its turn at the stone wall and McMillan's defenders. And then came one of the most memorable—and most ironic—events in the war. The second of Hancock's brigades to brave the deadly fire from the Rebel salient—the famed Irish Brigade of Thomas Francis Meagher—advanced with green flags flying, determined to take the graycoats by storm. But the obstinate Irishman directing the fire of the Rebels was just as resolved that they would not

AT THE STONE WALL AT FREDERICKSBURG. The Lochrane Guards, an Irish company from Macon, stood with Phillips' Georgia Legion in the sunken road at Fredericksburg. Irish immigrant Colonel Robert McMillan commanded the Georgia brigade that defended this part of the line. The Federal assault was one of the costliest in the war. (Library of Congress)

succeed. Spotting the Irish Brigade's green flag, the old colonel's eyes lit up. "That's Meagher's Brigade," he shouted. "Give it to them now, boys! Now's the time! Give it to them!" Colonel McMillan was constantly in motion, passing along the line, waving his sword, urging his men to keep down behind the wall, and animating them with shouts of support. Now and then the men of his regiment broke into cheers when he appeared. At one point, McMillan was struck in the neck by a spent shell. When his son Garnett saw his father clutch his neck, he called out "Pa, are you hurt?" The colonel was unconcerned. "Hit, but not hurt," he replied, waving Garnett aside. Then he reached down, scooped up the musket ball, and calmly put it in his vest pocket.[6]

As they had at Sharpsburg's Bloody Lane just three months earlier, the Federal Irishmen came up against an awesome firepower in a reckless type of charge that had become all too common in this devastating American conflict. According to one Federal officer, the Irish Brigade "charged the enemy, who were well protected behind a stone wall, and received a murderous fire from both musketry and artillery." He lamented, "It will be a sad, sad Christmas by many an Irish hearthstone in New York, Pennsylvania, and Massachusetts."[7]

Meagher's command was decimated. "It was not a battle," Irish Brigade staff officer David P. Conyngham reported, "it was a wholesale slaughter of human beings." "I feared the Irish Brigade was no more," Meagher wrote. The brigade lost 50 men killed, 421 wounded, and 74 missing, for a total of 545 casualties. Losses were even higher for other Federal brigades in the bloody slaughter at Marye's Heights. "Meagher met his match at Fredericksburg," the *Charleston Daily Courier* boasted, "in a gallant son of the Emerald Isle, Colonel Robert McMillan of the Twenty fourth Georgia."[8]

Credit for the Rebel victory also could go to a County Tyrone native, 27-year-old Major Joseph Hamilton, who assumed command of William Phillips' Georgia Legion after the other field officers in the regiment were disabled. But it was not only two Irish Confederate officers who helped defeat the Army of the Potomac's Irish Brigade at Marye's Heights. There were Irish Confederate enlisted men behind the stone wall as well, not only the handful of Irish in the McMillan Guards, but a full company of Irish in Phillips' Legion, which held the left of the line at the wall. Company F, the Lochrane Guards from the central Georgia town of Macon, had combat experience at Malvern Hill, Second Manassas, and Sharpsburg under their belts. They took their name from Osborn Lochrane, an Irish immigrant who became a prominent Georgia political figure.

The original captain of the Lochrane Guards was an Irish immigrant, Jackson Barnes, a 51-year-old bookbinder with five children. Health problems led to Barnes' resignation in September 1862, and Patrick McGovern commanded the company at Fredericksburg. The Lochrane Guards were filled with recruits from the small but responsive Irish community in Macon—men like red-haired Hugh Caughlin; Sergeant Francis Dever, 29; laborers Andrew and James Dowd, who lived with baggage master William Cronin and his wife and other Irish immigrants; 36-year-old Sergeant John Doyle, a bar keeper who lived at Patrick O'Byrne's boardinghouse; 25-year-old James O'Brien, a marble cutter who wound up a musician in the Phillips' Legion band; and 24-year-old 1st Lieutenant Michael S. Walsh, a printer for the *Savannah Morning News*.

A number of the Lochranes were no longer with the company. Dennis Drew, a 27-year-old laborer, lost his left leg at 2nd Manassas. Patrick Barry, a 37-year-old laborer who lived at O'Byrne's boardinghouse in Macon, was discharged with a hernia in September 1862. In the same month, 30-year-old gas fitter William Carroll, who lived with an Irish grocer and his wife and 4 other Irishmen, was wounded and captured at Sharpsburg. In the same battle John Kelly, a 29-year-old bar keeper, was wounded and later died.

Several of the Lochrane Guards became casualties at the stone wall—Neil S. Duggan, wounded in the ankle; John Flanagan, a 37-year-old laborer, wounded in the shoulder; Patrick Furlong, wounded in the wrist; Patrick McGuire, wounded in the head. Patrick Keating lost his left leg; he died later. Richard G. Gillespie, who had already been wounded at Sharpsburg, was wounded in the neck at Fredericksburg. At Gettysburg he would lose a leg and wind up a prisoner, only to die in a Federal hospital.

By mid afternoon, a lull came in the bloody slaughter at the stone wall—and then a new wave of attacks. In the late afternoon, Burnside broadened the assaulting Federal lines and threw five more divisions of troops into the killing field. But by now the Rebels had reinforced the stone wall and sunken road, and there were more troops there now from Joseph B. Kershaw's South Carolina brigade and John R. Cooke's North Carolina brigade. Nightfall finally brought an end to the disastrous Federal attacks on Marye's Heights.

Cobb's brigade lost 33 killed, 198 wounded, and 4 missing, for a total of 235 casualties at the stone wall. Phillips' Legion accounted for 13 killed and 55 wounded, while McMillan's 24th Georgia lost 5 killed and 31 wounded. McMillan praised the courage and determination of his Georgians. "The heaps of slain in our front," he noted, "tell best how well they acted their part." As for the old colonel, McMillan's division commander Major General Lafayette McLaws wrote that he "behaved with distinguished gallantry and coolness."[9]

Burnside finally had seen enough. He withdrew back across the Rappahannock, and for all practical purposes his tenure as commander of the Army of the Potomac was over. The latest Federal offensive was finished, and major operations in Virginia ceased until the following spring. Blue-coated bodies blanketed the ground at the foot of Marye's Heights. The Federals lost an astounding 12,500 dead, wounded, or missing. The Confederates lost 5,000.

The Army of the Potomac's disaster at Fredericksburg had a ruinous effect on Irish morale in the North. "The Battle of Fredericksburg," historian Kelly O'Grady asserts, "is the most important battlefield event of the war for many Irish-Americans today." The destruction of the Irish Brigade on Marye's Heights seemed to many Northerners, Irish and non–Irish alike, as the most needless of sacrifices. Irish journalists had already raised the specter of the Union command's use of the Irish and other immigrant soldiers as "expendable" cannon fodder. "We did not cause this war," the Boston *Pilot* editorialized," [but] vast numbers of our people have perished in it." The Irish Brigade never recovered from Fredericksburg. Meagher turned in his resignation in May 1863 and finished out his service in the war with an undistinguished record.[10]

There were other causes for unhappiness among the Irish in the North. The war brought economic hardships to Ireland, curtailing immigration to America and hurting the peasants back in the Emerald Isle. Irish families found the money sent back to them

TROOPS OF HARRY HAYS' LOUISIANA BRIGADE AWAIT A FEDERAL ATTACK AT HAMILTON'S CROSS-ING BELOW FREDERICKSBURG. Hays' brigade contained many Irish from New Orleans. They forged an impressive combat record during the war. (Library of Congress)

from relatives in America cut, ironically making them the forgotten casualties of the American Civil War. Fledgling cotton mills in Ireland suffered because of the Union blockade of Southern cotton ports. Irish public opinion in the North began to turn decidedly pro–Confederate.

Irish immigrants in the North had been hostile to slave emancipation as well, and racial tensions smoldered in many Northern cities. The final straw for the Irish was the introduction of conscription in the North, which many Irish perceived as further discrimination against poor Irish immigrants who could not avoid military service by hiring substitutes as well-to-do Northerners could. Discontent in the Irish community finally boiled over in the summer of 1863. The "draft riots" in New York City unfolded in four bloody nights of rampage in mid–July. Largely Irish mobs looted, burned, and lynched at least nineteen blacks in the worst example of civil unrest in American history. It took days for Federal soldiers to crush the uprising and restore order. When the smoke finally cleared, some one thousand Irish were dead.

Times change. In the years following the war, Irish nationalists sought United States support for Irish independence, and such support could be more readily gained by downplaying Irish discontent with the Union during the war. The legend of the Irish Brigade remained. The Irish Brigade had bled itself to death on the slopes of Marye's Heights, gallantly sacrificing itself for the Union. The wartime exploits of the Irish Brigade were romanticized and held up as the ideal, while the participation of thousands of Irish on the Confederate side in the war was expediently erased. These Irish Rebels became the forgotten soldiers of the Confederacy.[11]

8. "A Stubborn and Bloody Conflict": Gettysburg, July 1863

When ordinary men are swept into extraordinary events, legends often take root. The Irish soldiers of Company C, 1st Virginia Infantry—the Montgomery Guard—helped to forge such a legend when they stepped off with some 10,000 of their fellow gray-clad Virginians toward the center of the enemy line on the third day at Gettysburg, July 3, 1863. They were about to take part in the most celebrated assault of the entire war—Pickett's charge.

Moving into position at 7 a.m., the soldiers of Major General George E. Pickett's division had already witnessed burial details digging graves for victims of the previous day's fighting. Many of the dead had been horribly mangled by artillery fire, a grim testimony to the severity of the slaughter. "I pass very close to a headless body," wrote 21-year-old Lieutenant John Edward Dooley of the Montgomery Guard, "the boy's head being torn off by a shell is lying around in bloody fragments on the ground."

The Virginians reached the rear of the main Confederate lines on Seminary Ridge where they halted in the hollow of a field. They were unable to see Cemetery Ridge, their objective where the Union army was deployed. Surrounded by apple trees, shaded from the blistering July sun, Pickett's troops waited. Some of the boys spent the time pelting each other with small green apples. It was the last carefree moment that many of them would ever know.

By 11 a.m., the graycoats were up and moving again. Crossing Seminary Ridge, they halted behind the tree line in the rear of a long line of Confederate artillery. Just after 1 p.m. a signal gun boomed. The mighty cannonade—some 130 Rebel guns—was about to begin. Intended to soften up the Federal line before the attack, it would go on for two hours. All the Confederate foot soldiers could do during this time was wait and hug the trembling earth. More than 100 Yankee guns, responding from their position on Cemetery Ridge, overshot the Rebel artillery and did more damage to the graycoat infantry waiting behind. Many soldiers were killed where they lay, but there was nothing the men could do but hold on and wait. "Orders were to lie as closely as possible to the ground," Dooley wrote, "and *I like a good soldier* never got closer to the earth than on the present occasion."

When the artillery fell silent, it was time to move out. With almost a mile across an open valley to the Federal lines, there would be a clear field of fire for Union gunners massed on Cemetery Ridge. Many young Rebels would die today. They knew what they had to do, but it still seemed hopeless. "I tell you," Dooley explained, "there is no romance in making one of these charges.... [T]he thought is most frequently, *Oh, if I could just come out of this charge safely how thankful would I be!*"[1]

So many of the Montgomery Guard were gone now. Health problems forced the resignation of the Montgomeries' old captain, John Dooley, now a major in the 1st Virginia, in April 1862. Lieutenant James Mitchell, a 24-year-old clerk, replaced him as captain but left the service after being wounded at 2nd Manassas, the battle that claimed the life of Lieutenant John H. Donahue, a former laborer who died at the age of 30. Sergeant Michael Dornin, a 30-year-old carpenter, was gone, discharged in March 1862. A number of men had simply deserted, including Patrick McGee, who was captured and executed by firing squad in January 1863. The company lost a good many men in the fall of 1862, including Corporal Patrick Duffy, a 33-year-old laborer; John Dooley's older son, James Henry Dooley (a student at Georgetown University when the war started) who survived being wounded and taken prisoner at Williamsburg; and Sergeant Lawrence McCabe, a stone cutter whose career with the Montgomery Guard was a checkered one—wounded at Manassas, promoted to corporal and then to sergeant, listed as AWOL and reduced to private, captured in June 1862, exchanged and finally discharged.

So few remained. Only a handful of the original company members still answered the roll by April 1863. Conscripts had to be brought up to fill out the ranks, but there were still a few veterans left. John and Sarah Dooley's youngest son, John Edward Dooley, had enlisted as a private in the 1st Virginia and was now a lieutenant in his father's old company. Twenty-two-year-old James Hallinan, a former laborer who had also enlisted as a private, was now captain of the company. Twenty-three-year-old laborer Thomas Murphy and 24-year-old James O'Connor were both back now, having been discharged in the fall of 1862 but now reenlisted. Peter McCauley, a 35-year-old laborer who had been wounded and captured at Williamsburg, had been exchanged and returned to the company in August 1862. Benjamin J. McCary, new to the company since enlisting in February 1863, would be wounded and taken prisoner at Gettysburg. And there was prankster James McCrossen, a 24-year-old laborer who once surprised a dozen or so of his comrades at Sharpsburg by carrying their canteens off on a water run and returning—much later—with all of them filled with whiskey.[2]

There were Irishmen in two more companies in Pickett's division, although by now, like Richmond's Montgomery Guard, these companies were badly depleted. In Major Kirkwood Otey's 11th Virginia, which had been present with the 1st Virginia in Longstreet's brigade at Manassas, the Jeff Davis Guards (Company H) had attracted many Irish rail hands and laborers in the western Virginia rail center of Lynchburg. Colonel Henry Gantt's 19th Virginia had its own Montgomery Guards (Company F) formed from Irish recruits in Charlottesville. The company's officers included Captain Bennett Taylor, a 27-year-old former instructor who would be wounded and captured at Gettysburg, and Lieutenant James D. McIntire, a 20-year-old clerk and student at the University of Virginia when the war began.

Other Irish companies also complemented Virginia regiments at Gettysburg. In Stonewall Jackson's old brigade, now led by Brigadier General James A. Walker, there were the Virginia Hibernians, the color company of the 27th Virginia from Alleghany County, led by Captain John Payne Welsh, the son of a Scotch-Irish immigrant. As the

Rebels geared up for battle at Gettysburg, Welsh was confident of victory and felt that the Yankees had their fill of fighting. "I think they got anough of it at Fredericksburg," he wrote. Welsh would be wounded in the hip at Gettysburg and would die twelve days later. Ironically, his brother James Welsh joined the 78th Illinois in the war and served as a Federal soldier.[3]

Also in the Stonewall Brigade was the 33rd Virginia, with the Emerald Guard (Company E) from New Market in Shenandoah County. Officers in this mountain company included Captain George R. Bedinger and Thomas Doyle, who would soon make lieutenant. Earlier in the war, the Emerald Guard had gained a reputation as "unmanageable Irishmen" prone to drinking and brawling. In December 1861, Jackson had separated the company from the regiment and assigned it to temporary duty as field artillery. But by December 1862, the Emerald Guards had proved themselves a reliable company. "I never saw men in more glorious fighting condition," Bedinger wrote to his mother. "Marching and camping or lying upon the frozen earth, but not a man deserted his post.... I am very much pleased with the conduct of my Irishmen; they are enthusiastic and have at the same time obedience."[4]

Still fresh in the minds of the Rebel soldiers was the joy of Lee's greatest triumph, his victory at Chancellorsville two months earlier. The new commander of the Army of the Potomac, Joseph ("Fighting Joe") Hooker, was ready for yet another Federal lunge at Lee's forces at Fredericksburg, planning this time to outflank and envelop the Gray Fox rather than attack frontally as Burnside had done. With an awesome force of 130,000 men—twenty divisions, plus three more of cavalry—Hooker sent Major General John Sedgwick with 40,000 soldiers to cross the Rappahannock at Fredericksburg and keep the Rebels occupied there. Meanwhile, Fighting Joe with 73,000 men would cross the river above the town, move through the tangled dense forest called the Wilderness, and circle around Lee's left flank to envelop the Rebel army. Such was the plan.

Outnumbered more than two to one, Lee had just under 60,000 men—six infantry divisions and one of cavalry. He was short two divisions that Longstreet had taken to southeastern Virginia to repel an expected attack on the coast. In spite of the odds, Lee boldly moved to confront Hooker, leaving Jubal Early with 10,000 soldiers of his division to hold Marye's Heights, scene of the bloody slaughter in December. On May 1, 1863, Stonewall Jackson rushed north and launched an attack against Hooker's much larger army near the crossroads community of Chancellorsville. The first day of fighting surprised and stunned Hooker, who suddenly went from the offensive to the defensive.

Lee and Jackson conceived a brilliantly executed movement to turn the tables on Hooker and envelop *his* army—even though the plan was a dangerous gamble. Stonewall with 26,000 men pushed off on a wide fourteen-mile march to get behind Hooker's right flank. His three Rebel divisions struck the startled bluecoats of Major General Oliver O. Howard's corps in the Wilderness near nightfall on May 2.

In the first line in the Rebel attack, Irish-American officer Colonel Edward A. O'Neal led John B. Gordon's old Alabama brigade. O'Neal called the Wilderness "a dense and tangled forest," but the Alabamians grappled through the twisted undergrowth of brush and oak, overrunning one line of Federal earthworks, then a second, then a third of logs. The 6th Alabama lost 24 killed and 125 wounded in the assault, with 5 color-bearers shot down. The "Bloody Sixth"'s roll of honor included Sergeant Dennis Madigan of Company H (the Montgomery Greys), one of the color bearers for the regiment.

FIGHTING AT CHANCELLORSVILLE. **Irish Confederates played a conspicuous role in Lee's brilliant May 1863 victory over Joseph Hooker's Federals, a victory marred by the accidental shooting of Stonewall Jackson. (Frank Leslie,** *Famous Leaders and Battle Scenes of the Civil War,* **1896)**

In Alfred Colquitt's brigade, the 19th Georgia lost 3 killed and 40 wounded. Sergeant Peter Gavan of Atlanta's Jackson Guards perished in the brush fires set off by the fighting. His comrades discovered the 21-year-old Gavan, just promoted to sergeant, burned to death, still clutching his musket. Gavan was the only son of an Irish widow who died heartbroken two weeks later.[5]

Jackson's furious 30-minute onslaught crumpled Hooker's right flank and sent his troops reeling. The bluecoats fell back in confusion for two miles until they reached the Chancellorsville crossroads, where they regrouped and prepared a defense. Darkness had fallen now, but Jackson hoped to launch a strong night assault to finish Hooker. But before completing his preparations, Jackson was struck down in a volley of musket fire from his own pickets who did not recognize him in the dark as he rode through the lines with his staff. Tragically, he died a week later, becoming the greatest casualty of Chancellorsville. Stonewall would never be replaced.

"There is a great deal of gloom in our Brigade," Captain John P. Welsh of the 27th Virginia wrote his mother, "on account of Gen. Jackson's death." Captain George R. Bedinger of the 33rd Virginia was one of four brigade officers to draw up a petition on May 16 asking that the brigade be redesignated the Stonewall Brigade. On May 30, their request was granted. These Virginians became the only such command in the Confederate Army to be officially designated by a nickname.[6]

At Chancellorsville, Jackson's three Rebel divisions pressed their attack the next day, with cavalry chief J. E. B. Stuart taking the reins of command. Francis T. Nicholls'

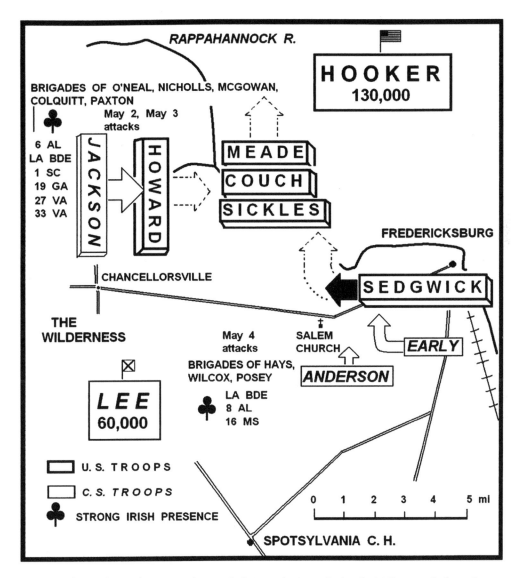

CHANCELLORSVILLE
May 2-4, 1863

Louisiana brigade took part in heavy fighting, losing 47 dead, 265 wounded, and many missing. The 10th Louisiana lost 50 men killed or wounded, including 6 color-bearers. Maxey Gregg's old South Carolina brigade was now led by Samuel McGowan, an Abbeville attorney and second generation Irish American, who was wounded in the fighting. The 1st South Carolina lost 12 killed and 88 wounded, Charleston's Irish Volunteers accounting for 6 of these. The Federals fell back to a new defensive position just north of Chancellorsville.[7]

Hooker was clearly on the ropes, but by then "Uncle John" Sedgwick's troops had overwhelmed Early's skeleton force left at Fredericksburg. Colonel William Monaghan's

6th Louisiana, aided by the 5th Louisiana, contested the Federals crossing the Rappahannock and managed to delay them for two hours, losing 89 men killed or wounded. At the stone wall on Marye's Heights, the Federals failed two times before finally overrunning the position. Early's troops retreated, and Sedgwick pressed on to join Hooker at Chancellorsville.[8]

Counting on the dazed Hooker to remain immobile at Chancellorsville, Lee whirled to confront Sedgwick advancing westward. In heavy fighting on May 3 and May 4, three Rebel divisions—including Early's men pulled back from Fredericksburg—smashed Sedgwick's corps in the densely wooded area near a modest, red-brick building called Salem Church.

Holding the road directly west of Salem Church, Cadmus Wilcox's Alabama brigade took the brunt of Sedgwick's attack but slowed down the Federal advance. The 8th Alabama lost 7 killed and 45 wounded, including Mobile Emerald Guards members John Cashin, J. H. Cochran, Patrick Crowley, and Cornelius Geary. Private Patrick Leary made the roll of honor. Captain Robert A. McCrary, a 27-year-old Selma clerk in Company D, was killed, "a valuable officer," Wilcox said. Casualties for the 9th Alabama, with the Irish company of Railroad Guards from Marshall County, were even higher, 23 killed and 89 wounded. Among the dead was Company A's Captain W. C. Murphy, "in the thickest of the fight, and in advance of his men."

Carnot Posey's Mississippi brigade attacked Sedgwick's Federals from the south. The 16th Mississippi lost 17 killed and 59 wounded, with the entire color guard out of action. The colors were passed to Corporal W. J. Sweeney of Company C who was struck down by grape shot and was carried to the rear still clasping the colors.[9]

Eager to be on the attacking end for a change after manning the works at Marye's Heights, Harry Hays' Louisiana brigade charged Sedgwick's troops dug in on a hilltop and took heavy fire. The Tigers gamely overran one line of defenses, then a second line above a sunken road, and pushed on to yet a third line drawn up on another hilltop, tougher works manned by Colonel Lewis Grant's Vermont brigade. The Louisianans plowed ahead. Eagerly observing the attack from a distant hilltop, Early and Lee were thrilled. Early threw down his hat. "Those damned Louisiana fellows may steal as much as they please now!" he whooped. Lee was more subdued. "Thank God!" he murmured. "The day is ours."

Lee had already won a remarkable victory. The icing on the cake would have been to surround and bag Sedgwick's corps, and the Rebels came close to doing just that. But Hays' brigade failed to take the last Yankee line. The boys from the Green Mountain State poured a devastating volley into the Tigers at point-blank range. Stopped in their tracks now, the Louisianans were too exhausted and too disorganized to go on, and 300 of them were taken prisoner. Sedgwick got away, leaving Hays' brigade with 63 dead and 306 wounded. Hooker withdrew his army north of the Rappahannock to safety.[10]

The aftermath of the brutal four-day combat that cost the Federals 17,000 casualties and the Confederates 13,000 was sobering, as the Confederate victors took in the extent of the carnage. "It is a slaughter pen," a member of the 16th Mississippi wrote. Captain William Fagan of the 8th Alabama recalled passing by the Chancellor House and witnessing "the most sickening sight I had ever beheld. Half buried in the mud were dead Federal soldiers, dismounted artillery, broken caissons, disemboweled horses, muskets, canteens, in fact, the whole paraphernalia of war in indescribable confusion."

In his second experience of seeing Federal wounded left behind to die in the fires set off in the woods, Lieutenant John Keely of the 19th Georgia translated his horror into action. He spotted an Irish soldier, most likely a member of the Philadelphia Irish in the 91st Pennsylvania, lying disabled with a broken thigh and trying pitifully to fight off the flames. Moved to compassion, Keely grabbed up the wounded soldier and carried him to safety. Keely reflected later on this act of mercy. "I paused not because he was an enemy," he wrote, "nor did I assist him because he was an Irishmen—I knew only that he was helpless, and in imminent danger, and that I could assist him—and I did."[11]

The Southern victory at Chancellorsville set the stage for the colossal battle of the war. Lee continued to seize the initiative to keep the Army of Northern Virginia's momentum going. In June, he launched his second offensive into the North and crossed the Potomac with an army of 72,000 men. Before the end of the month, Hooker resigned as commander of the Army of the Potomac and was replaced by George G. Meade. The two mighty armies maneuvered for a showdown at the small southern Pennsylvania town of Gettysburg.

On the opening day of the battle, the Confederates occupied Gettysburg and a low ridge running north to south called Seminary Ridge. Meade's army, some 94,000 strong, was strung out along the roughly parallel Cemetery Ridge to the east. Despite Meade's superiority in numbers, the Gray Fox was confident that the Federal army's flanks were vulnerable. The weak spots were two hills, Round Top and Little Round Top, on the southern end of Cemetery Ridge (the Federal left flank) and Culp's Hill and Cemetery Hill on the northern end, which Richard Ewell (Stonewall Jackson's successor) had failed to take the evening before. What Lee planned to do was to turn Meade's left flank. Longstreet's divisions of John B. Hood and Lafayette McLaws, plus R. H. Anderson, would attack the Round Tops. Ewell, with Edward Johnson's and Jubal Early's divisions, would attack Cemetery Hill and Culp's Hill.

Lee wanted the attacks to proceed early on July 2, but the Confederates were slow and only got underway very late in the afternoon. Hood's attacks on the Round Tops were furious but futile. The 1st Texas Infantry again lost heavily. The troops of McLaws and Anderson struggled for hours in bloody assaults farther west in a wheat field and a peach orchard where Union troops had unwittingly deployed in advance of the main line. They were unable to turn Meade's left.

The planned Rebel assault on the Union right flank also got underway late. About 8 p.m., Harry Hays' Louisiana brigade launched a determined and bloody attack on Cemetery Hill. The Tigers overcame a line of blue-coated infantry posted at the foot of the hill behind a stone fence, then two more lines along the slope. The Rebels drove back Adelbert Ames' mostly Ohio brigade and came close to overrunning Captain R. Bruce Ricketts' Pennsylvania battery on top of the hill. The Federal gunners hit the Confederates with grape, canister, and shrapnel, as Ricketts literally exhausted the battery's last round. The 9th Louisiana—with the Irishmen in Madison Parish's Milliken Bend Guards and Jackson Parish's Jackson Greys—fought their way into the battery. There was savage hand-to-hand combat, with the Yankee gunners using rammers, handspikes, pistols, and anything else they could lay their hands on. The Rebels took the hill and waited anxiously for reinforcements to consolidate their gains. But no support came. In the darkness, they could hear the sounds of large numbers of Federals massing for a counterattack. The bluecoats unleashed a deadly volley into the Tigers in the darkness. The fighting again was furious, but greater numbers prevailed. Hays' troops were rooted out and forced back down the hillside. By 10 p.m., it was over.

With proper support, the Tigers might have cracked Meade's lines on Cemetery Hill, but the manpower to follow up their initial breakthrough was sadly lacking now. Losses for Hays' Louisiana brigade were 26 men killed, 153 wounded, and 55 missing, for a total of 234 casualties, with the hardest hit being the 9th Louisiana with 57 casualties. Gettysburg left the Louisiana brigade shattered once again. Out of 1,626 men on hand on June 19, Hays had just 945 left on July 8.[12]

Meanwhile, Major General Edward Johnson's division attacked Culp's Hill. Colonel J. M. Williams' Louisiana brigade made its way among the boulders and trees along the slope of Culp's Hill toward the top. Fire from the top of the hill was intense and deadly, fighting was fierce, and there was confusion aplenty on the hillside as darkness came on. The 1st Louisiana—with New Orleans' Emmet Guards, Montgomery Guards, and Orleans Light Guards—forced the bluecoats out of part of their works, but Lieutenant Colonel Michael Nolan, the New Orleans grocer who had led the Irish rock throwers at Second Manassas, was killed.

The other Louisiana regiments could only take cover on the hillside and hope for the best. After four hours of this, the Louisianans had fired so many rounds that their muskets had become fouled. The graycoats used weapons taken off the dead and wounded, but they could make no headway. It was not until after midnight that firing died down enough for the Tigers to pull back down the hillside, leaving 43 men killed, 309 wounded, and 36 missing, a total of 388 casualties.[13]

The Stonewall Brigade made its attack on Culp's Hill in the pre-dawn hours of July 3, shrieking the Rebel yell as they clawed their way up the rock-clad slopes. By now the Federal defenders had been reinforced and had no intention of giving up the hill. Again attacks and counter-attacks swept the slopes. The graycoats were low on ammunition now. The Stonewall Brigade made four assaults with heavy losses, the last one around noon, but there were too many bluecoats. In the 33rd Virginia, Captain George Bedinger was killed and most of his Irish company, the Emerald Guard, was captured. The 27th Virginia lost 7 killed and 34 wounded at Gettysburg, while the 33rd Virginia lost 11 killed and 37 wounded.[14]

The savage fighting of July 2 had settled nothing, had failed to resolve the struggle. While all of this had played out, George Pickett's Virginia division was moving down the Chambersburg road to Gettysburg. But these graycoats were well aware of the intensity of the fighting going on to their south and had no illusions that they would avoid the slaughter. "It is a stubborn and bloody conflict," John Edward Dooley observed, "and we are sure if we escape tonight, tomorrow we will have our full share."[15]

The next day, July 3, Lee's final desperate gamble unfolded, a massive coordinated assault on the center of Meade's lines on Cemetery Ridge. Pickett's division was chosen to make the attack. Also taking part in the assault were the divisions of Brigadier General J. Johnston Pettigrew and Major General Isaac R. Trimble—North Carolinians, Alabamians, Tennesseans, and Mississippians, as well as Virginians. Waiting for them behind stout stone walls and barricades of wooden fence rails on Cemetery Ridge were the veteran soldiers of Major General Winfield Scott Hancock's Federal corps.

The long artillery duel was finally over, and the graycoats in Pickett's division began scrambling to their feet. But not all. Some of them lay dead or wounded from the Federal cannon fire, others prostrate from heat exhaustion. The men formed their lines and moved forward through the smoke still hovering over the ground, the smell of gunpow-

GETTYSBURG
July 3, 1863

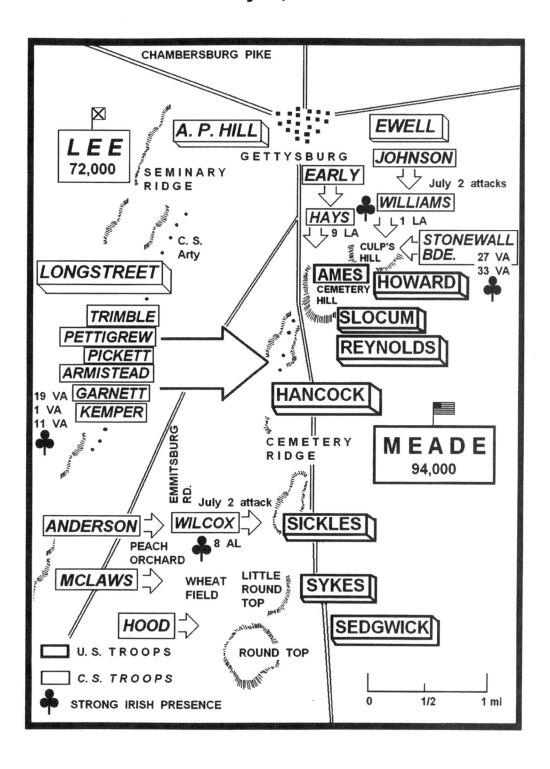

CHAMBERSBURG PIKE

A. P. HILL

EWELL

LEE 72,000

GETTYSBURG

JOHNSON

July 2 attacks

SEMINARY RIDGE

EARLY

WILLIAMS

HAYS | 9 LA

| 1 LA

C. S. Arty

CULP'S HILL

STONEWALL BDE. 27 VA 33 VA

LONGSTREET

AMES CEMETERY HILL

HOWARD

TRIMBLE
PETTIGREW
PICKETT
ARMISTEAD

SLOCUM

REYNOLDS

19 VA 1 VA 11 VA

GARNETT
KEMPER

HANCOCK

MEADE 94,000

CEMETERY RIDGE

EMMITSBURG RD.

July 2 attack

ANDERSON **WILCOX** 8 AL

SICKLES

PEACH ORCHARD

MCLAWS

WHEAT FIELD

LITTLE ROUND TOP

SYKES

HOOD

ROUND TOP

SEDGWICK

U.S. TROOPS
C.S. TROOPS
STRONG IRISH PRESENCE

0   1/2   1 mi

der still pungent. Rebel gunners raised their hats in salute and bid them good luck as they crossed the line of artillery. On the right was James L. Kemper's brigade, with the 1st Virginia in the center and the 11th Virginia just to their right. Next to Kemper marched Richard B. Garnett's brigade, with the 19th Virginia, and behind them Lewis A. Armistead's brigade. The other Rebel divisions were strung out farther to the left. The entire Rebel line stretched for a mile from end to end.

To the Federal troops waiting on Cemetery Ridge, the Rebels presented an awesome sight—a shimmering sea of bayonets studded with bright red flags amid the gray and butternut masses. "Onward they came," a Pennsylvania officer wrote, "and it would seem as if no power could hold them in check."

The orders were clear: No cheering, no Rebel yell, no firing. Save your strength and ammunition for the final assault. Dress your lines. Skirmishers out 200 yards in front. The graycoats marched forward, tin cups and canteens clanking, only the steady sound of the drum beat to mark their progress toward that "clump of trees" on Cemetery Ridge across the valley ahead.

The sun was blazing. The Rebels kept their formation well, even as the Federal artillery unleashed its response. Solid shot tore gaps in the Virginians' gray lines. The Virginians executed a half oblique, turning slightly to the left so as to close up the gap between the two attacking divisions. All the time the attackers were hemorrhaging, men falling right and left.

They reached the halfway point, a slight depression in the valley, halted, and closed up. The Rebels dressed their lines again and then proceeded ahead.

REBEL TROOPS ATTACKING CEMETERY HILL. Harry Hays' largely Irish Louisiana brigade attacks the Federal lines at Cemetery Hill, nearly cracking the Union defenses at Gettysburg. (Frank Leslie, *Famous Leaders and Battle Scenes of the Civil War*, 1896)

Kemper's brigade was drawing artillery fire from the Yankee guns across the valley and, even worse, from Federal artillery on Little Round Top to the south. Suddenly, a Vermont brigade swung out of the Federal line and turned to their right to fire into the flanks of Kemper's brigade. The 1st Virginia was presenting itself to the enemy at an angle and was taking deadly enfilade fire.

Four hundred yards to go. The graycoats reached the Emmitsburg road and began scaling the fences. A line of Yankee skirmishers got off a couple of volleys and then retired to the safety of their own lines to their rear. The Rebel lines were converging on the center, the low stone wall ahead of them, moving ahead. Now they were struck by canister, tearing into the gray-clad ranks, leaving behind a debris of mangled and dead men.

A hundred yards more to go. John Edward Dooley could see the Yankee guns looming up

LIEUTENANT JOHN EDWARD DOOLEY, 1ST VIRGINIA INFANTRY. The 21-year-old Montgomery Guard officer left a gripping account of the doomed Rebel assault on Cemetery Ridge, an action in which he was wounded and taken prisoner. (National Archives)

ahead. "[T]here is the line of guns we must take—right in front—but how far they appear! ... Behind the guns are strong lines of infantry. You may see them plainly and now they see us perhaps more plainly." The bluecoat infantry opened up now, many of them chanting, "Fredericksburg! Fredericksburg!" as more graycoats fell. The Rebs finally began to return fire. They were advancing up the gently rising slope to the Federal guns.

Now all became chaotic. The gray ranks were thinning. Flags were falling. Men were screaming. Close up! Close up! Captain James Hallinan was shot dead. Lieutenant Dooley was now in command of the Montgomery Guard. He would remember this brief, deadly moment for the rest of his life. "Volley after volley of crashing musket balls sweeps through the line and mow us down like wheat before the scythe." Thirty yards from the Federal works now, the graycoats raised the Rebel yell.

Kemper's bloodied brigade was slowing now, Garnett's brigade—with the 19th Virginia's Irish from Charlottesville—was moving ahead. Soon the two brigades merged, surging into the Federal works, Armistead's brigade close behind them. Kemper fell wounded. The color guard of the 1st Virginia was shot down. When the color-bearer was hit in the arm, Company D's 17-year-old Willie Mitchel—Irish nationalist John

Mitchel's youngest son—grabbed up the colors and was shot dead. The 1st Virginia's colors fell into the hands of the Federals. "Our poor Willy," John Mitchel would say. "He could not have fallen in nobler company, nor as I think, in a better cause."

John Edward Dooley did not make it into the works. Shot through the thighs, he lay listening to the sounds of battle, smoke and confusion. For an instant, he thought the graycoats had succeeded in breaking through, but the sound of fresh cheering told him the grim answer. "That huzza never broke from Southern lips," he wrote. "Oh God! Virginia's bravest, noblest sons have perished here today and perished all in vain!"

Possibly 300 or so graycoats, Armistead in the lead, continued bearing down on the clump of trees at the angle in the Union line. As a line of Pennsylvania soldiers fell back, the Rebs broke over the low stone wall and poured into the Federal works. The "high tide" of the Confederacy reached the Federal guns and—for just a fleeting moment in time—took the battery. But the bluecoats counter-attacked furiously, and there was desperate hand to hand combat. In the end, the weight of numbers was victorious. The Rebels were driven back, their assault broken.[16]

The Confederate attack was a disaster. Armistead and Garnett were killed. Kemper was wounded, along with every other brigade commander in the assault. Thousands were taken prisoner.

Amid the litter of dead and wounded covering the valley, the remnants of the doomed Confederate charge came limping back to Seminary Ridge. And yet there was fresh movement from the Rebel side. In a final pitiful epilogue to the tragic charge, two little brigades on the extreme right of the Confederate line—Cadmus Wilcox's Alabamians and Colonel David Lang's Floridians—began moving toward Cemetery Ridge. Intended to protect Pickett's right flank during the charge, the two brigades were finally being ordered forward. They already had lost many men in action the day before.

The 8th Alabama in Wilcox's brigade had been in the vanguard of the Rebel assault on Federal troops drawn up north of the peach orchard on the previous evening. The Alabamians had surged across the Emmitsburg Road, driving the bluecoats back and capturing several artillery pieces. But their elation had been short-lived, as Colonel William Colvill's 1st Minnesota Infantry came pouring down from their hilltop works in a desperate delaying action, hurling themselves at the Rebels—and losing more than two-thirds of their number in killed, wounded or missing to bring the assault to a stop. The Alabamians had held on for about thirty minutes hoping for reinforcements. None had come. Another lost opportunity. But as with the Louisiana brigade on July 2, there were not enough reserves available to exploit the advantage.

Now in the aftermath of Pickett's failed assault, the Rebel artillery was out of ammunition, and the Federal guns trained their fire on the two little brigades of Wilcox and Lang. Gaps began to open up in the ranks as the Alabamians steadfastly advanced to Pickett's support. "There was no longer anything to support," Confederate artillery chief E. Porter Alexander wrote. The futility of it all became obvious, and the graycoats were called back.

The 8th Alabama suffered 262 casualties, most of them on the second day at Gettysburg, the highest in Wilcox's brigade. Seventeen of the regiment's 26 officers were killed or wounded, including the Emerald Guards' Captain C. P. Branagan who fell with a shattered leg, was left in enemy hands, and later died. The roll of honor included Michael Duff and Michael Kane. John Cashin, Dennis Hall, and Patrick Kearny were killed; while Hugh McKeone, Patrick McNiff, and Thomas Smith were wounded. Nearly two dozen more of the Mobile Irish, most of whom were also wounded, were captured by the Federals.[17]

By 4 p.m. it was all over. Fewer than half of the soldiers who took part in the assault on Cemetery Ridge returned to their own lines. The 1st Virginia lost 120 men killed, wounded, or captured out of 160. Every officer was either killed or wounded, and there were no field officers left. The badly wounded Lieutenant Dooley spent the rest of the war in a Federal prison. There had been 29 men in the Montgomery Guard at the start of July, and by the end of August only 11 were left.[18]

The shattered Army of Northern Virginia withdrew across the Potomac beaten but not destroyed. While Federal casualties at Gettysburg numbered an appalling 23,000, more than 22,000 boys in gray were killed, wounded or captured in the three days of fighting. Lee's entire offensive campaign cost the Rebels over 27,000 men. Although a grand attempt by Lee to strike a masterful end to the war, Gettysburg marked the beginning of the end for the Army of Northern Virginia—but not the end of the war.[19]

9. "To No Avail": Wilderness to Appomattox, May 1864–April 1865

The South never recovered from the horrific losses inflicted on Lee's army at Gettysburg. The renewal of fighting in 1864 found the Army of Northern Virginia facing an enemy army nearly twice its size. Irish numbers in the Rebel army were steadily dwindling. In the 1st Virginia, Richmond's Montgomery Guard, which started the war with 90 men, was down to 28 by April 1864.[1]

The spring of 1864 brought the ultimate trial to the Army of Northern Virginia, where Lee was now opposed by the new commander of all the Federal armies, General Ulysses S. Grant. In a running series of brutal engagements through May and June, Lee and Grant battled their way south toward Richmond. For two hellish weeks without letup in May, the two armies were locked in a bloody grappling match at the crossroads site of Spotsylvania in the Wilderness west of Fredericksburg. This was a severe time for Lee's Confederate Irish, those few who were left now. Captain James Armstrong of Charleston's Irish Volunteers in the 1st South Carolina recalled that there was "as little rest as there were rations.... the men were seldom if ever out of the range of the enemy's guns.... There was no such luxury as a night's rest."[2]

On May 12, Federal troops assaulted a vulnerable point in the center of the Rebel works at Spotsylvania—an inverted V called the "Mule Shoe"—and threatened to break through. In heavy rain and mud, the Rebels launched furious counterattacks to seal the breach in their line at the place that would be called "Bloody Angle."

In dense fog and rain, Winfield Scott Hancock's 20,000-man corps launched the pre-dawn attack on the apex of the "Mule Shoe," overrunning J. A. Walker's Stonewall Brigade. "Remember your name!" Walker implored his troops. Lieutenant Thomas Doyle of the 33rd Virginia's Emerald Guard wrote that the fighting, much of it in furious hand-to-hand combat with clubbed muskets, "raged with inconceivable violence." In less than thirty minutes, the Stonewall Brigade, with the Irish and Scotch-Irish in the 27th and 33rd Virginia, was virtually wiped out as an effective combat unit. It would never fight again as an independent command. Most of the brigade was taken prisoner by the Yanks, among them Lieutenant Doyle, who summed up the graycoats' desperate defense this way: "All that human courage and endurance would effect was done by these men on this frightful morning, but all was to no avail."[3]

SEA OF VANQUISHED HUMANITY. Irish Confederates were among the hundreds of prisoners taken at Spotsylvania on May 12, 1864. The famous Stonewall Brigade and the Louisiana Brigade were practically annihilated in the fighting that, Lieutenant Thomas Doyle wrote, "raged with inconceivable violence." (Library of Congress)

The Louisiana brigades that contained so many of the New Orleans Irish also saw some of the worst of the fighting. The steady loss of manpower in the Wilderness had caused the two brigades to be consolidated into one, led by Colonel William Monaghan, with some regiments now the size of a company. Casualties in this command, also posted in the apex of Bloody Angle, were heavy, especially among field officers.

In the savage fighting that continued at the Bloody Angle throughout the day of May 12 and into the night, John B. Gordon's Rebel division spearheaded a counterattack that drove the Federals back and retook most of the Mule Shoe. Abner Perrin's Alabama brigade and Nathaniel Harris' Mississippi brigade were among the troops who counterattacked, taking heavy casualties in the process. The 8th Alabama lost 26 killed and wounded at the Bloody Angle. The brutal fighting of May and June 1864 claimed a number of the Emerald Guards from Mobile: 1st Sergeant James Jennings and Private Bernard Feeney, killed; Captain John McGrath, Sergeant Joseph F. Hart, Corporal Charles Cherry, Privates Francis McManus, Patrick McNiff, John Powers, and

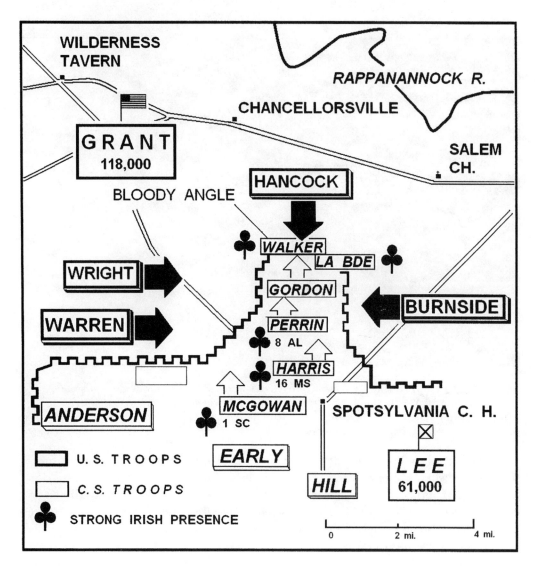

SPOTSYLVANIA
May 1864

Michael L. Regan, wounded; Sergeant Charles Hannon and Private Sylvester Russell, captured.[4]

In the 16th Mississippi, 16-year-old Buxton Rieves Conerly of Company E reflected on the misery that only a later generation of young Americans fighting in the trenches of France in World War I could appreciate: "The rain poured down upon us in torrents, and the ditches were filled with water reddened by the blood which flowed from the dead and wounded. We were forced to sit or stand on the bodies of the dead, covered with water." In the Adams Light Guards from Natchez (Company D), Privates Robert Currin, Timothy Carney, and Pat O'Donald were killed. The Jasper Grays (Company F) lost 12 men killed.[5]

Brigadier General Samuel McGowan's South Carolina brigade was also in the forefront of the Rebel troops rushed in to seal the gap at the Bloody Angle. "The trenches on the right in the Bloody Angle ran with blood," McGowan wrote, "and had to be cleared of the dead bodies more than once." While leading his brigade, McGowan was badly wounded, the fourth such wound he had suffered during the war. He called the struggle at the Bloody Angle "one of the most gallant and stubborn defenses recorded in history." Losses in the South Carolina brigade were dreadful—86 killed, 248 wounded (many fatally), 117 missing or captured. The 1st South Carolina's casualties—16 killed, 67 wounded—included

BRIGADIER GENERAL SAMUEL MCGOWAN. The trenches of Spotsylvania's Bloody Angle "ran with blood," McGowan wrote, as his South Carolina brigade fought desperately to stem the Federal onslaught. (Library of Congress)

Company I's 1st Sergeant Andrew F. O'Brien, who lost an arm, and in the Irish Volunteers (Company K) Private D. P. Cameron, killed in action, and Privates Michael McGuire and Michael Reilly, wounded. But the Rebels stemmed the deadly Federal assault at Bloody Angle, and the costly war in Virginia went on.[6]

Following the bloodbath at Spotsylvania—leaving more than 12,000 Rebels and over 18,000 Federals killed, wounded, or captured—Grant turned from attack to maneuver, side-stepping to Lee's right and moving south, forcing the Rebels to move south also to try to block him. The beginning of June found the Rebs confidently dug in east of Richmond at Cold Harbor, near the blood-soaked site of the battle of Gaines' Mill just two summers earlier.

On June 3, Grant ordered a massive 50,000-man frontal assault on the Rebel position at Cold Harbor. When the bluecoats managed to pierce one portion of the Confederate line, a Florida brigade led by Irish-born Major General Joseph Finegan—fresh from a victory over the Federals at Olustee in the Sunshine State—quickly moved in to seal the breach. When it appeared that the Floridians might be cut off, Finegan ordered Captain Charles Seton Fleming of the 2nd Florida to lead a charge against the enemy lines. Just five months earlier, Fleming—the grandson of Irish immigrants, a law student living on his father's plantation "Hibernia" in north central Florida—had persuaded the men of his regiment to re-enlist for the duration of the war. The young officer was struck down in a hail of gunfire, but the Rebels held their position. Grant's assault was a disaster. As at Fredericksburg, Rebel firepower decimated the attackers in droves, and 15,000 Federals became casualties, about half of that number in less than an hour. Confederate losses were less than 5,000.[7]

Grant now crossed the James River and moved quickly against Petersburg, the vital rail center 25 miles south of Richmond, hoping to sever Lee's army from its supply line to the Deep South. Attacking both with infantry and with cavalry forces, the Federals first attempted to cut the vital Weldon Railroad line south of Petersburg on June 22. A. P. Hill's corps successfully counterattacked and drove them back. The Federals attacked the railroad again on August 18, this time overcoming Rebel resistance and cutting the rail line. There still remained the Southside Railroad linking with Lynchburg to the west, however, and Grant had failed to completely isolate Lee's army. By the end of the summer, operations against Petersburg had settled into a prolonged siege—the longest in American military history—with the two armies locked in deadly combat across 37 miles of earthworks around the city.

One outfit that took heavy casualties at the Weldon Railroad was the 1st Confederate Infantry Battalion, formed in the spring of 1862, with three Mobile companies drawn from the Gulf City's Irish population. The battalion joined the Army of Northern Virginia in April 1864, after serving in Mississippi (where it took part at the bloody May 1863 engagement at Champion's Hill). Lieutenant Colonel George H. Forney was killed in the Wilderness, and Lieutenant Colonel Francis B. McClung, a 22-year-old railroad clerk from Tuscumbia, succeeded him as battalion commander. The battalion's roll of honor for the Wilderness and Spotsylvania included Corporal B. J. Hugan of Company B and Private Patrick Finegan of Company F. Captain Mike Donahue of the solidly Irish Company I was killed in the fighting at the Weldon Railroad, and the roll of honor for that engagement included Private John McNamara of Company I, Private John Dunnigan of Company D, and Sergeant J. Madden of Company F.[8]

The 8th Alabama fought the Yanks' cavalry raid on the Weldon Railroad on June 22–23. The Emerald Guards' Roll of Honor included Michael Cain, former blacksmith Michael Duff, and Hugh McKeone. In the 9th Alabama, the Railroad Guards' 22-year-old Captain Elias Jacobs—the son of an Irish mother and a German railroad contractor in Guntersville—was killed in action on August 30.[9]

Atlanta Irish in the 19th Georgia, now led by Colonel James Henry Neal, also sustained casualties in the Petersburg siege. In Captain John P. Keely's Jackson Guards, 37-year-old Irish-born Atlanta bar keeper John Ennis was killed, as was William Boyce. Sergeant Michael Haverty and Privates Martin Nally and Patrick Boyle were captured; Boyle later died from the amputation of his left leg.[10]

The 16th Mississippi fought at the Weldon Railroad on August 21, when Harris' brigade assaulted Federal entrenchments and was overwhelmed, losing many of its men captured. Colonel Edward C. Councill was fatally wounded. Sergeant T. J. Casey of Company A was killed in action, and Private Mike McGrath of Company D was fatally wounded. Casualties for the regiment were 6 killed, 28 wounded, and 59 missing or captured. The 16th Mississippi's colors were captured by Corporal H. A. Ellis of the 7th Wisconsin.[11]

In an attempt to breach the Rebel lines and bring the siege of Petersburg to an end, Federal soldiers devised a plan to construct an underground 511-foot-long tunnel laden with four tons of gunpowder beneath the Confederate defenses. The explosion on June 30 ripped a gaping hole thirty feet deep, 150 feet long, and 97 feet wide in the Southern lines. Blue-coated soldiers poured through the gap—only to become mired down in the crater, unable to advance. Rebel troops quickly counterattacked to retake the crater and seal the breach. "The heat was almost beyond human endurance," Captain William L. Fagan of the 8th Alabama wrote, "strong men fainted and were carried to the rear.... Hardly a word was spoken, for the Alabamians expected to die or retake the salient." Another

CAPTAIN CHARLES SETON FLEMING, 2ND FLORIDA INFANTRY. The young Irish-American officer died in action while leading a suicidal charge at Cold Harbor in June 1864. (State Archives of Florida Photographic Division)

savage combat, much of it in close quarters, played itself out in the crater. In the end, the Federals were forced to withdraw with heavy losses. "The crater was cleared of the dead and wounded," Captain Fagan wrote. "Men were found buried ten feet under the dirt." Among the Emerald Guards killed at the Crater were Moses Chafin (Chaffin), Patrick Crowley, and James Ryan.[12]

While Lee's army settled in for a long siege in Petersburg, Federal forces were gaining ground on other fronts. In Georgia, William Tecumseh Sherman's blue-coated legions were slowly but indisputably pushing toward Atlanta, the important industrial center of the Deep South. And in western Virginia, Union forces were once again threatening the Shenandoah Valley, posing a danger of cutting off vital foodstuffs from Lee's army. In July 1864, the Gray Fox dispatched Jubal Early, who had inherited Stonewall Jackson's old corps, to the Valley where Jackson had made his reputation. Soldiers in William Monaghan's Louisiana brigade marched with him. What was left of the old Stonewall Brigade went too, although now placed in a consolidated brigade with remnants of Ed Johnson's old division, now under command of Colonel William Terry.

Early won a victory over the Federals at Monocacy, near Frederick, Maryland, on July 9, and—as Jackson had done in 1862—he became a menace to Federal forces in the Valley. The Irish and Scotch-Irish soldiers in the Louisiana brigade and the decimated Stonewall Brigade revisited Jackson's 1862 Valley campaign in new clashes at Kernstown, Winchester, and Harpers' Ferry. Soon the Rebels were again threatening Washington, in hopes of diverting Yankee numbers away from Lee at Petersburg. It was not to be.

At the head of an army three times as large as Early's, Major General Philip H. Sheridan was sent to the Valley in August. Using tactics similar to those of Sherman in Georgia, Sheridan's troops burned their way across the Valley, destroying crops, waging a campaign designed to break the will of the Confederates. And he zeroed in on Early's forces as well. But Early was ever aggressive. On October 19, he attacked and nearly overwhelmed Sheridan's army at Cedar Creek, just north of Strasburg. But "Little Phil" was able to rally his troops and launch a successful counterattack that crushed the Rebel army.

Once more, battlefield losses steadily chipped away at the Irish element in the Virginia army. With more than 100 casualties in the Valley campaign, the already skeleton force that was the Stonewall Brigade had become yet a third smaller. Lieutenant Colonel William Monaghan, the 47-year-old former New Orleans notary public, died in a skirmish with Federal cavalry near Shepherdstown, Virginia, on August 25. His successor as commander of the Louisiana brigade, onetime *True Delta* reporter Joseph Hanlon, was captured at Strasburg. Colonel William R. Peck, the former captain of Madison Parish's Emerald Guards company, would next have his turn at command.[13]

In the fall of 1864, Early's corps returned to Petersburg. The veterans of the Valley campaign found Lee's ragged and hungry army worn down by months of attrition. The Federal noose was ever tightening around the city, and it was only a matter of time before Lee must evacuate. When that time came, Richmond must be evacuated also. News of the fall of Atlanta to Sherman on September 2 dealt a psychological blow to Southern morale—and a needed boost to Lincoln's re-election campaign. Now everything hinged on Lee. But "Marse Robert" did not intend to go out without a fight.

On March 25, 1865, Lee launched the Army of Northern Virginia's last feeble offensive, a surprise attack by John B. Gordon's troops on Fort Stedman, a key strong point in the Federal lines just east of Petersburg—and a high-stakes gamble at breaking out of siege. Lee hoped that he might force Grant to divert troops from his extreme left flank and thus open a door for the Army of Northern Virginia to slip away to the west. The Louisiana brigade (now led by Lieutenant Colonel Eugene Waggaman) spearheaded the pre-dawn assault—"on account of the valor of our troops," division commander Clement A. Evans had told Waggaman—and Virginians from the old Stonewall Brigade were part of the second wave of attackers. The Rebels achieved surprise, capturing the Union fort, but they could not hold it and were soon overwhelmed by superior numbers. A few days later, on April 1, Sheridan crushed the Confederate right flank at Five Forks, cutting the Southside Railroad, the remaining rail link to the south. Grant ordered a full scale assault on Petersburg the next day.[14]

Down to 150 men, the 16th Mississippi and 12th Mississippi regiments were among the defenders west of Petersburg at Battery Gregg, overrun by Federal troops of John Gibbon's corps on April 2, 1865. A battery of Rebel artillery had been ordered to hold the fort until Lee could evacuate his army across the Appomattox River. Harris' Mississippi brigade deployed as skirmishers in front of the fort, but when the massive wave of bluecoats surged toward them they fell back inside the works. Two heavy assaults failed to capture the fort, but the defenders knew that their time was short. "When the third assault came," the Jasper Grays' Sergeant J. B. Thompson wrote, "the fort was quickly filled by the enemy. We had no time to load and fire. We broke our guns and used the barrels for clubs. But what could we do against so many?" Thompson numbered only 27 out of 300 defenders left alive, 19 of them badly wounded. "The interior of the fort was a pool of blood," a New York soldier wrote, "a sight which can never be shut from memory. The rebels had recklessly fought to the last."[15]

The 8th Alabama's Captain William L. Fagan described the plight of the Rebels as they evacuated Petersburg and made a fruitless retreat westward — only to end at Appomattox: "Today's march was dreadful — the men slept as they walked, and when a temporary halt was made they fell down. Nobody laughs, and nobody comments. Officers ask no questions about their companies — each man seems absorbed in his individual suffering."

On April 9, 1865, Lee surrendered the Army of Northern Virginia. On hearing of the surrender, the 8th Alabama's color sergeant tore up the regiment's flag and distributed the pieces among the men. "You have never run in a battle," he cried, choking back tears, "and you don't surrender." There remained less than half a dozen of Mobile's Emerald Guards left to lay down their mus-

CAPTAIN WILLIAM FAGAN, 8TH ALABAMA INFANTRY. The 22-year-old teacher and farmer was the great-grandson of an Irish immigrant. Wounded at Second Manassas, Fagan saw action with the 8th Alabama in Virginia. In his diary, he described the Army of Northern Virginia's last bitter days before the surrender at Appomattox. (Alabama Department of Archives and History, Montgomery, Alabama)

kets. "[N]one of our companies," Colonel Hilary A. Herbert wrote of the Irish company, "were more thoroughly imbued with the spirit then animating the South."[16]

In the 6th Alabama, eleven Montgomery Greys were left at Appomattox, including Irish-born former corporal Lieutenant Philip E. Maher commanding; 22-year-old Corporal Michael Duffie, a color bearer who would later become a policeman in Montgomery; and Patrick Shevlin. The 10th Louisiana had only 16 men left at Appomattox. Of the two largely Irish Louisiana brigades in the Army of Northern Virginia, only 373 men remained. Nearly a quarter of them had died during the war. The remains of the old Stonewall Brigade numbered 110 soldiers at Appomattox, with no officer left above the rank of captain.[17]

Especially bitter was Richmond's Irish community that now witnessed the occupation of the Confederate capital. Captain Francis Potts of the Montgomery Guard called himself "a subjugated rebel, who has no nation, no rights, and no greenbacks." A prisoner of war since Gettysburg, John Edward Dooley returned in May 1865, sorrowful over the fate of his city and of the Confederacy that he and so many other Irishmen had fought for. "I shall not attempt to describe my feelings," he wrote. "The city in ruins and the hated and triumphant army of our malignant foes marching through the ruined city. With a raging headache and a swelling heart I reach my home, and here the curtain falls."[18]

PART III. THE IRISH IN THE ARMY OF TENNESSEE

10. *Hornets' Nest: The Irish at Shiloh, April 1862*

The bright, tranquil sunrise on Sunday, April 6, 1862, was deceiving to the blue-coated soldiers cooking their breakfast and moving about their tents on the ridge above Shiloh Branch. As the advancing Confederate army pushed toward them, most scarcely realized the danger they faced. But on the left of the Rebel line, the men in Brigadier General Patrick Ronayne Cleburne's brigade were alive with expectation, anticipating a great battle—a dawn attack on Major General Ulysses S. Grant's army encamped at Pittsburg Landing on the Tennessee River, a bold and ambitious bid to catch the Yankees napping and bag the whole bunch—and to reverse the chain of losses suffered by the Confederacy in the west in the first year of the Civil War.

Slogging through the tangled and overgrown underbrush of Shiloh Branch, Cleburne's soldiers found it difficult to even maintain formation. The brigade became separated as Cleburne with the 6th Mississippi and 23rd Tennessee regiments veered to the right, while the rest went to the left. The young Irishman himself had trouble negotiating the terrain, but a spill from his horse failed to slow him down for long. It was 7:30 when his troops came crashing into the camp of the 53rd Ohio, and the shrill Rebel yell rent the morning calm.

The first volleys quickly filled the air with the biting tang of gunpowder, blanketing the ground with smoke. A blizzard of rifle fire peppered Cleburne's men, who fell back to take shelter in a nearby ravine. Cleburne took it all in stride. "Boys," he yelled, "don't be discouraged; that is not the first charge that was ever repulsed; fix bayonets and give them steel." With a cheer, the Mississippians and Tennesseans were up again and at the blue-coats. They fell back again under heavy fire, but gradually the startled Yankees gave ground.[1]

At about 8 a.m., the rest of Cleburne's brigade came charging out of the woods in front of Colonel Ralph Buckland's untried Ohio brigade. Buckland's green recruits were taken by surprise, but still they put up a good fight. The Rebels hurled themselves three times at the blue-coated ranks drawn up along the ridge above Shiloh Branch, as casualties piled up. After losing 13 officers and almost 100 men killed and wounded out of 365, Colonel William Bate's 2nd Tennessee was out of the battle after this. Cleburne's old regiment, the 15th Arkansas, lost about as many, but stayed in.[2]

Pat Cleburne could number many of his Irish countrymen among the ranks of the Rebel army this day. Short of a majority they may have been, but they made their presence keenly felt. The 15th Arkansas, armed with new British Enfield rifles, contained some heavily Irish companies, particularly the Yell Rifles (Company C, Cleburne's old company from Helena), and the Phillips Guards (Company G). The tough Irish river-boat men of Company D (the Napoleon Grays) fought as skirmishers. One of them may have even been responsible for the hand wound given to none other than Brigadier General William T. Sherman, who commanded the division holding the right of the Federal line. Besides the Irish in the 15th Arkansas, Cleburne had the Helena Battery, an artillery company from his home town. Bate's 2nd Tennessee included an Irish company from Memphis.

And Cleburne's was not the only Confederate brigade to count many sons of Erin among its members. Coming up to the left of Cleburne was Bushrod Johnson's brigade. In this command, Colonel Knox Walker's 2nd Tennessee was full of lads from the poor Irish "Pinch" district in Memphis, so many that it was nicknamed the "Irish Regiment." The same Irish community contributed companies to Colonel Charles M. Carroll's 15th Tennessee and to the 154th Tennessee, where Captain Michael Magevney, Jr., would become colonel before the summer was out. The 154th Tennessee promptly went up against Captain Allen Waterhouse's troublesome Illinois gunners who had held up the Rebel advance for over an hour, but they only got within 300 yards of them.

The Rebels hurled themselves against Waterhouse's battery seven times but failed to root out the stubborn Yankees. At 9:30 the 154th Tennessee and Colonel A. K. Blythe's Mississippi Regiment moved forward once more, with the remnants of Cleburne's 23rd Tennessee and 6th Mississippi and two more Rebel brigades—Patton Anderson's and Robert M. Russell's—in support. It was a bloody encounter. A fatal gunshot wound toppled Blythe from his horse, and Bushrod Johnson was wounded by a shell fragment. This time the bluecoat line gave way, and the Illinois battery fell back. The Rebels now pressed on toward Shiloh Church as the right flank of the Yankee army disintegrated.

All of this came at a terrible price. Cleburne's brigade was a shambles, with 1,900 men out of 2,700 dead, wounded, or strayed away. Bushrod Johnson's brigade lost 62 percent. Scores of the "wild Irishmen" from Walker's 2nd Tennessee littered the ground. The 154th Tennessee also had suffered serious losses, and the 15th Tennessee counted 200 killed and wounded.[3]

To the east of this scene, Federal commanders were desperately trying to buy time for Grant to mount a defense at Pittsburg Landing, and they soon found a place to make their stand. Near the Federal center, Northern officers had come across an abandoned farm road and had quickly filled it with troops. The sunken road served as a natural fortification. In front of it were ravines and thickets, tangled underbrush, and open fields that the Rebels would have to cross. The battle began to focus on Federal resistance at this sunken road. Gray-clad veterans would later call it the "Hornets' Nest." They would make eight bloody attempts to capture it, four of them by Colonel Randall L. Gibson's brigade.

At noon Gibson's Louisiana/Arkansas brigade moved forward in line of battle toward the section of the sunken road held by Iowa and Missouri troops. The rattle of small arms to their front and the booming of artillery reminded one soldier in the 13th Louisiana of "a great thunder storm that shook the whole earth." The scrub oak here was so thick, another remembered, "it was almost impossible for a man to walk through it."[4]

In such a tangle of underbrush, where soldiers could scarcely see parts of their own

INTO THE HORNETS' NEST. **Colonel Randall Gibson's brigade, including many Irishmen from Arkansas and Louisiana, crashes through the underbrush to attack the stubborn Federal salient on the first day of fighting at Shiloh. A third of the brigade quickly became casualties. (Library of Congress)**

lines, it was easy to mistake one another for the enemy. Some of Gibson's soldiers fired on each other. In the 1st Arkansas (containing a goodly number of Irish) Colonel James F. Fagan shouted to an officer in the 4th Louisiana, "For God's sake, cease firing, you are killing our men, and we are killing yours."[5]

As Gibson's troops finally got to within a hundred yards of their objective, the Federal defenders opened up with "a perfect tornado of rifle fire," one Louisiana soldier wrote, "in our very faces." "Men fell around us like leaves," recalled an Arkansas soldier. In the 13th Louisiana (about 25 percent Irish, largely from New Orleans) Captain Stephen O'Leary, the former police chief of the Crescent City, was wounded. By the end of the day, he would be the senior officer in the regiment. "[I]n less than ten minutes in the 'hornets' nest' at Shiloh," Captain John McGrath of the 13th Louisiana wrote, "the appetite for fighting of nine-tenths of the regiment was satiated to repletion."[6]

But Gibson's soldiers would go back a second, third, and fourth time. By 2 p.m., they could do no more. At least a third of them were already lying in "heaps of killed and wounded," according to Fagan, thrown from his horse in the third charge. Gibson's men, Fagan wrote, "endured a murderous fire until endurance ceased to be a virtue."[7]

At 2:30, the Arkansas brigade of Brigadier General Thomas C. Hindman tried its hand at the Hornet's Nest. This outfit had already been engaged in two separate encounters with the enemy on other parts of the field that day. With the 2nd Arkansas (containing an Irish company from Helena) in the center and the 3rd Confederate Infantry (with Company D, the Shamrock Guards, largely Irish from Vicksburg) on the right, the brigade plunged through the thickets toward the Yankee stronghold. They only reached to within sixty yards of the enemy.

The final assault came at 3:30, when Brigadier General Patton Anderson's Florida-Louisiana brigade charged the Hornet's Nest. Once again the Rebels made no headway. Casualties were especially heavy in the 20th Louisiana, a regiment with four Irish companies from New Orleans.

Time was slipping away for the Rebels. What General Albert Sidney Johnston, the Confederate commander, had hoped for—and what should have been—was to have driven the Federal left clear back to Pittsburg Landing to envelop the entire army. Instead the Confederates had bogged down in a bloody contest at the Hornets' Nest. Scrambling to find another way to break the Yankee salient, Johnston seized on a different approach. Just east of the end of the sunken road lay a ten-acre peach orchard full of bluecoated troops. If he could take the peach orchard, Johnston could force the Yankees' left flank. Riding up to Brigadier General John S. Bowen's reserve brigade, Johnston directed them into line of battle. "Men!" he cried, "they are stubborn; we must use the bayonet. I will lead you!" At 2 p.m. the Rebel attack forged ahead, with Bowen's brigade in the center and Johnston riding in front. The graycoats would sweep Brigadier General Stephen Hurlbut's Federals from the peach orchard. But by 2:30 Johnston would be dead, shot down in the charge.[8]

COLONEL JAMES FLEMING FAGAN, 1ST ARKANSAS INFANTRY. Fagan's regiment was part of Gibson's brigade, which lay in "heaps of killed and wounded" after their fierce assault on the Hornets' Nest. The Irish-American officer later served in the Trans-Mississippi. (Library of Congress)

In Bowen's brigade, yet another Irish-tinged outfit, the 1st Missouri, led by 25-year-old Lieutenant Colonel Amos C. Riley, was in the thick of the fighting. In the 1st Missouri, Company D (the St. Louis Grays) was made up mostly of Irish firefighters, and Companies A and C also had large numbers of Irish. Moving forward under enemy fire through the mostly empty fields in front of the peach orchard, "taxed our patience and discipline very much," wrote Lieutenant Joseph Boyce. "It was the first fire the regiment was ever under and did not agree with our

SHILOH April 6, 1862

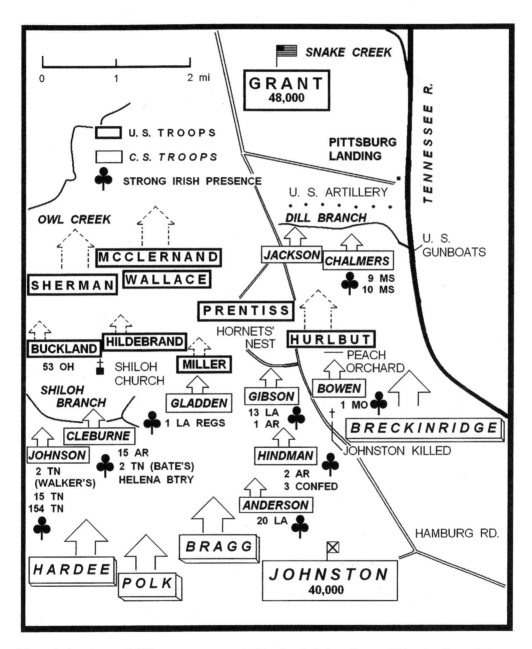

idea of a battle at all." Boyce was wounded in the fighting. It would be the first of eleven wounds that he would receive during the war.[9]

The fierce infantry assault on the Union left flank, combined with a determined artillery barrage—the greatest concentration of massed field artillery ever seen in North America up to that time—finally did the trick. This time the blue lines buckled, and the

Federals in the Hornets' Nest were surrounded. By sundown, Brigadier General Benjamin M. Prentiss' exhausted men, many of them out of ammunition now, surrendered. The Rebels captured the entire division.

The Confederates' savage but uncoordinated assaults on the Hornets' Nest had given Grant time to form a new defensive line at Pittsburg Landing. With night fast approaching, there was little opportunity now for a final push northward to capture the Yankees before reinforcements could reach them. Even now scores of Rebels were falling out from exhaustion and hunger, many of them stopping to forage for food and plunder in the captured Yankee camps.

At 6 p.m., the Rebels finally reached Pittsburg Landing and attempted to break through the Federal left flank there. James R. Chalmers' brigade and John K. Jackson's brigade made the final attack that day. On the extreme right, Chalmers' 10th Mississippi, three companies of which contained large numbers of Irish, exchanged fire with a Federal gunboat in the Tennessee River. But with a deep ravine filled with standing water to slush through and Federal batteries drawn up on the top of the hill beyond—plus Jackson's troops out of ammunition and only their bayonets to rely upon—the odds were too great. After twenty minutes, the attack ended.

Nightfall brought rest at last for the exhausted men. A cold drenching rain set in as the graycoats sought shelter in the abandoned tents of the Federals. The 1st Missouri appropriated the vacant camp of the 71st Ohio. Despite fatigue, hunger, and the sheer numbness of the bloody battle's aftermath, Lieutenant Boyce of the 1st Missouri wrote, "the feeling of exultation that we occupied and were to sleep in the camp of the enemy in a great measure restored our spirits."[10]

The Rebels felt that they had won a great victory, and some of them were in the mood for celebrating. Tickled pink to discover several jugs of Yankee whiskey in the camp, the 1st Missouri's Sergeant Tom Dwyer offered to mix up a bucket of punch to "drink the health of the 'poor divils' who had left such good whiskey behind them!" But there was no water, another soldier objected. "Niver mind, me boy;" Dwyer replied, "let the 71st keep all the water in the Tennessee river, we have the best part of the punch anyway. We have the whiskey and the sugar, and we'll make it a bit stronger."[11]

But their efforts that day were all for naught. Bright and early on the next morning, the Federals—bolstered by the timely arrival of reinforcements—launched a vigorous counterattack that drove the Rebels back over every inch of ground they had gained.

Even during the previous day's fighting, the Confederate brigades had become badly disorganized and intermingled. Near midnight a staff officer had located Cleburne calmly squatting on a stump and drinking coffee, but confessing that he had no idea of where most of his men had got off to and uncertain even as to where he was at that point. In the morning, the Irishman could only muster some 800 men, but still Cleburne's brigade had some fight in it. Ordered to move up in the face of advancing Federal troops, Cleburne led his brigade to near annihilation as his men were cut to pieces by artillery and rifle fire. While most retreated, the remnants of the faithful 15th Arkansas stayed to fight. Cleburne led them forward, captured some enemy cannon left behind in the previous day's fighting, collected some more reinforcements, formed another battle line, and launched a counterattack. The Yankees were momentarily stunned, their advance stalled, giving the Confederates time to withdraw. When they had used up all of their ammunition, the 15th Arkansas—with just 58 men left—also withdrew.[12]

In Bowen's brigade, the 1st Missouri also saw more hard fighting as part of the rear guard protecting the Rebel army's withdrawal. "Yesterday mornin' you were afeard you would nivir get into this battle," Corporal John O'Neil told some of his mates, "and I'm damned if I ain't afeard we will nivir get out av' it." The 1st Missouri lost a fourth of its men at Shiloh—48 killed, 130 wounded, 29 missing out of 850.[13]

Near Shiloh Church, where Rebel blood had bought the previous day's victory, Gibson's and Anderson's brigades—what was left of them—also put up a stiff resistance. A rear-guard action by the Alabama State Artillery, a largely Irish battery from Mobile, saved another Confederate brigade from annihilation.

As the Rebel army retreated back down the road to Corinth, Mississippi, the grisly tally of the two days of killing began to unfold, to the horror of observers North and South: over 23,000 casualties, 13,000 Union and 10,000 Confederate. Count up all the dead and wounded in all of America's wars fought up until that time, and you still cannot quite equal the losses in two days at Shiloh.[14]

And among the mangled dead littering the fields at Shiloh lay many with names like Eagan, Cassidy, Brennon, Gleason, Doyle, Malloy, Mahan, Donnelly, Kelley, Fogarty, and Meagher—sons of the Emerald Isle who, like Pat Cleburne, had cast their hopes and dreams with the Confederacy.

Shiloh set the tone for the Confederate army in the west. For three more years its story would continue to be one of extraordinary self-sacrifice and courage in the face of repeated defeats and setbacks—while in the east, the legendary Army of Northern Virginia forged an unequaled record of achievement on the battlefield. And in both Rebel armies—and in all parts of the war in the South—Irish soldiers would be in the forefront.

11. *"Gallantry and Courage":*
Perryville and Murfreesboro,
October–December 1862

The Army of Northern Virginia's two Louisiana brigades, with so many Irish from New Orleans, forged a reputation as some of Robert E. Lee's most reliable combat troops. But there was another Louisiana brigade with an Irish flavor, and it served with the Confederacy's major army west of the Appalachians, the Army of Tennessee. Daniel W. Adams' Louisiana brigade—so badly bloodied at Shiloh's Hornet's Nest—included Colonel Randall L. Gibson's 13th Louisiana, about 25 percent Irish, with former New Orleans police chief Steve O'Leary now a major. Gibson, the great-grandson of Irish immigrants, ultimately commanded the Louisiana brigade. O'Leary's old Irish company (the Southern Celts) was now led by Francis L. Campbell, and John McGrath led Company G (the St. Mary Volunteers). Colonel Augustus Reichard's 20th Louisiana, soon to be consolidated with the 13th Louisiana, contained a large number of Irish as well, with four Irish companies (G, H, I, and K) from New Orleans.

Also in Adams' brigade was a new outfit, Major John E. Austin's 14th Louisiana Sharpshooters Battalion. When the 11th Louisiana Infantry Regiment was broken up in August 1862, 200 of its men were selected for a small battalion of two companies to serve as skirmishers and sharpshooters for the Louisiana brigade. John E. Austin, formerly captain of the Cannon Guards from New Orleans, was assigned to lead the new battalion, at least half of which was Irish. The sharpshooters would earn a reputation as a hard-fighting command, often performing skirmisher duty in advance of the brigade.

While Lee's Army of Northern Virginia pursued its 1862 Maryland offensive, the Confederacy's major army west of the Appalachians launched an invasion of the Bluegrass State. General Braxton Bragg led the Confederate advance into Kentucky in September, and at first things went well for the Rebels. But on October 8, Bragg's forces—although still separated and not yet ready for a major action—stumbled into a violent encounter with the Federals at the little central Kentucky town of Perryville.

Largely in the dark about the true size and disposition of Major General Don Carlos Buell's Federal army, Bragg rashly attacked an enemy force nearly three times larger than his—and in the end was fortunate to withdraw with his own army intact. To compound things, the hot, dry summer of 1862 had brought to central Kentucky one of the worst droughts in its history. The shallow Chaplin River that ran through Perryville had nearly dried up, as had Doctor's Creek west of the town. It was the search for water that brought the two armies to Perryville.

Preliminary skirmishing on the morning of October 8 left Federal troops in possession of the western bank of Doctor's Creek, where they began forming a line of battle. At this point, Bragg ordered his generals to attack. The graycoats soon began to zero in on Major General Alexander M. McCook's Yankee troops west of Doctor's Creek, near the point where it intersected with the Mackville Road out of Perryville. Daniel W. Adams' Louisiana brigade was pressing them hard from the south. In the Rebels' path stretched rolling, uneven terrain, with blue-coated troops seemingly poised behind every rail and stone fence that crisscrossed the countryside.

It was John E. Austin's sharpshooter battalion that spearheaded the Louisiana brigade's assault on the Federal salient, first clashing with a party from the 42nd

BRIGADIER GENERAL RANDALL LEE GIBSON. The great-grandson of Irish immigrants, Gibson commanded the Army of Tennessee's Louisiana brigade, containing many Irish from New Orleans. (Alabama Department of Archives and History, Montgomery, Alabama)

Indiana foraging for water at a small spring south of Doctor's Creek, and later charging across the creek to hit the Federals from the south. As they raced toward the bluecoats at a rail fence, a Rebel artillery shell whistled through the air and struck a large barn nearby, which burst into flames. The sharpshooters pushed on through the smoke and searing heat and occupied a spot along the rail fence south of the Yankees, where they halted, fighting a gun battle before falling back to cover.

Following the lead of Austin's sharpshooters—moving "stealthily as a cat," one Federal soldier described them—the rest of the Louisiana brigade fell in behind the little battalion and made for the 10th Ohio, trapped now between Adams' Louisianans and Pat Cleburne's brigade closing in on them from the east. After overrunning the last of the Buckeyes, the two Rebel brigades continued pushing along the Mackville Road toward the 42nd Indiana back near the Dixville crossroads at yet another rail fence position.

Gibson's 13th Louisiana—a "hard looking set," according to one Federal soldier—lost four color bearers in as many charges on the 42nd Indiana's position. Still they advanced "steadily; apparently as if on drill in camp." A Louisiana soldier remembered the confusion of battle, the "perfect storm" of "the sound of musketry never ceasing ... the roar of cannon rolling without a break.... the yelling ... the dead and dying.... loose horses ... running in all directions ... wounded men ... crying for help." Only a surprisingly determined and desperate bayonet charge by the 42nd Indiana stopped the Louisianans and sent them falling back to cover.[1]

The Louisiana brigade lost 6 killed, 78 wounded, and 68 missing, for a total of 152 casualties. Adams particularly commended the 13th Louisiana's Colonel Gibson and Major Austin of the Sharpshooters for "gallantry and courage."[2]

An unusual amount of battlefield chaos marked the bloody, hard-fought engagement at Perryville. There was disorder at all levels of command, with troops mistakenly firing into each other and with poorly coordinated attacks that led to whole brigades breaking up. The Confederate attacks started at about 2 p.m., when Major General Benjamin Franklin Cheatham's division crossed the Chaplin River and struck the Union left flank hard, driving back the surprised Federals of McCook's corps and killing both a Yankee division commander and a senior brigade commander in the first volleys. Major General Simon B. Buckner's Confederate division followed up Cheatham's assault with an attack on McCook's brigades farther south along Doctor's Creek.

While Adams' Louisiana troops were hurling themselves at the bluecoats, Bushrod Johnson's Tennessee brigade that had seen such hard fighting six months earlier at Shiloh stormed across the steep banks of Doctor's Creek to attack Colonel William H. Lytle's Federal brigade from the east. On the left of Johnson's line of battle and not far from Austin's Louisiana sharpshooters, Colonel James A. Smith's 300-man regiment of Irishmen from Memphis—the newly created 5th Confederate Regiment—advanced between a rail fence on their left and a stone fence on their right. From behind the stone fence suddenly came a volley that staggered the grad-clad line and momentarily hurled it back. Captain Charles W. Frazer, a 28-year-old Scottish-American attorney from Memphis, led Company B in the attack. "The shock was terrific," Frazer remembered, "the line swayed as one body, leaving a track of dead and wounded to mark its former position." Smith's men were under fire from Buckeyes of the 3rd Ohio up ahead behind the fence and from fellow Irishmen of Lieutenant Colonel Joseph Burke's 10th Ohio Infantry to their north across the Mackville Road. Up and charging forward again, the Tennesseans scaled the stone fence and drove off the bluecoats. They held their position against several attempts by the Federals to dislodge them as dead and wounded continued to pile up in front of the wall.

The 5th Confederate—with the other Tennessee regiments in Johnson's brigade—advanced to occupy a second wall. After two hours of fierce fighting that would cost the 5th Confederate 5 men killed and 34 more wounded, the Rebels had pushed the Buckeyes back past a farmhouse considerably to the west of the creek, but now they were running low on ammunition. Alarmed, Smith spied a swarm of blue-coated troops outflanking the Tennesseans and moving down the hill toward their rear. Suddenly a fierce Rebel yell ("Federals always *cheered*," Frazer noted) told them that these were not

PERRYVILLE Oct. 8, 1862

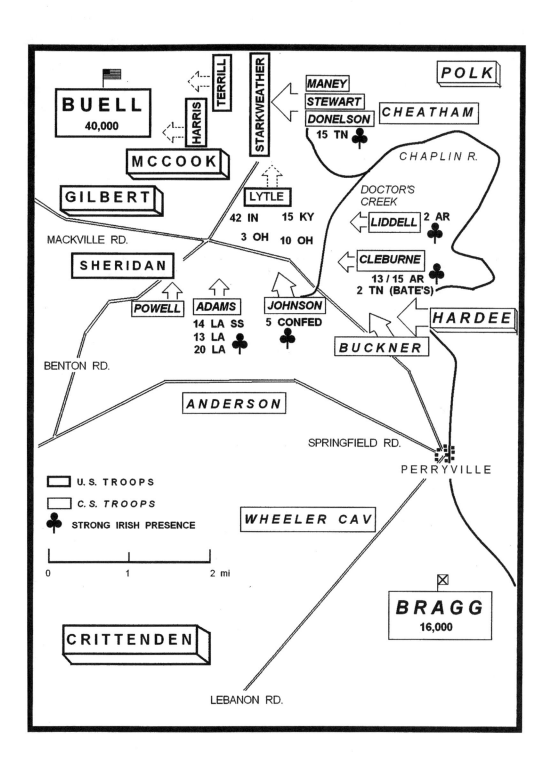

enemy troops after all, but Pat Cleburne's brigade, many of its members wearing blue Yankee clothing captured several weeks earlier at Richmond, Kentucky.[3]

Cleburne's brigade advanced up the dry creek bed of Doctor's Creek to support Johnson's Tennesseans. In his brigade, the 13th Arkansas and his old regiment, the 15th Arkansas, had been consolidated into one regiment now, because of their heavy losses at Shiloh. It would be the first of many such consolidations during the war. Cleburne ordered his Irish skirmishers, led by Captain George Dixon of the Napoleon Grays— with regimental flags flying—to fan out just ten paces ahead of his main battle line. As the Rebels reached the top of a hill, the Federals—the 10th Ohio, making a determined stand after their comrades in the 3rd Ohio and 15th Kentucky had withdrawn—were deceived into believing that the whole Rebel battle line was upon them and promptly let loose with a volley. Before they had time to reload, Cleburne's main battle line had reached them and quickly overran their position, sending the Buckeyes flying to the rear. The Irishman had improvised quickly to meet the conditions of battle and to use the rolling ground to his advantage. He was demonstrating his growth as a leader.

Cleburne took a fall when his favorite horse "Dixie" was struck and killed by an enemy cannon ball. Immediately he was on his feet again, waving his sword and shouting, "Give 'em hell boys." Cleburne received a serious wound in the ankle but refused to leave the field. Meanwhile his men pushed on, overwhelming the 42nd Indiana near the Dixville crossroads about a mile west of Doctor's Creek. Captain Edmund O'Neill of the 2nd Tennessee took the wounded Colonel William Lytle prisoner. Fighting until sunset and with ammunition nearly all spent, Cleburne's brigade finally could advance no farther.[4]

The Confederates finally broke the Yankee resistance at the crossroads. As night fell, with a full moon rising, St. John R. Liddell's Arkansas brigade attacked. The 8th Arkansas' 24-year-old Colonel John H. Kelly took an enemy officer prisoner—Colonel Michael Gooding of the 22nd Indiana.

The hard-fighting Rebels of Adams', Johnson's, Cleburne's, and Liddell's brigades had forced McCook's Federals a mile back from Doctor's Creek. This key sector appeared shattered now, but farther south Brigadier General Philip H. Sheridan's division of Charles C. Gilbert's corps still held fast. To the north, Colonel John C. Starkweather's brigade had finally brought Ben Cheatham's attack to a grinding halt, and the Federal line was stabilizing. Southwest of Perryville, yet a third Federal corps under Major General Thomas L. Crittenden hovered, waiting to enter the fray but held at bay by Colonel Joe Wheeler's cavalry brigade—and unaware of the extent of the slaughter unfolding to their north.

So victory eluded the Confederate army at Perryville. With the Federals finally holding their battered lines, Bragg at last realized that his 16,000 troops were facing a much larger enemy army, and he could not risk potential annihilation. He disengaged and withdrew from Perryville that night. The Confederacy's invasion of Kentucky was over, and with it any chance of recapturing that state. Ironically, Lee's invasion of Maryland had ground to a halt three weeks earlier at Sharpsburg.

Bragg's army made its way back into Tennessee, finally taking up a defensive position at the small town of Murfreesboro, about thirty miles south of Nashville. In December 1862 the veteran Confederate army that had fought so hard only to have victory slip from its grasp at Shiloh and Perryville received the name that it would carry for the rest of the war—the Army of Tennessee. Pat Cleburne also received a promotion; he was now a division commander Meanwhile, the Federal army welcomed a new commander, Major General William Rosecrans, and settled in at Nashville to make ready for a fresh offensive. By the day after Christmas, Rosecrans was moving south along muddy, rain-soaked roads toward Murfreesboro, and Bragg was preparing to give battle.

The bloody engagement known in the South as the battle of Murfreesboro and in the North as the battle of Stones River began early on the morning of December 31, 1862. By coincidence and unknown to each other, both opposing commanders—Bragg and Rosecrans—had planned to attack the other's right flank. As it happened, Bragg was quicker, and 10,000 soldiers in John P. McCown's and Pat Cleburne's divisions hit the Federal right—by coincidence Alexander M. McCook's corps, the same troops that they had engaged at Perryville—just before daybreak.

Murfreesboro also bore an eerie similarity to Shiloh. The two sides began the battle hungry and soaked from a previous night's rain, but this time a cold, bone-chilling rain. Also as at Shiloh, the dawn Rebel attack struck the Federals just as they were preparing breakfast. The bluecoats were taken by surprise, and although they put up a stiff fight, by 8 a.m. they were overwhelmed and thrown back, and Rosecrans was frantically pulling troops from his left flank—troops that had already crossed Stones River for the planned attack on the Rebel right—to bolster his own crumbling right.

Moving forward in the chilly morning mist, Cleburne's division—with the his old largely Irish brigade, now including the 5th Confederate Regiment as well, on his right—crossed the Franklin Road west of Murfreesboro and encountered a line of Federal troops from Illinois, Ohio, and Wisconsin. In a fierce fight lasting half an hour, the Rebels triumphed and the Federals broke and fell back. The Federals formed a second battle line in the woods and open pasture land behind their former position, and Cleburne's troops promptly hit that line with equal determination, capturing a half dozen cannon as well as ammunition and inflicting deadly casualties.

The bluecoats retreated again, this time to a new battle line drawn up south of the Wilkinson Pike. Taking cover under heavy fire, the 5th Confederate received the order, "Fix bayonets as you lie." Then they were up again running and yelling as they overwhelmed the Federal line, capturing several more pieces of artillery. The Federals made another stand in the woods north of the Wilkinson Pike, and again the Rebels drove them back. The 1st Arkansas' Lieutenant Colonel Don McGregor (whose old company, "Clan McGregor," contained Scottish, Scotch-Irish, or Irish men from Pine Bluff) was killed. A hundred yards to the north, the bluecoats drew up yet another defensive line, but Cleburne's men plowed on, pushing the Yankees back again. "[T]he Confederate line," a Federal officer wrote, "came sweeping on like a resistless tide."[5]

In fact, the speed of the Rebel advance was remarkable, although Cleburne conceded that it was "rapid, but not very orderly." The makeup of the terrain west of Stones River, with its gloomy thickets and fields criss-crossed by wooden rail fences, played havoc with any attempt to maintain an orderly battle line. At one point, when his brigade ran short of ammunition, Lieutenant James M. Dulin of the 6th Arkansas hustled forward with two horse-drawn ordnance wagons and lost track of where the brigade was. Dulin wound up in advance of the brigade, clattering through a corn field and frightening a line of blue-coated Federal soldiers, who broke and ran for cover. The unassuming Dulin became probably the only soldier on the field that day who could claim to have led two ordnance wagons in a successful charge against enemy infantry.[6]

Finally the Federals drew up their last defensive line south of the Nashville Pike, a line that they must hold or face annihilation. Both sides by now were exhausted, but Rosecrans had managed to bolster his line with reinforcements. Not so with the Rebel attackers. "[I]t was now after 3 o'clock," Cleburne wrote, "my men had had little or no rest the night before; they had been fighting since dawn, without relief, food, or water … their ammunition was again nearly exhausted." Still, the graycoats tried once more, but they couldn't break this final line. They were driven back.

In nine hours of grueling fighting, Cleburne's troops had pushed the bluecoats back for nearly three miles. Where the Federal battle line before had resembled a straight one, now it had been bent back like a jackknife half opened, with the blade bent parallel to the Nashville Pike. But the cost in lives was enormous. Cleburne's division lost 2,081 men killed, wounded, or missing out of 6,045. In Cleburne's old brigade, now led by Lucius Polk, 347 men were killed, wounded, or missing; the 1st Arkansas accounted for 102 of these casualties, the 5th Confederate for 83, and the 13th/15th Arkansas for 68. Captain Charles W. Frazer of the 5th Confederate saw half of his company killed or wounded. "It was a long day," he wrote, "and that night we bivouacked on the bloody field, both sides exhausted, and neither desiring to disturb the dying or exert themselves by further strife."[7]

Over to Cleburne's right, Phil Sheridan's division stubbornly held a sector of the Federal line that refused to give. Sheridan's troops held off attacks by three more Con-

REPULSING CLEBURNE AT MURFREESBORO. **Samuel Beatty's Federal brigade attempts to bring the Rebel juggernaut to a halt on the first day of fighting at Murfreesboro. Colonel Lucius Polk's largely Irish brigade is to their front. (Library of Congress)**

MURFREESBORO Dec. 31, 1862

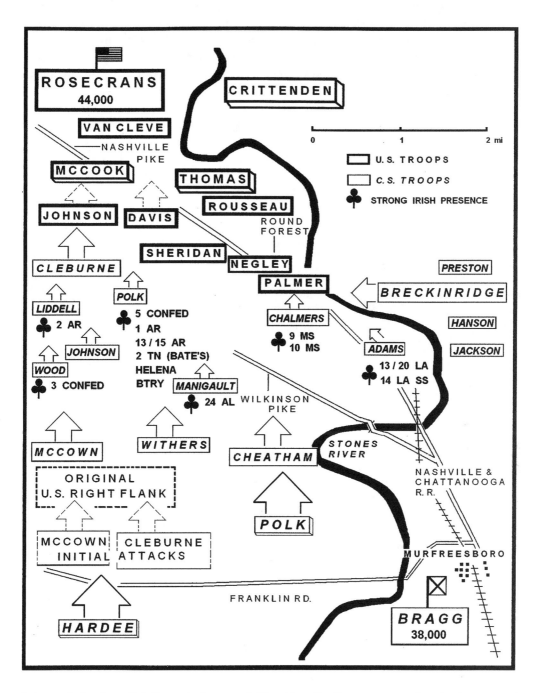

federate brigades, all delivered piecemeal. Sheridan finally gave ground, swinging around to face the south, when Cleburne's troops collapsed the rest of the Union right flank.

One of the Rebel commands that took on Sheridan's troops was the 24th Alabama in Arthur Manigault's brigade, and it was here that the Emmet Guards (Company B) saw their first major combat action with the Army of Tennessee. A solidly Irish company (like the Emerald Guards in the 8th Alabama), the Emmet Guards' first commander was Irish immigrant Barney O'Connell, a successful builder and a veteran of the Mexican War. The 49-year-old O'Connell had made a good life for himself as a carpenter in Mobile and lived with his wife Catherine, who worked as a milliner. One of the Irish couple's three children, John, was a 25-year-old marine engineer who served with the 24th Alabama as a sergeant before accepting a commission as a lieutenant in the Confederate navy. Of the ten residents living in the O'Connell household, three young Irish women were dress makers, and one Irishman was a laborer. Such arrangements were common in Irish communities in the South, and more affluent immigrants often took in boarders from among their more needy countrymen.

Besides the Emmet Guards, there were 25 or so Irish names in Companies A and H in the 24th Alabama, also from Mobile. At Murfreesboro, two members of the Emmet Guards made the Rebels' roll of honor for their part in this bloody engagement—Captain William J. O'Brien, a 25-year-old Mobile attorney who took over command of the company after O'Connell's resignation, and Private Martin Duggan, a 29-year-old Irish immigrant who worked as a waiter at Mobile's Battle House inn. The 24th Alabama lost 20 men killed and 95 wounded.[8]

With Cleburne's strength spent now, the focus of the battle shifted to the point in Rosecrans' line where the jackknife bent, a grove of trees between the Nashville Pike and the railroad tracks called the "Round Forest," held by a cluster of determined blue-clad Midwesterners. Rosecrans reinforced the salient with artillery and entrenched infantry until he had massed an amazing amount of firepower.

Brigadier General James R. Chalmers' Mississippi brigade that had ended the fighting on the first day at Shiloh was the first to go up against the Round Forest. Chalmers' brigade contained the 9th, 10th, and 44th Mississippi regiments, each with a complement of Irish recruits from Natchez, Port Gibson, and other river towns.

In the 9th Mississippi, the first of the state's "war regiments" formed early in 1861, many Irishmen had joined Captain John P. Holahan's Company B. About 65 or so Irish names appear on the company's roster. Holahan had enlisted as a private in Company K, the Panola Guards, in 1861, but became the captain of Company B when the 9th Mississippi was reorganized in early 1862. His lieutenants, Robert E. McCarthy and Michael William Shanahan (a 22-year-old Irish immigrant from Senatobia, Mississippi) both had served as enlisted men in other companies in the regiment. There also were 25 or so Irish names on the rolls in Captain S. S. Calhoon's Company D and Company E from Vicksburg.

The 10th Mississippi contained the Port Gibson Rifles (Company F), led by Captain William McKeever, a 35-year-old carriage painter who gave his origin simply as "born at sea." Thirty or so Irish names appear on Company F's rolls, and there were at least as many in Company K, led by Captain Moses McCarley, from Yazoo County. Company A, the prestigious Mississippi Rifles from Jackson, also carried 25 or so Irish names on roll. In the 44th Mississippi was Company L, the Tom Weldon Rebels from Natchez, with 40 or so Irish names on roll. Officers in this company included Lieutenant Thomas O'Hea, who had tried unsuccessfully to form an Irish company in Natchez early in 1861.

The Mississippians had already endured a miserable night and had been under tension for 48 hours. Dug in on the extreme right of Bragg's lines, Chalmers' brigade was to have been the pivot that the entire Rebel left wing swung on. Because they had occupied a position next to Stones River in view of the enemy, the Mississippians had orders to light no camp fires and had spent the night cold and wet in their trenches. The brigade was short of decent rifles, and most of the soldiers in the 9th Mississippi found that they could not even fire their weapons, because the rain of the night before had left them too wet. Still, at about 10 a.m., Chalmers' brigade surged forward through a cotton patch and on past a burned out farm house, headed for the Round Forest—800 yards away through open fields. "[T]hey came on like a pack of hounds in full cry," a Union officer wrote.[9]

Federal cannon and musket fire quickly thinned the Mississippians' ranks, and the gray-clad troops fell back. The noise of the guns was so unbearably loud that many of the soldiers stooped and picked cotton to stuff in their ears. They charged a second time, and Chalmers' ranks were decimated, with some regiments losing as many as six color-bearers. Chalmers himself became a casualty when he was wounded by a shell fragment. A third of his brigade—542 men—lay dead or wounded. The 9th Mississippi and 10th Mississippi each lost 84. The 44th Mississippi lost 52. Captain James Garrity's largely Irish Alabama battery (the Alabama State Artillery) from Mobile, attached to the brigade, lost 23. To Chalmers' men the Round Forest became known as "Mississippian's half acre," and to many others as "Hell's Half Acre."[10]

An attack by Daniel S. Donelson's Tennessee brigade at noon also failed to break the Union stronghold. Bragg would now have to wait until John Breckinridge's division arrived, and it was well into the afternoon before he could try again. At 1:30 p.m., Daniel W. Adams' Louisiana brigade was ready to make the attempt.

With the recently consolidated 13th/20th Louisiana on their right, Adams' men stepped off proudly, "a magnificent brigade," one Federal soldier described them, "the most daring, courageous, and best-executed attack which the Confederates made." As the Louisianans neared the Federal lines, they lowered bayonets and rushed forward giving the Rebel yell.

The Federals opened fire into the oncoming gray ranks with one volley after another. The 13th/20th Louisiana began taking heavy fire from the bluecoats entrenched in the Round Forest ahead and also from two regiments of Indiana troops and their artillery posted near the river to their right. After thirty minutes, they were unable to advance in the crossfire, but tried to hold on to allow the rest of the brigade to withdraw. Major Austin moved his Irish sharpshooters up and formed along a fence parallel to the railroad to provide covering fire. Colonel Gibson wrote that the 13th/20th Louisiana "behaved throughout like veterans," commending Captains John McGrath and Thomas M. Ryan for bravery. The 13th/20th Louisiana suffered 187 casualties out of 620 men engaged. Adams was wounded in the arm by a shell fragment and was out of action. It was Shiloh's Hornet's Nest all over again.[11]

Piecemeal attacks, one brigade after another, brought only heavy casualties and still failed to take the position. The Rebel troops had accomplished wonders, but if only there had been more of them, they might have destroyed the Federal army. "If ... a fresh division could have replaced Cleburne's exhausted troops," Rebel general William J. Hardee wrote, "the rout of Rosecrans' army would have been complete."[12]

The Confederates had failed to break "Hell's Half Acre," but the overall battering that they had given the Yankees had been stunning, and they had inflicted heavy losses. By nightfall, the Federals appeared beaten, and Bragg was satisfied that by morning they would be gone, headed back to Nashville. He telegraphed news of a great victory to Richmond and rejoiced that, "God has granted us a happy New Year."[13]

The New Year was far from happy for the survivors of the bloody day's fighting. A cold rain that had set in again whipped at them through the night. Shivering, drenched, dog-tired, and hungry, they were in no mood for celebrating. Mutilated dead and wounded soldiers cluttered the field. Search parties spent the night gathering together the wounded, both Rebs and Yanks, laying them in rows side by side with campfires between each row to keep them from freezing to death.

When daylight came, to Bragg's chagrin, the Federal army had not budged. New Years Day passed with little activity with both sides too worn out to fight again.

On January 2, Bragg's troops made one more heroic attempt to stun the Federals into retreating. At 4 p.m., they struck four brigades of Rosecrans' left flank that had crossed Stones River to the north of the Round Forest and were holding the heights there. Breckinridge's division made the attack, and once again the Louisiana brigade, with Gibson commanding now, threw itself against the enemy. After half an hour of savage fighting, the Federals broke and began streaming back across Stones River. Gibson's Louisianans gave chase, storming across the river. They saw the end and triumph in sight.

But suddenly victory was snatched away, as 45 Union guns concentrated on the heights west of Murfreesboro opened up on the Rebels—vulnerable now in the open— in a shooting gallery. The end of the slaughter saw dead Confederates littering the field. The rest of the division retreated back across the river. The attack was over. Breckinridge's division suffered 1,700 casualties out of 5,000 engaged. Once again, the 13th/20th Louisiana was hit hard, suffering 129 more casualties. To the soldiers in the Army of Tennessee, Breckinridge's repulse meant another chance for victory gone. After this, the 5th Confederate's Captain Frazer wrote, "the world looked cold."[14]

Reluctantly, Bragg withdrew to the south. The Confederacy had lost eastern Tennessee. Casualties at Murfreesboro were over 24,000, more than in the two days at Shiloh—a bloody slaughter that gained the Confederacy nothing. The timing could not have been better for the Lincoln administration. Coming close on the heels of the Army of Northern Virginia's lopsided victory over the Federals at Fredericksburg, Murfreesboro gave Lincoln positive news that he desperately needed. His ambassador to Britain was quick to cite the Federal victory as proof to the Europeans that the North would win the war.[15]

Of the 88 Confederate regiments at Murfreesboro, 23 sustained more than 40 percent casualties. Like Lee in Virginia, Bragg had continued to rely on the tried-and-true tactics of massed assault, tactics that had worked well when they were young officers during the Mexican War but which now resulted in appalling casualties because of the increasingly deadly accuracy of improved rifles. Shiloh, the Seven Days, Sharpsburg, Perryville, and now Murfreesboro had witnessed the same headlong charges, and each time the Confederacy lost more young men that it could ill afford to lose. Of the soldiers to die on so many fields, no group would be more decimated than the Confederate Irish.[16]

12. The Contest for Chattanooga: Chickamauga to Ringgold Gap, September–November 1863

There were many children of Erin who hailed from the boisterous river towns along the lower Mississippi—towns that were all under Federal occupation after the summer of 1863. The largest Irish enclave was found in Memphis, where Emerald Islanders made up close to a quarter of the city's population. In Memphis the older Scotch-Irish families had achieved social and political clout, and early Irish Catholic immigrants had assimilated as well. Eugene Magevney helped found the city's public school system, and journalist Edward Carroll helped start the city's first daily newspaper, the *Memphis Daily Eagle*.

In contrast to the "lace curtain Irish," the flood of "Famine Irish" immigrants in the 1840s found work at the busy waterfront, navy yard, and rail yards of Memphis. Segregated in the unhealthy, crime-ridden, flood-prone area called "the Pinch," the poorest ward in the city, it was these newcomers who had to hurdle greater obstacles in the Know-Nothing unrest of the Fifties. When 200 Irish immigrant laborers arrived in 1854, hired to work on the Memphis and Ohio Railroad, rumors spread that hundreds more were soon to follow. The city's mayor called out the local militia. John McClanahan, editor of the *Memphis Appeal*, branded nativist fears "humbugery and nonsense" and explained that the laborers' stay in Memphis would only be for a few months.

The Memphis Irish overcame native intolerance. They formed volunteer militia companies like the Montgomery Guard and the Jackson Greens, named for Andrew Jackson (a hero to both Irish and Scotch-Irish alike). In January 1861, pro-secession members of the Irish community held a meeting to discuss the current secession crisis. Upwardly mobile young middle class Irishmen—like grocery clerk Michael Magevney, Jr., (Eugene's nephew—and current captain of the Jackson Greens), firefighter Edward O'Neil, carpenter Michael Fisher, and brass molder Sam Tighe—were there, all casting their futures and fortunes with the South. They adopted this resolution: "In the event of the federal powers attempting to coerce any or all other seceding states, we pledge ourselves to buckle on our armour and do battle in defense of our southern homes and southern institutions." Mike Magevney was destined to see action soon, as the Jackson Greens would become one of three Irish companies in the 154th Tennessee, a regiment that he would ultimately command.[1]

It was in Memphis that one of the Confederacy's most solidly Irish commands, Colonel Knox Walker's 2nd Tennessee Infantry (the "Irish Regiment"), was mustered in with solemn ceremony at the Ancient Order of the Druid Hall. When the 2nd Tennessee was consolidated with the 21st Tennessee (about a third of them also Irish from Memphis) in July 1862, the result was one of the Confederacy's great unsung commands—the 5th Confederate Infantry Regiment, led by Colonel James A. Smith. Keeping these rambunctious Irishmen in line posed a challenge to any commander, and Smith would remember his experience with mixed feelings. "I had a good deal of trouble with them," he recalled, "but they never failed to respond in the hour of danger. Whenever the command 'Forward' was given it was replied to with a yell."[2]

For the 5th Confederate especially, there would be a close relationship with "Old Pat." "The hero-worship," Captain Charles W. Frazer wrote, "that existed between this regiment and Cleburne was remarkable." Other regiments in the division felt the same way toward their commander. Cleburne's old regiment, the 15th Arkansas, presented him with an elegant sword (carried by a Southern blockade runner from Bermuda) made of choice Damascus steel with a shamrock on the hilt. Cleburne never carried the valued sword into battle.[3]

Because companies in the Southern army tended to be formed of young men from the same communities, a high degree of unit pride evolved early in the war. As in the Army of Northern Virginia, the leadership of outstanding officers like Cleburne helped to forge a bond of unity and camaraderie that made the Army of Tennessee the never-say-die outfit that it became. Patriotism may bring many men under arms, but when the shooting starts soldiers do not really fight for cause or country; they fight for each other. This great sense of esprit de corps and primary group cohesion was especially strong in Cleburne's division.

Cleburne's soldiers carried a distinctive blue battle flag with a white border and crossed cannons in a white circle in the center. In May 1863, the Congress at Richmond decreed that all Confederate regiments were to carry the newly-adopted national flag. Cleburne's men received permission to retain their unique blue flag, the only division in the Army of Tennessee allowed to do so. "Friends and foes," General Hardee remarked, "soon learned to watch the course of the blue flag that marked where Cleburne was in the battle."[4]

The year 1863 witnessed the rise and the fall of the South's fortunes, and with it the hopes of the Confederate Irish. Heart-rending losses at Gettysburg and at Vicksburg in July dealt fatal blows to the South, although the will to fight was still strong. Now in September 1863, eyes were focused on the important rail center at Chattanooga, where Braxton Bragg's Army of Tennessee had taken up yet another defensive position.

In a surprising move, Major General William S. Rosecrans' Federal army lunged southward in an attempt to cut Bragg's supply line to Atlanta. Bragg withdrew from Chattanooga and began moving south into northern Georgia. Rosecrans' 60,000-man army initiated a pursuit, hoping to destroy the Rebel army once and for all. What Rosecrans did not know was that reinforcements from Mississippi and from Virginia (two veteran divisions under James Longstreet on loan from Lee in Virginia) had just reached Bragg, bolstering the Army of Tennessee's strength to 70,000—more than evening the odds for a change. The tables were about to be turned, as Bragg—no longer in retreat as Rosecrans surmised—prepared to launch an attack on his pursuers. He intended to strike

Rosecrans' left flank and sever his communications line to Chattanooga, forcing his entire army south against the mountains. The attack began on September 19 at an obscure place called Chickamauga Creek.

Chickamauga—what the Cherokees called "river of death"—was heavily wooded, and the dense foliage made it difficult for armies to carry out complicated maneuvers. Chickamauga would be called a "soldiers' battle"—one that didn't go according to the commanders' plans—and would witness some of the deadliest combat of the war. The fighting here would quickly spiral into a confusing bloodbath, with casualties on both sides steadily mounting.

The fighting that erupted west of Chickamauga Creek and escalated all through the afternoon of September 19 was savage, confusing, and inconclusive—a see-saw action in the dense undergrowth, where Lieutenant Colonel John Edward Murray of the 5th/13th Arkansas wrote that it was "impossible to see the enemy until we were very close upon him."[5]

It was late in the day when Pat Cleburne's division went in, attacking a Federal division of Major General Alexander M. McCook's corps at dusk. Cleburne's division now included James Deshler's Arkansas-Texas brigade, S. A. M. Wood's Alabama-Mississippi brigade, and Lucius Polk's Arkansas-Tennessee brigade (Cleburne's old command).

The veteran brigade that Polk inherited from "Old Pat" was now largely an Irish command. The 5th Confederate was there—consolidated (yet again) with the 3rd Confederate Infantry, where Vicksburg's Shamrock Guards made up a company. Also in Polk's brigade was Colonel John W. Colquitt's 1st Arkansas Infantry (led at Shiloh by James F. Fagan, now a brigadier general serving west of the Mississippi) with a large number of Irish from Little Rock, Pine Bluff, and El Dorado. And there was Colonel W. D. Robison's 2nd Tennessee (William Bate's old regiment at Shiloh), with an Irish company from Memphis. Temporarily on duty with Daniel Govan's brigade in St. John R. Liddell's division, but soon to rejoin Cleburne's division, were Cleburne's old regiment, the 2nd/15th Arkansas (with many of the Helena Irish), Lieutenant Colonel John E. Murray's 5th/13th Arkansas, and the Warren Light Artillery from Vicksburg.

Cleburne formed his line of battle with care. It took half an hour to do so, and it was 6 p.m. when it moved forward—Deshler's brigade on the left, Wood's in the center, Polk's on the right, near a sawmill. They passed through the worn-out Rebel brigades of Govan and Edward C. Walthall, who had seen heavy fighting all afternoon. "Boys," one of Govan's soldiers piped up, "we're glad to see you, but there is more fighting Yankees right up there than a little."

As Wood's brigade emerged from the dark pines into an open cornfield—the same field that Walthall's brigade had crossed earlier in the day and where gray-clad bodies still lay from the previous fighting—a volley from the opposing side quickly blanketed the already darkened field with smoke. In the chaotic twilight, one thing helped sustain the Rebels more than anything else. A firm believer in training, Cleburne had drilled his soldiers so often to load, fire, and reload their weapons quickly that the act now came naturally to them, and they alarmed the Yanks with the sheer swiftness of their fire, their muskets flashing in the dark. Confusion reigned as the Rebels struggled to advance under fire, unable to see the enemy or each other. As some units fell behind, they fired into friendly units ahead of them. Cleburne described the scene: "For half an hour the firing was the heaviest I had ever heard. It was dark, however, and accurate shooting was

CHICKAMAUGA Sept. 20, 1863

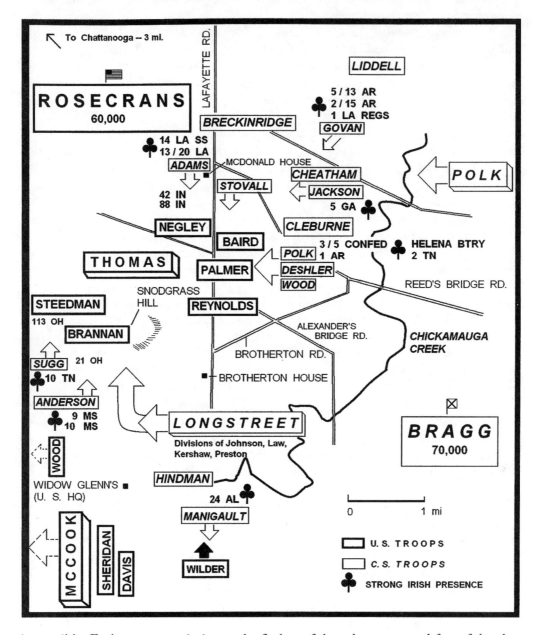

impossible. Each party was aiming at the flashes of the other guns, and few of the shot from either side took effect."

Quick thinking from Cleburne's artillery officers, Lieutenants Thomas Key and R. W. Goldthwaite, helped to move the advance forward. The two Rebel field batteries, Key's Helena Battery and Goldthwaite's Alabama battery, unlimbered their pieces and began firing at the Federals behind their hastily thrown up fortifications—a wooden fence reinforced with tree limbs and rocks—just sixty yards away. Lieutenant Key's Helena Irish gunners were already gaining recognition for their rapid firing and accuracy, and

Privates James McCourtney and George McMillon made the Confederate roll of honor for bravery in this engagement. Soon the Rebels were scrambling over the barricade, and the bluecoats were in full retreat.

But by now there was so much chaos in the gathering darkness that Rebel commanders could not re-form their units, and the Federals—although in equal disarray, firing into the gloom, often at each other—were managing to throw together another line of battle. But they were not prepared for Polk's Rebels, who plowed into them from the east and routed them. Polk's brigade suffered 60 casualties, but took 50 Yankee prisoners and three cannon. The Federals had put up a tough fight, though, and this was as far as Polk would go that night.[6]

After the first day's fighting subsided, the cold, hungry troops endured a miserable night at Chickamauga. Wounded soldiers in gray and blue lay among the dead in the woods as the commanders of both armies revised their battle plans and prepared to renew the struggle on the morrow. Bragg reorganized his army into a right wing (under Leonidas Polk) that would attack the Federal left and a left wing (under Longstreet) that would strike the center.

Leonidas Polk hit the bluecoats, who had entrenched now behind formidable log breastworks near the junction of the Lafayette Road and Alexander's Bridge Road—first with John C. Breckinridge's division at 9:30 a.m., then at 10 a.m. with Cleburne's, attempting to turn Rosecrans' left flank and cut the Lafayette Road to the north. In Breckinridge's division, Daniel Adams' Louisiana brigade attacked the Federals on their extreme left.

Adams' brigade—with Major John Austin's 14th Louisiana Sharpshooters battalion acting as skirmishers and Colonel Randall Gibson's 13th/20th Louisiana on the extreme right—pushed forward just east of the Lafayette Road, and the 13th/20th Louisiana quickly encountered skirmisher fire from one of two Indiana regiments posted near the McDonald house. The Hoosiers were isolated from the rest of the Federal army that lay a quarter of a mile south along the Lafayette Road. Adams' soldiers quickly swarmed through the breach and cut off the Yankees, and the 13th/20th Louisiana fell on the Hoosier regiments which disintegrated and fled into the woods, tossing down their weapons and equipment. The New Orleans Irishmen captured about eighty of them.

Adams' brigade promptly shifted to their left and assembled for a push down the western side of the Lafayette Road to hit the left flank of George Thomas' Federal corps. They soon made contact with the bluecoats, but this time the going was much rougher, because the Yankees had thrown up a stout breastwork of tree limbs and lay in wait behind them—ready to pour on fire at the Confederates before they realized they were there. The Louisianans had become reckless after their earlier quick success at the McDonald farm, and they were racing impulsively toward the enemy when suddenly their ranks were staggered by a heavy volley. The 13th/20th Louisiana's color bearer, Sergeant J. C. McDavitt, was killed when he was hit in both legs by canister. Nearly 40 percent of the 13th/20th Louisiana (16 killed, 50 wounded, and 35 missing) were casualties. The commander of the 19th Louisiana was killed, leaving Captain Hyder A. Kennedy of Claiborne in charge of that regiment. In what Kennedy called "the most desperate and bloody charge that troops were ever called on to make," the 19th Louisiana suffered 153 casualties out of 349—nearly half of the regiment. Adams was wounded and was taken prisoner by the Yankees, and command passed to Randall Gibson, who ordered the broken brigade back to the McDonald farm. M. A. Stovall's brigade, which had advanced down the eastern side of the road, met the same fate.[7]

Cleburne attacked the bluecoats farther south along the Lafayette Road. But his three brigades ran into even stiffer resistance than Adams and Stovall, for here they came up against 4,000 Yankee troops crammed together behind stout breastworks that were almost invisible to the Rebels in the woods. From those breastworks came a devastating fire that cut through the gray-clad ranks like a scythe. The difficulty that the troops had in maintaining their alignment in the dense undergrowth only added to the chaos. In Lucius Polk's brigade, 350 soldiers became casualties in a matter of minutes. It was like a shooting gallery for the Federals, whose losses were incredibly slight. "The strife at this point was fearful," wrote Colonel James A. Smith of the Irish 3rd/5th Confederate. "Such showers of grape, canister, and small-arms I have never before witnessed." And yet, the Rebels kept at it for three hours, huddling behind the crest of a hill, refusing to withdraw. Stubborn and tenacious as ever, still they never got any farther. For the second time in two days Cleburne's division was repulsed.[8]

James Longstreet's troops would play the critical role now, thanks to a misunderstanding in orders by a Federal division commander. When the Rebel general discovered that a Yankee division had vacated its place along the Lafayette Road, leaving a yawning gap in the defensive line just waiting to be occupied, Longstreet pounced at the chance. His three divisions under E. M. Law, Joseph B. Kershaw, and Bushrod Johnson struck the gap in the Federal line at just the right moment around 11:30 a.m., shot past the Brotherton house and penetrated far beyond the Lafayette Road. Thomas Hindman's division followed, peeling back the remnant of the Federal right wing, isolating Rosecrans from the rest of his army. The Federal right wing was routed.

In Arthur Manigault's brigade of Hindman's division, the 24th Alabama, including many Irish Mobilians, gamely charged the Federals near the burning house of Widow Eliza Glenn (recently used by Rosecrans as his headquarters but now hastily vacated), overran the enemy position, and captured their guns. But their joy turned to distress as heavy gunfire to their south announced the arrival of Colonel John T. Wilder's "Lightning Brigade," the hard-riding Federal mounted infantry of Indiana and Illinois troops, armed with the rapid-fire Spencer repeaters. Outgunned, the Alabamians fell back to the Lafayette Road. Captain William J. O'Brien of Company B (the Emmet Guards of Mobile) was killed. The 24th Alabama lost 22 killed, 91 wounded, and 3 missing—116 out of 381.[9]

Soon to be known as the "Rock of Chickamauga," Major General George Thomas, commanding the Federal left wing, made a stubborn stand to the north, on Snodgrass Hill and Horseshoe Ridge. During the afternoon, Longstreet attacked this final Federal line with four of his divisions. J. P. Anderson's brigade of Hindman's division went into action but experienced the same frustratingly superior Yankee firepower that had stymied Manigault's brigade to the south. The Irish in the 9th, 10th, and 44th Mississippi regiments tried their hand at cracking the Federal line for two hours, only to be checked and driven back by the Colt repeating rifles of the 21st Ohio. Although the Buckeyes' rifles were overheating and they were running out of ammunition, the Mississippians were low as well, and the 10th Mississippi's commander, Lieutenant Colonel James Barr, noted that his men's rifles were so clogged that "the men were compelled to force the balls home by hammering the ends of their ramrods against trees." Barr mentioned the bravery shown by two of his Irish soldiers in Company F (the Port Gibson Riflemen),

Sergeant D. O'Brien and Private Barney McCabe, who "died within reach of his bayonet of the enemy."[10]

Now it was Bushrod Johnson's turn to attack. In his division was the 10th Tennessee, the "Sons of Erin" from Nashville, new to the Army of Tennessee and among the reinforcements that Bragg had just received from Mississippi. After the death of Colonel Randal McGavock at Raymond, Mississippi, four months earlier, command of the 10th Tennessee had passed to Colonel William ("Battling Billy") Grace. The 10th Tennessee had seen combat the previous day at Chickamauga, and earlier in today's fighting they had stormed two Federal batteries. The Sons of Erin captured the Yankees and their cannon, but they were left with several of their best officers wounded or killed.

The Irish lads' path to Horseshoe Ridge took them past a homestead where a farmer, his wife, and their three attractive daughters spilled out of the home to greet the troops. It seemed that they had been afraid to come out for fear of the Yankees. As the women whooped with delight at the sight of the gray-coated deliverers, the soldiers tarried there a moment to set the ladies' minds at rest. One Rebel officer wistfully recalled them as "four very nice looking ladies."

The Sons of Erin's respite was short-lived. At 4 p.m., the graycoats ran into Lieutenant Colonel Darius Warner's 113th Ohio, part of Rosecrans' reserves just now committed to reinforce Thomas' beleaguered line. "Battling Billy" immediately formed a line of battle to receive the Yankee attack, and the 10th Tennessee's sharpshooters, led by Major John ("Gentleman Johnny") O'Neill, fought off the bluecoats. But a second attack by the Buckeyes succeeded, and the Sons of Erin were pushed back, as the rest of the Confederate regiments also retreated under heavy pressure from the Federal reinforcements. During the withdrawal, Federal sharpshooters picked off Colonel Grace's horse. In falling, the Irishman injured his back and lay on the ground in pain as the bluecoats closed in. But the Sons of Erin had no intention of letting their commander be taken. While O'Neill's sharpshooters laid down covering fire, Lieutenant Robert Page Seymour sped forward, hauled Grace up on his saddle, and galloped to safety to the cheers of the Irishmen.[11]

In some of the fiercest fighting of the day, Cleburne's division made one more assault late in the afternoon, striking the knot of Federal resistance still holding on east of the Lafayette Road. Lucius Polk's brigade went forward, and soon his troops were scrambling over the Federal barricades that had given way at last. With the aid of the Helena battery's deadly accurate fire, Polk's troops overran three lines of breastworks. The successful charge cost the brigade 200 casualties. The 1st Arkansas lost nearly half its soldiers. Losses were also heavy in the 3rd/5th Confederate, and Captain Charles Frazer wrote, "The regiment never did better work than here." Colonel Smith reported the deaths of Captain George Moore of Company H and Company E's Captain James Beard, "the best and bravest soldier I ever saw."[12]

The Federals were in full retreat, but Thomas' stand had saved them from annihilation. The bluecoats had made a remarkable defense, delaying the Rebels while the bulk of Rosecrans' army slipped away, and at nightfall they began to withdraw toward Chattanooga. The Rebel victory had come at a high price—for the Federals, 16,000 men dead, wounded, or missing, over a quarter of their army, and for the Rebels, more than 18,000 casualties, nearly a third of their army. Cleburne counted 36 percent of his division as casualties.[13]

But Bragg's failure to capitalize on his triumph at Chickamauga made the Confed-

HIGH POINT OF THE WAR FOR THE ARMY OF TENNESSEE. **The Rebel victory at Chickamauga was won at the price of nearly a third of their army in killed and wounded. Irish Confederates saw action on many parts of the battlefield. (Library of Congress)**

erate victory even more hollow. First he hesitated to finish off Rosecrans' beaten army, then he watched while the bluecoats retreated into Chattanooga to lick their wounds. While the Army of Tennessee laid siege to the strategic city—it was really more of a "half-siege" since the Rebels occupied only Lookout Mountain and Missionary Ridge, the high ground south of the town—the Federals continued to receive reinforcements, as well as a new commander, General Ulysses S. Grant, the stubborn victor at Shiloh and Vicksburg.

At Missionary Ridge, Cleburne was pleased to recommend an Irish-American, Colonel John H. Kelly of the 8th Arkansas, for promotion to brigadier general. Orphaned at the age of 7 and raised by his grandmother, Kelly would have graduated from West Point with the class of 1861, but instead he resigned to take a commission in the Confederate army. He had fought well at Shiloh and Perryville and had been badly wounded at Murfreesboro but returned to the field at Chickamauga. "I know no better officer of his grade in the service," Cleburne wrote. The 23-year-old Kelly became the Confederate army's youngest general officer on November 16, 1863, and took command of a brigade of gray-clad cavalry. Just eight months later, he would die while leading a cavalry charge near Franklin, Tennessee.[14]

Two months after the Confederacy's wasted opportunity at Chickamauga, Grant stunned the Army of Tennessee and turned the tables on Bragg by breaking out of siege at Chattanooga. On November 24, he launched massive assaults at both the ends of the Rebel line, capturing first Lookout Mountain on the south and sending William T. Sherman to secure Tunnel Hill, the northern end of Missionary Ridge. Sherman's troops crossed the Tennessee River and seized what they thought to be their objective, only to learn that they had taken a separate hill detached by a considerable stretch of open ground from Tunnel Hill, held by none other than Cleburne's division.

After the Federal capture of Lookout Mountain, Cleburne had awaited the order for the army to withdraw from Missionary Ridge. He was surprised when word reached him to stand and fight, but he immediately prepared to do so, ordering axes to be distributed so his troops could begin fortifying. A ghostly eclipse of the moon made the night very dark as the soldiers went about their work. James A. Smith now commanded a brigade of Texas troops entrenched high on Tunnel Hill facing the separate hill that Sherman's troops had occupied. (The 10th Texas Infantry contained perhaps a dozen or more Irish Americans in several of its companies; and it would be an Irish-American officer, Captain Reuben D. Kennedy, who would command the regiment by December 1864.) Returned to Cleburne's division now was Daniel C. Govan's brigade (including the 2nd/15th Arkansas and Colonel John E. Murray's 5th/13th Arkansas, which lost close to half its men in casualties at Chickamauga) holding the eastern side of the ridge.

Cleburne posted Irish-American Mark Lowrey's Alabama-Mississippi brigade north of Govan's troops near Chickamauga Creek. Lucius Polk's brigade (including the 3rd/5th Confederate, the 1st Arkansas, and Colonel William D. Robison's 2nd Tennessee) would guard the East Tennessee and Georgia Railroad bridge over Chickamauga Creek to secure a vital route of retreat. Lieutenant Harvey Shannon placed the four 12-pounders of his Warren Light Artillery on top of Tunnel Hill. Farther south, Lieutenant Thomas J. Key's Helena battery occupied the top of the ridge over the railroad tunnel.

The hazy dawn of November 25 gave way to a fine, cloudless day. Sherman attacked at 10 a.m. Outnumbering Cleburne's defenders four to one, four divisions of blue-coated troops stepped off smartly and swarmed toward the base of Tunnel Hill. They had to cross several hundred yards in the open, but Cleburne held his troops ready until they actually began climbing the ridge. As the Yankees approached, they were pounded by Cleburne's artillery, and the Federal guns responded in kind. Cleburne's soldiers watched until the bluecoats reached the foot of the ridge and were out of their view.

And then Cleburne's men began to see patches of blue and the glint of steel moving among the dark pines as the Federals scrambled up the rocky, wooded slope. Soon they were almost upon them, and the Rebel infantry and cannon let loose with everything they had. Shannon's gunners of the Warren Light Artillery loaded their pieces with canister and fired directly into the Yankees just fifty paces away. They were too close for comfort, and Colonel Smith's Texas troops swarmed over the earthworks near the battery and drove the bluecoats back down the ridge in desperate fighting at the point of the bayonet.

STUBBORN FIGHT FOR TUNNEL HILL, NOVEMBER 1863. Wartime sketch by Albert Waud captures the chaotic fighting at the northern end of Missionary Ridge, where Cleburne's defense marked the only bright spot for the Confederacy at Chattanooga. (Library of Congress)

Thirty minutes later, the Federals charged up the slope again, trying to reach Shannon's guns. Again they came within paces of the breastworks and were thrown back by heavy fire from both front and flank. Although badly outnumbered, Cleburne had used the terrain of Tunnel Hill to the fullest advantage, placing his meager forces skillfully, so as to maximize his firepower. As the morning wore on, there were more Federal assaults, and more Rebel counter-assaults to drive them back, with Cleburne himself leading some of them. Federal fire took its toll on Shannon's battery, wounding Lieutenant Shannon, killing and wounding several others, leaving a corporal in command.

It must have been a novel experience for Cleburne's troops, so accustomed to throwing themselves at the enemy in desperate headlong attacks—at Shiloh, Perryville, Murfreesboro, and Chickamauga—to find themselves for once on the receiving end. By noon, both sides seemed to have had enough for the present. Cleburne used the lull in the fighting to move the 2nd/15th Arkansas to the top of Tunnel Hill behind the Vicksburg gunners. At the same time, he ordered the Helena battery up to the top of the hill.

In the early afternoon, the Federals renewed their attacks on Tunnel Hill, hitting Shannon's and Key's batteries with what Cleburne called "one continuous sheet of hissing, flying lead." There were a half dozen charges and counter-charges. The Helena gunners depressed their pieces as low as they could, belching canister and shell at the bluecoats, and some of the graycoats rolled lighted artillery shells down the hill at them. The Yankees were gradually gaining a foothold, as groups of them began to ease their way closer to the Rebel works. Running short on ammunition and unable to fire at the Federals taking advantage of cover on the hillside, the Irish in the 2nd/15th Arkansas resorted to rolling boulders and large stones downhill at them.

And so things stood until about 4 p.m., when Cleburne ordered a bayonet charge in strength down the ridge, spearheaded by the 36th and 56th Georgia regiments of Carter Stevenson's division (who occupied the western side of the ridge atop the railroad tunnel), and including the 2nd/15th Arkansas, out of ammunition and relying only on the bayonet. The fierce hand-to-hand fighting finally broke the deadlock for control of Tunnel Hill. The bluecoats gave way, and the Rebels chased them to the foot of the ridge. Cleburne's division had won the day, but the victory had cost them 42 men killed and 178 wounded.[15]

But while Cleburne's troops were savoring their victory, elsewhere on Missionary Ridge things were turning out very differently, as the very center of the Army of Tennessee's defensive line suddenly and inexplicably crumbled before the Federal onslaught.

Rebel soldiers in the rifle pits at the base of Missionary Ridge watched in amazement as four more Federal divisions—20,000 strong—in a front two miles wide launched their attack at noon. George Thomas' well-drilled troops were like an unbroken blue mass coming steadily closer across the open fields. "It was indeed a grand spectacle," remarked an awe-struck Ralph J. Neal of the 20th Tennessee. Yelling, "Chickamauga! Chickamauga!" the onrushing Federals overwhelmed the lightly defended rifle pits, but they didn't stop there. They next charged up the side of Missionary Ridge and overran both the Confederates' uncompleted second line halfway up the slope and the final line at the crest.

Why for the first time in its history did the Army of Tennessee crack under pressure? Historian James Lee McDonough places much of the blame on the Rebel commanders, who had thought the position on Missionary Ridge to be much stronger than it actually was. There were flaws in the Confederate defenses: insufficient reserves to plug gaps in the line; too many places on the approach to the crest where Union attackers could rest and receive more troops before resuming the attack; no reserve line behind the crest where the defenders could re-form, the eastern slope undefended; too many troops posted at the base, instead of near the crest where Rebel firepower could have been massed.

When the blue-coated wave hit the first defensive line with full force, the line gave way. Rebel soldiers scrambled up the slope, discarding knapsacks, blankets, and rifles in the panic to reach the top. Many never did, but were killed or captured in the process. Joseph E. Riley of the 33rd Tennessee was struck in the left side by a piece of shell that broke several ribs as it tore out of his body below his right shoulder. Remarkably, Riley lived, but he was too weak to get to his feet and was taken prisoner. Many of the Confederates who did manage to reach the crest were so exhausted that they were unable to fight.[16]

MISSIONARY RIDGE
Nov. 25, 1863

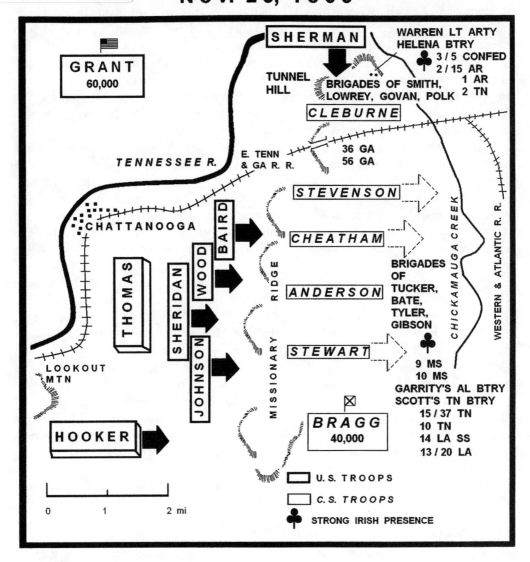

Manning part of the rifle pits was the 15th/37th Tennessee, part of William Bate's old brigade. Of the Irish-dominated 15th Tennessee (which contained three companies of Memphis Irish, including the old Montgomery Guard), barely 140 men had been left in the regiment when it was consolidated with the 37th Tennessee in June 1863. While most of the Rebel soldiers in the rifle pits obeyed the orders passed on to them by General Bragg—to get off one quick volley before withdrawing quickly uphill—the 15th/37th Tennessee, still containing a few of the Memphis Irishmen who had enlisted back in June 1861, stubbornly kept firing at the advancing bluecoats until they were nearly right on them, then they too joined the mad rush up the slope of Missionary Ridge.[17]

For the Rebel artillery at the crest of Missionary Ridge—like James Garrity's Alabama battery, left as the sole company occupying a 150-yard-wide gap in the Rebel line with no infantry support—there was nowhere to go. Gunners either defended their pieces to the end or fled. One of the Rebel batteries to be overrun was an Irish company from Memphis, Captain William L. Scott's battery that had already suffered heavy losses at Chickamauga. Federal troops overwhelmed and captured the battery on Missionary Ridge, although the gunners remained by their guns fighting to the end. Many of them were killed and wounded or captured, and those few who were able to escape were not enough to form a new company. The battery was disbanded at the end of the year. A few of those remaining were transferred to the Warren Light Artillery.[18]

Among the routed Confederates in the center were the Irish companies of the 9th, 10th, and 44th Mississippi regiments (now in Colonel William Tucker's brigade), and Gibson's Louisiana brigade, for the first time retreating rather than attacking. As the soldiers of the 19th Tennessee scrambled down the eastern slope in a desperate effort to get away, Irishman Tom Kennedy—with bullets zipping around him—took off his hat and shook it at the bluecoats who had gained the crest, as if to ward off evil spirits rather than flesh-and-blood Yankees. A Rebel band struck up "Dixie," and a few graycoats tried to make a stand along the eastern slope, but to no avail.[19]

In the Rebel center, Bate's division managed to give a good account of itself, keeping formation and making a decent withdrawal. Bate formed two lines of battle—with skirmishers from Major John E. Austin's 14th Louisiana Sharpshooters on the left and from Major John M. Wall's 15th/37th Tennessee on the right—and conducted an hour's holding action to allow the rest of Breckinridge's corps to withdraw. Clinging to their earthworks like bulldogs, Nashville's "Sons of Erin," the 10th Tennessee—just 103 strong—led by Major John O'Neill, kept firing at the blue-coated troops steadily overrunning Missionary Ridge. They were the final Rebels to abandon the line in the Confederate center, and their stand cost them nearly a third of their numbers in casualties. Four "Sons of Erin" were killed—Lieutenant John McCullough, Sergeant Patrick Kennedy, and Privates Patrick Delaney and Philip McDermott.[20]

Now it fell to Cleburne's division, which had held fast on the Confederate right flank, to form a rear guard and protect the Rebel army as it made its escape from the disaster on Missionary Ridge. Learning the shocking news of the collapse of the army's center and left, Cleburne took command of the Rebel divisions on the right flank and formed a line of battle across the ridge to stop the Federal advance northward along the summit. He posted Govan's brigade along the road leading to the bridge across Chickamauga Creek and placed Polk's brigade at the bridge itself to hold the Rebels' only route of retreat.

As night fell, one Rebel division after another, ending with Cleburne's, came down from the heights of Missionary Ridge and made for the rendezvous point on the rail line to the east. Lying dead or wounded on the slopes of Missionary Ridge were more than 6,000 of their gray-coated comrades. Falling sleet and cold made the retreat more depressing. Cleburne's boys covered the withdrawal, and when all were across Chickamauga Creek, they set fire to the bridge and joined the beaten remnants of Bragg's army at Chickamauga Station.

The Federals had a golden opportunity to destroy the Army of Tennessee by launching a vigorous pursuit. On the morning of November 27, as the Confederates retreated southward to Dalton, Georgia, Cleburne's division again had to save the army from annihilation. Against four-to-one odds, Cleburne drew up his 4,000 troops across the narrow pass at Ringgold Gap, about twenty miles south of Chattanooga, as the rapidly gaining Federal army closed in. The road south passed alongside Chickamauga Creek and the Western and Atlantic rail line through a narrow gap only a half mile wide.

Cleburne positioned his forces shrewdly to defend the strategic gap. On Taylor's Ridge, the sharp hill to his left, Cleburne stationed the 16th Alabama and in front of them, three companies of the 6th/7th Arkansas under Lieutenant James M. Dulin, the officer who had "charged" the enemy with ordnance wagons at Murfreesboro. On White Oak Mountain to the right of the gap, Smith's Texas brigade took up a defensive position. And in the gap itself, Cleburne posted four lines of his Arkansas infantry, with Colonel John E. Murray's 5th/13th Arkansas in front, along with a section of two guns of Lieutenant Goldthwaite's Alabama battery. In the rear rank was the 2nd/15th/24th Arkansas (including Cleburne's old company from Helena). On watch behind the gap in case they were needed on the vulnerable right flank was Lucius Polk's brigade.

Behind him, Cleburne could see the last of the Rebel cavalry and slow-moving wagon train struggling along the muddy road south, and already the enemy was appearing to his front. Concealed by branches piled in front of their position, Cleburne's Alabama gunners and infantry in front of the gap let loose a sheet of lead at the first column of bluecoats fifty yards away. A half dozen quick discharges of canister forced the Federals back to the shelter of the railroad embankment. But to Cleburne's right, the Federals had fanned out and were pressing against White Oak Mountain.

Lucius Polk acted quickly to reinforce Cleburne's right flank, sending in the 1st Arkansas who arrived just in time to drive the bluecoats back within mere yards of the top of the ridge. The 1st Arkansas continued to stand firm against repeated enemy charges, even flinging rocks at the bluecoats when they ran low on ammunition. (Later on, one of the Yankee prisoners, an Irishman, recognized Chris "Kit" Cleburne, the teenage brother of the general, as one of the graycoats who had pelted him with rocks on White Oak Mountain: "Ah, you are the little devil who smashed me jaw with a rock!" The general found it amusing.) Soon the 3rd/5th Confederate and 2nd Tennessee, along with the remaining Alabama-Mississippi regiments of Mark Lowrey's brigade, joined them, checking the enemy's attempt to turn Cleburne's right.

Now the Federals moved against Cleburne's left. Dulin's Arkansas skirmishers held their ground, keeping them in check. Finally the Federals gained the cover of some nearby houses and made a charge on Govan's Arkansas skirmishers to the left of the railroad track. But Cleburne's gunners swept the field with canister and solid shot, and the bluecoats withdrew, leaving several dead along with a stand of colors. Captain Valentine M. McGehee of the 2nd Arkansas eagerly offered to take a squad of his men out to recover the flag. This was typical of the brave and reckless McGehee, one of the many young Irishmen who had enlisted in Cleburne's home town of Helena. Just five months earlier, McGehee had been seriously wounded in an engagement at Liberty Gap, but he had refused to leave the field and had to be carried off by force. The young Irish officer now had his eyes on that Yankee flag, but Cleburne vetoed him, arguing that it was not worth the risk to the lives of his soldiers.[21]

When Cleburne received word at noon that the Rebel wagon train was in the clear, he began pulling his division out and moved south to join them. Stung by the unexpected repulse of their advance troops, the enemy made no attempt to follow. The Army of Tennessee would live to fight another day, and the Confederate Congress would vote a resolution praising Cleburne's division and crediting them for saving the army from disaster at Ringgold Gap.

13. The Contest for Atlanta, May–September 1864

On March 22, 1864, a freak late winter storm dropped a blanket of snow nearly half a foot deep on the Georgia mountains, and Confederate soldiers in winter quarters at Dalton had a frolic. Cooped up for four months with no fighting to be done and itching to let off some steam, the Rebels decided to have some fun. The Army of Tennessee had its first all-day snowball battle.

It started innocently enough early in the morning, as soldiers of two neighboring regiments began hurling snowballs at each other in good-natured play. But the play soon escalated into full scale mock combat involving whole brigades and divisions. Some soldiers even took to horse, commandeered cannons, and assumed the role of commanders. Thousands became involved, and even the generals were sucked into the horseplay.

The snowball fight soon spread to Pat Cleburne's division. Helena Irish and Memphis Irish cheerfully whacked each other with snowballs in the cold Georgia mountain air. "Old Pat" led Lucius Polk's brigade against Daniel Govan's brigade, and at one point the general fell captive to Govan's boys. Cleburne was a strict disciplinarian, and some of the lads used the occasion to turn the tables on him for once. "Arrest that soldier," one of them cried, "and make him carry a fence rail!" Cleburne was able to secure a "parole," but he re-entered the battle when Polk's brigade began losing. Govan's boys won the day, though, vanquishing Polk's brigade and pursuing Cleburne to his quarters, where they threatened to "court-martial" him and dunk him in an iced-over creek. Cleburne was able to persuade them to spare him by arguing that he was a first time offender. Then he ordered whiskey for all of his men.[1]

The Great Snowball Battle wasn't as tame as it might sound. It was only a game, but it was a rough game. More than a few snowballs concealed rocks, and there were plenty of bloody noses and missing teeth to testify to just how seriously the soldiers took their play. There would be real combat soon enough.

The ranks of the Irish in the Army of Tennessee were thinning drastically. The 1st Arkansas and Cleburne's old 15th Arkansas (already consolidated with the 2nd and 24th Arkansas) each numbered about 300 men in December 1863, while the Helena Battery was down to 71 soldiers. The 3rd/5th Confederate (the old Memphis "Irish Regiment") mustered only 338 men, and the 10th Tennessee counted just 80 of Nashville's "Sons of Erin," only half of them with muskets. New Orleans' 13th/20th Louisiana mustered fewer than 200 men, with arms for just a little more than a third of them, and of the 61 men left in the 14th Louisiana Sharpshooters Battalion only half were armed. The heavily Irish 1st Louisiana Regulars was down to 68 men now and had been assigned as a company-sized headquarters guard for the Army of Tennessee since Chickamauga.[2]

In April 1864, the war that many had expected to be over in ninety days was entering its fourth year, and the original enlistments of most of the troops in the Army of Tennessee were running out. In Ben Cheatham's division, the Memphis-based 154th Tennessee, with many Irish members from the Pinch district, set the trend by unanimously re-enlisting for the war. Other Irish-tinged units like the 10th Mississippi (with numbers of Irish from Port Gibson and Jackson) also re-enlisted for the war. The men of Cleburne's division re-enlisted almost to a man. Considering that most of these men had not seen their homes and families in Arkansas and Texas in three long years, it is a testament to their affection and regard for Old Pat.[3]

Morale had improved since the calamitous loss of Chattanooga. Braxton Bragg was gone now. In an accumulation of resentment stemming from the Army of Tennessee's missed opportunities at Perryville, Murfreesboro, and Chickamauga, Bragg's corps and division commanders (Cleburne included) had lost confidence in his leadership. After the disaster at Missionary Ridge, the embattled Confederate commander came under increasing criticism for incompetence, and Jeff Davis accepted his resignation in December 1863. Bragg's replacement was General Joseph Johnston, who was much more popular with the rank and file. "Joe Johnston knows how to manage the Yanks," wrote Captain Samuel Camp Kelly, an Irish-American officer in the 30th Alabama Infantry. "I say Johnston has the confidence of nine-tenths of the army."[4]

Revitalized and ready for renewed fighting, the Army of Tennessee passed in review for their new commander on a sunny day late in April 1864. The army boasted nearly 60,000 men in two corps of infantry and one of cavalry. The spring campaign got underway on May 6 as William T. Sherman's Federal army—three times the size of the Army of Tennessee—began to move south on a relentless drive to capture the key industrial center of Atlanta, and it did not let up for three months.

Only too aware of his weakness in numbers—and the painful reality that the South could no longer replace the precious lives lost—Johnston followed a practical strategy of defensive maneuver, digging in to force Sherman to either attack or to go around him in the movement south. He hoped to catch the Yanks off guard, to take advantage of any mistake and strike them a damaging blow.

The first clash in the Atlanta campaign occurred on May 14 after Sherman bypassed the strong Rebel defenses at Dalton and moved south to the little village of Resaca. Fighting continued here the next day, and Johnston withdrew to a stronger position to the south. In a rear guard action, the 10th Tennessee's Major John O'Neill became one of the battle's casualties when he was shot through both lungs. Thanks to Irish-born Captain John L. Prendergast, another of the Sons of Erin's crack sharpshooters, O'Neill was removed from the battlefield—in bad shape but still alive. Private Patrick Flaherty, a farmer from the Irish community at McEwen, Tennessee, was killed. Private John McElroy, a member of Prendergast's company from Clarkesville, received wounds to his right eye, jaw, and groin, but he would live for nearly half a century. Still ailing from his back injury, Colonel William Grace returned to command now.[5]

In an unexpected and welcome pause after Resaca, Cleburne received a Federal courier riding under a flag of truce. The courier bore a letter from fellow County Cork native General Thomas W. Sweeny, a hot-tempered officer who was said to be fluent in English, Irish-American, and Profane, but most proficient in the latter. Sweeny offered his fellow Irishman an unusual proposition: join with him once the war was over and help recruit an army of Irish combat veterans from both Rebel and Union armies to liberate Ireland from the British—an appealing proposition to Cleburne the Irish patriot, but not an appetizing one to Cleburne the veteran of three years of punishing warfare. Old Pat sent a reply to Sweeny: both of them will have had far enough of fighting, once the war was over, to last them for the rest of their lives.[6]

Johnston and Sherman repeated their flanking and maneuvering after the Confederates took up another strong position along the railroad through strategic Allatoona Pass. Sherman swung fifteen miles to the west and south hoping to outflank the Rebel army but instead ran into stubborn resistance at New Hope Church, where once again the Sons of Erin did yeoman duty as sharpshooters. North of New Hope Church on May 25, the 14th Louisiana Sharpshooters once more deployed as skirmishers. They fought a costly engagement, losing 15 men killed or wounded, and at the end of the day only 30 soldiers were left fit for duty. Sergeant Major Augustus O'Duhigg was badly wounded, and Major Austin mentioned Sergeant James Delaney and Privates John Hagan, Richard Kieley, and J. B. McGraw for bravery. The 13th/20th Louisiana was down to 71 members now, while the minuscule 1st Louisiana Regulars no longer even mustered the numbers to effectively engage in combat.[7]

When Sherman saw an opportunity to turn Johnston's right flank on May 27, his soldiers came up against Cleburne's veterans who awaited an attack amid the tangled underbrush near Pickett's Mill. In a series of uncoordinated attacks before sundown, three Federal brigades threw themselves headlong against the graycoats with reckless loss of life—against gunfire so intense that it seemed, according to one Yankee officer, "like hail in sheets"—and failed to budge them. On the Rebel side, most of the fighting was done by Hiram Granbury's Texans, but John Kelly's cavalry division leant a hand, as did the Irish in the Helena Battery and Warren Light Artillery, who delivered punishing fire of canister, shells, and solid shot. The Federals left some 1,600 men killed, wounded, or missing.[8]

The two armies withdrew farther south to Kennesaw Mountain, where the Rebels dug in and waited for an attack. Colonel Virgil S. Murphy of the 17th Alabama wrote on June 21 that the Rebels were so well entrenched that "it would take more Yankees than you could pack into a fifty acre field to move us from our position." And this proved to be true. His patience giving out now, Sherman ordered a disastrous frontal assault on June 27. In the blazing Georgia heat, with temperatures rising to one hundred degrees, the Federals sacrificed some 3,000 men in futile charges against the well-entrenched Confederates.[9]

All along the ground in front of Cleburne's division, dug in snugly to the south of Kennesaw, Yankee dead and wounded soldiers began to pile up. Brush fires started by the intense artillery fire were spreading frighteningly close to the Federal wounded, lying helpless. Killing the enemy was one thing, but sitting by calmly and watching men burn to death was not the humane thing to do. In Govan's brigade, Lieutenant Colonel William H. Martin of the 1st/15th Arkansas ordered his troops to cease firing, mounted a parapet, and waved a ramrod with a white handkerchief tied to the end. "Come and get your wounded," he yelled, "they are burning to death; we won't fire a gun till you get them away. Be quick!" The Federal guns fell silent, and cautiously small parties of Yankees

SHORT-LIVED TRUCE. **Irish members of the 1st/15th Arkansas observe a cease-fire to allow Federals to retrieve their wounded at Kennesaw Mountain in June 1864. (Library of Congress)**

began coming forward to retrieve the wounded. In this unusual act of compassion, the gray-coated soldiers of the 1st Arkansas crept down from their entrenchments and pitched in to remove the Yankee wounded. Once they were done, both sides went back to firing away at each other. In the lopsided battle in front of Cleburne's division that day, the Federals lost 300 men killed and 500 wounded, while Old Pat's soldiers lost only 2 killed and 9 wounded.[10]

Failing to take Kennesaw Mountain, Sherman reverted to the turning maneuver that he had used for the past several weeks. By July 17, the Army of Tennessee took up a defensive position south of the Chattahoochee River on the northern outskirts of Atlanta and prepared to defend it against the Federals.

Impatient with Johnston's failure to defeat Sherman's army, Jefferson Davis removed him on July 17 and replaced him with John B. Hood, a more aggressive but less experienced officer. Cleburne called it a "disaster" for the Army of Tennessee and for the Confederacy. Sadly, Davis also remembered Cleburne's proposal to recruit African Americans, and he refused to consider the Irishman for promotion even to corps command. Cleburne had another reason to be sad. Word had just reached him of the death of his younger brother Chris, now a cavalry officer serving in Virginia. "He was unusually gloomy," Hardee wrote to his wife, "and he had quite enough to make him so." But there would be much more sadness ahead, as the climactic battle for Atlanta loomed near.[11]

Bald Hill is a piece of high ground that lies well within metropolitan Atlanta today, but in 1864 it was just a mile and a half east of the city. The possession of this hill would determine the fate of the vital industrial city of Atlanta, most important in the South next to Richmond. Federal troops occupied Bald Hill on the morning of July 21 and began throwing artillery shells into Atlanta and at Cleburne's division just to the west of the hill. The bluecoats attacked while Cleburne's boys were still digging in, but the gray-coats counter-attacked and beat them back in time to complete their breastworks. Gunners of the Helena battery and the Warren Light Artillery leant a hand. Cleburne called the fighting here that went on all day in the intense heat, with Federal guns continually pounding the Rebels, the "bitterest" of his life. Particularly deadly were the 20-pounder Parrott guns of Captain Francis De Gress's 1st Illinois battery posted just north of the rail line from Atlanta. Colonel James A. Smith, commanding Hiram Granbury's brigade, recalled, "I have never before witnessed such accurate and destructive cannonading." The Irish 5th Confederate regiment lost 1 man killed and 3 wounded and were grateful when night fell.[12]

When Hood pulled back into Atlanta after heavy losses on the south side of Peachtree Creek on July 20, Sherman thought he might be evacuating the city. But Hood had a new plan, and had fortune favored him on July 22, he would have achieved possibly the greatest victory of the war. The Army of Tennessee's new commander envisioned a bold, aggressive maneuver to duplicate the success of Lee and Jackson in their brilliant victory at Chancellorsville in Virginia. Hood would try to exploit the gap between Sherman's two main armies, led by George Thomas and James B. McPherson, and strike and destroy the Federal left flank before they could join. William J. Hardee's corps would make a hard fifteen-mile night march south and east of the city, wheel back to the north, and then his four divisions would attack McPherson east of Bald Hill and roll up the Federal left flank, which Hood believed to be unfortified.

Unforeseen problems and delays doomed the plan from the start. Just about all of the commands were late, the men exhausted from the previous day's fighting and from lack of sleep. "The march lasted until daylight when we rested for two hours," Georgia officer William Dixon wrote. "How we got here is more than is known." Hardee's attack, planned for dawn, did not get underway until shortly after noon. When the Rebels did reach their objective, the ground to the east of Bald Hill, what they expected to find was McPherson's flank hanging in air. Instead, what they found was two Federal divisions, John Fuller's and Thomas W. Sweeny's, well dug in along Sugar Creek and supported by artillery. Worst of all, Hardee's four divisions were unable to coordinate their assaults and threw themselves piecemeal against the bluecoats.[13]

William B. Bate's division, the farthest Rebel unit to the east, with the 10th Tennessee's Sons of Erin on its far right flank, launched the first Rebel assault, against the Union division of fiery Irishman Thomas W. Sweeny. Emerging from the swampy eastern bank of Terry's Mill Pond, knee-deep in mud in some places, the division pushed north through difficult underbrush, its formation broken, the men worn out. Still they managed to form two lines of battle and "burst from the woods in truly magnificent style," as one Federal officer put it. The graycoats immediately came under artillery fire. They exchanged several volleys with the bluecoats, then gave the Rebel yell as they lunged forward. Raked by canister, Bate's troops were unable to maintain their momentum and fell back, no more to attack that day. The Sons of Erin, along with the rest of Thomas Benton Smith's brigade, received new orders and peeled off from the division to move farther east toward Decatur to support Confederate cavalry in a projected strike against

CONFEDERACY'S HIGH WATER MARK AT ATLANTA, JULY 22, 1864. At a key moment in the battle for the Gate City, Arthur Manigault's Confederate brigade overruns a Federal battery. (*The Mountain Campaigns in Georgia*, 1890)

McPherson's supply wagons there. The 10th Tennessee lost 2 men killed, Privates Patrick Conry and William A. Mentiss, and 7 other Irishmen wounded. The Sons of Erin were down to 53 men by the end of the day's fighting.[14]

To the west of Bate's division, struggling out of the morass on the other side of Terry's Mill Pond was William Walker's division. As Bate's troops advanced on the east of Sugar Creek, Walker's men did the same on the west, moving north toward Fuller's division. Just as the column reached the northern end of the pond, Walker was struck dead by a Federal musket ball, and Brigadier General Hugh Mercer of Georgia assumed command. Mercer's division formed line of battle poorly, not properly coordinated with Bate's, and two of its brigades launched furious piecemeal assaults against the right of Sweeny's division and the left of Fuller's, only to be pushed back with heavy losses.

At this point, Mercer's own Georgia brigade entered the fray, but it did not get very far either. Acting commander Colonel William Barkuloo reported, "We found the enemy drawn up in three lines of battle on the crest of the hill and supported by two batteries.... ground was open and afforded no shelter for an advance.... They were distant about 500 yards, and their lines outflanked ours both to the right and left." Barkuloo decided the odds were too great and withdrew, losing 15 men killed and wounded.[15]

Mercer's brigade now contained the Army of Tennessee's largest concentration of Irishmen—his own 1st Georgia Volunteers. Drawn from Savannah's volunteer militia companies, the 1st Georgia boasted the Irish Jasper Greens, the pride of the city's Irish, as well as the older Republican Blues with many Irish and Scotch-Irish members, and the more recently formed Irish Volunteers. Today marked their biggest taste of battle to date in the war. Until now, the 1st Georgia Volunteers had served in the Savannah area, occupying nearby Fort Pulaski in January 1861 and defending Fort McAllister from Federal assaults in late 1862 and early 1863. But the Savannah boys had yearned for service in the larger theaters of the war. With the opening of Sherman's Georgia offensive, they got their chance. The 1st Georgia Volunteers left Savannah on May 27 to an enthusiastic send-off by local townspeople.

To troops used to garrison duty, the rigors of marching in the field were something new, and the Republican Blues' Captain William Dixon admitted, "they are not used to marching." During the first two weeks of June, Savannah's Irish lads had more than their fill of marching, digging in, and fending off attacks by the Federals—a pattern of maneuvering and fighting that had become commonplace in the Army of Tennessee. The Savannah boys' first major combat occurred in a running engagement between June 15 and June 18, when the bluecoats stormed the 1st Georgia's line at Lost Mountain, a phase of the Kennesaw Mountain fighting. In a series of Federal attacks and Rebel counterattacks, Irish Jasper Greens Captains John Flannery and James Dooner were wounded slightly, and Sergeant James McGowan lost his left arm. The end of this fighting found 7 Irish Jaspers wounded and 49 missing, many of whom were either captured or deserted to the enemy.[16]

The news of Joe Johnston's replacement by Hood in July was greeted with less than enthusiasm by the war-weary Savannah boys. "The Army is very much dissatisfied with the change," William Dixon wrote. The Bald Hill assault of July 22 brought the full reality of the new commander's attack-and-die policy home to the Savannah Irish. "The fight was heavy," Dixon wrote. It would not be the last action they would see that day.[17]

Bate's and Mercer's failed attacks took all of forty-five minutes and never penetrated within one hundred yards of the Yankee lines. The Federals were fresher, although largely unfortified they had artillery support, and they made quick work of uncoordinated attacks by the exhausted Rebels.

Now it was Cleburne's turn. But first, there was a fateful encounter between the young Federal commander James McPherson and members of the 5th Confederate regiment, reduced now to just 91 men and reassigned to James Smith's Texas brigade. Fearing that a major attack was underway on his lightly defended left flank, McPherson had set out on horseback with two of his aides to reconnoiter the situation when he rode into a group of Rebel skirmishers from the 5th Confederate—Lieutenant Richard Beard, Corporal Robert Coleman, and Asher Stovall—just emerging onto the road. Beard called out for the Federal party to halt. As McPherson wheeled his horse and tried to make a run for it, Coleman took aim and fired, and McPherson fell dead.[18]

Cleburne launched his attack at about 1 p.m., to the west of Bate's and Mercer's futile attacks. Cleburne's division advanced up the eastern side of Flat Shoals Road to strike the left flank of Giles Smith's Federal division south of Bald Hill. Cleburne's veterans had expected to reach—and to overrun—the exposed, unfortified rear of the Federal left flank east of Atlanta. Instead, the unpalatable sight of Yankee entrenchments—two lines of breastworks fronted by formidable abatis of felled trees—was the first thing that greeted Daniel C. Govan's brigade, the vanguard of Cleburne's division. Waiting behind those entrenchments were the tough veteran Iowa soldiers of Colonel William Hall's brigade. Govan's boys—with the Helena Irish of the 1st/15th Arkansas, the remnants of the Vicksburg Irish in the 3rd Confederate, and supported

CAPT C. W. FRAZER

CAPT J. H. BEARD

MAJ. R. J. PERSON

CAPT W. E. SMITH

CORPORAL ROBERT COLEMAN

Officers of the 5th Confederate Infantry

by four guns of the Helena battery—would have to fight their way through the jumble of felled trees, navigate fifty yards of open ground, and then assail the bluecoats' log-and-earthen breastworks, while all the time braving small arms and artillery fire.

But still Govan's troops surged forward, giving the Rebel yell as they went. They reached the abatis, and then came a burst of canister and small arms fire that ripped through their first line of battle. Following closely on the heels of the first wave, a second line of graycoats made it through the abatis, but with the same deadly losses. As the Iowa soldiers loaded and fired their weapons into the gray masses as fast as they could—the barrels of their rifles heating up so rapidly that cartridges ignited and flashed as soon as they were put in—Govan's third wave of Arkansans with part of James A. Smith's Texas brigade as well made it to within a few yards of the Yankee breastworks. They could go no farther, but they could not retreat either.

Some of Govan's soldiers in desperation began to raise white flags, and the Iowans began to cease firing. Then abruptly, Smith's Texans penetrated the Federal defenses at the northern end of their rampart, isolating the 16th Iowa and taking most of the regiment prisoner. With the rest of the Iowa brigade falling back now, Smith's Confederates pushed ahead while Govan's troops, too exhausted to go on, remained behind. Colonel John Edward Murray of the 5th/13th Arkansas was killed in this action. The loss of this promising young officer, Govan recorded, "cast a gloom over the whole command, where he was universally beloved." Murray would probably have been made a brigadier general had he lived through this battle.[19]

Since the Iowans had abandoned their works, Smith's brigade now was actually in the rear of the Federal left flank at Bald Hill. Now Cleburne's troops from Smith's and Mark Lowrey's brigades hit the Federals from the south, while two brigades from George Maney's division—the Tennessee brigades of Colonel Michael Magevney, Jr., and O. F. Strahl—struck from the west along Flat Shoals Road. It was a critical moment in the battle, because for once the Rebels were managing to deliver simultaneous attacks on both the front and rear of the Federal position, but could they break through and punch a dangerous hole in the bluecoats' line?

It was not to be. The soldiers of Mortimer Leggett's Federal division reversed their position and shifted their battle line to the rear of their westward-facing trenches to meet Smith's attack. In fierce fighting, they began beating back the Rebel attackers whose numbers were simply too few and, according to one Federal officer, "slaughtered the rebels by the hundreds." When Smith sent for reinforcements that failed to come, the outcome of the struggle became clear. A stiff counter-attack by two Federal regiments overwhelmed the 5th Confederate, capturing 10 officers and 38 enlisted men as well as the regiment's colors. All but one of Smith's regimental commanders were killed, wounded, or captured, and he himself was badly wounded.[20]

Mark Lowrey's brigade attacked again and again just south of Bald Hill but could not hold what little ground it gained. The Federals there greeted the Rebels in the same manner as Leggett's troops, reversing their position and digging in their heels behind

Opposite: CLEBURNE'S FAVORITE COMMAND, THE 5TH CONFEDERATE INFANTRY. The hard-fighting 5th Confederate was composed mainly of Irish Americans from Memphis. Captain Charles W. Frazer (top left) was captured in Setpember 1863 and remained a prisoner until the end of the war; Captain James H. Beard (top right), the son of a Presbyterian minister, was killed at Chickamauga; and Corporal Robert Coleman (bottom right) is believed to have fired the shot that killed Federal General James B. McPherson at Atlanta. (*Military Annals of Tennessee*, 1886)

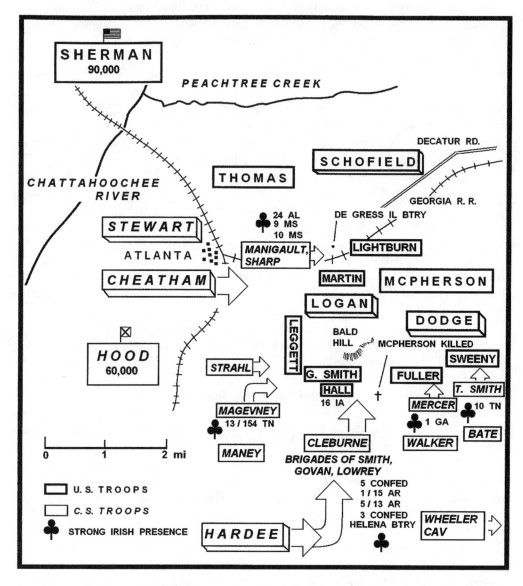

ATLANTA July 22, 1864

SHERMAN
90,000

PEACHTREE CREEK

DECATUR RD.

CHATTAHOOCHEE
RIVER

SCHOFIELD

THOMAS

GEORGIA R. R.

STEWART

24 AL
9 MS   DE GRESS IL BTRY
10 MS

ATLANTA   MANIGAULT,   LIGHTBURN
                 SHARP

CHEATHAM   MARTIN   McPHERSON

                 LOGAN

                              DODGE

                 BALD
                 HILL   McPHERSON KILLED

HOOD   SWEENY
60,000

STRAHL   LEGGETT   G. SMITH   FULLER
                      HALL   T. SMITH
MAGEVNEY   16 IA   MERCER   10 TN
13 / 154 TN   1 GA
                                   WALKER   BATE
0   1   2 mi
            MANEY   CLEBURNE
                      BRIGADES OF SMITH,
                      GOVAN, LOWREY

   U.S. TROOPS   5 CONFED
                               1 / 15 AR
   C.S. TROOPS   5 / 13 AR
                               3 CONFED   WHEELER
   STRONG IRISH PRESENCE HARDEE HELENA BTRY   CAV

the westward-facing side of their earthworks. They poured a murderous fire into the
attacking graycoats. Some of the Rebels made it into the Federal works, only to be over-
powered and killed or taken prisoner. There were heavy losses, and many men fell out
from sheer exhaustion in the intense heat. Lowrey's men were finally forced to retreat
at the cost of 578 killed, wounded, or missing, nearly half of their numbers. The 3rd

Opposite: IRISH-AMERICAN VETERANS FROM MEMPHIS' 154TH TENNESSEE INFANTRY. Colonel Michael
Magevney, Jr. (2nd row, left), who commanded the regiment for much of the war and was wounded at
Franklin, was a grocery clerk and bookkeeper in Memphis; Private James E. Clary (4th row, right) was
chief of the Memphis fire department after the war; and Private Thomas B. Turley (bottom) became
a successful attorney and eventually a U.S. Senator. (*Military Annals of Tennessee,* 1886)

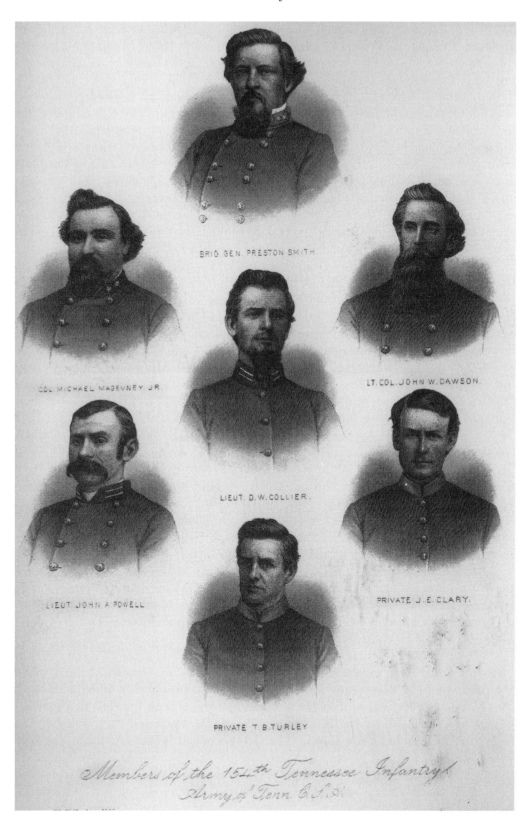

BRIG. GEN. PRESTON SMITH

COL. MICHAEL MAGEVNEY, JR.

LT. COL. JOHN W. DAWSON.

LIEUT. D. W. COLLIER.

LIEUT. JOHN A. POWELL

PRIVATE J. E. CLARY.

PRIVATE T. B. TURLEY.

Members of the 154th Tennessee Infantry, Army of Tenn. C.S.A.

Mississippi Battalion, with a small number of Irish, lost 2 killed and 33 wounded, with 2 officers missing. A 35-year-old Irish-American officer from Mississippi, Lowrey summed up as well as anyone who was there the reason for the Confederate failure, writing, "they failed to take the works simply because the thing attempted was impossible for a thin line of exhausted men to accomplish."[21]

But Govan and Magevney were still not through and again hit the Federal line, the former now east of Flat Shoals Road and the latter striking from the west. After three hours of the toughest fighting, the Rebels finally had achieved a breakthrough and were coming at Giles Smith's division from the front, the rear, and the left flank. The blue-coats were unable to fend off Magevney's Tennesseans hitting from the south and west and Govan's Arkansans pummeling them from the east. South of Bald Hill, Federal resistance disintegrated. Rebels occupied the works formerly held by Giles Smith's division. Cleburne's boys had succeeded in breaking through the half-mile-wide gap between the two Federal corps (Blair's and Dodge's) around Bald Hill.[22]

Frank Cheatham's corps was moving now, ordered into the fray by Hood, who wanted to support Hardee's gains. Arthur Manigault's and Jacob Sharp's brigades followed the Georgia Railroad eastward, overran a large white house near the railroad tracks, and captured the four Parrott guns of Captain Francis De Gress's Illinois battery. Manigault's troops swarmed over the white house and spilled up into the second floor where they began firing from the windows and balcony at an Ohio brigade entrenched to the east. While this was happening, Sharp's 9th, 10th, and 44th Mississippi regiments were moving swiftly up the rail line south of the house, penetrating the left flank of Colonel James S. Martin's brigade and shattering through the center of J. A. J. Lightburn's division, punching an opening right into the center of the Federal XV Corps.[23]

Sensing the danger of the Rebel breakthrough, the Federals launched a furious counter-attack that pushed Manigault and Sharp back. An alarmed Sherman himself personally took charge of all of the artillery that he could gather together and led them to a hill near his headquarters north of the Troup Hurt house where he directed their fire. The Yankees began shelling Manigault and Sharp, as four brigades of bluecoats scurried to attack the Rebels and close the rupture. Manigault and Sharp held their position as long as they could, but no reinforcements came to their aid, and they fell back. In fifteen minutes, the Federals had retaken the position.[24]

Around sundown, the final Confederate assault lurched forward. Having breached the Yankee lines south of Bald Hill, Govan's and Magevney's brigades continued to assail from the south, and now Colonel F. M. Walker's Tennessee brigade and Mercer's Georgia brigade struck from the east. The Rebels faced a new line drawn up by Leggett and Giles Smith's troops in the rear of Bald Hill.

While Walker's Tennesseans made some initial headway, Mercer's Georgians met a quick end, managing to take the first two lines of earthworks but not the third, where the Yanks were only thirty paces away. Both sides blazed away at each other, but by now the Georgia brigade was so disorganized and its regiments so intermingled that the officers were unable to reform their commands, and the attack stalled right there. The Georgians fell back in total confusion. The Georgia brigade's losses for the day were 32 killed, 122 wounded, and 14 missing. Savannah's 1st Georgia Volunteers lost 9 killed, 18 wounded, and 1 missing. In the Irish Jasper Greens, Sergeant Laughlin McSorley and Privates Michael Doherty and John Fitzpatrick were captured, and Private John H. Muller was wounded.[25]

Govan's hard-fighting Arkansans had punched their way to the southern slope of Bald Hill, and now they tangled with the Buckeyes of Leggett's division in savage hand-to-hand fighting—the most desperate of the day—at the rail barricade that the Yankees had thrown together, but were overcome by sheer numbers. Govan's losses for the day were 499 casualties out of 772—86 killed, 322 wounded, 91 missing. The 1st/15th Arkansas lost 15 killed, 67 wounded, and 3 missing out of 144. The 5th/13th Arkansas lost 16 killed, 89 wounded, 7 missing out of 120. Hood's daring gambit had failed.[26]

The bloody battles of the 20th and 22nd—"better never fought," lamented the 5th Confederate's Captain Charles Frazer—cost the Army of Tennessee some 5,500 casualties, 1,388 of them in Cleburne's division. But really the cost for the Confederacy was much higher. The outcome of the war itself may have been decided, since the fall of Atlanta virtually assured Abraham Lincoln's re-election as President and the end of any chance of a political settlement to end the war.[27]

The fighting was not over, though. On July 28, west of Atlanta at Ezra Church, the Army of Tennessee attacked again, to the delight of Sherman. "[T]hey'll only beat their brains out," the Federal commander gloated. Total Rebel losses were nearly 3,000. Randall Gibson's Louisiana brigade—once more with John E. Austin's Irish sharpshooters doing good duty as skirmishers—suffered particularly, losing heavily in an unsupported assault. Lieutenant Colonel Thomas Shields of the 30th Louisiana was killed. Of the 600 casualties in Henry Clayton's division, 480 came from the Louisiana brigade. (One month later, on August 31, this same brigade would lose half its number in fifteen minutes of fighting at Jonesboro).[28]

A small victory on August 6 showed clearly that Confederate Irishmen could still fight. West of Ezra Church along the banks of Utoy Creek, Ohio Irish-American Brigadier General James W. Reilly sent out a skirmish line that clashed with Thomas Benton Smith's 450-man brigade sent to thwart Federal attempts to lunge against the Macon and Western Railroad line south of Atlanta. The bluecoats pushed across Utoy Creek and advanced on the Rebel logworks atop a hill one hundred yards east of the creek. Reilly made three ill-conceived assaults on the stubborn Rebel line, where Irish Confederates manned the right flank. "Battling Billy" Grace, commanding the Confederate right, led the Sons of Erin, two Irish companies from the 4th Kentucky, and the Memphis Irish of Company E, 2nd Tennessee in a counter-charge that drove the bluecoats back across Utoy Creek. The six hour engagement was a minor one, but it turned out to be the Army of Tennessee's last decisive infantry victory in the war.[29]

There remained one final bloodbath before John Bell Hood was forced to concede defeat and abandon Atlanta. On August 31, the battered Confederates attacked Sherman's forces south of Atlanta at Jonesboro. Cleburne commanded Hardee's corps in this engagement, and Mark Lowrey led Cleburne's division. The outcome for the Army of Tennessee was disastrous. In stubborn hand-to-hand fighting in the Rebel works, the Federals overwhelmed Govan's brigade, many of whom died by the bayonet or the rifle butt. The bluecoats captured Govan and more than 600 of his brigade, plus the Helena and Vicksburg batteries and their eight guns, and the entire 3rd Confederate regiment—down to the size of a company now and commanded by Vicksburg's Captain Mumford H. Dixon. Govan's brigade also lost 26 men killed and 68 wounded. Among the captives was Irish immigrant Thomas Flynn, a carpenter, one of the original Napoleon Grays (Company D of the 15th Arkansas) who transferred to the Helena battery at the end of 1862 and had served with it ever since. The 1st/15th Arkansas was captured, along

Left: LIEUTENANT LOUIS ALEXANDER CONO-
LEY, 29TH ALABAMA INFANTRY. A grandson of
Scotch-Irish immigrants, Conoley was not yet
20 years old when he died from wounds received
at Resaca during the Atlanta campaign. He was
the son of Colonel John Francis Conoley and
had worked as a clerk in his father's law office.
(Alabama Department of Archives and History,
Montgomery, Alabama)

Above: CAPTAIN SAMUEL CAMP KELLY, 30TH
ALABAMA INFANTRY. A veteran of the Mexican
War, Kelly was 37 years old when he enlisted in
the 30th Alabama at the start of the Civil War.
One of the few of the regiment's officers to sur-
vive the fighting, he was a major during the
Atlanta campaign. (Alabama Department of
Archives and History, Montgomery, Alabama)

with their regimental flag. Captain Valentine M. McGehee of the 2nd Arkansas was
wounded. Govan and his soldiers, who had
never before surrendered in battle, remained
prisoners until September 9, when they were
released in a prisoner exchange.[30]

Just transferred into Cleburne's division,
the 1st Georgia Volunteers—"We all expect hot times now," William Dixon wrote in his
diary—lost 1 man killed, 3 wounded, and 1 missing at Jonesboro. The Savannah regiment's
total losses between July 20 and September 1 were 11 killed, 31 wounded, and 6 missing.[31]

In the 10th Tennessee, Colonel Grace became a fatal casualty, shot through the intes-
tines. "Do not move me," Grace mumbled. "I am suffering and cannot live long. Let me
die here." The 33-year old Son of Erin died just short of realizing his promotion to brigadier
general. Also killed was Father Emmeran Bliemel, the Catholic chaplain who performed
last rites over him. The 32-year old Bliemel was the only Catholic chaplain to be killed in
the war on either side and the first American Catholic military chaplain ever to be killed
in combat. Sons of Erin color-bearer Sergeant James Hayes was killed; he had carried the
regimental flag since the organization of the regiment. Eight men were wounded, including Captain John L. Prendergast, hit by a piece of metal from an exploding shell. Seven
other Sons of Erin fell captive, leaving only 35 Irishmen to carry on.[32]

The Atlanta campaign had taken a high toll of the Army of Tennessee's manpower. In the 1st Georgia Volunteers, the Republican Blues had started off from Savannah with 79 men in May; now they were down to 25. After Corporal David McLeod was killed on September 4, Captain Dixon wrote in the company daybook, "One more of our faithful few gone." "It was a hot time," the 30th Alabama's Captain Samuel Camp Kelly wrote after Jonesboro. "The regiment lost heavily." Kelly had been the senior captain in his regiment back in May, had been acting major all this time, and his company of just 30 men was still the largest in his regiment.[33]

The Army of Tennessee evacuated Atlanta on the night of September 1. One of the last rear guard units to leave was Francis Cockrell's Missouri brigade, with many Irish Confederates from St. Louis, marching away as rail cars of exploding ammunition rocked the Gate City and crowds of drunken men wreaked havoc among the burning buildings. "We were saddened by the announcement that Atlanta must be given up," Lieutenant Joseph Boyce of the 1st Missouri wrote. "Such destruction was going on that it really appalled us, veterans as we were... It was the dark side of war."[34]

14. "Carnival of Death": Franklin, November 1864

The Confederate Irish in the Army of Tennessee were destined to fight one more great battle. John Bell Hood sought to strike at Sherman's supply line in Tennessee and targeted the Union supply center at Nashville. In October 1864, he invaded the Volunteer State. Sherman, in the meantime, dispatched troops back to Tennessee to oppose the Rebels and started off on his march across Georgia to the sea, leaving Atlanta in ruins.

The decisive battle of Hood's doomed campaign unfolded at the little town of Franklin, just eighteen miles south of Nashville, on November 30, 1864. Refusing to wait for one of his three corps and nearly all of his artillery to catch up with the army, Hood ordered a suicidal assault on Federal General John M. Schofield's well-entrenched Federals south of the town. This would be the Army of Tennessee's last major assault in the war.

On a hilltop south of Franklin, Pat Cleburne surveyed the formidable enemy works through the telescopic sights of a sharpshooter's Whitworth rifle. "They have three lines of works," he noted. The Federal earthworks stood as high as eight feet in some parts of their line, with broad ditches on both sides. "And they are all completed," he added. The Irish general contemplated the work ahead with grim determination. Brigade commander Daniel Govan guessed that few of them would make it back to Arkansas. "Well, Govan," the Irishman replied, "if we are to die, let us die like men."[1]

It was now 4 p.m., the time for the attack to commence. The day had been warm and sunny, a late Indian Summer day. The Rebels could see the sun going down in the west, the sky turning red. The Army of Tennessee stepped off proudly, 25,000 men in three lines of battle, with bayonets glittering and battle flags flapping. It was a grander spectacle than Pickett's charge at Gettysburg, and in fact the Rebels' numbers today exceeded it. Gray-coated and butternut-coated troops stretched as far as the eye could see and was, in the words of St. Louis veteran Captain Joseph Boyce, "a beautiful sight."[2]

As Boyce's outfit, Francis Cockrell's Missouri brigade, shuffled into line of battle on the Confederate right, a voice from the ranks quoted Admiral Nelson at Trafalgar: "England expects every man to do his duty." "It's damned little duty England would get out of this Irish crowd," Sergeant Denny Callahan retorted. There was hearty laughter from this band of hardened veterans, who marched proudly ahead. Even the Missouri brigade's brass band of eleven men, led by Professor John O'Neil, fell into line now, although Boyce noted it was "rather an unusual thing for the 'tooters' to go up in a charge with the 'shooters.'" The band struck up "The Bonnie Blue Flag" and later changed to "Dixie." "[N]ever in all our history," Corporal William H. Kavanaugh later wrote, "had we gone into battle with better discipline or prouder step than on this occasion."[3]

Wearing his new gray uniform jacket, Cleburne rode up and down the line in his division, urging his men to conserve their ammunition and to "use the bayonet." At about 200 yards from the enemy works, he brought his division to a halt, pulled in his skirmishers, and gave the order to fix bayonets. Next came the command: "Right shoulder shift; forward; double-quick; march!" Cleburne's division moved forward east of the Nashville-Columbia pike, Govan's Arkansas brigade (with 1st/15th Arkansas, 5th/13th Arkansas, and 3rd Confederate) on the right and Brigadier General Hiram B. Granbury's Texas brigade (with the remnant of the 5th Confederate) on the left. Mark Lowrey's Alabama-Mississippi brigade (with the 3rd Mississippi battalion) brought up the rear.[4]

In the Federal works, Colonel Henry Stone watched the enemy coming on "as steady and resistless as a tidal wave." Rabbits and quail fluttered away in the path of the oncoming machine. The Federals took in the awesome spectacle, another officer wrote, "spellbound with admiration," but painfully conscious that in a matter of minutes "all that orderly grandeur would be changed to bleeding, writhing, confusion."[5]

Because now the moment had come. The graycoats shifted from marching to attacking formation, lowering bayonets and rushing forward. "They were coming on the run," a Federal soldier wrote, "emitting the shrill rebel yell, and so near that my first impulse was to throw myself flat on the ground and let them charge over us."[6]

The battle was really three uncoordinated assaults: On the Confederate right, Alexander P. Stewart's corps would assault near the Harpeth River and strike the Federal left. In the center, Cleburne's and John C. Brown's divisions would advance up both sides of the Nashville-Columbia Pike and hit the Federal center. On the far left, William Bate's division would hit the Federal works from the west. Before reaching the enemy lines, the Rebels faced the daunting prospect of marching across an open rolling plain for two miles, and they surely would be under enemy artillery and small arms fire for much of the way.

George D. Wagner's Federal troops—two brigades—occupied an advanced position south of the main Federal lines, and they were the first to feel the fury of the Confederate assault. The initial Yankee volley stunned the graycoats, and the second volley forced them back under the crest of a small hill, where they reformed and came on again. It took just fifteen minutes before Cleburne's and Brown's men plowed into the Federals from front, right, and left. The Rebels overran the exposed earthworks, and the bluecoats fell back almost immediately, heading for the main works less than half a mile away and safety. As the Rebels pursued, some of them began shouting, "Go into the works with them!"[7]

An abatis of locust branches lay between them and the main works just south of the brick Fountain Branch Carter house. The obstructions slowed the fleeing Federals down, and their comrades behind the breastworks ahead held their fire to let them get through. They also let the Confederates through as well. Govan's Arkansans and Granbury's Texans raced to the works. George W. Gordon's brigade of Brown's division, which included Michael Magevney's 154th Tennessee, broke across the Columbia pike to become intermingled with Granbury's brigade. "[T]he triumphant Confederates," Colonel Stone wrote, "now more like a wild, howling mob than an organized army, swept

"CARNIVAL OF DEATH." The remnants of the Army of Tennessee's Irish took part in a suicidal frontal assault on Federal defenses at Franklin, November 30, 1864. (Library of Congress)

on to the very works, with hardly a check from any quarter." The Rebels captured eight cannon in the Yankee lines, turning some of them against the enemy. As it had so often before, victory seemed to be just within their grasp.[8]

But the elation of Cleburne's veterans was short-lived. Colonel Emerson Opdyke's mostly Illinois brigade came tearing out of the Federal works in a furious effort to beat back the Rebel assault and seal the breach near the Carter house. There was desperate hand-to-hand fighting with bayonet and rifle butts, but the stubborn Rebels were gradually beaten back out of the main works.

In front of a cotton gin east of the Columbia pike, Cleburne's troops were caught in a vicious cross-fire. From the right, Colonel John Casement's Federal brigade, with the 65th Indiana armed with Henry repeating rifles—"sixteen shooters," they called them—poured a deadly fire into them. And in front, Brigadier General James W. Reilly's brigade, with the 12th Kentucky also armed with repeaters, did equal destruction. "The wonder is," one bluecoat wrote, "that any of them escaped death or capture."[9]

Cleburne's troops held on to the outer ditch of the Federal earthworks south of the cotton gin for the rest of the night, with Reilly's and Casement's Federals in the inner ditch. Gordon's, Granbury's, and Govan's brigades even mounted a second brief assault on the Federal works near the cotton gin before dark, but this too was beaten back. The rest of the night became a matter of brutal sniping back and forth across the works. In reality, the Rebels were trapped, unable to retreat and unable to push forward. Cleburne's troops continually attempted to beat their way through one embrasure in the Federal works and were driven back in desperate hand-to-hand fighting, Yankee gunners using bayonets, rifle butts, picks, and axes to fend them off. Along the outer side of the earthworks, the Rebels fired under the Federal headlogs and even flung dirt at the enemy. Reilly reported that Cleburne's soldiers, even after dark, made "various and continual assaults," which "were each time repulsed with fearful slaughter."[10]

So many officers were dead that any command structure ceased to exist. Cleburne's division counted 14 brigade and regimental commanders as dead, wounded, or taken prisoner. Three of Govan's regimental commanders were casualties. Granbury was dead. Cleburne's troops awaited the order from Cleburne to attack—an order that never came. It could only mean one thing—the Irishman must be dead.[11]

Cleburne's mood had taken on a more fatalistic bent as he prepared for the Tennessee offensive. After the exhausting fighting around Atlanta, he had looked forward to spending some time with his fiancee Susan Tarleton, possibly even marrying, in October, but the couple's hopes were dashed by Hood's plans to invade Tennessee. The Confederacy had lost so many irreplaceable men in the previous months that to launch another offensive seemed almost suicidal, and defeat seemed almost a certainty. "If this cause that is so dear to my heart is doomed to fail," Cleburne had told his men, "I pray heaven may let me fall with it, while my face is toward the enemy and my arm battling for that which I know to be right."[12]

Cleburne fell in the first assault. About eighty yards from the main works, as he galloped among his troops racing in pursuit of Wagner's fleeing men, Old Pat's brown horse stumbled, hit by Federal cannon fire. A nearby courier quickly leapt from his horse and offered it to Cleburne. As Cleburne tried to mount up, the horse was killed by another cannonball. Undeterred, the Irishman continued forward on foot, waving his cap. He went forward in the midst of the old 5th Confederate "Irish" regiment, only 21 of whom would be left in the morning. No one saw him again that night. Some veterans of the Irish regiment had already vowed to conquer to die that day. They found the body of one of them, Dick Cahill, lying a few feet inside the Federal inner works with four bayonet wounds in him.[13]

Cleburne's brigade was a shambles. Mark Lowrey wrote that the incessant Federal firing was "the most destructive fire I witnessed ... about half my men had fallen, and the balance could not scale the works. It would have been certain death or capture to every one of them.... [W]hen I saw that nothing more could be done, I went to the rear, and began the work of gathering up the fragments of our division."[14]

On the other side of the Columbia pike, Brown's troops had opened a gap west of the Carter house but were being pushed back also with heavy losses. Blue-coated soldiers began firing from the windows of the Carter house and outbuildings, and the Federal 44th Missouri, which suffered heavy losses, formed a second, retrenched line near

FRANKLIN Nov. 30, 1864

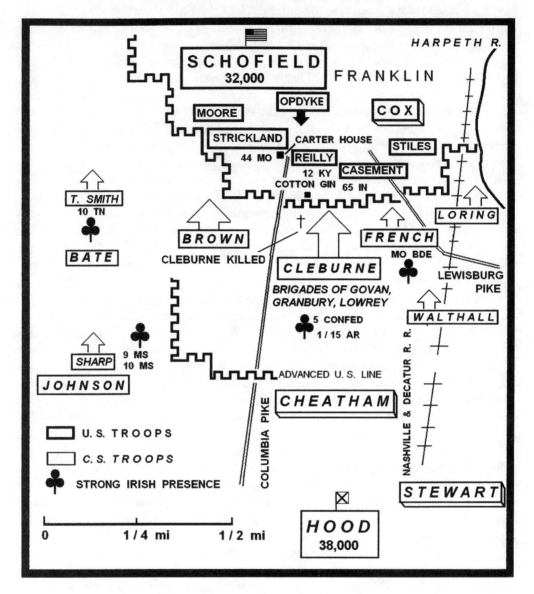

the Carter house. The Rebels were stubborn and made a determined stand at the Federal earthworks, refusing to give ground. For a time, there was only a brutal deadlock with neither side able to push the other off. In fact, the Federals never regained that part of their works that Brown's troops had captured, and the Rebels remained there for the rest of the night. But like Cleburne's men, they were exposed to a withering cross-fire, and by day's end Brown and all four of his brigade commanders would be either killed, wounded, or captured. Bodies piled up in the ditch, and the survivors had to stand on top of them to continue the fight.

On the Confederate right, the Missouri brigade spearheaded the attack of Stewart's corps, penetrating the Federal works east of the cotton gin. With orders not to fire until they reached the Federal lines 900 yards away, the Missouri brigade plowed forward. There were heavy casualties. "Men commenced dropping fast from the start," Captain Boyce reported.

"By the time we got within 500 or 600 yards of their works," Corporal William H. Kavanaugh wrote, "we began to lose heavily. Their artillery from the parapets would tear great holes through our ranks with shot, shell, and canister. But immediately and just like clockwork these gaps would close up, and forward we pressed reserving our fire for close quarters."[15]

Henry Guibor's Missouri battery, a largely Irish outfit from St. Louis, supported the Missouri brigade. One of only two Confederate artillery units on the field at Franklin, the St. Louis gunners shoved two cannon by hand up to the advanced Federal line and opened fire on the bluecoats.[16]

The Missourians probably hit the Federal line just before Cleburne's troops directly to their west. They delivered a volley and then surged ahead with the bayonet. Lieutenant Henry Gillespie of the 2nd/6th Missouri, hefted an ax—his sword had been broken earlier in the fighting in Georgia—and lit into the foe. Ensign Joseph T. Donavan, hit by a shell fragment, dropped the Missouri colors, scooped up by John S. Harris and Robert Bently who were killed moments later. Sergeant Denny Callahan picked it up and carried it into the Federal works.[17]

As he mounted the parapet, Captain Boyce glanced behind him and noticed that "the ground in the rear was all too thickly covered with the bodies of our comrades.... As we crossed the rifle pits our line was delayed a moment, when, finding myself alone, I cried out: 'Who is going to stay with me?'" Denny Callahan, carrying the flag, was soon at his side, along with Lieutenant A. B. Barnett, Dick Saulsbery, and Robert Bonner. As the little band entered the works, Boyce recalled, "we all went down together." Boyce swiped at a Federal with his sword but was wounded in the leg and fell on top of the parapet, his sword flying out of his hand. He retrieved his sword and tried to go on, but he was barely able to walk and fell again. Some of his comrades helped him back to the rear.[18]

Boyce recounted the Missouri brigade's destruction on the Federal parapet: "With empty guns, without officers, out of breath, our thin line rested a few seconds, when it was assailed by the enemy's second line.... A solid wall of blue infantry advanced at the double-quick and poured in a volley. It was too much. Our brave fellows came out of the works as quickly as they had entered them and sought refuge behind the rifle pits a short distance back." Like Cleburne's unlucky troops, the Missouri brigade encountered the same deadly repeating rifles of Casement's and Reilly's soldiers. And like Cleburne's troops, they huddled in the outer ditch of the Federal works while the Yankees, packed five or six ranks deep, held firm on the other side, the men in front rank firing and passing their weapons back to the men in the rear to reload. It went on throughout the night, as the Rebels made sporadic unsuccessful assaults.[19]

Captain Patrick Canniff, acting major for the 3rd/5th Missouri, was one of the saddest casualties. Just thirty feet from the Federal works, a bullet hit the auburn-haired veteran in the right shoulder, and he fell from his horse. Struggling to get to his feet, he was hit in the head by a second bullet and died on the field. The career of the Missouri brigade's finest skirmisher officer was over.[20]

The Missouri brigade sustained the highest losses (60.2 percent) of any brigade at Franklin and the fourth highest of any Confederate brigade in the war (The other three fought at Gettysburg and Antietam.) The Missourians lost 19 officers and 79 enlisted men killed; 31 officers and 198 enlisted men wounded; 13 officers and 79 enlisted men missing; total 419 casualties.[21]

There were also heavy casualties in the other brigades on the Confederate right. The 17th Alabama's Colonel Virgil S. Murphy, captured during the fighting, wrote of the savageness of the combat that "raged with unexamplid fury." The Federal works, Murphy wrote, were "wet with human gore, and men disfigured mutilated and dying lay upon them while the carnage raged around them. It was the carnival of death."[22]

On the Rebel left, Bate's division, with more ground to cover than the other divisions, was the last to attack. Thomas Benton Smith's brigade, with the 10th Tennessee, deployed on the left, near the Widow Rebecca Bostick's house. The attack quickly degenerated into a series of uncoordinated failed assaults. Lieutenant Colonel John G. O'Neill hadn't time even to send out his skirmishers before Federal troops counter-attacked and overwhelmed the small band that was now down to 36 men, wounding or capturing a third of them. Private Martin Fleming was killed. Drummer boy Danny McCarthy, the youngest lad in the Sons of Erin—he had been just 14 when he had enlisted and had received the first pair of shoes he had ever owned given him by members of the company that first Christmas—was shot in the chest and was taken prisoner. McCarthy would survive and would live to be the last of the Sons of Erin, dying in 1939 at the age of 92.[23]

Major General Edward Johnson's division of Stephen D. Lee's corps had now arrived on the scene and was sent in to support Bate's troops near the Bostick house at about 7 p.m. Johnson's men stumbled forward in the dark over dead and wounded men lying by the thousands. Some of the wounded even would reach out to them, grabbing onto pants' legs, trying to stop them and telling them that what they were heading for ahead was sure death. About an hour after dark, Jacob Sharp's brigade (with the 9th, 10th, and 44th Mississippi regiments) actually penetrated the Yankee works for a brief moment before being pushed back in heavy hand-to-hand combat.[24]

The fighting along the line died down after 9 p.m. There only remained the cries of thousands of wounded and dying soldiers through the night. Soon the temperature dropped to below freezing. "My foot was shot entirely off," wrote Private James Riley Campbell of the 8th Arkansas. "I lay on the battlefield all night with one blanket for cover. My company had the doctor come see me on the battlefield about 10:00. He gave me whiskey and morphine. I lay there nearly 12 hours without care."[25]

Daybreak revealed the hideous cost of Hood's assault at Franklin. Joseph Boyce recoiled at the "ghastly sight" of piles of Rebel dead, some of them having died standing because there was no room to fall. "Our army," Boyce declared, "was a wreck." "I could have trodden on a dead man at every step," wrote Tennessee chaplain James McNeilly. "The dead were piled up in the trenches almost to the top of the earthworks." Even the Federals were appalled by the carnage. "I never saw the dead lay near so thick," Colonel Emerson Opdyke wrote. "I saw them upon each other, dead and ghastly in the powder-dimmed star-light."[26]

The Federals began withdrawing after midnight and by daybreak they were gone, prompting many of the Rebels to feel they had won a great victory—but at what cost? The Army of Tennessee lost probably 7,000 men at Franklin—1,750 killed, 4,500 wounded, 702 captured. Hood had lost a third of his infantry in five hours, and his army was destroyed as an effective fighting force. The last hopes of the Confederacy in the west were as good as dead.[27]

They found Cleburne's body around dawn where he had fallen just south of the cotton gin. He had been shot once through the heart. The Irishman was on his back with his cap partly covering his eyes. His boots, sword belt, and watch were gone. Cleburne had fallen near the cotton gin house in front of fellow Irish-American James W. Reilly's Federal brigade.[28]

Rebel soldiers carried Cleburne's body to the home of Colonel John McGavock a mile or so to the east and laid it on the porch next to Granbury and two of the four other Confederate generals killed at Franklin, Otho Strahl and John Adams, who also was the son of Irish immigrants. All through the morning, groups of Old Pat's soldiers came to the house to look at the popular general one last time. Cleburne's face was covered by a blood-spattered handkerchief. One of his staff officers, Lieutenant Leonard Mangum, produced an embroidered handkerchief. "Cover his face with this," he said, "it was sent him from Mobile and I think he was engaged to the lady."[29]

COLONEL VIRGIL S. MURPHY, 17TH ALABAMA INFANTRY. This Irish-American officer was captured in the fighting at Franklin in November 1864. After the war, he resumed his law practice in Montgomery. (Alabama Department of Archives and History, Montgomery, Alabama)

Susan Tarleton heard of the general's death six days later. As she was strolling in her garden, she heard a newsboy singing out the evening headlines—"Cleburne and other Generals Killed!"—and her world shattered. She was grief-stricken for months, and eventually she married a classmate of her brother's. She died in 1868 of an "effusion of the brain."[30]

Cleburne was buried in the cemetery of St. John's Episcopal Church not far from Columbia, Tennessee. He had earlier remarked that it was "a beautiful spot" to be buried in. Confederate soldiers throughout the Army of Tennessee mourned the Irish general's passing. Captain Joseph Boyce in the Missouri brigade called him "the model soldier." The Army of Tennessee never recovered from the loss of this fine officer, known as the "Stonewall of the West," nor could it ever recover from the bloodbath at Franklin.[31]

The fighting went on, though. Despite having lost an appalling one third of his army at Franklin, Hood pushed on to Nashville where he sought to draw Major General George H. Thomas' Federal army out of its strongly prepared entrenchments. Hood succeeded in provoking Thomas to attack. Unfortunately for him, the Federals now had twice his numbers. On December 15, Thomas' blue-coated troops came swarming out of their works and in two days of fighting nearly annihilated the Rebel army. Only a stubborn rear-guard action by Randall Gibson's veteran Louisiana brigade and Lieutenant William J. McKenzie's Alabama battery (the Eufaula Light Artillery) saved the Army of Tennessee from complete destruction.

Hood withdrew from Nashville under cover of darkness and began the army's retreat from Tennessee. Bitter cold, heavy rain turning to sleet and snow, roads turning to mud, and the sting of bitter defeat made the march south one of the most wretched that any American army ever endured. Whole regiments were without arms, without blankets or tents, without hope. The Louisiana brigade continued to do good duty as part of the rear guard, fending off pursuing Federal cavalry. "Hard fighting and harder marching," wrote Captain Sam Kelly of the 30th Alabama. "Some of the troops are barefooted, all hungry and tired, it was one of the worst retreats I ever saw." On January 3, 1865, the beaten and demoralized remnants of Hood's army straggled into Tupelo, Mississippi, just a third of what it had been two months earlier.[32]

The end of the war was just four months away, but Southern hopes weren't entirely extinguished, even though the Army of Tennessee no longer posed a threat and although Grant had a strangle-hold on Lee's Army of Northern Virginia at Petersburg. Joe Johnston returned to command the Army of Tennessee in mid–January, and its remaining troops followed him into the Carolinas in a futile effort to slow down Sherman's juggernaut and possibly unite with Lee. But the end was near. On March 19, 1865, Johnston fought his last battle with Sherman at Bentonville, North Carolina, realized that it was useless to try to go on, and finally gave in to the inevitable. The Army of Tennessee surrendered on April 26. "My heart is heavy," Captain Sam Kelly wrote, "I can not write." This was the young officer's last letter. He was going home.[33]

About 5,000 soldiers from the Army of Tennessee did not go to the Carolinas but were transferred to the Gulf Coast to aid in the defense of Mobile, the last seaport still in Confederate hands. Gibson's Louisiana brigade braved a thirteen-day siege at Spanish Fort, which fell to the Federals on April 8, 1865. As at Nashville, the Louisiana brigade, its consolidated commands greatly reduced in numbers, covered the Confederate retreat to Mobile. The Missouri brigade withstood a fierce Federal assault on Fort Blakely, the last of the war, on April 9. Colonel James McCown and the remains of his 3rd/5th Missouri Infantry were the last of the Rebel troops to surrender there. On the same day that Fort Blakely fell, Lee surrendered the Army of Northern Virginia.

The surrender of the Confederate armies found only handfuls of the Southern Irish left. Few remained of the Helena Irish who fought with Cleburne. Every Arkansas command was consolidated into one small regiment. Only five of the original Napoleon Grays were left at the surrender on April 26, including 1st Sergeant William D. Weller, drummer James McGehee, and Privates Charles Cohen, John Shea, and Jacob Warfield. Less than a dozen of Savannah's Irish Jaspers remained, half that number for the 1st Georgia's Irish Volunteers, and just 14 for the Scotch-Irish Republican Blues. Augusta's Irish Volunteers numbered around 15.[34]

When New Orleans' 13th/20th Louisiana laid down its arms on May 8, 1865, there were 22 men left, and roughly the same number remained in the 14th Louisiana Sharpshooters. Out of the original 109 men in the 13th Louisiana, 41 of them had been killed, wounded, or died of disease, 9 had deserted, and 53 had been captured or had transferred to other units.[35]

There were only 10 men left in the 5th Confederate regiment at the surrender on April 26, and probably no more than 100 of the original members were still alive. Of the 10th Tennessee Sons of Erin, Lieutenant Colonel John G. O'Neill, Captain Lewis R. Clark, and Lieutenant Robert Paget Seymour were captured at Bentonville. That left only Commissary Master Sergeant Barney McCabe, who served as a cook until the surrender, when all four men were paroled and sent home. During the long conflict, 30 Sons of Erin had been killed, 26 more had died in prison, and 10 had died from disease.[36]

PART IV. THE IRISH IN THE COASTAL STRONGHOLDS

15. *"Up-Hill Work": Charleston, Savannah, and Fort Fisher*

At dusk on Morris Island, in a rude earthwork fortress off the coast of Charleston, South Carolina, on July 18, 1863, watchful gray-clad soldiers peered out from behind their sand barricades to scan the dunes of the beach and the blue Atlantic beyond. It was hot, humid, the air stagnant. Captain William H. Ryan and the soldiers of his Charleston Irish company swatted at sand fleas as they loaded their weapons. They knew that their works were about to be stormed by a large force of Yankee infantry. The enemy had landed troops at the southern end of the island and had made his way north to Battery Wagner. The bluecoats had already attempted one direct assault, and it had failed. But the Rebel defenders had been hurt as well.

From early in the morning until sundown—twelve hours continuously—Wagner's garrison had been under a heavy bombardment by both the Federal army and the guns of their naval vessels offshore. Now those guns had suddenly become silent.

Darkness was falling, and now here came the enemy! Indistinct but visible in the hazy twilight, masses of blue-clad troops were moving up the beach. The first wave of attackers was the 54th Massachusetts, a regiment of African-American soldiers eager to prove themselves. The beach was narrow, and the troops jammed together made an easy target. The Rebel gunners opened up on the advancing columns with grape shot and canister, tearing vicious holes in their ranks. But the bluecoats kept coming. Captain Ryan's soldiers poured a volley of musket fire into the onrushing Federals, but still they came.

The 54th Massachusetts' young white colonel, Robert Gould Shaw, and a handful of black soldiers made it through the fort's moat and up to the top of the parapet where they were struck down in a hail of gunfire. As the riddled black troops fell back, the next wave of attackers—white soldiers this time—raced to the attack. Once more they penetrated the Rebel works, and the desperate struggle continued as graycoats and Yankees fought hand to hand.

Battery Wagner was the key to the Federal capture of Charleston. Defiant Charleston, the birthplace of secession, had been under a Federal naval blockade and siege for four years. Charleston was a symbol of Southern resistance, and Battery Wagner was the linchpin in its defenses. That was why the Federals were so determined to take it. And that was why the Rebels were equally determined that it must not fall.

The story of the black 54th Massachusetts' heroic sacrifice at Battery Wagner is well known. Few recall their gray-clad opponents who defended the fort, among them many from Charleston's Irish community.

Lieutenant Colonel Peter C. Gaillard's 1st South Carolina Infantry Battalion (called the Charleston Battalion) contained older companies from the city's pre-war volunteer militia, one of them Captain William H. Ryan's Old Irish Volunteers. Ryan, a 29-year-old engineer, replaced the company's original commander, Edward Magrath, in April 1862 when Magrath resigned for health reasons. The oldest of the Irish companies in Charleston, the Old Irish Volunteers could point to a proud record of service since the 1790s. They had held out the longest for the formation of an Irish battalion from Charleston, and when this failed to materialize they joined the Charleston Battalion, destined to serve for most of the war in the defenses around Charleston. The city's other Irish companies, consolidated into Captain Edward McCrady's "new" Irish Volunteers, joined Maxey Gregg's 1st South Carolina Infantry in Virginia.[1]

The Charleston Battalion was active throughout 1862 and 1863 as the Federals began to tighten the screws on their siege of the Rebel city. Taking Charleston was not an easy thing to do, however, as the Yankees had learned. A ring of formidable defenses, secured on mighty Fort Sumter in the harbor, protected the city from attack by sea and land.

In June 1862, the Rebels thwarted Federal plans to occupy James Island south of the city and thus bypass the Fort Sumter defenses. At a small earthwork south of Secessionville, the Rebel garrison of 500 troops under Colonel T. G. Lamar repulsed the Federals in a bloody engagement on June 16. A steady barrage of grape and canister from the seven guns in the little fort stopped the bluecoats cold.

The Old Irish Volunteers saw steady fighting at Secessionville. Captain Ryan helped man one of the guns, and Lieutenant Alexander A. Allemong braved Federal fire several times to bring up ammunition. The Charleston Battalion lost 10 men killed and 30 wounded out of 100 at Secessionville. Also in action at Secessionville was Lieutenant Colonel John D. McEnery's 4th Louisiana Infantry Battalion, which lost 6 killed and 22 wounded. McEnery, the son of Irish immigrants, raised the largely Irish Ouachita Blues (Company B) from Monroe in the northern part of the Pelican State.[2]

A year later the Charleston Battalion was stationed on Morris Island, part of a 1,300-man Rebel garrison at Battery Wagner that also included two North Carolina infantry regiments and some South Carolina artillery, under the command of Brigadier General William B. Taliaferro. The Irish Volunteers were one of three battalion companies posted in the southwestern part of the works.

Having failed in their operations on James Island, the Federals tried to force their way into Charleston harbor with a naval armada of ironclads and steamers in April 1863, but the guns of Fort Sumter and the other coastal batteries forced them to turn back. The next thing to try was an assault on Battery Wagner. If Wagner could be taken, then Fort Sumter and Charleston would be in range of the Federals' heavy guns. Major General Quincy A. Gillmore landed troops at the southern end of Morris Island and advanced northward for an attack on the fort.

The assault was preceded by an intense artillery bombardment. The shelling cut the halyards on the garrison's flag, sending it blowing over into the fort. Major David Ramsay, Sergeant William Shelton of the Irish Volunteers, and Private John Flynn of Company F of the Charleston Battalion, and Lieutenant William E. Readick of the

THE 54TH MASSACHUSETTS STORMS BATTERY WAGNER. **The key linchpin in the Rebel defenses around Charleston, the earthen fort was defended by members of the Charleston Battalion, including the Old Irish Volunteers.** (*Harper's Weekly,* **August 8, 1863**)

63rd Georgia grabbed the flag and lashed it onto a makeshift staff, replacing it on the works.

Nightfall brought the Federal assault. The attackers were raked by grape and canister from the fort and by blistering musket fire from the Charleston Battalion and 51st North Carolina. The Rebels held their position stubbornly. After the black 54th Massachusetts was cut down in the vanguard of the Federal assault, succeeding waves of white troops of the 6th Connecticut and 48th New York penetrated the works and fought with the Rebels.

The bluecoats were able to gain a foothold in the southeastern corner of the battery. To dislodge them, a Rebel infantry company was needed to go in and root them out, and Captain Ryan's Irish Volunteers made the attempt. In the lead of his boys, Ryan was shot down and killed, and the charge fell apart. But the Rebels kept up a steady fire on the bluecoats, who finally surrendered.

Brigadier General George C. Strong, leading the Federal attack, was killed, and there were many more Union casualties. The ditch in front of the fort was filled with dead soldiers, both white and black. Federal losses were disastrous—more than 1,500 killed, wounded, or captured. The Rebel garrison suffered 181 casualties. The Charleston Battalion lost 6 killed and 43 wounded, and Major David Ramsay was badly wounded.[3]

After the debacle of July 18, the Federals fell back on the longer but more reliable method of siege warfare. For the next six weeks, Federal guns continued to hammer Battery Wagner as the bluecoats tunneled ever closer to the fort. The grueling attrition took a heavy toll on the fort's garrison, as the Rebel works were gradually reduced to ruins. Seven more Charleston soldiers lost their lives, and 27 more were wounded. On the night of September 6, the Rebels evacuated Battery Wagner. The Yankees occupied the fort the next day.[4]

While they were bombarding Battery Wagner into oblivion, the Federals had also been battering Fort Sumter ruthlessly, and Sumter—an older, brick masonry fort built many years earlier in a different era—had been pounded to a pile of rubble. The fort was so badly damaged that the Rebels had withdrawn their big guns, leaving only infantry there as a token defense force. Fort Sumter now became the Charleston Battalion's home. The Irish Volunteers, 43 men now under Captain James M. Mulvaney, a 37-year-old Charleston policeman, settled in for another hard fight.

And a new fight was not long in coming. Less than forty-eight hours after the Charleston Battalion took up residence at Fort Sumter, the Federals launched an attack on the night of September 8. Five hundred blue-coated Marines and sailors attempted a landing on the southern and southeastern sides of the fort. The Charlestonians fought back with muskets, hand-grenades, and fire balls. The Rebel ram *Chicora* and the batteries on James Island and Sullivan's Island also pounded the landing force which withdrew.[5]

At the end of September 1863, the badly used up Charleston Battalion was consolidated with the 1st South Carolina Sharpshooters to form the 27th South Carolina Infantry. The new command was transferred to Virginia, where it faced more combat with Lee's veteran army. The Federals did not give up on Charleston, though, and beginning on September 22, they began shelling the city itself. The Confederates did not evacuate Charleston until February 1865 as William T. Sherman's army closed in after a triumphant sweep through Georgia.

The Federal naval blockade of the long Southern coastline and offensive operations against Southern seaports was a lengthy and often tedious but significant part of the Civil War. Events like those at Battery Wagner and Fort Sumter were played out many times during the four years of war, and it was determined little bands of Rebel gunners like the Irish Volunteers that tenaciously contested every Union gain.

Savannah had always been home to an Irish element. Early Scotch-Irish settlers made their dwellings downtown, while the more recent middle class "Old Fort Irish" lived east of the city near Fort Wayne, an old fort of the Revolutionary War period. The poorer "famine Irish" immigrants lived west of the city in the Yamacraw section, near the railroad depot. It was Savannah's early Scotch-Irish community that formed the Hibernian Society in 1812 to further Irish culture and traditions. With a membership of Irish professionals and businessmen, the Hibernians sponsored Savannah's annual St. Patrick's Day festivities as well as charitable activities to uphold bonds of loyalty to Ireland while helping the immigrant make the material adjustment to life in America.

The middle class Irish also took the lead in forming a volunteer militia company in Savannah. The city's older Scotch-Irish community already had a military company, the Republican Blues, formed in 1808. In 1842, a group of young men representing the "New Irish" met downtown above John Riordan's store to organize a new volunteer militia company, the Irish Jasper Greens. On their charter, the members crossed out the words "an Irish" from "an Irish military company," feeling that an *exclusively* Irish unit might not be appropriate for democratic America. But Irish the company was—from its dark blue uniform with green trouser stripes and brass buttons engraved with an Irish harp to its green silk flag with the Irish harp on one side and the Georgia state seal on the other. The young patriots named their company for Sergeant William Jasper, a South Carolina soldier killed at the Revolutionary War siege of Savannah in 1779.

Typical of Irish volunteer militia companies, the Irish Jasper Greens held scheduled drills, marksmanship contests, dances, and banquets, parading on St. Patrick's Day, Independence Day, and other special occasions. While the Greens drew many members from the poorer working class of recent immigrants, many of its officers also served in the more prestigious Hibernian Society, which the Greens traditionally escorted in the St. Patrick's Day parade. The Irish Jasper Greens served in the Mexican War of 1846–1848, the only military company from Savannah to do so.

Tempers flared during the Know-Nothing troubles in August 1854, when an officer in one of the non-Irish military companies in the city wrote a letter to the editor of the *Savannah Republican* accusing members of the Irish Jasper Greens of plotting to "attack any procession of Americans that might parade the streets." The writer threatened to enlist "an equal number of native born Americans ... to prove once and for all which is the better." The Greens' Lieutenant John Murphy denied the charges in a letter in the next edition of the newspaper, branding them "street rumors" and insisting that any enemies of native born Americans were also "the enemies of the Irish Jasper Greens individually and collectively."

The Savannah Irish enthusiastically embraced Southern independence in 1861. On St. Patrick's Day, the city's military companies (including the Irish Jasper Greens) marched to St. Andrew's Hall, where Father Jeremiah O'Neill gave a lively speech in support of the Confederacy. British newspaperman William H. Russell noted in May, "there is a considerable population of Irish and Germans in Savannah, who to a man are in favor of the Confederacy, and will fight to support it." Their devotion would be sorely tested as part of the 1st Georgia Volunteers at Atlanta in July 1864.[6]

Like the Irish Volunteers in Charleston, Savannah's Irish Jasper Greens intended to organize an ethnic "Irish Battalion," but this never came to pass. Instead, the Jaspers expanded into two companies, A and B of the 1st Georgia Volunteers. Also in Savannah's 1st Georgia was the older Scotch-Irish unit, the Republican Blues (Company C), and the recently formed Irish Volunteers (Company E). Two more Savannah Irish companies, the Montgomery Guard and Emmett Guard, later went into the 22nd Georgia Artillery Battalion (as Companies E and F) and saw garrison duty on the Georgia coast. The Telfair Irish Grays became Company H, 25th Georgia Infantry Regiment and fought with the Army of Tennessee.

Elements of the 1st Georgia Volunteers (including the Irish Jaspers, the Blues, and Irish Volunteers) served garrison duty at Fort Pulaski—the imposing fortress on Cockspur Island that guarded the entrance to the Savannah River—on a rotating basis from January 1861 to April 1862. Constructed in 1846 (much of the design was done by Robert E. Lee while serving with the U. S. Army Engineers), Fort Pulaski was encircled by a moat, had brick walls seven and one half feet thick, bristled with close to 50 guns, and was considered one of the strongest fortresses on the eastern seaboard. But the fort's invincibility proved to be a sad illusion. On April 11, 1862, Federal troops on nearby Tybee

Island, armed with the newer, more powerful rifled artillery, reduced the fort to rubble and forced its surrender after thirty hours of bombardment. The Irish Jaspers were not among the 400-man Rebel garrison when Fort Pulaski fell.

Under the direction of Captain John McCrady of the C. S. Engineers, the Confederates erected Fort McAllister, fifteen miles south of Savannah at the mouth of the Ogeechee River, in July 1861. Like Charleston's Battery Wagner, it was an earthen fort, smaller than Fort Pulaski and equipped with 10 large-caliber guns. Fort McAllister would withstand seven separate Federal naval bombardments over a two and one half year period. A shelling by three Federal ironclads on March 3, 1863, lasted eight hours and failed to destroy the fort although it did do some damage.

Fort McAllister, Battery Wagner, and other defensive works along the Georgia and South Carolina coasts became familiar sites to detachments of the 1st Georgia Volun-

FORT MCALLISTER, GATEWAY TO SAVANNAH. The strategic fort on the Ogeechee River south of Savannah was manned by Irish companies in the 22nd Georgia Artillery before its capture by Federal forces in December 1864. (Library of Congress)

teers—including the Irish Jasper Greens, Irish Volunteers, and Republican Blues—who served rotating tours of duty there at various times during 1863 and 1864. By May 1864, these troops were on their way to Atlanta for service with the Army of Tennessee—and their first encounter with truly deadly combat. Remaining to man the big guns at Fort McAllister were members of the 22nd Georgia Artillery Battalion.

The 22nd Georgia Artillery was organized in November 1862. Major John B. Gallie, a Scottish immigrant and prominent Savannah merchant, was killed at Fort McAllister on February 1, 1863, in the first enemy naval attack. The Montgomery Guards (Company E) and Emmett Guards (or Emmett Rifles) (Company F) were both Irish companies from Savannah that served early on with the 1st Georgia Volunteers and later with the 22nd Georgia Artillery.

Fort McAllister was not built to withstand a land assault—although it was protected by a 15-foot-deep moat and an abatis of tree limbs, as well as land mines—and it took only fifteen minutes on December 13, 1864, for General William Hazen's Federal division of Sherman's army to storm the little fort and overwhelm the 230-man Rebel garrison, which included the Emmett Rifles. Fort McAllister had protected the southern approaches to Savannah, and Confederate General William Hardee, faced with an investment of his forces, evacuated the city on December 21. Now at the end of his "march to the sea," Sherman offered Savannah to Lincoln as "a Christmas gift."

Older brick and mortar fortresses like Fort Sumter and Fort Pulaski that dotted the eastern coast of the United States had become obsolete because of advances in rifled artillery. These forts had been designed to withstand the impact of the largest guns in use at that time, 8-inch Columbiads. Now in the fourth year of the war, both sides had weapons far more powerful and with far greater range. But the Confederacy's last fortress to fall, the massive Fort Fisher on the North Carolina coast, demonstrated that the Rebels had taken these lessons to heart.

By the end of 1864, Wilmington, North Carolina, was the Confederacy's last open seaport. Here blockade runners landed badly needed supplies for Lee's army in Virginia. And guarding this important link with the outside world was Fort Fisher at the entrance to the Cape Fear River. But Fisher was no Fort Sumter, no Fort Pulaski. The Confederacy's largest fort, this gigantic earthwork—shaped like the number 7—lay on a narrow neck of land with the Atlantic Ocean on one side and the Cape Fear River in its rear. Constructed of heavy logs, earth, and sand, which absorbed the impact of shells better than brick walls, the fort's extensive works stretched for a mile on its sea face and a third of a mile on its narrow land side. And it was still not completely finished. At the southern end of the peninsula was a small four-gun earthwork, Battery Buchanan.

Fort Fisher's garrison was commanded by Colonel William Lamb, who had designed the fort with an eye to replicating Russia's Malakoff fort at the Black Sea port of Sevastopol. During the Crimean War, that fortress had held allied French and British forces at bay for a year, and the comparison gave rise to Fort Fisher's nickname as the "Sevastopol of the South." Fort Fisher's thick 20-foot-high ramparts and its 47 big guns provided formidable protection from any assault, and the beaches beyond the fort's walls were seeded with land mines.

Wilmington itself was home to a large Irish community. In May 1861, many of these sons of Erin enlisted in Captain Edward D. Hall's company in the 2nd North Carolina Infantry. "[N]o better or more loyal men, or better soldiers could be found in any company," Hall remembered. "When work or fighting was to be done, they were always ready, and would go wherever ordered." After serving with the Army of Northern Virginia in the Seven Days campaign, Hall's company was detached in September 1862 and was converted to artillery, serving under Captain Calvin Barnes as Company H of the 3rd North Carolina Artillery stationed in the defenses around Wilmington. Also here was the Wilmington Horse Artillery, a largely Irish company now serving in the 1st North Carolina Artillery.[7]

From Bladen County, Company B (the Bladen Guards) of the 2nd North Carolina Artillery contained 45 to 50 Irish, Scottish, or Scotch-Irish names recruited near the communities of Tar Heel and Dublin. The company was transferred to the 18th North Carolina Infantry and saw service with the Army of Northern Virginia. Also from Bladen County were 45 or so Irish or Scotch-Irish names in Captain George C. Buchan's Company G (formerly the Herring Artillery) of the 3rd North Carolina Artillery.

Fort Fisher's second-in-command was an Irish immigrant who would also make his home in Wilmington, 43-year-old Major James Reilly, called "Old Tarantula" by his soldiers. Hailing from County Westmeath, Reilly had run away from home at age 16 to join the British army, and when he later immigrated to America, he enlisted as a U. S. soldier. Reilly fought in the Mexican War and saw service on the western frontier. The outbreak of the Civil War found him stationed at Fort Johnston, a small outpost on the North Carolina coast, where he was serving as an ordnance sergeant in charge of a small detachment of regulars. Reilly surrendered the fort to the Confederates, the same side that he joined shortly afterwards. He was commissioned captain of the Rowan Artillery, Company F of the 10th North Carolina. Reilly's battery earned a reputation as an excellent artillery unit in the Army of Northern Virginia, while its men would remember their commander as "rough, gruff, grizzly, and brave."[8]

The Federals made an assault on Fort Fisher on Christmas Eve, 1864, but this attempt failed. They tried again two weeks later. On January 12, 1865, Major General Alfred H. Terry landed 8,000 Federal soldiers on the beach north of the fort, while 627 guns of 59 naval vessels began an artillery bombardment that was heavy and unrelenting, concentrating on the fort's land face. Federal ironclads offshore hammered the fort all day on January 13, all day and night on January 14.

Inside the fort were 800 men of the 2nd North Carolina Artillery, 100 of them in no shape to fight. Captain George Buchan's Company G of the 3rd North Carolina Artillery was also on hand. Reinforcements brought up on January 13 raised the number of defenders to 1,500. (The Irish Volunteers of the 27th South Carolina—the old Charleston Battalion—nearly made it to Fort Fisher in time for the climactic battle of January 15, but by then the Federal bombardment was so heavy that they were prevented from landing.) The Federal shelling exacted a terrific toll. The nightmarish pounding that never seemed to stop was so heavy that the defenders couldn't repair the damage done to the fort or even bury their dead. By now every big gun in the fort was disabled, except for one 8-inch Columbiad. Some 200 of the garrison had been killed.[9]

After twelve more hours of furious naval bombardment, Terry launched the Federal attack on the afternoon of January 15. The Rebels spotted three heavy lines of bluecoated infantry grimly advancing across the beach, while the ironclads offshore provided supporting fire. The Federals assaulted the northern land face of the fort in two waves. A swarm of sailors and Marines that hit the northeastern angle of the land wall distracted the Confederates, but the real assault—made by a division of tough New York

ASSAULT ON FORT FISHER. Major James Reilly, an Irish immigrant and veteran soldier, directed the Rebel defense of Fort Fisher, protecting the Confederacy's last open seaport in 1865. (Library of Congress)

and Pennsylvania infantry under Brigadier General Adelbert Ames—struck the western end of the wall where Major James Reilly commanded, with a fury.

Major General William Whiting, who was badly wounded while leading a Rebel counterattack at Fort Fisher, called it "an assault of unprecedented fury, both by sea and land." The shelling was so brutal that the defenders, whose numbers were so small that they couldn't man the entire works anyway, were not even able to mount the parapets. The bluecoats managed to gain a foothold on the left, getting into the fort's traverses.[10]

At the head of another band of Rebels trying to seal the bluecoats' penetration, Colonel Lamb fell with a wound to the hip, and this left James Reilly in command of the beleaguered fort. "Reilly came," Lamb reported, "and promised me that he would continue the fight as long as a man or a shot was left, and nobly did he keep his promise." Now the defense was up to "Old Tarantula."

But the battle, as Reilly recalled, was all "up-hill work." Hopelessly outnumbered, the old Irishman kept up a stubborn resistance for six more hours. As complete darkness fell, the graycoats fought desperately in hellish hand-to-hand combat with the Yankees, contesting every inch of the works. The fighting raged until 9 p.m. Finally the bluecoats had wrested control of so much of the fort that further Rebel resistance seemed hopeless.

Reilly and his "gallant little band of Tar Heels"—fewer than 50 men, including the wounded Whiting and Lamb—fell back to Battery Buchanan under the cover of darkness with the Federals close on their heels. But when he reached the little outpost and found that the detachment of troops stationed there had spiked their guns and evacuated, any hopes of mounting a last-ditch defense were dashed. With the bluecoats closing in, Reilly stepped out onto the beach, raised his sword with a white handkerchief on the end of it, and, "with a heart of deepest depression," surrendered.[11]

The Confederacy's last lifeline was severed. The Fort Fisher garrison, including the Irish companies in the North Carolina artillery, as well as Major James Reilly, were now prisoners of the Federal government. For them, the war was over. But there still were Confederate armies in the field, and fighting must continue until their final defeat. For the Confederate Irish, there still were painful sacrifices ahead.[12]

16. To the Last Ditch: From Fort Pickens to Fort Blakely, 1861–1865

Ready and eager for their first military action, the young Rebel soldiers raced breathlessly along the sandy beaches on narrow, 40-mile long Santa Rosa Island on the night of October 8, 1861. Their objective was Fort Pickens, the Federal stronghold that occupied the western end of the island—and that dominated the entrance to Pensacola Bay. After the fall of Fort Sumter in April 1861, Fort Pickens remained the only major fort still in Federal hands on the Southern coast, and its defiant refusal to surrender was an affront to youthful Confederate pride. The Rebels had landed 1,000 troops by steamer and barge on the eastern end of the island. Surprise would be their ally. With advance parties dispatched to pick off drowsy, unsuspecting Federal sentries, three columns of Rebel infantry pushed on toward the fort. The first thing they encountered as they stumbled along in the darkness was the bodies of these unlucky Federal sentries. For most of them, it was their first unsettling look at death in war.

About a mile east of Fort Pickens, the attackers surprised the camp of the 6th New York Infantry—a largely Irish outfit described by one Union officer as "thieves, plug-uglies, and other dangerous characters gathered from the slums of New York City"—and stampeded the startled Yankees, overrunning the camp and lingering to pillage and burn. "[W]e fired a volley into the very heart of their camp," wrote a member of one Rebel company, the Irish Volunteers from Augusta, Georgia. "You ought to have heard the groans of the dying devils."[1]

Alerted now, four companies of U. S. regulars poured out of Fort Pickens to launch a counterattack. The Rebels were already exhausted from marching through miles of deep sand and thickets, and dawn was already breaking. Having lost the element of surprise, they fell back and returned to the mainland. Rebel losses were 18 killed, 39 wounded, and 30 missing or captured. The engagement was only a skirmish compared to the bloodbaths to follow, but it was the first taste of combat for most of these young men, and for the Rebels it raised their spirits, even though the raid had been repulsed. "We returned home," the Irish Volunteer proudly wrote, "after teaching them how to fight."[2]

Captain John H. Hull's Irish Volunteers, which became Company C of the 5th Georgia Infantry, represented Augusta's large Irish community. The company included men like 1st Sergeant Henry P. Haney, a 26-year-old Pennsylvania-born moulder who lived with three Irish immigrants. Haney would rise to the rank of captain in May 1862, but would resign due to disability in July. Second Lieutenant Michael J. O'Connor, Jr., a 21-year-old Irish immigrant who worked as a clerk, would succeed Haney as captain, serving until the end of the war and the surrender of the Army of Tennessee in North Carolina in 1865. For 26-year-old Irish-born laborer John Stanton, Santa Rosa Island marked his first and only experience under fire; he was killed in the action. Edmund Flynn was wounded.[3]

Irish-Americans could be found in other Rebel detachments that fought at Santa Rosa Island. Three companies of Colonel Daniel E. Adams' 1st Louisiana Regulars—about one fourth of them Irish from New Orleans—also took part in the action. In the 10th Mississippi Infantry, the Irish communities in Port Gibson, Jackson, and Yazoo City contributed at least 30 Irish names each to Companies C (Captain William McKeever's Port Gibson Rifles), A (the Mississippi Rifles), and K (the Yazoo Minute Rifles). There were at least 15 to 20 Irish names in each of the 10th Mississippi's other original companies.

Colonel Henry D. Clayton's 1st Alabama Infantry, which did most of its duty as heavy artillery in the Rebel shore batteries on the northern side of Pensacola Bay, contained Company D, the Alabama Rifles (or Talladega Rifles), one of two companies from the regiment to take part in the Santa Rosa Island raid, with at least 40 Irish or Scotch-Irish names on roll. The sizeable population of recent Irish immigrants in the thriving river town of Eufaula probably accounted for the numbers of Irish names in Companies A (Pioneer Guards), B (Eufaula Rifles), and F (Clayton Guards).

Even sparsely settled Florida, largely ignored by strategists (although an enthusiastic Confederate state), boasted a scattering of Irish-American soldiers. There were no distinctly Irish companies, but the 1st Florida Infantry counted at least 15 Irish names on the rolls of Companies B, E, H, and K (Pensacola Guards). One of two Florida companies to take part in the Santa Rosa Island fight, the Pensacola Guards represented a small but old Irish presence in Pensacola. Commanded by Captain A. H. Bright, the Pensacolans later had an Irish-American officer, Augustus O. McDonell, as their captain. The Floridians lost 6 killed, 8 wounded, and 12 missing on Santa Rosa Island.

Part of the chain of masonry forts built to protect the U. S. coastline, Fort Pickens had been completed in 1834. To the north of Santa Rosa Island lay the town of Pensacola, the U. S. Navy Yard, and one of the best harbors on the Gulf Coast. Rebel forces had occupied the Navy Yard and shore installations at Fort Barrancas and Fort McRee in January 1861. The fledgling Confederacy was in desperate need of a fine harbor like Pensacola's for constructing ships for its infant navy. For the Union, holding Pensacola was critical for any successful blockade operations against Mobile and New Orleans. The closest alternate port, Key West, was too far away to be used with effect. The Civil War nearly began at Fort Pickens, rather than Fort Sumter.

Throughout the spring and summer of 1861, the situation at Pensacola Bay remained tense. There were many who expected an attack on Fort Pickens to be the war's first major battle. Confederate troops, placed under command of Brigadier General Braxton Bragg, gradually increased to more than 8,000. With U. S. naval warships still in control of the Bay, Federal reinforcements continued to filter into Fort Pickens. Both sides observed an informal truce for months.

The problem for the Rebels was that they lacked the firepower to reduce Fort Pickens. Unlike the Rebel-occupied Forts Pulaski and Sumter, Pickens was in no danger of

Top: ALABAMA RIFLES AT PENSACOLA, APRIL 1861. The roll of this volunteer company from Talladega contained a large number of Irish surnames. At Pensacola, they manned mortars and became part of the newly formed 1st Alabama Infantry. (State Archives of Florida Photographic Division).

Right: 1ST LIEUTENANT AUGUSTUS O. MCDONELL, 1ST FLORIDA INFANTRY. The Irish-American officer, a 22 year-old railroad clerk from Archer, Florida, commanded the Pensacola Guards, a company in the 1st Florida Infantry. (State Archives of Florida Photographic Division)

being leveled by the new longer ranged rifled artillery. The Yankee garrison enjoyed a clear superiority in firepower, and the Santa Rosa Island raid only demonstrated the futility of a Confederate land attack. On November 22 and 23, an intense artillery duel left Fort McRee (just a mile distant from Fort Pickens across the entrance to Pensacola Bay and garrisoned at the time by Georgia and Mississippi troops) a pile of rubble. The Federals fired 5,000 rounds of ammunition at the Rebel works and sustained very little damage from the 1,000 rounds fired by the Rebels in return. On January 1 and 2, 1862, the Yankees pounded Fort McRee again, this time setting off an explosion in the fort's powder magazine, which rendered the fort practically useless.

The tedious siege that had dragged on through the summer months of 1861 saw the new recruits drilling, working on the sand batteries, and passing the time playing cards. Stifling heat and humidity took its toll, and a number of soldiers died from heat exhaustion. In the 1st Alabama, 17-year-old Edward Y. McMorries (a great-grandson of Irish immigrants from County Antrim) learned that, "The warm spring brought clouds of mosquitos, and fleas of prodigious size and blood-thirsty intent became as numerous as the sands of the seashore." As camp illnesses like measles, malaria, and typhoid fever ran rampant, sick soldiers crowded the marine hospital at the Navy Yard. "Nearly one hundred of our regiment died in less than three months from diseases," an Alabama officer wrote. Each day, dead soldiers would be carried from the hospital to the "dead house" for burial or for shipment back home, and youthful soldiers completely unacquainted with the callousness of war were appalled. "A man can die and be buried here," one wrote, "with the least ceremony and concern I ever saw."[4]

The anticipated great battle for Fort Pickens never materialized, and in the spring of 1862 attention shifted to western Tennessee, where the horrendous clash at Shiloh was shaping up. The skeleton Rebel force remaining in Pensacola burned the Navy Yard and evacuated the town on May 9, and U. S. forces occupied it the next day. By the end of the war, Pensacola had become a staging area for operations into the interior of Florida and against Mobile. For the Rebel and Yankee soldiers at Pensacola in the summer of 1861, it represented their first experience with war, their first time away from home, and their loss of innocence. None could have foreseen what was to follow.

The brutal reality of war was not long in coming to many of the Pensacola veterans. At Shiloh, the 1st Florida Infantry (reduced to about 250 men and downscaled to a battalion) suffered heavy casualties. Major Thaddeus A. McDonell, who was commended for his skill in handling the battalion, was badly wounded. The mostly–Louisiana brigade to which the Floridians belonged lost over one fourth of its 1,633 men in killed and wounded. In the same bloody clash, the 1st Louisiana Regulars was decimated after just twenty minutes of heavy fighting, with only about 100 men left in the entire regiment who were present for duty at the end of the first day of fighting. The Regulars would see more costly combat with the Army of Tennessee.[5]

The 10th Mississippi and its sister command, the 9th Mississippi, suffered dreadful losses in some of the bloodiest fighting at Shiloh, Murfreesboro, Chickamauga, and Atlanta. As part of the Rebel garrison at Island Number Ten across the Mississippi River from New Madrid, Missouri, the 1st Alabama was captured in April 1862 after sustaining 150 casualties during the siege; 150 more died in prison before prisoners were exchanged in September. The Alabamians were captured again at Port Hudson, the Louisiana outpost on the lower Mississippi, in July 1863, were exchanged in the fall, and lost half of their numbers with the Army of Tennessee in the fighting at Atlanta.[6]

Augusta's Irish Volunteers became the color company of the 5th Georgia Infantry. In the vicious fighting at Chickamauga in September 1863, the 5th Georgia suffered 60 percent casualties, and the Irish Volunteers were hit hard. Sergeant Jeremiah D. O'Connor, Corporal George Lawless, Private John O'Donnell, and Private John Sullivan were killed. Corporal Bernard Carroll, Private William Lanier, and Private Patrick Powers were badly wounded.[7]

After Pensacola, Florida saw little military action. The only major battle fought in the Sunshine State during the Civil War unfolded at Olustee (or Ocean Pond), fifteen miles east of present-day Lake City, Florida, on February 20, 1864. After occupying Jacksonville, about 5,000 Federal troops (including the old hands of the 7th Connecticut and the black veterans of the 54th Massachusetts) under Brigadier General Truman Seymour marched inland toward a Rebel army of about equal size under Irish-born 50-year-old Brigadier General Joseph Finegan.

Finegan had settled in the Atlantic coast town of Fernandina, where he ran a sawmill and became an attorney—and a close colleague of prominent Florida political leaders. He had no military training, but his political connections landed him a position as brigadier general in command of Confederate defenses in the Department of Florida. At Olustee, the military amateur managed to scrape together two brigades of Georgia and Florida troops—many of them combat veterans who had served in other theaters of the war—to win a hard-fought victory over the Federal invaders and send them hastening back to Jacksonville.

One of the seasoned Rebel outfits that fought at Olustee was Colonel James Henry Neal's 19th Georgia Infantry with its Irish color company (and Neal's old command), the Jackson Guards (Company B) from Atlanta. While serving with the Army of Northern Virginia, the 19th Georgia had suffered heavy losses at Second Manassas and Sharpsburg and was overrun at Fredericksburg. The regiment's casualties at Olustee were 8 killed and 88 wounded, including the Jackson Guards' Private Patrick Breen.[8]

Another veteran command was the 1st Georgia Regulars, formed in April 1861 with men from recruited from Atlanta and Brunswick and a few other areas of the state. The Emmet Rifles (Company B) was an Irish company led by Captain William Martin, who was later promoted to field command. Company G was also largely Irish. "We have a good many Irish in the regiment," Sergeant W. H. Andrews wrote, "and while they are good hardy soldiers, they are hard to control." The 1st Georgia Regulars served with the Army of Northern Virginia in 1862, taking heavy casualties at Second Manassas, and they transferred back to Georgia in 1863 to recruit. Captain Henry A. Cannon was killed while leading the regiment at Olustee. The Georgians lost 3 killed and 25 wounded.[9]

A section of Captain Robert H. Gamble's Leon Light Artillery, a Tallahassee battery with 25 to 30 Irish names on roll, also saw action at Olustee, where it lost 2 men killed and 3 wounded. Captain Henry F. Abell's company of the Milton Light Artillery from Apalachicola (with at least 30 Irish names on roll) fought as infantry with the 1st Georgia Regulars, having been overrun earlier in the campaign with the loss of their five cannon. Sergeant Andrews was impressed with them, writing, "The Florida Artillery Company placed in the Regulars fought like veterans and was highly complimented by the Regulars for their gallantry."[10]

The Federal threat to Florida appeared to be over, and Olustee established Finegan's reputation as a commander, leading to his transfer to the Army of Northern Virginia. The military novice had fought a bloody engagement at Olustee, one of the war's costliest. Finegan reported 93 Rebels killed and 841 wounded. The Federals lost somewhat more.[11]

OLUSTEE Feb. 20, 1864

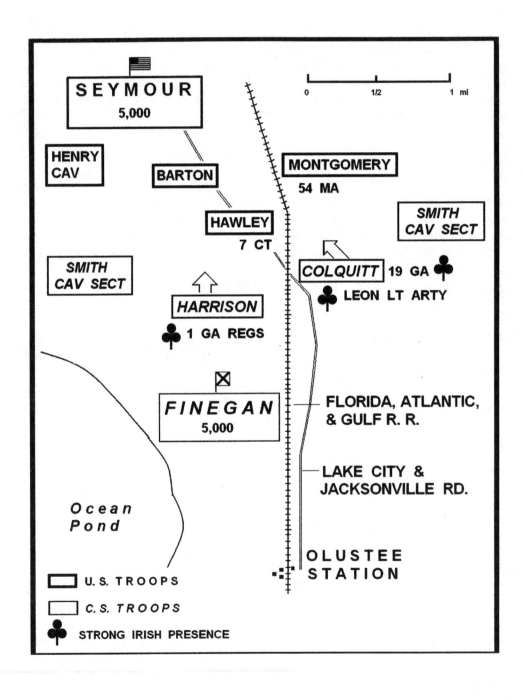

SEYMOUR
5,000

HENRY
CAV

BARTON

MONTGOMERY
54 MA

HAWLEY
7 CT

SMITH
CAV SECT

SMITH
CAV SECT

COLQUITT 19 GA

LEON LT ARTY

HARRISON

1 GA REGS

FINEGAN
5,000

FLORIDA, ATLANTIC,
& GULF R. R.

LAKE CITY &
JACKSONVILLE RD.

Ocean
Pond

OLUSTEE
STATION

0   1/2   1 mi

U. S. TROOPS

C. S. TROOPS

STRONG IRISH PRESENCE

Following the capture of New Orleans in April 1862, Mobile became the primary Federal target on the Gulf Coast, but operations against the Alabama seaport were delayed until the summer of 1864. After the Federals' failed Red River campaign in western Louisiana came to a close in May 1864, Union Admiral David G. Farragut finally had the manpower to strike against Mobile.

Farragut crushed the Confederates' small naval squadron in the battle of Mobile Bay on August 5, 1864. The victory gave the Federals control of the gateway to Mobile. But the city still had formidable land defenses. Thirty miles south of Mobile, the Federals initiated operations against the two coastal forts at the entrance to Mobile Bay—Fort Morgan at the tip of a narrow peninsula of land on the eastern side of

BRIGADIER GENERAL JOSEPH FINEGAN. An Irish immigrant who made his home in Jacksonville, Florida, Finegan scored an impressive victory over the Federals at Olustee. Later he commanded a brigade in Lee's army in Virginia. (Library of Congress)

the bay, and Fort Gaines on Dauphin Island to the west.

On August 3, Major General Gordon Granger, a tough Federal officer who had helped save his army from destruction at Chickamauga, landed 1,500 blue-coated infantry on the western end of Dauphin Island and moved against Fort Gaines. The fort was held by just six companies of the 21st Alabama Infantry Regiment, a command recruited in Mobile, and one of the companies was Irish.

The city's Irish community that had sent its sons to battle with the Army of Northern Virginia and the Army of Tennessee also furnished a company of men to serve on the Gulf coast. Captain John O'Connor's Montgomery Guards, Company B of the 21st Alabama, drew its recruits from middle and working class Irish of the Gulf City. Lieutenant Colonel James M. Williams of the 21st Alabama commented on the Montgomery Guards in a letter to his wife in January 1862: "I pause from our letters for another laugh at our Irish neighbors the 'Montgomery Guards'—one of their sergeants was calling the eight-o'clock roll—he had got about half way down his alphabet and was among the O'Flannigans and O'Flahertys when suddenly the rain began to fall briskly and we could hear them all scampering off to their tents."[12]

The 21st Alabama Infantry saw its first combat at Shiloh in April 1862, and its initiation was a bloody one. Six color-bearers were shot down, and the regiment lost 200 killed and wounded out of 650. Williams became especially fond of the Irish company, who he wrote, "stood by my side in the battle of Shiloh." The 21st Alabama spent the rest of the war garrisoning forts on Mobile Bay and doubling as heavy artillery.[13]

Fort Gaines surrendered on August 8, 1864, after Granger's troops, aided by Federal ironclads, shelled the fort for five days. The Montgomery Guards, including Captain John O'Connor and former 1st Sergeant (now Lieutenant) Michael Burke, were among the Rebel prisoners taken at Fort Gaines. The prisoners went to Ship Island, a desolate prison camp off the Mississippi coast.

The capture of Fort Morgan, on the opposite side of Mobile Bay, took a while longer. The largest of the Alabama coastal forts, a five-sided brick structure with 86 guns under the command of Brigadier General Richard L. ("Ramrod") Page, Fort Morgan withstood an eighteen-day siege. The primary garrison here, in addition to two companies of the 21st Alabama and some Tennessee artillery, was the 1st Alabama Artillery Battalion.

Company A of 1st Alabama Artillery contained 30 or so Irish-Americans from Mobile, and there were nearly as many in Company D from Macon and Madison Counties. A well disciplined little command, the Alabama artillerists were highly regarded even by the Federals.[14]

Granger's infantry and Farragut's naval vessels outside the Bay pounded Fort Morgan ruthlessly for days, and on the night of August 22 the Union shelling set off a fire inside the fort. A Rebel officer wrote, "Six or eight shells could be counted in the air at once and every shot appeared to take effect.... The interior of the fort had become a mass of smoking ruins."[15]

The Alabama artillerists handled the cannon at Fort Morgan until all but two of the big guns were disabled, and 150 of their members were killed and wounded. When the fires threatened to spread to the powder magazine, and much of the fort's gunpowder had to be sacrificed, Page made the reluctant decision to surrender the fort. The Rebels raised the white flag the next day.

The Fort Morgan garrison, with its Irish gunners in the 1st Alabama Artillery, went to a Federal prison in Elmira, New York. Half of them died there from smallpox. The Fort Gaines garrison, with the Montgomery Guards, returned to Mobile as part of a prisoner exchange in January 1865.[16]

The capture of Forts Morgan and Gaines gave the Federals control of Mobile Bay, ended the Gulf City's usefulness as a Rebel seaport and haven for blockade runners, and provided a welcome boost to Lincoln's campaign for reelection as U. S. president. Mobile Bay was just one in a string of Federal victories in the late summer and autumn of 1864. With the fall of Atlanta and with Lee's army on the ropes at Petersburg, Southern hopes for independence were withering like dry fruit on a barren vine, and most realized at long last that the end was in sight. As Confederate morale plummeted, Southern cities were hit by food shortages, and Rebel soldiers deserted in droves. But not all.

By March 1865, Major General Edward R. S. Canby had some 45,000 U. S. troops available for the long-planned assault on the city of Mobile, the last armed Rebel stronghold on the Gulf coast. A massive Federal war machine lumbered north from Pensacola and Mobile Bay, zeroing in on the key forts in the city's defenses, Spanish Fort and Fort Blakely, where die-hard Rebel garrisons were resigned to fight to the last ditch.

Brigadier General Randall L. Gibson commanded the 2,800-man garrison at Spanish Fort on the eastern side of Mobile Bay, a line of earthen works two miles long with six batteries or redoubts protected by abatis and rifle pits and a ditch eight feet wide and five feet deep. His veteran Louisiana brigade, down to about 500 men, had been transferred to Mobile after the ruinous Nashville campaign. Now a skeleton command of consolidated regiments, the Louisiana brigade still contained a number of the New Orleans Irish and Louisiana Sharpshooters and could boast a proud record of service in the Army of Tennessee. James T. Holtzclaw's Alabama brigade now included the 21st Alabama. This badly depleted little command contained the handful of Irish—by this time *all* Rebel companies were handfuls—in the Montgomery Guards, who would number just fourteen men when they finally surrendered in May 1865. Captain James Garrity's fine battery with many Irish gunners from Mobile held a portion of the Rebel center. Flapping defiantly over the Rebel works, tattered battle flags bore testimony to hard-fought battles from Shiloh to Franklin.

Canby's forces began siege operations against Spanish Fort on March 27. In the following thirteen days—which Gibson described as "digging all night and fighting all day"—four years of experience in military science were put to work as Rebels and Yankees dug trenches, probed, conducted occasional sorties, and dodged mortar shells and snipers' bullets. The Rebel defenses were holding, but while the graycoats' supplies of ammunition and manpower were steadily dwindling, every new day brought the Federals closer to their works.[17]

Accompanied by one of his men, Captain James Garrity stole stealthily up to enemy lines on the chilly night of April 7. By the light of the moon, the artillery officer observed a Federal work party busily digging away, close enough to the two men that a shovelful of dirt cascaded down on Garrity's head—and close enough to hear one Federal declare, "We'll give the rebels hell tomorrow."[18]

The next day, after a sustained pounding by Federal artillery and gunboats on the upper part of Mobile Bay, the bluecoats launched an assault that penetrated the Rebel left at Spanish Fort shortly after nightfall, capturing 350 gray-clads. Gibson evacuated the doomed fort and slipped away by a pre-arranged escape route during the night of April 8. As they had done at Nashville, the Louisiana brigade acted as a rear guard while the garrison withdrew.

Now only Fort Blakely stood. Just three miles north of Spanish Fort on the eastern bank of the Tensas River, Blakely was an earthen fortress covering three miles of works, crowned with nine redoubts and forty pieces of artillery. This final Rebel stronghold was protected by ditches four to five feet deep, rifle pits and abatis, and land mines made with 12-pound artillery shells. Brigadier General St. John R. Liddell, the grandson of an Irish immigrant, commanded the garrison of 3,500 troops, most of them teenage Alabama reserves stoically bracing themselves for a full-scale enemy assault. But veterans were here too.

Francis Cockrell's Missouri brigade, reduced now to 400 men, held the center of the Rebel works at Fort Blakely and was stretched so thin now that the men were forced to deploy at intervals of ten paces. Gone now were many of the St. Louis Irish, especially Captain Patrick Caniff, the impulsive skirmisher leader of the "Fighting Irish Company" who had fallen at Franklin. Consolidated regiments in the Missouri brigade were now led by junior officers. "All wore a saddened, softened look," veteran officer Joseph Boyce now reflected. "[I]t looked like refined cruelty to ask men to fight again."[19]

The massive assault by 16,000 Federal troops—the last grand charge of the war—rolled forward at about 5:30 p.m. on April 9. Resistance centered on Redoubts 3 and 4,

the sector of the line held by the Missouri brigade, the strongest and best fortified part of the Rebel works. In the rifle pits in front of these works, the soldiers had been ordered to stand their ground and fight. Corporal William H. Kavanaugh, a 20-year-old Irish-American farmer from central Missouri, dolefully considered, "skirmishers with such orders seldom live to run in." Now as waves of bluecoats poured out of the Federal trenches, quickly overwhelming the Rebel rifle pits, Corporal Kavanaugh sprinted for the safety of the fort. "It appeared to me that all hell had turned loose," Kavanaugh wrote, "that every man in the U. S. was practicing on us with repeating rifles."[20]

Top: BRIGADIER GENERAL ST. JOHN R. LIDDELL. The stubborn commander of Fort Blakely at the close of the war, Liddell was the grandson of an Irish immigrant. (Library of Congress). *Bottom:* THE LAST GREAT CHARGE OF THE WAR, FORT BLAKELY, APRIL 9, 1865. Federal troops storm Fort Blakely, the last stronghold defending Mobile. The best defended part of the Rebel works was held by the veteran Missouri brigade, which contained many Irish Americans from St. Louis. (*Harper's Weekly,* May 27, 1865)

Some of the most savage close combat in the war took place in Redoubts 3 and 4 as the bluecoats overran the outnumbered defenders. Defiant to the end, 24-four-year-old Captain Joseph H. Neal cried out, "No quarter to the damn Yankees," just before he was nearly decapitated by a Federal musket blast.[21]

Colonel James McCown's 3rd and 5th Missouri Infantry fired one last volley at the Federals in the captured fort, then turned and made a run for the Tensas River landing. There they were overtaken, and McCown raised a white handkerchief on the end of a stick, bringing to a sad end the story of the St. Louis Irish Confederates who had forged such an excellent combat record in the Rebel army. The storming of Fort Blakely had taken twenty minutes, at the cost of 500 Rebels killed and wounded and nearly 3,400 captured. Federal losses were about 600. Just six hours earlier, Robert E. Lee had surrendered the Army of Northern Virginia.[22]

COLONEL JAMES C. MCCOWN, 5TH MISSOURI INFANTRY. The son Irish immigrants, McCown commanded the 5th Missouri throughout the war and was among the remnant of this band to surrender at Fort Blakely, Alabama, on April 9, 1865. (Collection of Dr. Tom and Karen Sweeney, General Sweeny's Museum, Republic, MO)

PART V. THE IRISH IN THE MISSISSIPPI AND TRANS-MISSISSIPPI CAMPAIGNS

17. The Struggle for the Mississippi

They were a thousand miles away from the Southern disaster at Gettysburg, but just a day after Lee's stunning defeat Irish Confederates were facing another calamity at Vicksburg, Mississippi. It was July 4, 1863.

The siege of Vicksburg, the last Confederate stronghold on the Mississippi, had dragged on for seven exhausting weeks. Federal artillery had shelled the city relentlessly day and night. To escape the bombardment, civilians had retreated into caves dug into the bluffs along the river. Food had given out, and both townspeople and soldiers had resorted to eating mules. Sergeant Thomas Hogan, a young Irish immigrant in the 5th Missouri Infantry, adopted a philosophical attitude about this. "[I]f you did not know it," he maintained, "you could hardly tell the difference, when cooked, between it and beef."[1]

Debilitated and famished, the Rebel defenders were no longer able to hold out, and—despite all hopes to the contrary—there were no reinforcements coming. By 10 a.m., the Federals could see white flags flapping all along the Confederate lines. Columns of Union soldiers began to file into the Rebel works while sullen and emaciated graycoats looked on. Up went the United States flag over the courthouse at Vicksburg, for the first time in two and a half years.

Soon the Confederates began filing out of the works. Unit by unit, they halted and stacked arms. There was no cheering by the Federals, no humiliation for the Rebels. And for the beaten army, there would be no prison in the North, only a battlefield parole. Both sides were thankful that the long siege was over. As for the Rebels, they were just glad to be given something to eat—a little hard-tack, some coffee, some sugar.

The Rebs had put up a good fight and had nothing to be ashamed of. Colonel Francis M. Cockrell's Missouri brigade, tough veteran troops who had fought on battlefields on both sides of the Mississippi, was especially proud of its combat record. The war was not over for these soldiers, many of them Irish, and Cockrell avowed that they were "in no wise whipped, conquered, or subjugated."[2]

The loss of the fortress at Vicksburg would give Northern forces complete control of the Mississippi, splitting the Confederacy asunder. It was the end of a struggle that had its beginnings two and one half years earlier.

As a border slave state with sharp divisions between Northern and Southern sympathizers, Missouri held the key to the control of the upper Mississippi. Five years before the first gun was fired at Fort Sumter, Missourians had already been affected by civil war, as bloody frontier raids between pro-slavery and anti-slavery settlers spilled across the border from Kansas. Federal forces were determined to hold Missouri in the union, and Confederates were equally committed to winning the state for the Confederacy. Caught up in the turmoil was Missouri's Irish population, found in large numbers in St. Louis but also scattered in rural areas of the state.

The experience of the Irish in St. Louis was unique. Early in the nineteenth century Irish immigrants, mostly skilled workers and merchants, had settled in the Mississippi river port when it was still a French Catholic city. With Anglo Americans moving in at the same time, the Irish found greater acceptance and equality than in eastern cities of the United States. A middle class Irish community came to be firmly established in the section of town known as Market Street, while the flood of largely unskilled famine immigrants that came decades later—shanty Irish—settled farther west in the section known as "Kerry Patch," St. Louis' most notorious slum.

Irish immigrants in St. Louis found work in the dozens of new saw mills, flour mills, foundries, and machine shops in that growing western city. The St. Louis levees offered work too. In the first half of 1854 alone, 3,307 boats had docked at the St. Louis wharf. Like Savannah and New Orleans, a large pool of Irish immigrant labor was forming in St. Louis, which boasted nearly 30,000 Irish residents by 1860.[3]

The Irish formed their share of volunteer militia companies in St. Louis. The bulk of Captain Martin Burke's St. Louis Grays, formed in 1832, were Irish firefighters in the city. Captain Daniel Morton Frost's Washington Guards, formed in 1853, wore a gilt harp wreathed with shamrocks on their dress caps. Captain Joseph Kelly's Washington Blues, formed in 1857, and Captain William Wade's Emmet Guards represented the young, upwardly mobile Irish middle class in St. Louis. Dublin-born Father John B. Bannon of St. John's parish in the Market Street neighborhood served as chaplain to the volunteer militia. These volunteer companies would rush to join the Confederacy with the coming of war.

The Irish in other Mississippi River towns responded to the outbreak of war with equal enthusiasm. Farther down the Mississippi was Helena, Arkansas, and below it the wild riverboat town of Napoleon. These were still frontier communities, rowdy, lawless—rife with crime, gambling, and prostitution. But they all had their complement of Irish immigrants, anxious to fight.

There were many Irishmen in Pat Cleburne's company, the Yell Rifles of Helena, and Cleburne saw to it that they were well drilled, enlisting the aid of fellow Irishman and Helena resident J. H. Calvert, a former sergeant in the U. S. regular army. Calvert served as Cleburne's drillmaster and later became captain of the Helena Artillery, a company of mostly Irishmen (from Helena and from Memphis) who would serve closely with Cleburne's brigade.

In Vicksburg, where Irish residents made up more than 11 percent of the city's population, Irish immigrant planter Felix Hughes organized the Sarsfield Southrons, named for seventeenth-century Irish patriot Patrick Sarsfield. The company's flag, the Confederate first national "Stars and Bars," contained a wreath of shamrocks and the Gaelic war cry "Faugh a Ballagh" on the front. As part of the 22nd Mississippi Infantry Regiment, the Sarsfield Southrons fought at Shiloh and later with the Army of Tennessee. Hughes' promising career was cut short in August 1862 when he was killed in action while leading his regiment during the battle of Baton Rouge. Other Vicksburg Irish joined the Warren Light Artillery and Captain John Crump's Shamrock Guards (Company E, 3rd Confederate Regiment), both of which served in the Army of Tennessee.

Rebel soldiers would worship at Father Jeremiah O'Connor's St. Paul's Church during the siege of Vicksburg in the summer of 1863.[4]

St. Louis was already experiencing violence even before the outbreak of the Civil War. When a detachment of 40 U. S. regulars led by Lieutenant Thomas W. Sweeny, a one-armed veteran of the Mexican War, occupied the well stocked state arsenal in January 1861, pro–Confederates threatened to take the armory by force. "I'll blow it to hell first," the fiery-tempered Sweeny replied, "and you know I'm the man to do it." Tension in St. Louis remained high, and in May 4,000 Federal volunteers led by Brigadier General Nathaniel Lyon swooped down on nearby Camp Jackson, overwhelmed the 900-man pro–Confederate state volunteer militia there, and then marched their prisoners through the streets of the city toward the arsenal. Angry crowds gathered, gunfire broke out, and several civilians were killed including six Irish residents, three of them children. The event triggered civil war in Missouri.

The Camp Jackson incident also underscored a deep-seated hostility between ethnic groups, with St. Louis' large German community supporting the Union and the Irish supporting the Confederacy. Federal Missouri regiments were heavily German—the pro–Confederate Missourians called them "Hessians"—while Confederate Missouri regiment contained large numbers of Irish. Former members of the pro–Confederate state militia in Missouri—men like Joseph Kelly, Patrick Canniff, Joseph Boyce, Daniel Frost, and Father John Bannon—enlisted in Major General Sterling Price's Missouri State Guard.[5]

Lyon and the Federals attacked Price at Wilson's Creek in the southwestern corner of the state on August 10, 1861. But the Missouri Guard had been bolstered by the arrival of reinforcements from Arkansas led by Brigadier General Ben McCulloch, former Texas Ranger, veteran of the Texas War for Independence and Mexican War, and a great-grandson of Irish immigrants. Although McCulloch and Price didn't exactly see eye to eye on all matters, they were able to coordinate a successful defense and inflict a defeat on the Unionists. Lyon was killed.

An officer whose conduct shone at Wilson's Creek was a 45-year-old Texas cavalry officer, Lieutenant Colonel Walter Paye Lane. A native of County Cork, the Irishman now made his home in the East Texas town of Marshall. He had fought in the battle of San Jacinto, the decisive victory of the Texas War for Independence from Mexico in 1836. Since then Lane had been an Indian fighter, a teacher, a gold miner, a crewman on a Texas privateer, and an officer of rangers in the Mexican War of 1846–1848. Lane's horse was shot out from under him at Wilson's Creek, but this didn't deter him. He led his men forward on foot and remounted when another horse became available. Lane would go on to serve in campaigns west of the Mississippi, including the Red River campaign in 1864 in which he was wounded.

The Rebels' victory at Wilson's Creek did little for their cause. Seven months later Union forces inflicted the death blow to Southern hopes in Missouri. In a hard-fought engagement at Elkhorn Tavern (or Pea Ridge) in northwestern Arkansas on March 7 and 8, 1862, Major General Samuel R. Curtis's Federal army smashed Major General Earl Van Dorn's Rebels. Ben McCulloch was shot and killed. Price's State Guardsmen fought well, but they were never able to regain control of Missouri. Even though the Confederacy acknowledged Missouri with one of the thirteen stars on her flag, Union forces held the state for the rest of the war. The St. Louis Irish could not go home now.

The Missouri State Guard was dissolved, but many of its veterans—including the St.

BATTLE OF WILSON'S CREEK, AUGUST 10, 1861. St. Louis Irish elements formed a significant part of General Sterling Price's Missouri State Guard, which won a badly needed victory over Federal forces at Wilson's Creek in southwestern Missouri. (Library of Congress)

Louis Irish—enlisted in Francis Cockrell's Confederate Missouri brigade that continued the struggle east of the Mississippi River. There it became one of the Confederacy's best combat units, although a "foreign legion" destined never to return to their home state. All too many of these young soldiers are buried in unmarked graves east of the Mississippi.

The 1st Missouri Infantry, known as the "Camp Jackson Regiment," contained the St. Louis Grays (Company D) with a large number of Irish from that city, and there were a good many sons of Erin in Companies F and H as well. The Suchet Guards (Company A) was actually a company of Louisiana Irish transferred to the Missouri regiment, a company in exile within a regiment in exile. Irish recruits from Memphis bolstered the ranks of Company C. Colonel Amos C. Riley, a young Missouri planter and graduate of the Kentucky Military Institute, commanded the regiment. Junior officers included former bookkeeper Martin Burke and Joseph Boyce, both of the St. Louis Grays. Boyce would become the historian of the Missouri brigade.

BATTLE OF PEA RIDGE, MARCH 8, 1862. **The Missouri State Guard rallies around Sterling Price near Elkhorn Tavern, site of the battle of Pea Ridge in northwestern Arkansas, shortly before being routed by the Federals. Henry Guibor's largely Irish battery from St. Louis is shown in action to the right. The Rebel defeat at Pea Ridge lost Missouri for the Confederacy.** (*Battles and Leaders of the Civil War,* **1887**)

Colonel James C. McCown, whose parents had immigrated from Ireland to Virginia, commanded the 5th Missouri Infantry. A prominent farmer and politician in Francis Cockrell's home community of Warrensburg, Missouri, the 45-year-old McCown had made his pro-secession feelings known early. Before the war, McCown's son had killed a pro–Union man in a fight, and in March 1861 Cockrell had to defend both McCowns from a pro–Union lynch mob. Even while McCown was serving in the Confederate army, Unionists back in his home state didn't forget his sympathies. In March 1862, in an act that was all too typical in the brutality of Missouri's civil war, the Federals burned his home, depriving his wife and children of a place to stay in the cold of winter.

McCown's 5th Missouri was also home to the "Fighting Irish Company" (Company F) led by Captain Patrick Canniff, a 24-year-old saddle maker from Ireland whom Cockrell called "a fearless and skillful officer." Noted for his distinctive Irish brogue and mane of long auburn hair, Canniff had served in the volunteer militia in St. Louis and had seen combat with the Missouri State Guard at Wilson's Creek and at Pea Ridge. The "Fighting Irish" often advanced in front of the brigade as skirmishers, almost always in the hottest of the action. Although consistently suffering high casualties, they continued to serve as skirmishers, the best in the Missouri brigade. One officer called them "the best soldiers on duty and the worst off, the best fighters and the most troublesome men in the army." They were just as likely to be found roaring drunk on Saturday night or devoutly attending religious services on Sunday morning. The 5th Missouri contained a large number of Irish in Companies E and H as well.

BRIGADIER GENERAL BEN MCCULLOCH. A former Texas Ranger and soldier—and a great-grandson of Irish immigrants—this veteran officer of the Lone Star State was killed at Pea Ridge. (Library of Congress)

Unlike other skirmisher companies, the "Fighting Irish" used whistles as a signal instead of bugles. This innovation was the idea of Martin Burke of the 1st Missouri, and it allowed the Irish skirmishers to distinguish themselves from the skirmishers of the enemy. The "Fighting Irish" were well drilled, fearless of danger, and always dependable in a pinch.[6]

Company F also boasted dependable NCOs like Sergeant Thomas Hogan and Color Sergeant William W. Walsh. Hogan had come to America with his family to escape the potato famine in Ireland. In St. Louis, the Hogans struggled to make a place for themselves in this new country. Through hard work Thomas, the oldest son, and his father were able to provide a good life for their large family. When the war broke out, Thomas was working alongside his father as a clerk in a St. Louis general store. Walsh was a 28-year-old Irish immigrant who dabbled in poetry, some of which had been published in St. Louis newspapers, when his merchant business in St. Louis permitted.[7]

Captain Henry Guibor's battery provided artillery support for the Missouri brigade and saw action at Wilson's Creek and Pea Ridge. Some 50 or so Irish names, many of them from the rough streets of St. Louis, graced the company's roster. Major General John S. Bowen, their division commander, called it "the best volunteer company of artillery in this country." Another dependable artillery company serving with the Missouri brigade was William Wade's 1st Missouri Light Artillery, mostly Irish, veterans of combat at Pea Ridge, Farmington, Iuka, and Corinth. Bowen called Wade, killed in action at Grand Gulf in April 1863, "one of the bravest and best of my command." Wade was succeeded by Irish-born Lieutenant Richard C. Walsh.[8]

Combat in Mississippi—especially the bloody engagement at Corinth in October 1862, where Canniff's Irish company lost over 70 percent of its men—exacted a deadly toll on the Missouri brigade. Still General Joseph E. Johnston praised the courage and steadiness of these veteran troops, noting that he had "never [seen] better discipline, or men march more regularly." And a newspaperman wrote, "These veteran soldiers never falter in battle. They are never whipped!"[9]

The Missouri brigade saw some very rough service in the 1863 campaign in Mississippi, as Lieutenant General John C. Pemberton, the Confederate commander at Vicksburg, opposed Major General Ulysses S. Grant, the Federal victor at Shiloh. In a brilliant campaign of maneuver, Grant out-generaled and out-gunned Pemberton in his campaign to take the Mississippi's last Rebel post at Vicksburg. The Confederates made a valiant effort to stop the bluecoats.

On May 12, James B. McPherson's Federal corps ran headlong into a stubborn little Rebel brigade holding the town of Raymond, 15 miles southwest of Jackson, the Mississippi state capital. Brigadier General John Gregg put up quite a fight before breaking off the encounter and withdrawing to Jackson.

Gregg's command contained the 10th Tennessee Infantry, the "Sons of Erin," led by Colonel Randal W. McGavock. The young red-haired mayor of Nashville, "Randy Mack" had organized the Sons of Erin from the rough-hewn Irish of that area. The unit's green flag bore a gold harp and the inscriptions "Sons of Erin" and "Where Glory Waits You." Most of the 10th Tennessee's companies hailed from Nashville's Irish community, plus three Irish companies from railroad towns like McEwen (known as "Little Ireland"), Clarksville, and Pulaski. Probably the best company in the regiment was Company A, a solidly Irish company from McEwen led by 22-year-old Captain John G. ("Gentleman Johnny") O'Neill.

Fighting in the heavily wooded country south of Raymond, the Sons of Erin made a dogged stand against incredible odds. While urging his men on in this engagement, Colonel McGavock was killed, and a half dozen of the 10th Tennessee's officers were cut down as well. Lieutenant Colonel William ("Battling Billy") Grace took command of the Sons of Erin, and Major John G. O'Neill's company of sharpshooters laid down covering fire to aid in the brigade's withdrawal. The 10th Tennessee lost 8 men killed, 37 wounded, and 7 captured or missing.[10]

McGavock died in the arms of a young lieutenant, Pat Griffin, who had enlisted as an underage drummer boy in Randy Mack's original company in Nashville. Born in Galway, Pat had come to America with his parents. When the war broke out, he was working as a timekeeper with the Southeastern Railroad in Nashville, the same firm where his father had worked. Pat was wounded twice in the war and eventually became captain of the company.

When Griffin saw that McGavock had been hit in the chest, he caught him and lowered him to the ground. "Griffin," Randy Mack gasped, "take care of me!" But nothing could be done. McGavock died in five minutes. Griffin had idolized McGavock—"God's own gentleman," he called him—and now he determined to bury the colonel in Raymond. But before Griffin and his small detachment of the 10th Tennessee reached the town, they were overtaken by the bluecoats.

Griffin's two litter bearers were all for dropping the body and running. "Damn it, boys," Pat stormed, "die by your colonel!" Finally he told them to go on while he remained to be taken prisoner by the Federals. An enemy officer, also an Irishman, allowed Griffin to give McGavock a proper burial, and Pat later wrote, "I am convinced that if ever there was a good Yankee he must have been Irish." On his way north to a Federal prison, Pat was able to make his escape when his naval transport was stopped at Memphis. Griffin got out through the boat's wheelhouse and swam the river to shore.[11]

Following the Rebel defeat at Raymond, Grant went on to take Jackson on May 14. Next he turned on Pemberton's 22,000-man army about halfway between Jackson and

Vicksburg. Pemberton's three divisions had taken up a strong defensive position at Champion's Hill, in the bend of Baker's Creek, and when Grant's two corps—32,000 soldiers—attacked on May 16, 1863, one of the most critical engagements of the war unfolded, one in which the Irish soldiers of the Missouri brigade would play a key role.

The day was sweltering hot, the woods and fields wet from rain on the previous evening. At first the Rebels seemed to be holding their own, but by 1 p.m. Federal troops from Alvin P. Hovey's division began to drive back the thin line of graycoats from Carter L. Stevenson's division holding Champion's Hill. Major General John S. Bowen's division—with Cockrell's Missouri brigade on the left and Martin Green's Arkansas brigade on the right—rushed to counter-attack.

Early in the day, the Rebels had formed a five-company battalion of skirmishers under Lieutenant Colonel F. L. Hubbell (who was mortally wounded in the fighting), including Patrick Canniff's "Fighting Irish Company" from the 5th Missouri and Captain Martin Burke's St. Louis Grays from the 1st Missouri. The skirmishers had stayed busy all day, and now they were called back to the brigade to take part in the attack. Rushing back to their lines, they passed by a house where a group of women began singing "Dixie," and Canniff's Irishmen responded with the Rebel yell.

CAPTAIN PAT GRIFFIN, 10TH TENNESSEE INFANTRY. Irish immigrant Pat Griffin enlisted in the Sons of Erin as an underage drummer boy. It was he who cradled the dying Colonel Randal McGavock in his arms at Raymond, Mississippi, in May 1863. (*Confederate Veteran*, 1905)

With the skirmisher battalion adding badly needed weight to the Rebel assault, Bowen counterattacked, and after half an hour of savage, close-in fighting, the graycoats had retaken Champion's Hill. Private Patrick Monahan, one of Canniff's boys, stole up behind a squad of Yankees posted behind a log, pounced on the unsuspecting bluecoats with a mighty roar, and dispatched them one by one, swinging his rifle like a club, waging his own private vendetta against the bluecoats whom he blamed for the wrongs done to the St. Louis Irish.

The Rebels had not long to enjoy their triumph, however, as Federal reinforcements finally surged in. The Missouri brigade plunged down the hill in a furious attempt to repel the bluecoats. Riley's 1st Missouri and McCown's 5th Missouri literally hurled themselves at the Yankees with all their might and actually came near to

SAVAGE COMBAT AT CHAMPION'S HILL SEALS THE FATE OF VICKSBURG. Desperate fighting by Irish-American units in the Missouri brigade, at the cost of a third of its numbers in casualties, failed to save the Confederate army in Mississippi, which was bottled up in Vicksburg by mid–May 1863. (Library of Congress)

breaking the Federal assault. The Missouri soldiers used up all of their 40 rounds of ammunition, then they rummaged through cartridge boxes and haversacks of the dead and wounded to retrieve more and continued firing. But when Federal artillery unleashed a devastating volley into the flanks of the Missouri brigade, this brought the Rebel assault to a halt.

After fighting continuously for more than two hours, the exhausted Missourians were finally played out. The Rebels' left flank was shattered, and Bowen was forced to pull back. Cockrell's troops got out the best way they could, with the batteries of Henry Guibor, Richard Walsh, and John Landis providing covering fire to delay the bluecoats long enough for their Missouri comrades to break free.[12]

Pemberton managed to withdraw his army and retreat to Vicksburg. In the end, even Grant conceded that Baker's Creek was "a hard-contested battle." It had cost the Missouri brigade a third of its soldiers. Colonel Amos Riley's 1st Missouri lost 29 killed, 94 wounded, and 52 missing. Colonel James McCown's 5th Missouri lost 4 killed, 49 wounded, and 37 missing.[13]

Grant's next objective was the capture of Vicksburg itself, where Pemberton's army was bottled up. The bluecoats tried two direct assaults on Vicksburg, May 19 and May 22, but both failed to break through, and the Missouri brigade played a big part in checking them. So did a stubborn little band of graycoats from Thomas N. Waul's Texas Legion. When the Federals seized part of the Rebel works and planted their colors on the parapet, 20 volunteers from Captain L. D. Bradley's Company B (containing a large

CHAMPION'S HILL
May 16, 1863

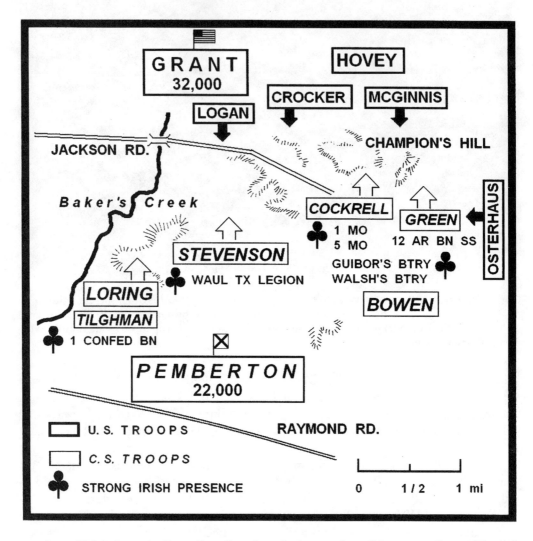

number of Irish from the Lone Star State), and 15 more from Lieutenant James Hogue's Company C launched a furious counterattack and drove the Yanks out. "A more gallant feat than this has not illustrated our annals during the war," Confederate Major General Carter L. Stevenson wrote.[14]

So Grant settled down for a siege. Throughout the siege, regiments of the Missouri brigade dashed from point to point trying to shore up the Rebel defenses. As the siege passed by slowly, the monotony of the hot steamy days punctuated by sniper fire and artillery bombardment, the Missouri Irish attended St. Paul's Church, where Father John Bannon, their old priest from St. Louis, held Mass. Bannon was a frequent visitor at Captain Canniff's tent, where he listened to confessions, gave communion, and provided comfort to the men.[15]

The Federals tried everything in their bag of tricks to break through the Rebel lines. On June 26, they blew up a mine that they had tunneled under the redan north of the Jackson road. The explosion left a crater twenty feet deep and recalls the more famous "Battle of the Crater" during the siege of Petersburg, Virginia, a year later. The 6th Missouri and 5th Missouri rushed in to seal the breach. Once more there was vicious fighting and an all too familiar case of Irishmen against Irishmen as Pat Canniff's company fought against St. Louis Irish in the Federal 7th Missouri whom they hated and considered "renegades."[16]

During the siege, the Missouri brigade lost another third of its men, over 60 percent in the entire Vicksburg campaign. At Vicksburg the 1st Missouri lost another 18 killed and 70 wounded, while the 5th Missouri lost 20 killed and 52 wounded. In the end, it was starvation and exhaustion as much as another anticipated Federal assault that finally led Pemberton to agree to lay down arms. "If I had 10,000 more Missourians," the Rebel commander declared, "I would have won and carried the war." By the end of the summer the Missourians were exchanged. The newly reorganized Missouri brigade would take an active part in the fighting in Georgia the following year.[17]

18. West of the Sabine:
The Irish in Texas

Even as far away as the distant Texas frontier, Irish immigrants made homes for themselves, fleeing the harsh economic conditions and repressive political environment of the Emerald Isle. By 1830, the government of Mexico had granted a tract of land north of Copano Bay to Irish *empressarios* James Power and James Heweston, who settled many of their countrymen in present-day Refugio, Texas. Just to the south near Corpus Christi Bay, John McMullen and James McGloin established a second Irish colony in San Patricio. In the early 1830s, a Scotch-Irish settlement of staunch Presbyterians called "Little Ulster" grew up at Staggers Point in Brazos County. By the 1840s, a sizeable community of Irish immigrants had settled in the "Irish Flats" area of San Antonio.

By 1860, the earlier Irish enclaves in Refugio and San Patricio had been outstripped by larger, expanding Irish communities in Galveston and Houston, as well as San Antonio, Beaumont, and Corpus Christi's "Irishtown." The Irish population in Texas grew from 1,403 to 3,480 between 1850 and 1860. Not surprisingly, Irish Texans gave the same enthusiastic support to the Confederacy as their fellow immigrants in other Southern states. The Texas Ordinance of Secession in 1861 contained the signatures of 18 Irish settlers, and the names of many Irish members appeared on the rolls of volunteer militia companies like Galveston's Wigfall Guards and San Antonio's Alamo City Guards, a unit that took part in the Rebel seizure of the federal arsenal in that city on February 18, 1861. The scattered, violent clashes between Rebel and Union forces in this vast Trans-Mississippi area would extend from the Red River to the remote New Mexico Territory and as far south as the Rio Grande.[1]

In a hard-fought campaign ultimately intended to secure Confederate control of California, Brigadier General Henry Hopkins Sibley's 3,500-man Texas army invaded New Mexico in February 1862. Sibley scored a victory over the mostly-untrained Federal troops led by Colonel Edward R. S. Canby at Valverde on February 21, then the Texans went on to occupy Santa Fe and Albuquerque. But this encouraging beginning for Southern arms was short-lived. Reinforced by 900 Colorado volunteers, Canby defeated Sibley's army, under the field command of Colonel William R. Scurry, at Glorietta Pass (the "Gettysburg of the West"), 30 miles southeast of Santa Fe, on March 28. Canby smashed Sibley again at Peralta, 20 miles south of Albuquerque, on April 15.

Crippled now by manpower shortages and a lack of food and supplies, Sibley's ragged, hungry troops withdrew to Fort Bliss. The New Mexico campaign, largely overlooked today but momentous in the war's course in the Trans-Mississippi, was over.

Cavalry was the dominant branch of arms in the Lone Star State, and in the Texas mounted commands raised at the beginning of the war, more than a few of these hard riding, hard fighting, shotgun-toting troopers hailed from the Emerald Isle or boasted Irish heritage. While there were no "green flag" units with distinctive Irish names like those found in the Army of Northern Virginia and the Army of Tennessee, there still were enough Irish soldiers to provide a significant Gaelic presence. Many of them were veteran Texas Rangers with years of experience in frontier warfare against Mexicans and Native Americans.

Lieutenant Colonel John R. Baylor's 2nd Texas Mounted Rifles (one soldier quipped that they should have been called "Texas Mounted Shot Guns") formed in May 1861 (later to become the 2nd Texas Cavalry Regiment) established a Confederate military presence in New Mexico before the arrival of Sibley's army. There was no outwardly Irish company in this regiment, but half of the companies in the regiment contained 15 or more Irish names on the rolls. One of these, Company A led by Captain Peter Hardeman, was among the troops mentioned by Colonel Scurry as "in the last brilliant and successful charge, which decided the fortunes of the day" at Valverde.[2]

Colonel James Reily commanded the 4th Texas Mounted Volunteers (later 4th Texas Cavalry) in the New Mexico campaign. A 51-year-old Houston politician, Reily was an officer in the prestigious Milam Guards volunteer militia company, a veteran of the Mexican War, and a former diplomat for the Republic of Texas. A gifted speaker, Reily had also served as U. S. consul to Russia, and while the 4th Texas was fighting in New Mexico he was in Mexico on a diplomatic mission for the Confederacy. His attempt to win support for the Confederacy from Mexico was unsuccessful. Reily returned to lead his regiment, and he was killed in action at Franklin, Louisiana, on April 14, 1863, during the Bayou Teche campaign. Major General Richard Taylor called him "a gallant and chivalrous soldier, whose loss I deeply regret."[3]

Lieutenant Colonel William R. ("Dirty Shirt") Scurry held field command of the 4th Texas in New Mexico while Reily was absent. A brave soldier and a veteran of the Mexican War, he was much admired by his men. The Clinton, Texas, attorney was promoted to brigadier general in September 1862. Among the 4th Texas companies that served under Scurry in New Mexico was Company B, Captain Andrew J. Scarborough's Davis Guards (or Davis Rifles) from DeWitt County, which contained 20 or more Irish names on its rolls. The DeWitt County boys rescued a disabled field piece and hauled it off by hand while under enemy fire at Valverde. In the same engagement, gunners in a battery of Texas artillery commanded by Lieutenant John Reily (Colonel James Reily's son) used the salvaged gun to good advantage against the enemy, and Scurry reported that "this brave little band performed the duty assigned them."[4]

When the Civil War began, Galveston was the largest city in the Lone Star State. Large numbers of Texas Irish hailed from this major seaport, a city with a large immigrant population. The Irish were avid backers of the Confederacy. On April 18, 1861, near Matagorda Bay, Confederate troops on the Rebel naval vessel *General Rusk* (including members of the Wigfall Guards, an Irish volunteer militia company in Galveston led by Captain James McGrath) captured the *Star of the West*, which had already been fired upon by Rebel forces in Charleston on January 9 when it attempted to reinforce Fort Sumter.

Galveston became a major focus of military activity during the war, and U. S. naval operations began in July 1861 as a blockade was established. Federal forces occupied Galveston in late 1862, and Rebel General John B. Magruder was determined to recapture it for the Confederacy. His plan called for William R. Scurry to lead a land assault with veterans of Sibley's New Mexico campaign, supported by two Confederate "cotton-clads"—actually former commercial steamboats, the *Bayou City* and the *Neptune*, reinforced with cotton bales and recently-mounted guns. An array of Rebel land batteries—including largely Irish companies of the Galveston-based 1st Texas Heavy Artillery under Captains Richard Dowling (Company F), O. G. Jones (Company A), J. V. Riley (Company B), Charles M. Mason (Company D), and M. V. McMahan (Company E)—would pound the Federals on Galveston Island with artillery fire.

The Rebel assault began on New Year's Day, 1863. After the land attack by dismounted troopers of James Reily's 4th Texas Cavalry was stalled by Federal naval fire, the two Confederate "cotton-clads" headed out toward the U. S. ships in Galveston Bay. Enemy fire soon sank the *Neptune* and knocked out the *Bayou City's* gun. But the pilot of the latter craft, Irish-born Michael McCormick, steamed straight for the Federal gunboat *Harriet Lane*, and—under punishing enemy fire—rammed the vessel. A boarding party of "horse marines" from Sibley's expedition armed with shotguns and cutlasses then stormed onto the *Harriet Lane* and captured it. The remaining Union gunboats withdrew. Without the firepower of the supporting naval vessels, the Federal garrison in Galveston raised the white flag. The Rebels retained control of Galveston for the rest of the war, although Federal ships still kept the city under blockade.[5]

Besides splitting the South and depriving the eastern Confederates of badly needed supplies from west of the Mississippi, the July 4, 1863, fall of Vicksburg—and of Port Hudson five days later—opened the door for more aggressive Federal operations west of the river. In September 1863, Union forces captured Little Rock and Fort Smith in Arkansas.

Plans were also in the works for operations against Texas. Major General Nathaniel P. Banks (Stonewall Jackson's hapless opponent in the 1862 Shenandoah Valley campaign in Virginia) was scheduled to lead a Federal expedition against Shreveport, Louisiana, considered a springboard for an invasion of the Lone Star State. Banks hoped to avoid the toilsome march up the Red River by making a strike directly at the Texas coast. The target was Sabine Pass at the mouth of the Sabine River, which separated Louisiana and Texas. Once the mouth of the Sabine was secured, the bluecoats would move on Galveston and Houston, which was connected to Sabine Pass by rail. But Banks' plans were ruined by a small company of 43 Irish artillerymen led by a red-headed 26-year-old lieutenant, Richard (Dick) Dowling.

Dowling's company, the Jefferson Davis Guards (Company F of the 1st Texas Heavy Artillery Regiment) was an Irish company recruited in Houston and Galveson. Its soldiers were men like Ohio-born Corporal R. C. O'Hara, the grandson of an Irish immigrant who had fought in the Revolutionary War. A cabinetmaker, O'Hara settled in Houston in 1859. Michael ("Mickie") Carr, born in Ireland, immigrated to America in 1848. The fun-loving Mickie worked on railroads and was fond of poetry and ballads. Lieutenant Dowling, a County Galway native, came to America to escape the famine in 1846, becoming a tavern owner in Houston.

The Davis Guards garrisoned Fort Griffin, an unfinished earthwork that guarded Sabine Pass. The fort had only six cannon: two 32-pounder smooth-bores, two 24-pounder smooth-bores, and two 32-pounder howitzers. Two of the 32-pounders were barely fit to use and had recently been repaired in Houston. The range of the guns was short, their ammunition low. The Davis Guards were hardly prepared to hold a Federal invasion fleet at bay.

The Federal armada that came sailing into the mouth of the Sabine on the morning of September 8, 1863, was impressive—22 transports carrying 5,000 troops, escorted by 4 naval gunboats. Captain Frederick Odlum, the Davis Guards' commander, felt it would be best to spike the fort's guns and withdraw to the little town of Sabine Pass about a mile and a half above the fort. But when Lieutenant Dowling relayed the order, the men urged him to let them stay. Dowling sent a message back to Odlum: "The men are refusing to leave the fort. What shall I do?" Odlum finally agreed to mount a defense. The little fort didn't even have a Confederate flag. A courier brought in a small one that the men could fly over the works. Dowling declared, "Dick Dowling is a dead man before that flag shall come down!"

At 6:30 a.m., the Federal gunboat *Clifton* opened fire on Fort Griffin. The *Clifton* fired 26 shells at the fort. Most either fell short or overshot the fort, but enough of them hit their mark, and since the *Clifton* was out of range of the fort's guns, all the Rebel gunners could do was to lay low. Occasionally one of them would take a shovel and clear off the sand that exploding shells had thrown up around the guns.

By 11 a.m., a Rebel gunboat, the *Uncle Ben*, made its appearance, steaming downstream toward the fort. The Federal gunboat *Sachem* opened fire, its 30-pounder Parrott gun firing three shots that missed the *Ben*. The Federal fleet drew off out of range. By 3:40 p.m., the *Sachem* and *Arizona* began moving ominously up the Louisiana channel of Sabine Pass. When they were within 1,200 yards of the fort, Dowling gave the order to open fire with everything they had. One of the fort's guns ran off its platform on its second recoil, rendering it useless.

Through a combination of good gunnery and good luck, Dowling's men managed to disable two of the gunboats. One of the garrison's shots—Dowling credited it to expert gunner Private Michael McKernan—struck the *Sachem*'s boiler which exploded, killing and wounding many of the crew, and the bluejackets ran up the white flag. A shot to the *Clifton*, entering the Texas channel, tore away her tiller rope, causing the gunboat to go aground 500 yards from the fort. Dowling trained all of his guns on the *Clifton*, pounding the craft for half an hour. The Davis Guards used up nearly all of the fort's ammunition.

The Yankees fired back, unleashing grape-shot and musket fire at the fort. Then the white flag went up. The third Yankee gunboat, the *Arizona*, also ran aground.

The remaining gunboat, the *Granite City*, and the Federal transports were stymied outside of the mouth of the Sabine. With three of his gunboats out of commission and his troops unable to land, the Federal commander, General William B. Franklin, felt that he had no choice but to abandon the operation. "The enemy's battery," he wrote, "commanded the whole landing, and he could, with his battery and gunboats, have destroyed us at any time."

Dowling boarded the *Clifton* and inspected the boat's magazines, which he found well stocked and secure. Not having any small boats to board the *Sachem*, Dowling left that task to the crew of the *Uncle Ben* who towed the gunboat away. The Confederates took about 350 prisoners in the brief engagement. There were no casualties among the Davis Guards. "All my men behaved like heroes," Dowling reported, "not a man flinched from his post. Our motto was 'victory or death.'"

Lieutenant Henry C. Dane of the *Sachem* expressed surprise on meeting Dowling, "a modest, retiring, boyish-looking Irish lad." "And do you realize what you have done, sir?" he stammered, "you and your forty-three men in your miserable mud fort in the rushes have captured two Yankee gunboats carrying fourteen guns, a good number of prisoners, many stands of small arms, and plenty of ammunition—and all that you have done with six popguns."[6]

News of the victory at Sabine Pass was a breath of fresh air to a Confederacy that had seen all too many disasters in the summer of 1863. Magruder called it "the most extraordinary feat of the war." And a resolution by the Confederate Congress expressed "gratitude and admiration" to the Davis Guards for "one of the most brilliant and heroic achievements in the history of this war." Dowling's successful action at Sabine Pass prevented the Federals from occupying east Texas. The Rebels continued to hold Fort Griffin until the end of the war.[7]

By March 1864, General Nathaniel Banks was at last ready to launch the long-planned Federal invasion of Texas by way of the Red River. Banks' 30,000-man army made its way toward Shreveport, the Confederate capital of Louisiana, while a flotilla of 12 Federal gunboats steamed upriver to provide support. On April 8, 35 miles southwest of Shreveport, Rebel forces under Richard Taylor (although outnumbered two to one) defeated Banks at Mansfield (or Sabine Cross Roads). Elements of Thomas Green's Texas cavalry led by Brigadier General Hamilton Bee, with the 1st Texas Cavalry on the extreme right, played an important role in attacking and routing the Federal left.

Formed on the Rio Grande in May 1863 to protect the cotton trade and to defend the southern border against enemy invasion, the 1st Texas Cavalry Regiment included Company F, Captain James A. Ware's Partisan Rangers from San Patricio County. "Ware's Tigers," as the men were sometimes known, carried at least 25 Irish names on roll and included men who worked in the south Texas cattle business: 23-year-old Corporal Alden McLaughlin, a stock raiser from Corpus Christi, whose wife Marie sewed the company's flag; 2nd Lieutenant Patrick F. Murphy; and Sergeants Patrick Burke and John Mahoney, both stock raisers. Irish immigrants Lawrence Dunn and Patrick McMurray, as well as the Gallaher brothers (Barnard, Michael, and Thomas) also worked in the cattle business. James Fields and John Harding were former sailors, both born in the Emerald Isle. Corporal Thomas Brady, a fellow Irish immigrant, was a brick mason. "Ware's Tigers" were described by Major A. M. Hobby at Corpus Christi in 1862 as a "fine cavalry company ... present and eager for the fray."[8]

"Ware's Tigers" had seen their share of fighting before the beginning of the Red River campaign. They had shown their mettle in a skirmish in San Patricio County on March 13, 1864, when a 62-man Texas force led by Major Matthew Nolan came across a larger (125-man) force of enemy cavalry camped in a dense mesquite area. Nolan's detachment, which included Ware's company, attacked and in a skirmish that lasted fifteen minutes—but according to Nolan was "well-contested" and "a desperate fight"— the rebel force completely routed the bluecoats. Ware "acted with conspicuous gallantry," in this engagement, and his "men behaved coolly and bravely."[9]

Although there was no conspicuously Irish company on the field at Mansfield on

April 8, 1864, the Gaelic presence was also felt in companies A and C of the 1st Texas Cavalry, each of which carried at least 15 Irish names on roll. Captain Bartholomew Donnelly, a 64-yr-old Irish immigrant from Lawrence, Kansas, commanded Company C. (The regiment also contained a German company, and Colonel August Buchel, the commander of the 1st Texas, was a veteran of the Prussian army.) In Colonel Xavier B. Debray's 26th Texas Cavalry, a command with an excellent reputation for discipline, three companies (C, G, and K) had at least 15–20 Irish names on roll. Captain M. V. McMahan's Texas artillery battery, with 25 or so Irish names on roll, was the only Rebel artillery unit in action at Mansfield, and Taylor said that it "rendered excellent service." Not so fortunate was Captain William Edgar's largely Irish battery (the former Alamo City Guards) from San Antonio which had been overrun and captured by the Federals just two weeks earlier.[10]

Although a Confederate victory, Mansfield was a costly triumph. Leading a Texas cavalry brigade on the left flank of Taylor's army, Irish-born veteran soldier Walter Paye Lane was seriously wounded. Colonel George W. Baylor, in temporary command of Lane's brigade, praised the Irishman, saying, "we wish for no braver or more experienced officer to command us." In March 1865, Lane would be commissioned brigadier general, one of five Irish-born officers to achieve this rank in the Confederate army.[11]

Also among the badly wounded Rebel soldiers was 21-year-old Captain Leander H. McNelly, chief of a scout company of Texas Rangers. The son of Irish immigrants, McNelly was a veteran of Sibley's New Mexico campaign, where he was commended for gallantry at Valverde, and he also fought in the 1863 battle of Galveston. His most famous exploit took place on June 23, 1863, when a detachment of 15 to 20 of his scouts surprised and captured the Federal garrison at Brashear City, Louisiana, bagging 380 Yankee soldiers. Recovering from his wound at Mansfield, McNelly returned to duty in May and continued to scout and annoy the Federals in southern Louisiana. After the war he resumed his service in the Texas Rangers.

After the rout of his army at Mansfield, Banks fell back to Pleasant Hill, 14 miles to the south, and fought a holding action against the Rebels the next day. Taylor attacked, and Thomas Churchill's Missouri-Arkansas division hit the Federal left, making quick progress as they overran the bluecoats and pushed on to General Andrew J. Smith's corps that held the Union center. John Walker's Texas division, with veteran officer William R. Scurry now a brigadier general (Three weeks later he would be killed in action at Jenkins Ferry, Arkansas), struck the center along the Mansfield Road. In a particularly bloody phase of the battle, Hamilton Bee's cavalry attacked on the left, in an effort to turn Banks' right. "From one single volley," a soldier in the 1st Texas wrote, "one half of our men fell." Colonel Buchel became one of the 2,600 Rebel casualties in these two costly days of fighting, and the old Prussian died three days later.[12]

The decisive point of the day was reached when Smith's troops launched a furious counter-attack and drove Churchill's men back in confusion. Banks' army was saved, and the Federals—only too lucky to evacuate the gunboats that were nearly marooned by falling water levels in the Red River—abandoned the campaign. The Rebels had thwarted the Federal invasion, regarded as one of the most ill-conceived of the war, but at a high price in human lives.

With the collapse of the Federals' Red River offensive, the focus of military activity in the Trans-Mississippi shifted much farther south. The Rio Grande frontier was important to both sides, even late in the war, because it remained the only open door to outside aid for the Confederacy. Supposedly neutral, the Mexican port of Matamoros, across the river from Brownsville, witnessed tons of war supplies being unloaded from European ships—all on their way to the Confederacy. U. S. and Confederate relations with Mexico were complicated by the brutal civil war raging there between the French army backing Emperor Maximilian on the one hand and the forces of Mexican president Benito Juarez on the other. Balancing the problems of dealing with rival political factions in Mexico, keeping the flow of goods to the Confederacy open, defending the area from Federal invasion, and fending off raids by armed bands of renegade Mexicans and Native Americans called for someone particularly savvy in frontier warfare and in possession of astute military and diplomatic skills. Texas found such an officer in Colonel John Salmon ("Rip") Ford, a highly seasoned Texas Ranger commander whose nickname came from his practice of writing, "May his soul rest in peace (later shortened to R. I. P)" on the death notices of his Rangers killed in action. Ford was also a distant kinsman to the O'Neal clan of Ireland.

CAPTAIN LEANDER H. MCNELLY, TEXAS RANGER SCOUT. McNelly served with distinction in New Mexico and in the Red River campaign. After the war, his hard-hitting Rangers sometimes crossed the Rio Grande into Mexico to bring lawbreakers to justice. Tuberculosis ended McNelly's action-filled career in 1877. (Courtesy of the Texas Ranger Hall of Fame and Museum, Waco, TX.)

To defend Texas' southern frontier, Ford raised the Rio Grande Regiment, which included a largely Irish company from San Patricio County under Captain William H. Redwood, in February 1861 and immediately struck south to capture the Federal post at Brazos Santiago Island, which guarded the strategic mouth of the Rio Grande. Soon afterwards, he secured the surrender of every Federal outpost on the Rio Grande from Brownsville to El Paso. Ford's regiment later became the nucleus for the 2nd Texas Mounted Rifles, formed in May 1861.[13]

Surprisingly, Ford was relieved in the fall of 1861 and was reassigned as chief of the Texas Conscript Bureau. Command of the 2nd Texas Mounted Rifles fell to Ford's second-in-

CLIMAX OF THE RED RIVER OFFENSIVE. BATTLE OF PLEASANT HILL, LOUISIANA, MAY 1864. A scattering of Irish Texas horsemen and gunners were engaged in this hardfought action in which Nathaniel Banks' retreating Federal army managed to stave off destruction by Richard Taylor's Confederates. The Federals' plans to seize Shreveport were effectively thwarted. (Library of Congress)

command, Lieutenant Colonel John R. Baylor, who led the regiment in Sibley's failed New Mexico offensive in the spring of 1862. Following the debilitating campaign, the 2nd Texas was reorganized as the 2nd Texas Cavalry Regiment under Colonel Charles L. Pyron, and saw action in the defense of Galveston. One of several companies in the 2nd Texas to contain a significant number of Irish names was Company G, a Corpus Christi outfit led by Captain Matt Nolan.

An Irish orphan born in 1833, Nolan arrived in Corpus Christi with his younger brother Tom and older sister Mary in 1845. When he was only 13 years old, he enlisted as a bugler in the 2nd U. S. Dragoons during the Mexican War. Later he served in the

Texas Rangers under Rip Ford and was elected sheriff of Nueces County. When Ford raised the Rio Grande Regiment early in 1861, Nolan joined him, bringing a volunteer company he recruited in Corpus Christi. Although Nolan's company disbanded in the fall of 1861, many of its members re-enlisted and served under Nolan in Company G, 2nd Texas Cavalry. Nolan's company was among the Rebel "horse marines" who boarded and seized the Federal gunboat *Harriet Lane* at Galveston on January 1, 1863. Promoted to major early in 1864, Nolan led his company in periodic skirmishes and raids around Federal-occupied Corpus Christi. Although still a Confederate officer, Nolan won re-election as sheriff of Nueces County in August 1864. Near the end of December, he was gunned down by the stepsons of a Federal collaborator. Only 31 years old, he died with eight shotgun slugs in his side.

Frustrated in his attempts to invade Texas at Sabine Pass, General Nathaniel P. Banks had sent a 6,000-man Union force to seize Brazos Santiago in November 1863. Encountering no resistance from outnumbered Rebel troops, the Federals went on to occupy Corpus Christi, Brownsville, and other posts westward along the Rio Grande. They stopped the flow of supplies into Texas directly from Matamoros, but the Rebels diverted it farther upriver to areas outside Union control. In December 1863, Rip Ford was recalled to organize another Rebel cavalry force to re-conquer the Rio Grande valley. Meanwhile, with Banks' attention diverted by the opening of the Red River campaign, Federal troops withdrew to Brazos Santiago and Brownsville.

Rip Ford launched his counter-offensive to retake the Rio Grande Valley in March 1864. The previous month he had organized the Cavalry of the West (or Rio Grande Expeditionary Force), a cavalry brigade composed of assorted Texans, Tejanos, Arizonans, and Mexicans, many of them either too old or too young for service in Confederate units. Among the commands were Matt Nolan's company from Corpus Christi and units from San Patricio under Captain James A. Ware and Captain James Dunn. Lieutenant Colonel George H. Giddings' small Texas Cavalry Battalion contained at least 50 Irish names, and Captain O. G. Jones' 6-gun battery of artillery (the Dixie Grays from Galveston, formerly Co. A, 1st Texas Heavy Artillery) had 30 or so Irish names on roll.

Ford's horsemen left San Antonio in March 1864 and proceeded to Corpus Christi and westward to Laredo. In June, Ford's troops forced the withdrawal of all Federal troops from Laredo to Brownsville. During one skirmish, Captain James Dunn was killed while leading a cavalry charge. The Federals eventually pulled back to Brazos Santiago, and Ford occupied Brownsville. By the end of September 1864, the Federal threat seemed to be over, and Ford's command dwindled down to six companies of Giddings' battalion and a few other mounted companies at scattered outposts around Brownsville.[14]

With Robert E. Lee's Army of Northern Virginia worn down by attrition in the siege of Petersburg, Virginia, and Joseph E. Johnston's Army of Tennessee on the verge of collapse in the Carolinas, military operations in the war appeared to be winding down in early 1865. Federal and Rebel military commanders on the Rio Grande struck an informal truce in March 1865. In early May, news of Lee's surrender finally reached the isolated Rebel stations in south Texas. Soldiers of Giddings' Texas cavalry battalion (Captain William N. Robinson temporarily in command) posted near Ford's outpost at Palmito Ranch learned of the surrender from a copy of the *New Orleans Times* delivered by a steamboat making its way up the Rio Grande to Brownsville.

The last battle of the war was fought near Brownsville at Palmito Ranch on May

12–13, 1865. The Federal commander at Brazos Santiago, Colonel Theodore H. Barrett, broke the cease-fire on May 11, when he sent an expeditionary force of 250 soldiers from the 62nd U. S. Colored Infantry and 50 men from the Federal 2nd Texas Cavalry to attack Rebel outposts as a prelude to an occupation of Brownsville. On May 12, they overran a Confederate camp at Palmito Ranch and skirmished with Captain Robinson's 190-man detachment, which continued fighting guerrilla-style, hitting the bluecoats from cover. Barrett arrived on the morning of May 13 with 200 reinforcements from the 34th Indiana Infantry, skirmished with Rebel detachments (Robinson's men again, fighting Indian-style), destroyed supplies at Palmito Ranch, and withdrew to the Rio Grande to camp for the night. At 4 p.m., Ford attacked with his cavalry (300 more troopers from the 2nd Texas Cavalry, Colonel Santos Benavides' largely Hispanic cavalry regiment, and Giddings' battalion, plus Captain O. G. Jones' battery), and the bluecoats drew up a line of battle.

Rip Ford conducted his attack as if it were the first of the war instead of the last, deploying his artillery to the best advantage, and a skillfully executed mounted charge by the Rebels soon scattered Barrett's infantry. Lieutenant J. Mayrant Smith with a section of Jones' battery launched an aggressive pursuit of the retreating bluecoats, and as they retired to the safety of Brazos Santiago, he personally fired the final defiant artillery shot of the war. Ironically, the last engagement of the Civil War was a Confederate victory. Casualties at Palmito Ranch were probably around 30 killed and wounded for both Rebels and Federals, but more than 100 bluecoats were captured.[15]

Epilogue: "Their Bones Lie on Every Battle-Field"

The Irish in the South felt the sting of defeat more than other Southerners because the impact of slave emancipation hit them the hardest. They now had to contend with their worst fear economically—direct competition from free African Americans for low-paying jobs. Soon the Irish would be supplanted by blacks in unskilled and semi-skilled jobs, and the monopoly that they once had in this type of work would be over. With their economic opportunities curtailed now, every Irish community in the South would experience a drop in population.[1]

New Orleans, the city with the South's largest concentration of Irish, declined as the major transportation center and gateway to the West, being replaced by St. Louis with its access to northern rail lines. There were other obstacles to the growth of Irish communities in the South. Memphis was hit by a catastrophic yellow fever epidemic in the 1870s that claimed over 2,000 Irish lives. And the Irish population in large cities was dropping at the same time that the African-American population was increasing. By 1870 the Irish population in New Orleans had decreased from over 24,000 to less than 15,000, and by 1880 it would be less than 12,000. At the same time the black population in the Crescent City grew from 6,000 to 13,000.[2]

The percentage of immigrants in Southern cities as a whole dropped dramatically in the remaining decades of the nineteenth century—from 8 percent to 1 percent in New Orleans, from 21 percent to 6.3 percent in Savannah, from 13 percent to 3.4 percent in Richmond. By 1890, the Irish population in Arkansas would be 2,021, just 14.1 percent of the state's foreign-born; in 1860 it had amounted to 35 percent. Irish communities in all of these areas would no longer grow, because there no longer would be the pre-war flood of immigrants from the Emerald Isle, even though Irish communities would still exist in larger cities like Richmond, New Orleans, and Memphis. The great Irish immigration to the South was over.[3]

The changing economic and social conditions in Southern cities made for deteriorating relations between Irish and African Americans that led to racial clashes. The nastiest incident was the Memphis race riot of May 1, 1866. The trouble started when black U. S. soldiers celebrating their discharge in South Memphis confronted a group of Irish policemen, with the two sides trading racial insults. What unfolded was three days of bloodletting that left 46 African Americans and 2 whites dead. There were shootings, beatings, and rapes as the white mob, led by Irish policemen and firefighters, burned 89 black homes, 4 black churches, and 12 schoolhouses. Federal soldiers finally restored order.[4]

Meanwhile, the Irish in the South joined with their Northern brethren in a cause dear to all their hearts. It was the same cause that had led Union General Thomas W. Sweeny to contact Pat Cleburne during the war—the goal of an independent Ireland. Even while the Civil War was going on, members of the revolutionary Fenian Brotherhood were actively recruiting followers among both Union and Confederate armies. Irish Americans in Tennessee actually sent delegates to the first Fenian convention in Chicago in 1863, and in 1866 former Nashville resident Thomas J. Kelly became the leader of the Irish Republican Brotherhood in Ireland.[5]

Fenian cells in cities like New Orleans, Savannah, and Charleston were active in raising funds to support a war of independence in Ireland, as well as a scheme to launch a U. S.-based invasion of British Canada. New Orleans' Patrick Condon was a tireless organizer for the Fenian movement and launched similar circles in Montgomery, Mobile, and Brownsville. Condon sold Fenian bonds to help finance the coming military actions. Even though many balked at purchasing *any* bonds—the sour experience of the now worthless Confederate bonds was still fresh in their minds—New Orleans Irish made unselfish contributions. Some 800 members of the Fenian Brotherhood were active in New Orleans alone; their largest cell—the Emmet Circle—had 250 members in the city's heavily Irish third ward. The radicals named one of the Fenian circles in Louisiana after Pat Cleburne, whose name, Patrick Condon remarked, had "a talismanic effect" on Irish Southerners. It would seem that the defeat of the South had not dampened the Irish zeal for rebellion.[6]

Fenian recruits assembled in Memphis in May 1866 for the planned invasion of Canada, orchestrated by Cleburne's old foe General Sweeny. Led by ex–U.S. Army Colonel John O'Neil of Nashville, a 500-man Fenian force crossed the border near Buffalo and seized the Canadian town of Fort Erie, then defeated one of two Canadian militia forces sent against them. But the invasion as a whole collapsed. O'Neill and his men awaited reinforcements that never came. Instead, U. S. forces intervened, sending sailors aboard the steamship *Michigan* to Fort Erie to arrest the Fenian leaders and to confiscate weapons. O'Neill withdrew back across the border and was taken prisoner, but the Irish Fenians in Nashville raised $10,000 to bail him out of jail. Although they carried out two more Fenian raids across the Canadian border in 1866 and in 1870, the conspirators never came this close again. Poor preparations, splits in the movement's leadership, and the activity of British infiltrators doomed the operations, and the illusory dream of an Irish military enclave in Canada faded away like the Celtic mist.

The Irish continued their involvement in Southern military affairs. With the end of Reconstruction, they reorganized many of their old volunteer militia companies like Richmond's Montgomery Guard, Charleston's Irish Volunteers, Nashville's Burns Light Artillery, and the St. Louis Grays. Irish veterans in Alabama helped reorganize the Montgomery Greys and the State Artillery Company (Garrity's battery) of Mobile, where John Maguire, a member of the wartime company, became the first post-war captain. The Savannah Irish reorganized the Irish Jasper Greens, led by former wartime officer John Flannery, who became a prominent banker and cotton merchant. These military organizations continued to play an important role in the social life of Southern cities and did their patriotic part in the Spanish American War of 1898.

Irish social and political leaders continued to contribute to American and Southern life. Newspaperman Henry Grady of Atlanta became a spokesman for the "New

South," promoting reforms in agriculture—crop diversification—and the development of Southern industry. In fact, even though the percentage of Irish-born was decreasing in the South, the participation of second-generation Irish Americans in public affairs was growing as the Irish assimilated into the Southern mainstream.

Because they concentrated in Southern cities, the Irish had a profound impact on urban institutions, and in the larger cities they remained a major part of urban life. John P. Grace became mayor of Charleston in 1911, running on a platform of municipal reform. Andrew J. McShane became mayor of New Orleans. During the Populist movement in 1894, Socialist reformer Dan Hogan sought the governor's office in Arkansas. Irish pride is still strong in New Orleans, with its preservation of the Irish Channel neighborhood, and in Charleston and Savannah, where the St. Patrick's Day celebration draws thousands every year.

The silver lining in the plight of Irish Confederates after the war may have been that it helped to nudge them more into the American mainstream. As African Americans took over the menial jobs that Emerald Islanders had dominated before the war, Irish Southerners were moved to compete for work that required more skills, forcing more of them to move out of their poverty-ridden urban enclaves into the middle class suburbs, leading them to assimilate into the larger Southern society. Many of them also joined the migration to the western states, the last American frontier, in the late nineteenth century.[7]

But the Irish Confederates remain the neglected warriors of the South. So many of them sacrificed their lives for their adopted country, and so few survived to tell their story. The Memphis Irish 5th Confederate's Captain Charles Wesley Frazer summed up the Irish legacy as well as anyone. "The Irish name," he wrote, "is associated with all that is true to allegiance and gallant in arms, and while no monumental brass commemorates their deeds in the New World, their friends across the Atlantic are assured that the name and fame were upheld by the Fifth Confederate. Their bones lie on every battle-field from Belmont to Bentonville, and at the last roll-call they can proudly answer to their names."[8]

Appendix 1: Irish Commands in the Confederate Army

Service: ANV = Army of Northern Virginia
AT = Army of Tennessee
M = Mississippi
TM = Trans-Mississippi
AC = Atlantic Coast
GC = Gulf Coast

ALABAMA

Eufaula Light Artillery. AT. Although not an Irish command, this company organized in Eufaula (with the third largest Irish population of any Alabama city) contained at least 30 Irish, Scottish, or Scotch-Irish names on roll. One of the Army of Tennessee's most reliable units, the battery saw action at Murfreesboro, Chickamauga, and Nashville. Captains were John W. Clark, W. A. McTyre, McDonald Oliver (killed in the Atlanta campaign), and William J. McKenzie.

Garrity's Battery. AT. This was the pre-war Alabama State Artillery Company, formed in Mobile in 1836. Captain James Garrity, a Mobile merchant who led these gunners throughout most of their service, was wounded at Murfreesboro (where the battery lost 27 men killed and wounded) and during the Atlanta campaign. There were 60 or so Irish names on the roll.

Phelan's Battery. AT. Captain John Phelan's company from Tuscaloosa lost 28 men killed or wounded at Chickamauga. There were at least 30 or so Irish, Scottish, or Scotch-Irish names on the rolls. Phelan was wounded at Resaca.

1st Alabama Artillery Battalion. GC. Company A (recruited in Mobile and Montgomery) had 30 Irish names on roll. Company D (recruited in Macon and Madison Counties) had 25. Most of them were captured at Fort Morgan.

1st Alabama Infantry Regiment. AT. Company D, the Alabama Rifles from Talladega, contained at least 40 Irish or Scotch-Irish names on roll. There also were at least 25 Irish or Scotch-Irish names in Companies A, B, and F.

6th Alabama Infantry Regiment. ANV. The 30 or so Irish names on the roll of Company H (Montgomery Greys) may be the remnant of a disbanded Irish company. After the war, some referred to the Greys as the "Irish Greys," although it was not a majority Irish company. The

Montgomery Greys were the color company of the 6th Alabama. Their commander, Captain John B. McCarthy, was killed at Seven Pines.

8th Alabama Infantry Regiment. ANV. A solidly Irish company recruited in the Gulf City, the Emerald Guards (Company I) was the color company for the 8th Alabama. Company commanders were Patrick Loughry, C. P. Branagan, John McGrath, and Andrew Quinn. There was also a scattering of Irish in Companies C, E, and H from Mobile.

9th Alabama Infantry Regiment. ANV. With 80 Irish names on roll, the Railroad Guards (Company B) hailed from Jackson and Marshall Counties and were largely workers on the Tennessee and Coosa Railroad. Captain Elias Jacobs, whose father was German and mother Irish, was wounded at Gettysburg and was killed in action in August 1864. There were also some 20 Irish names on the rolls of Company A from Mobile and Company K from Marshall County.

21st Alabama Infantry Regiment. GC. The Montgomery Guards (Company B) saw action at Shiloh, but spent most of the war garrisoning the forts on Mobile Bay. Captain John O'Connor commanded this company recruited from middle and working class Irish in Mobile.

24th Alabama Infantry Regiment. AT. Another wholly Irish company from Mobile, the Emmet Guards (Company B) was organized by Bernard O'Connell, a successful builder and a veteran of the Mexican War. Later the company was led by Captain William J. O'Brien, a fine officer killed at Chickamauga. There were 25 or so Irish names in Companies A and H as well, also from Mobile.

1st Confederate Infantry Battalion (Forney's). M, ANV. Company I, from Mobile, was a solidly Irish company, and there was a strong Irish presence in Companies A and C as well. The battalion fought at Champion's Hill, was captured at Vicksburg, was exchanged, and served the rest of the war in Virginia.

ARKANSAS

Helena Artillery. AT. Enlisted mostly in Helena and Memphis, at least 50 or so Irish sons served as gunners in this hard-fighting command, first led by Captain John H. Calvert and later by Captain Thomas J. Key.

1st Arkansas Infantry Regiment (Fagan's). AT. Companies A, D, and F (El Dorado Sentinels, Clan McGregor from Pine Bluff, and Ettomon Guards from Little Rock) each boasted 30 or so Irish names, and there were at least 20 Irish members each in Companies G and H. The 1st Arkansas lost heavily at Shiloh and was consolidated with the 15th Arkansas during the Atlanta campaign.

2nd Arkansas Infantry Regiment (Hindman's / Govan's). AT. There were 50 or so Irish names in Company B from Helena, with a liberal scattering of Irishmen in Companies D, F, G, and I.

12th Arkansas Battalion of Sharpshooters. M. A handful of Irish crack shots leant a hand in Company A, commanded by Captain Griff Bayne. The unit did good duty during the siege of Vicksburg.

13th Arkansas Infantry Regiment. AT. Captain Thomas Fletcher's Company A, which often performed skirmisher duty, boasted 40 or so Irishmen, most of them recruited in Memphis. The 13th Arkansas was consolidated with the 15th Arkansas in late 1862 and with the 5th Arkansas in 1863.

15th Arkansas Infantry Regiment (Cleburne's). AT. Old Pat's original command carried 30 or more Irish names on the rolls of Companies C, D, and G (Yell Rifles, Napoleon Grays, and Phillips Guards). The Napoleon Grays especially were conspicuous as skirmishers. Their commander, George Dixon, drowned near Chattanooga in July 1863. A successor, Irish-born James B. Kennedy, was wounded and captured at Franklin. The 15th Arkansas was consolidated with the 13th Arkansas in late 1862 and with the 1st Arkansas in 1864.

18th Arkansas (3rd Confederate) Infantry Regiment. AT. Captain John Crump's Shamrock Guards (Company D) and Captain Mumford H. Dixon's Swamp Rangers (Company H), both from Vicksburg, were heavily Irish. Consolidated with the 5th Confederate Infantry during 1863 and part of 1864.

FLORIDA

Leon Light Artillery. GC. Not an Irish command, but this Tallahassee company that saw action at Olustee in February 1864 carried 25–30 Irish and Scotch-Irish names on roll.

Milton Light Artillery. GC. Formed in Apalachicola, this company contained 30 or so Irish names on roll. A section of the battery saw service at Olustee in 1864.

1st Florida Infantry Regiment. GC, AT. There were no real Irish commands in this regiment, but Companies B, E, H, and K each carried at least 15 Irish names on roll. Lieutenant Colonel Thaddeus A. McDonell was wounded at Shiloh.

GEORGIA

22nd Georgia Artillery Battalion. AC. Company E (Montgomery Guard) and Company F (Emmet Rifles) were both Irish companies from Savannah. They served on the Georgia coast at Fort McAllister and joined the Army of Tennessee for the North Carolina campaign of 1865.

1st Georgia Regular Infantry. ANV, GC, AT. The Emmet Rifles (Company B) was an Irish company led by Captain William Martin (promoted to field command). Company G was also largely Irish. The 1st Georgia Regulars served with the ANV and fought in South Carolina and Florida before joining the Army of Tennessee for the final campaign in North Carolina in 1865.

1st Georgia Volunteer Infantry Regiment (Mercer's / Olmstead's). AT. Volunteer militia companies from Savannah made up this regiment that served on the Georgia coast until the Atlanta campaign of 1864. Companies A and B (Irish Jasper Greens) and Company E (Irish Volunteers) were purely Irish units, while Company C (Republican Blues) contained 40 or so Irish or Scotch-Irish names.

5th Georgia Infantry Regiment. AT. Irish recruits from Augusta formed the Irish Volunteers (Company C) led first by Captain John H. Hull (seriously wounded at Chickamauga) and later by Captain Michael J. O'Connor. They were the color company of the 5th Georgia, which suffered heavy casualties at Chickamauga.

10th Georgia Infantry Regiment. ANV. Companies F (Thompson Guards from Columbia County) and K (Pulaski Guards from Richmond and Chatham Counties) each had some 30 Irish names on roll. Companies D (Independent Blues from Augusta) and H (Wilcox Guards from Wilcox County) had about 20.

19th Georgia Infantry Regiment. ANV, AT. An Atlanta Irish company, the Jackson Guards (Company B) was the color company of the 19th Georgia and served in Virginia until 1865. Company commander James Henry Neal became lieutenant colonel of the 19th Georgia and was killed at Bentonville in the Army of Tennessee's last battle of the war.

20th Georgia Infantry Regiment. ANV. The Montgomery Guards from Augusta (Company K) was the Irish company in this command. Captains were Jesse Cleveland and Irish immigrant William Craig (promoted to field command).

24th Georgia Infantry Regiment. ANV. Irish immigrant Robert McMillan (promoted to field command) led Company K (the McMillan Guards from Habersham County), whose handful of Irish, including McMillan's three sons, saw action at the stone wall at Fredericksburg's Marye's Heights.

25th Georgia Infantry Regiment. AT. Formed from Irish in the Savannah vicinity, the Telfair Irish Grays (Company H) fought at Chickamauga, Chattanooga, and in the Atlanta campaign.

Phillips Legion, Infantry Battalion. ANV. The south-central Georgia town of Macon furnished the Lochrane Guards (Company F), an Irish company that saw action at the stone wall at Fredericksburg. Commanders were Jackson Barnes, Patrick McGovern, James Meara, and Michael S. Walsh.

KENTUCKY

9th Kentucky Infantry Regiment. AT. Company H, with some 60 Irish surnames on roll, was probably the remnant of the old Jackson Guards from Louisville. Lieutenant Peter H. O'Connor was one of the officers. The 9th Kentucky, part of the famed Orphan Brigade, was distinguished during the Atlanta campaign.

LOUISIANA

Madison Light Artillery ("Madison Tips"). ANV. Irish levee workers from County Tipperary enlisted as a body in Captain George V. Moody's artillery company formed in Madison Parish, across the river from Vicksburg. The battery did good service at Sharpsburg and at Gettysburg.

1st Louisiana Cavalry Regiment. AT. There were 30 or so Irish names in Company F from Concordia Parish. The troopers distinguished themselves in an engagement at Big Hill near Richmond, Kentucky, on August 23, 1862. The regiment saw much action at Murfreesboro and Chickamauga.

1st Louisiana Regular Infantry. AT. The whole regiment was about 25 percent Irish from New Orleans. There were 75 to 80 Irish names each in Companies C, E, F, and G. The 1st Louisiana Regulars sustained heavy casualties at Shiloh, Murfreesboro, and Chickamauga.

1st Louisiana Infantry Regiment. ANV. Recruited in New Orleans, at least a fourth of this regiment was born in the Emerald Isle. Two of the companies were solidly Irish: the Emmet Guards (Company D), first led by James Nelligan (promoted to field command), and later by Albert N. Cummings and Henry R. Kenna; and the Montgomery Guards (Company E), led by Michael Nolan (promoted to field command), Michael B. Gilmore (killed in June 1862), and Thomas Rice. Also with a strong Irish presence was the Orleans Light Guards (Company F) led by Patrick O'Rourke, Samuel H. Snowden, and James Dillon.

1st Louisiana Special Battalion (Wheat's Tiger Battalion). ANV. Raised by C. Roberdeau Wheat, this colorful battalion of Zouaves was made up largely of Irish dock workers in New Orleans. Fearless in battle but dreaded for its reputation for bad conduct, the command was disbanded in August 1862 after Wheat's death.

2nd Louisiana Infantry. ANV. Captain John Kelso's Moore Guards (Company B) was an Irish company from Alexandria in Rapides Parish. Kelso's successor, Michael Grogan was later promoted to field command.

4th Louisiana Infantry Battalion. AT. Company B (Ouachita Blues) contained 30 or so Irish from Ouachita County, first commanded by Captain John McEnery, later the battalion commander. The battalion first joined the Army of Tennessee at Chickamauga, where it took part in heavy fighting.

5th Louisiana Infantry. ANV. According to one member, the 5th Louisiana was mostly composed of "uneducated Irishmen," but there was no distinctly Irish company. Most of the members were common laborers from New Orleans, and nearly 100 listed Ireland as their place of birth. Irish immigrant John McGurk commanded the Chalmette Guards (Company B), and James Garrity led the Orleans Cadet Company (Company E).

6th Louisiana Infantry. ("Irish Brigade"). ANV. New Orleans laborers comprised the bulk of this regiment, over half of them born in Ireland. Two of the regiment's colonels, Henry B. Strong and William Monaghan, were Irish immigrants, and both were killed in action. The Calhoun Guards (Company B) was first led by Strong and later by Thomas Redmond. Irish Brigade "Co. B" (Company F) was led by Monaghan and Michael O'Connor. Irish Brigade "Co. A" (Company I) was led by Samuel L. James and Joseph Hanlon (both promoted to field command), and Blayney T. Walshe. Hanlon and Walshe, a newspaperman and a clerk respectively, were both born in Ireland.

7th Louisiana Infantry ("Pelican Regiment"). ANV. Described as a "crack regiment," the 7th Louisiana listed clerks, laborers, and farmers (most from New Orleans) among its members, a third of them Irish-born. The Sarsfield Rangers (Company C) of New Orleans was led by Irish immigrant Jonathan Moore Wilson (promoted to field command), McGavock Goodwyn, and Charles Cameron. The Virginia Guards (Company D) and the Virginia Blues (Company I) were largely Irish, as was the Irish Volunteers (Company F) from Assumption Parish.

8th Louisiana Infantry. ANV. Colonel Henry B. Kelly commanded this regiment, with more than a tenth of its members born in Ireland. The Cheneyville Rifles (Company H) from Rapides Parish was led by Irish immigrant Patrick F. Keary. There also were a number of Irish in Companies B, D, and G.

9th Louisiana Infantry. ANV. A significant number of Irish made up this command. The conspicuous Irish company here was the Emerald Guards or Milliken Bend Guards (Company E) from Madison Parish, led by Captain William R. Peck (promoted to field command). There were also 20 or so Irish names on the rolls of the Jackson Greys (Company K) from Jackson Parish.

10th Louisiana Infantry. ANV. In this largely Irish command, there were the Shepherd Guards (Company A) from New Orleans, led by Jewish officers Jacob A. Cohen (killed in action in August 1862) and Isaac Lyons, and later by Patrick Barron, Michael Carroll, and Daniel Mahoney; the Derbigny Guards (Company B), led by Lea F. Bakewell; Hewitt's Guards (Company C), led by Richard M. Hewitt and later by Thomas N. Powell (promoted to field command); Hawkins' Guards (Company D); and Orleans Blues (Company H) from New Orleans.

13th Louisiana Infantry Regiment. AT. This whole regiment was about 25 percent Irish, especially Company A (Southern Celts from New Orleans) and Company G (St. Mary Volunteers from St. Mary Parish). Consolidated with the 20th Louisiana, the command saw much action throughout the war—with especially heavy casualties at Shiloh, Murfreesboro, and Chickamauga—and was one of the last to surrender in 1865.

14th Louisiana Infantry. ANV. There were no distinctly Irish companies in this command, but six of them had an Irish majority. Irish immigrant John Fennelly, a New Orleans plasterer, enlisted in Company H, was promoted to lieutenant and later to adjutant of the regiment, and was killed at Spotsylvania.

14th Louisiana Battalion of Sharpshooters. AT. With 35 or so Irish names each in Companies A and B, Major John E. Austin's battalion formed a hard-fighting command that often performed skirmisher duty.

15th Louisiana Infantry. ANV. Although there was no distinctly Irish company, more than 100 soldiers in this regiment were Irish-born.

18th Louisiana Infantry Regiment. TM. The sizeable Irish community in St. Mary Parish contributed some 40 names to Company D (Hays Champions). The unit fought at Shiloh and Corinth and later in the Trans-Mississippi, seeing action at Mansfield and Pleasant Hill during the Red River campaign.

19th Louisiana Infantry Regiment. AT. Company C (Claiborne Volunteers) boasted 30 or so Irish or Scotch-Irish names. The company was led by Captain Hyder A. Kennedy, who later became lieutenant colonel of the regiment. The 19th Louisiana suffered especially heavy casualties at Chickamauga.

20th Louisiana Infantry Regiment. AT. Four Irish companies (G, H, I, and K from New Orleans) were later consolidated with the 13th Louisiana Infantry.

MARYLAND

2nd Maryland Artillery Battery (Baltimore Battery). ANV. There were 35 or so Irish members in this unit led by Captain John B. Brockenbrough and later by Captain William H. Griffin.

3rd Maryland Artillery Battery. ANV. Captain Henry B. Latrobe's company contained 45 or so Irish members.

1st Maryland Infantry Regiment. ANV. The regiment was formed from disbanded companies of Baltimore's pro-Confederate volunteer militia. Companies B and E each had 25 or so Irish members.

MISSISSIPPI

Warren Light Artillery. AT. This aggressive little Vicksburg command, led by Lieutenant Harvey Shannon, contained at least 25 or so Irish names and saw heavy action at Chickamauga and Tunnel Hill.

9th Mississippi Infantry Regiment. AT. Company B, Captain John P. Holahan's company, carried 60 or so Irish names on roll. The lieutenants were Robert E. McCarthy and Michael William Shanahan. Holahan was seriously wounded at Kennesaw Mountain. There were 25 or so Irish names in Companies D and E.

10th Mississippi Infantry Regiment. AT. There were at least 30 Irish names each in Company A (Mississippi Rifles from Jackson), Company C (Port Gibson Rifles), and Company K (Yazoo Rifles).

12th Mississippi Infantry Regiment. ANV. The Natchez Fencibles (Company B) contained some 30 Irish names, and there were 25 or so in Companies C and G.

16th Mississippi Infantry Regiment. ANV. The Jasper Grays (Company F) from Paulding, led by Captain James J. Shannon, was chiefly Irish. There were also a number of Irish names on the rolls of Company D (Adams Light Guard), Company A, and Company I.

19th Mississippi Infantry Regiment. ANV. There were a significant number of Irish in Company C, the Warren Guards from Vicksburg.

22nd Mississippi Infantry Regiment. AT. The Sarsfield Southrons (Company C) from Vicksburg, first commanded by Captain Felix Hughes, was solidly Irish. There were also 30 or so Irish names in Companies D and I.

44th Mississippi Infantry Regiment. AT. Company L from Natchez carried 40 or so Irish names on roll. The 44th Mississippi sustained heavy casualties in fighting at Chickamauga and Atlanta.

45th Mississippi Infantry Regiment (3rd Mississippi Infantry Battalion). AT. Company E (McNair Rifles) from Pike County, with 25 or so Irish or Scotch-Irish names, served in Mark Lowrey's brigade in Cleburne's division. The captains were R. H. McNair, killed at Shiloh, and William M. McNulty.

MISSOURI

Kelly's Battery. TM. Captain Ephraim V. Kelly's Irish company was transferred from the Missouri State Guard to Confederate service in March 1862 and served in the Corinth campaign before being disbanded in June.

Wade's Battery. TM, M. Captain William Wade's light artillery company contained mostly Irish-American veterans of combat at Pea Ridge, Farmington, Iuka, and Corinth. After Wade was killed in April 1863, Irish-born Lieutenant Richard C. Walsh commanded the battery during the Vicksburg siege.

Guibor's Missouri Battery. TM, AT. This St. Louis artillery company carried 50 or so Irish names on its roster. Commanded by Captain Henry Guibor, the unit was distinguished in the Atlanta campaign and at Franklin.

1st Missouri Infantry Regiment. AT. Company A (Suchet Guard), mustered 85 or so Irishmen from Louisiana; Company C had 40 or so Irish, many from Memphis; Company D (St. Louis Grays) had 35 or so; also 20 or so Irish each in Companies F and H. Outstanding Irish officers included Colonels Martin Burke and Amos C. Riley. Wounded eleven times during the war, Captain Joseph Boyce led the St. Louis Grays. Consolidated with the 4th Missouri in 1862, this hard-fighting regiment earned a reputation as one of the South's finest combat units, serving with distinction in the Atlanta campaign, at Franklin, and in the last major battle of the war at Fort Blakely, Alabama, on April 9, 1865.

5th Missouri Infantry Regiment. AT. Company F ("Fighting Irish Company" from St. Louis) became one of the Confederacy's most outstanding skirmisher units; its Captain Patrick Canniff—called "a fearless and skillful officer" by brigade commander Francis Cockrell—was killed at Franklin. There were also 20 or so Irish names in Company E and 35 or so in Company H. The regiment was consolidated in 1863 with the 3rd Missouri, which had at least 30 Irish members in its Company D. Remnants of the command fought at Fort Blakely under Colonel James McCown.

NORTH CAROLINA

2nd North Carolina Artillery (36th North Carolina State Troops). AC. The original Company B (Bladen Guards) contained 45–50 Irish, Scottish, or Scotch-Irish names. Company A (Wilmington Horse Artillery) boasted 30 or more.

3rd North Carolina Artillery (40th North Carolina State Troops). AC. Company H, Captain Calvin Barnes' company from Wilmington (formerly Company A, 2nd North Carolina Infantry), was heavily Irish. There were also 45 or so Irish or Scotch-Irish names in Captain George C. Buchan's Company G (formerly Company I, 2nd North Carolina Artillery).

SOUTH CAROLINA

3rd South Carolina Artillery Battalion. AT. Company B (Columbia Flying Artillery) had 30 or so Irish names on roll. Under Captain John Waties and R. B. Waddell, the detached battery fought at Chickamauga, Missionary Ridge, and in the Atlanta campaign.

15th South Carolina Artillery Battalion. AC. Company C (Captain Theodore B. Hayne's company) had 35–40 Irish members. There were also 20 or so Irish names in Companies A and B.

1st South Carolina Infantry Regiment. ANV. The Irish Volunteers (Company K) was the color company of the 1st South Carolina. Under company commanders Edward McCrady, Jr., Michael Parker, and James Armstrong, Jr., the Irish Volunteers saw much action in Virginia. There were also some 20 Irish names in Company I (Richardson Guards).

1st South Carolina Infantry Battalion (Charleston Battalion) (27th South Carolina Infantry Regiment). AC, AT. Captain Edward Magrath's Old Irish Volunteers from Charleston (Company C), served at Fort Sumter early in the war, with the Army of Northern Virginia in 1864, and ended the war with the Army of Tennessee in 1865. Captain William H. Ryan was killed at Fort Wagner.

TENNESSEE

Fisher's Battery (Nelson Artillery). M. Captain James A. Fisher's company from Nashville carried 45 Irish names on roll. The battery saw service in Mississippi during the Port Hudson siege.

McClung's Battery (Caswell Artillery). Captain Hugh L. W. McClung's battery hailed from Knoxville and boasted some 35 Irish names on roll. With the exception of service in Kentucky and at Shiloh in 1862, this unit spent most of the war in East Tennessee and Southwestern Virginia.

Morton's Battery (Burns Light Artillery). AT. Named for Irish immigrant entrepreneur Michael Burns, Captain John W. Morton's largely Irish company from Nashville saw much service with Nathan Bedford Forrest's cavalry.

Rutledge's Battery (Company A, 1st Tennessee Artillery). Captain Arthur M. Rutledge's battery from Nashville contained some 40 Irish names on roll. The unit served in Kentucky and at Shiloh, after which it was consolidated with McClung's Battery.

Scott's Battery. AT. Memphis Irish formed the nucleus of Captain William L. Scott's battery that saw heavy fighting at Shiloh, Murfreesboro, and Chickamauga. These were the stubborn gunners who fought to the last and were practically annihilated at Missionary Ridge.

Winston's Battery. M, GC. Captain William C. Winston's company enlisted at Nashville contained 60 or so Irish names on roll. The unit served on the Mississippi and in the defenses around Mobile.

2nd Tennessee (5th Confederate) Infantry Regiment (Walker's/Smith's). AT. The "Irish Regiment" from Memphis, this command was consolidated with the 21st Tennessee Infantry to form the 5th Confederate Infantry. A hard-fighting Irish outfit, these lads forged an exemplary combat record during the war and were with Cleburne in his last charge at Franklin. The unit was consolidated with the 3rd Confederate Infantry during 1863 and part of 1864.

2nd Tennessee Infantry Regiment (Bate's). AT. Company E boasted 55–60 Irish members of the Memphis Fire Department. The 2nd Tennessee suffered heavy casualties at Shiloh, Chickamauga, and Nashville.

10th Tennessee Infantry Regiment. AT. Colonel Randal McGavock's "Sons of Erin" contained Irish companies from Nashville, McEwen, Clarksville, and Pulaski. Under strong officers like William Grace and John G. O'Neill, this command built a solid reputation as a hard-fighting and dependable outfit.

15th Tennessee Infantry Regiment (Carroll's / Tyler's / Wall's). AT. Memphis Irish Americans contributed Companies C (Montgomery Guard), B, and H to this regiment that suffered heavy casualties at Shiloh, Chickamauga, and Missionary Ridge. Consolidated with the 37th Tennessee in 1863.

21st Tennessee Infantry Regiment. AT. Irish companies from Memphis consolidated with 2nd Tennessee Infantry Regiment (Walker's).

32nd Tennessee Infantry Regiment. AT. Company G, led by Captain William P. O'Neal, contained 30 or so Irish names from the town of Belfast in Marshall County. The 32nd suffered heavy losses at Chickamauga.

34th Tennessee Infantry Regiment. AT. Captain Michael Fitzpatrick's company from the Nashville area, Company F (Acklen Rifles), carried 30 or so Irish names on roll. The regiment lost 40 percent of its men at Chickamauga.

154th Tennessee Infantry Regiment. AT. Company C (pre-war Jackson Guards) and Company H (Crockett Rangers) were two Memphis Irish companies, and Company F (Henry Guards) was a largely Irish company from Paris, Tennessee. This volunteer militia command served for much of the war under Colonel Michael Magevney, Jr., and suffered heavy casualties at Shiloh and Murfreesboro. Consolidated with the 13th Tennessee in 1863.

TEXAS

1st Texas Heavy Artillery Regiment. TM. The Jefferson Davis Guards (Company F), an Irish company from Houston, won fame as the 43-man detachment that foiled a Federal invasion of east Texas at Sabine Pass in September 1863. Two other companies had 30 or more Irish names on their rolls: Company D, led by Captain Charles M. Mason, and Company E, led by Captain J. W. Bennett and later by Captain M. V. McMahon.

Captain William Edgar's Battery (Alamo City Guards). TM. Some 55 Irish names were on the roll of this San Antonio company, attached to Waul's Texas Legion. The battery was captured in March 1864 during the Red River campaign.

Captain O. G. Jones' Battery. TM. Jones' company was the Dixie Grays from Galveston (formerly Co. A, 1st Texas Heavy Artillery, detached from that command in June 1863). There were 30–35 Irish names on roll. Gunners of Jones' battery fired the last shot of the war at Palmito Ranch on May 13, 1865.

1st Texas Cavalry Regiment. TM. Captain James A. Ware's Company F (formerly Ware's Company of Partisan Rangers or "Ware's Tigers") contained 25 or so Irish names from the Celtic enclave in San Patricio County.

2nd Texas Cavalry Regiment. TM. There was no distinctly Irish company, but Companies A, B, D, G, and H each contained 15 or more Irish names. Irish orphan and self-made Texas soldier Matthew Nolan was promoted to major.

Giddings' Texas Cavalry Battalion. TM. Lieutenant Colonel George H. Giddings' small 300-man cavalry command was formed late in the war and saw action in the last battle at Palmito Ranch. Giddings' battalion contained at least 50 Irish names, company distribution unknown.

1st Texas Infantry Regiment. ANV. The premier regiment of Hood's Texas Brigade contained two companies with 20 or more Irish-American names on roll: Company C, Captain A. G. Dickinson's Palmer Guards from Houston, and Company L, Captain Alfred C. McKeen's Lone Star Rifles from Galveston.

11th (Spaight's) Battalion Texas Volunteers. TM. Company E, formed by Captain George Washington O'Brien, contained 20–25 Irish or Scotch-Irish names from the Beaumont area. An important community leader after the war, O'Brien bankrolled the Spindletop oil field, which sparked the Texas oil boom.

Waul's Texas Legion. M. Although Company A was considered a German unit, there were at least 60 Irish names on roll. Companies B, C (also mostly German), and F each contained 35 or so Irish names.

VIRGINIA

19th Battalion Virginia Heavy Artillery. ANV. The Irish Volunteers of Alexandria (Company C) served in this command which spent most of the war in the defenses around Richmond.

1st Virginia Infantry Regiment. ANV. Richmond's Montgomery Guard (Company C) was the city's premier Irish volunteer militia company, formed in 1850 and molded into shape by County Galway native Patrick T. Moore. Company commanders during the war were John Dooley (promoted to field command), William English, James Mitchell, James Hallinan (killed at Gettysburg), and John Edward Dooley.

1st Virginia Infantry Battalion (Irish Battalion). ANV. Four of the battalion's five companies were Irish, recruited in Richmond, Lynchburg, Norfolk, Alexandria, and Covington. Under Major David B. Bridgford, the Irish Battalion became the provost guard for the ANV.

11th Virginia Infantry Regiment. ANV. The Jeff Davis Guards (Company H) was recruited from Irish rail workers and laborers in Lynchburg.

15th Virginia Infantry Regiment. ANV. Another Irish company from Richmond, the Emmet Guard (Company F), served during the Peninsular Campaign. It was disbanded in June 1862.

17th Virginia Infantry Regiment. ANV. Alexandria's Emmet Guards (Company G) and O'Connell Guards (Company I) were two Irish companies in this unit.

19th Virginia Infantry Regiment. ANV. The Montgomery Guards (Company F) was recruited from Irish in Charlottesville. James D. McIntire, who was a 20-year-old clerk and student at the University of Virginia when the war began, served as company commander for much of the war.

27th Virginia Infantry Regiment. ANV. Mountainous Alleghany County was the home of the Virginia Hibernians (Company B), an Irish company that served under Captain John P. Welsh. There were also some 25 Irish or Scotch-Irish names in Company A (the Alleghany Roughs), Company C (the Alleghany Rifles), Company H (the Rockbridge Rifles from Rockbridge County).

33rd Virginia Infantry Regiment. ANV. The Emerald Guard (Company E) was organized in New Market from Irish rail laborers.

CONFEDERATE REGULARS

1st Regular Confederate Light Artillery Battery. TM. Captain Oliver J. Semmes's command contained 40 or so Irish members. Semmes said that most of his men were Irish and Germans, former U. S. regulars. The battery was active in the Confederate attack on Baton Rouge in August 1862 and afterward in the Trans-Mississippi. They left a good record of service.

1st Regular Confederate States Cavalry, Company A. TM, AT. About 25 percent of this command was Irish, recruited from U. S. Army deserters in Texas at the beginning of the war. Following rugged service west of the Mississippi, this hard-riding company joined the Army of Tennessee for cavalry operations at Chickamauga, in eastern Tennessee, and in the Atlanta campaign.

Captain Jules V. Gallimard's Company of Sappers and Bombardiers. M, GC. With 40 or so New Orleans Irish names on roll, this unit worked on fortifications around the Crescent City, at Fort Pillow and Island No. 10, and in the Mobile Bay forts. Most of the men were captured at Fort Morgan.

3rd Confederate Engineer Regiment, Company D. AT. With 30–35 Irish surnames on roll, this unit played an active role in the Atlanta campaign both in erecting fortifications and occasionally in combat. In a nutshell, they did the same things that many of these soldiers probably had done in their civilian days—pick-and-shovel work and fighting.

Appendix 2: Some Irish-American Field Commanders in the Confederate Army

ALABAMA

Brigadier General Alpheus Baker. Baker was born in South Carolina, but his mother was a native of Ireland. An attorney in Eufaula, Alabama, he was captain of the Eufaula Rifles company. Later he became colonel of the 54th Alabama Infantry and commanded a brigade in the Atlanta campaign.

Colonel John Francis Conoley, 29th Alabama Infantry. Born in 1811 in North Carolina, Conoley was the son of Scotch-Irish immigrants. An attorney and county sheriff in Selma, Alabama, Conoley was seriously wounded at Resaca.

Brigadier General James Hagan. Born in County Tyrone in 1821, Hagan came to America as an infant with his parents. He later became part of his uncle's merchant business in Mobile. A veteran of the Mexican War, where he became an officer of dragoons, Hagan took command of the 3rd Alabama Cavalry shortly after Shiloh. He led a cavalry brigade under General Joseph Wheeler and was wounded several times during the war.

Major Samuel Camp Kelly, 30th Alabama Infantry. Born in 1825 in Tennessee, Kelly was educated on his father's plantation in Calhoun County, Alabama. He served in the Mexican War. At the start of the Civil War, he commanded a company from Calhoun County that became part of the 30th Alabama, and he was promoted to major during the Atlanta campaign.

Lieutenant Colonel James McGaughey, 16th Alabama Infantry. McGaughey first commanded a company from Franklin County and was later promoted lieutenant colonel of the 16th Alabama. He was killed at Chickamauga.

Colonel Virgil S. Murphy, 17th Alabama Infantry. Born in South Carolina in 1838, Murphy became an attorney in Montgomery, Alabama. During the war he was colonel of the 17th Alabama and in the spring of 1864 served as a brigade commander. Health problems forced Murphy to go on sick leave in June 1864. He returned to command of the 17th Alabama in October 1864 but was captured at Franklin the following month.

Colonel Theodore O'Hara. The son of Irish immigrants, O'Hara based his poem "The Bivouac of the Dead" on his experiences as a young officer in the Mexican War. His diverse background in civilian life included a career as an attorney and as editor of the *Mobile Register*. O'Hara commanded the 12th Alabama Infantry in Virginia and later served as a staff officer to

General Albert Sidney Johnston and was with him at his death at Shiloh. He was also chief of staff to General John C. Breckinridge, a friend from school days. He died in Alabama in 1867.

Brigadier General Edward A. O'Neal. Born in 1818, the son of an Irish immigrant, O'Neal was an attorney in Florence, Alabama. As colonel of the 26th Alabama Infantry, he was a veteran of the fighting in Virginia and was wounded at Seven Pines and at Boonsboro. O'Neal joined the Army of Tennessee as a brigade commander for the Atlanta campaign in 1864. After the war, he resumed his law practice and became active in state politics. He served two terms as governor of Alabama.

ARKANSAS

Major General Patrick R. Cleburne. Born in Ireland in 1828, Cleburne served in the British army before immigrating to America in 1849. He settled in Helena, Arkansas, where he managed a drug store and later became a successful attorney. He led the Yell Rifles, before being chosen to command the 15th Arkansas and rose rapidly in rank to become the most capable division commander in the Army of Tennessee. The only Irish-born Confederate to attain the rank of major general, he died at Franklin in November 1864.

Major General James Fleming Fagan. Born in Kentucky, Fagan was the grandson of Irish immigrants and a veteran officer who served in the Mexican War. He led the 1st Arkansas Infantry at Shiloh and was later promoted to brigadier general and served in the Trans-Mississippi.

Colonel Harris Flanagan, 2nd Arkansas Mounted Rifles. Flanagan was the grandson of an Irish immigrant. An attorney and land speculator in Arkadelphia, he became active in state politics. He led the 2nd Arkansas Mounted Rifles in operations of the Army of Tennessee in the summer and fall of 1862, resigned his commission to run for governor of Arkansas, and was elected in November.

Colonel D. A. Gillespie, 7th Arkansas Infantry. While a lieutenant in Company G, this Scotch-Irish officer from Smithville was commended for bravery at Shiloh. He was promoted to command of the 7th Arkansas at Perryville. Wounded at Chickamauga, he died in October 1863.

Brigadier General John Herbert Kelly. Born in Carrollton, Alabama, in 1840, Kelly was orphaned at an early age. At age 17 he was admitted as a cadet to the U. S. Military Academy at West Point, but he left shortly before graduation to enlist in the Confederate army. Kelly led the 8th Arkansas Infantry at Shiloh and Perryville, was wounded at Murfreesboro, and commanded a brigade at Chickamauga. He became the youngest Confederate general at age 23 in November 1863. After leading a cavalry brigade in the Atlanta campaign, he died in a mounted raid near Franklin, Tennessee, in August 1864, at age 24.

Major John C. McCauley, 7th Arkansas Infantry. McCauley was originally captain of Company A from White County and was a merchant in Searcy.

Colonel James H. McGehee, McGehee's Arkansas Cavalry Regiment. At the head of his mounted regiment in the Trans-Mississippi, McGehee was seriously wounded in hand-to-hand combat with a Federal officer in the battle of Westport (present-day Kansas City,) Missouri, on October 23, 1864.

Lieutenant Colonel John Edward Murray, 5th/13th Arkansas Infantry. Murray was born in 1843 in Virginia and moved to Pine Bluff, Arkansas, in the 1850s. A highly regarded officer, he would have become the youngest Confederate brigadier general had he not fallen during the Atlanta fighting on July 22, 1864.

Lieutenant Colonel James McCarney O'Neill, 1st Arkansas Cavalry. A Drew County farmer, born in Tennessee in 1823, O'Neill served with this regiment in the Trans-Mississippi before turning in his resignation in April 1864.

FLORIDA

Brigadier General Joseph Finegan. Born in Ireland in 1814, Finegan settled in Jacksonville, Florida, where he became a successful planter and lumber mill owner. As commander of Confederate forces in Florida, Finegan won an important victory at Olustee on February 20, 1864. He was then transferred to the Army of Northern Virginia, where he commanded a Florida brigade at Cold Harbor and at Petersburg.

Lieutenant Colonel Thaddeus A. McDonell, 1st Florida Infantry Battalion. Born in Florida in 1831, McDonell was an attorney in Gainesville. At the head of the Florida battalion, he was seriously wounded at Shiloh in April 1862.

GEORGIA

Major Peter Brenan, 61st Georgia Infantry. Born in Ireland in 1811, Brenan was a merchant in the western Georgia hamlet of Georgetown and commanded Company F in the 61st Georgia. He was killed at Gettysburg in July 1863.

Major William Craig, 20th Georgia Infantry. Craig immigrated to the United States from Ireland and became a merchant in Augusta, Georgia. He commanded the Montgomery Guards, an Irish company from that city, before being promoted to field command.

Major John Foley, 1st Georgia Volunteer Infantry (Mercer's / Olmstead's). Foley was captain of the Irish Jasper Greens of Savannah at the start of the war. He was promoted to major in January 1862.

Lieutenant Colonel Martin J. Ford, 1st Georgia Volunteer Infantry (Mercer's / Olmstead's). A lieutenant in the Irish Jasper Greens at the start of war, Ford became lieutenant colonel of the regiment during the fighting around Atlanta.

Lieutenant Colonel Joseph Hamilton, Phillips' Legion, Infantry Battalion. Hamilton was born in County Tyrone in 1836. He led Company E in Phillips' Legion and commanded the Legion at the stone wall at Fredericksburg after all the field officers were disabled. He was promoted to major and soon after to lieutenant colonel, and he commanded the battalion for the remainder of the war.

Major Michael Lynch, 21st Georgia Infantry. Born in Ireland in 1835, Lynch settled in Lumpkin, Georgia, where he became a dairy farmer. He raised and commanded Company I in the 21st Georgia, and by 1864 he had been promoted to major. Lynch was wounded at Chancellorsville.

Colonel Robert McMillan, 24th Georgia Infantry. A native of County Antrim, McMillan immigrated to America and settled in mountainous Habersham County in northern Georgia. His most distinguished service was at the stone wall at Fredericksburg, where he led the 24th Georgia in an impressive defense against Federal assaults. He resigned in January 1864 for health reasons.

Major Robert Emmet McMillan, 24th Georgia Infantry. Field command came early to the son of Colonel Robert McMillan. The younger McMillan was wounded at Sharpsburg and resigned in January 1864.

Lieutenant Colonel William Martin, 1st Georgia Regulars. Martin commanded the Emmet Rifles (Company B) at the start of the war and was promoted to lieutenant colonel in February 1862. Tuberculosis took his life in October 1864.

Lieutenant Colonel James Henry Neal, 19th Georgia Infantry. Neal was captain of the Jackson Guards from Atlanta at the start of the war. He was promoted to colonel in August 1863. Neal was killed at Bentonville in March 1865.

Louisiana

Major John E. Austin, 14th Louisiana Sharpshooters Battalion. Austin was the former captain of the Cannon Guards from New Orleans (Company D, 11th Louisiana Infantry) before becoming commander of the 14th Louisiana Sharpshooters. He received a number of commendations for his service.

Lieutenant Colonel Michael Grogan, 2nd Louisiana Infantry. An Irish-born machinist in New Orleans in 1861, Grogan was an officer in the Moore Guards (Company B). He led the 2nd Louisiana at Fredericksburg, where he was commended for his actions. Grogan was promoted to lieutenant colonel in May 1864; he was wounded in November 1864.

Lieutenant Colonel Joseph Hanlon, 6th Louisiana Infantry. An Irish immigrant, Hanlon became a newspaper reporter in New Orleans. He became captain of Company I (Irish Brigade "A") in the 6th Louisiana. Hanlon quickly advanced in rank and was lieutenant colonel by June 1861. He commanded the regiment at Gettysburg in July 1863.

Colonel Henry B. Kelly, 8th Louisiana Infantry. Kelly commanded the 8th Louisiana that saw service in Virginia, but he spent much of 1862 and 1863 absent due to sickness. In April 1863 he was re-assigned to military court duty with Pemberton's army in Mississippi.

Lieutenant Colonel Hyder Kennedy, 19th Louisiana Infantry. Born in 1840, Kennedy moved with his family from Georgia to Louisiana, where his father had a plantation near Homer. Captain of the Claiborne Volunteers (Company C) at the start of the war, Kennedy was promoted to lieutenant colonel in November 1863. He was the younger brother of Robert Cobb Kennedy (of the 1st Louisiana Regulars), who was executed as a spy in March 1865 for his part in a conspiracy to set fire to buildings in New York City.

Lieutenant Colonel John D. McEnery, 4th Louisiana Infantry Battalion. The son of an Irish immigrant, McEnery led the Ouachita Blues (Company B) at the start of the war and was promoted to lieutenant colonel in May 1862. He mounted an unsuccessful bid as the Democratic candidate for governor of Louisiana in 1872. His brother Samuel D. McEnery was elected governor in 1884.

Colonel William Monaghan, 6th Louisiana Infantry. A New Orleans notary public, the Irish-born Monaghan was the captain of Company F (Irish Brigade "B") of the 6th Louisiana. By 1862 he had been promoted to colonel. When the Federals overwhelmed his command at Rappahannock Bridge, Virginia, in November 1863, Monaghan avoided capture by swimming the river. He commanded Hays' Louisiana brigade in May 1864 at Spotsylvania, where he was in the thickest of the fight. Monaghan was killed in action in August 1864.

Lieutenant Colonel James Nelligan, 1st Louisiana Infantry. Irish immigrant Nelligan was an auctioneer in New Orleans when the war started and was captain of the prestigious Emmet Guards (Company D). He was soon promoted to lieutenant colonel, was wounded in June 1862 during the Seven Days Battles, was wounded again at Chancellorsville in May 1863, and was captured in 1864.

Colonel Michael Nolan, 1st Louisiana Infantry. A native of County Tipperary, the amiable New Orleans grocer enlisted in the distinguished Montgomery Guards (Company E), but he soon rose in rank. By August 1862, he was in command of the 1st Louisiana and led the regiment at Sharpsburg, where he was wounded in September 1862. Nolan's promising career was cut short when he was killed at Gettysburg, just before he was to be promoted to brigadier general.

Major Stephen O'Leary, 13th Louisiana Infantry. O'Leary was the former New Orleans police chief and was captain of the Southern Celts (Company A) at the start of the war. Promoted to major in April 1862, he resigned his commission in December 1862.

Major Patrick R. O'Rourke, 1st Louisiana Infantry. The captain of the Orleans Light Guards (Company F), Irish immigrant O'Rourke was an inspector in the Crescent City when the war began. He was wounded at Sharpsburg, where he lost his left arm. Appointed to a staff position, O'Rourke spent the balance of the war in the Trans-Mississippi.

Brigadier General William R. Peck. A planter in Madison Parish, Peck became captain of the Emerald Guards (Company E of the 9th Louisiana) at the outset of the war. He became colonel of the regiment in October 1863, and he made brigadier general by February 1865.

Major Thomas N. Powell, 10th Louisiana Infantry. A New Orleans planter, Powell joined Hewitt's Guards (Company C) when the war started and was soon promoted to 2nd lieutenant. He was promoted to major in May 1864.

Colonel Henry B. Strong, 6th Louisiana Infantry. An Irish immigrant clerk in New Orleans, Strong was the captain of the Calhoun Guards (Company B). His leadership abilities put him on the fast track to promotion, and by September 1862 he commanded Hays' Louisiana brigade at Sharpsburg, where he was killed while leading his troops.

Major Johnathan Moore Wilson, 7th Louisiana Infantry. Born in Ireland, Wilson was a 30-year-old merchant in New Orleans at the start of the war. He commanded the Sarsfield Rangers (Company C). Promoted to major, Wilson was wounded at Winchester in June 1863. He commanded the regiment by 1864 and was captured at Spotsylvania.

MARYLAND

Lieutenant Colonel R. Snowden Andrews. The son of an Irish immigrant, Andrews was a Baltimore architect in 1861. He organized the Maryland Flying Battery (1st Maryland Artillery) and later was lieutenant colonel of a battalion of Maryland and Virginia artillery. Twice wounded during the war, Andrews constructed railroads in Mexico after the conflict and later returned to Maryland.

MISSISSIPPI

Colonel William A. Feeney, 42nd Mississippi Infantry. A saddler in Senatobia, Mississippi, Feeney first served as an officer in the 9th Mississippi before being transferred to the 42nd where he was promoted to field command. He was seriously wounded at Gettysburg and the Wilderness.

Captain Felix Hughes, 22nd Mississippi Infantry. Hughes raised the Irish Sarsfield Southrons from Vicksburg. He was in temporary command of the regiment when he was killed in action at Baton Rouge in August 1862.

Brigadier General St. John R. Liddell. The grandson of an Irish immigrant, Liddell was born on his father's plantation in Mississippi. A veteran of combat with the Army of Tennessee, the hotheaded officer commanded Fort Blakely near Mobile—one of the very last strongholds to fall to the Federals in April 1865.

Major General Mark P. Lowrey. The son of Irish immigrants, Lowrey was born in Tennessee in 1828 and settled in Tishomingo County, Mississippi, in 1845. He was a veteran of the Mexican War, a self-educated brick mason, and a Baptist minister. Lowrey served as a brigade commander in Cleburne's division.

Lieutenant Colonel James J. Shannon, 16th Mississippi Infantry. The son of Irish immigrants, Shannon hailed from Paulding where he recruited the Jasper Grays (Company F). He received his promotion to lieutenant colonel in April 1862, but health problems forced him to resign by the end of the year.

MISSOURI

Lieutenant Colonel Martin Burke, 1st Missouri Infantry. A former St. Louis bookkeeper, Burke was captain of Company D (St. Louis Grays) at the beginning of the war and later became lieutenant colonel of the regiment.

Brigadier General Daniel Morton Frost. The captain of a St. Louis Irish volunteer militia company (the Washington Guards), Frost was born in New York and was a veteran of the Mexican War. He served in the Missouri State Guard and fought at Pea Ridge.

Colonel Joseph Kelly, Missouri State Guard. Kelly was the former captain of the Washington Blues, an Irish-majority company in St. Louis. He commanded a regiment in the Missouri State Guard and fought at Wilson's Creek.

Colonel James McCown, 5th Missouri Infantry. The son of Irish immigrants, McCown was born in Virginia and moved to Missouri, where he became a well-to-do landowner and outspoken pro-secession political leader in Warrensburg. He commanded the 5th Missouri from the beginning of the war to the end and was among the very last to surrender at Fort Blakely in April 1865.

Colonel Emmett McDonald, 10th Missouri Cavalry. Born in Ireland in 1838, McDonald was captain of the St. Louis Light Artillery and fought at Wilson's Creek. Later he commanded the 10th Missouri Cavalry. He was killed in action at Hartsville, Missouri, in January 1863.

Colonel Amos C. Riley, 1st/4th Missouri Infantry. Riley was a young planter who took command of the 1st Missouri after its original commander was killed at Shiloh. He led the regiment during the Atlanta campaign.

NORTH CAROLINA

Major James Reilly, 10th North Carolina Infantry. Known as "Old Tarantula," Reilly was born in County Westmeath. A former U. S. regular soldier and veteran of the Mexican War, Reilly commanded the Rowan Artillery (Company F, 10th North Carolina) in Virginia. He had the unpleasant duty of surrendering Fort Fisher to the Federals after a spirited defense in January 1865.

SOUTH CAROLINA

Colonel William G. Burt, 22nd South Carolina Infantry. Irish immigrant Burt was a stonecutter who enlisted in the 22nd South Carolina and rose to field command by 1864. He served in Virginia.

Brigadier General James Conner. Born in Charleston in 1829, this Irish-American attorney was captain of the Montgomery Guards, an Irish volunteer militia company in that city. During the war he commanded Hampton's Legion and the 22nd North Carolina Infantry, was wounded at Gaines' Mill, and lost a leg at Cedar Creek in 1864.

Lieutenant Colonel Edward McCrady, Jr., 1st South Carolina Infantry. McCrady commanded Charleston's Irish Volunteers. He led the 1st South Carolina at 2nd Manassas, where he was wounded.

Brigadier General Samuel McGowan. An attorney in Abbeville, South Carolina, McGowan was the son of Irish immigrants. He was a veteran of the Mexican War, commanded the 14th South Carolina Infantry in the Seven Days Battles and 2nd Manassas, and led Maxey Gregg's South Carolina brigade for the rest of the war. He was wounded four times during the war.

Major Charles C. O'Neill, 16th South Carolina Infantry. A young officer from Greenville, O'Neill was killed while on picket duty during the Atlanta campaign.

TENNESSEE

Brigadier General John Adams. The son of Irish immigrants, Adams was born in Nashville in 1825. A former regular army officer, he served in the Mexican War. Adams' brigade saw action in the Atlanta campaign. Killed in action at Franklin, his body was placed next to Cleburne's on the porch of the McGavock house.

Brigadier General William H. Carroll. The grandson of Irish immigrants, Carroll was a postmaster at Memphis. He commanded the 37th Tennessee Infantry at the start of the war and was promoted to brigadier general in October 1861. Braxton Bragg accused him of incompetency and drunkenness, and Carroll resigned from the army and emigrated to Canada where he died in 1868.

Colonel David M. Donnell, 16th Tennessee Infantry. The son of a Presbyterian minister, this Scotch-Irish officer was captain of Company C from Warren County. He led the 16th Tennessee at Perryville, Chickamauga, and Chattanooga.

Colonel Edward Fitzgerald, 154th Tennessee Infantry. Fitzgerald first commanded Company F, the Henry Guards from Paris, Tennessee. He was promoted to colonel after Shiloh but was killed in Kentucky in August 1862.

Colonel William Grace, 10th Tennessee Infantry. Burly "Battling Billy" Grace was an aggressive and well respected Nashville officer who led the "Sons of Erin" at Chickamauga and in the Atlanta campaign. He was killed at Jonesboro in 1864.

Colonel David Campbell Kelley, 3rd Tennessee Cavalry. Born in Tennessee in 1833, Kelley was a Methodist minister in Madison County, Alabama. The cavalry company that he organized, "Kelley's Troopers," became Company F in Nathan Bedford Forrest's 3rd Tennessee Cavalry, which Kelley later commanded.

Colonel Michael Magevney, Jr., 154th Tennessee Infantry. This nephew of Irish immigrant educator Eugene Magevney was the captain of Memphis' Jackson Guards (Company C) at the start of the war. He was promoted to lieutenant colonel after Shiloh, and he commanded a brigade in the Atlanta campaign.

Major General John Porter McCown. Born in Tennessee in 1815, McCown was a West Point graduate and an artillery officer during the Mexican War. His Confederate division saw action at Murfreesboro, but he ran afoul of Braxton Bragg, who charged him with insubordination and had him transferred out of the Army of Tennessee. McCown served the balance of the war in Mississippi.

Colonel Randal W. McGavock, 10th Tennessee Infantry. The young mayor of Nashville, McGavock organized the "Sons of Erin" from the city's Irish populace. "Randy Mack" was killed in action at Raymond, Mississippi, in May 1863.

Colonel John P. McGuire, 32nd Tennessee Infantry. Originally the captain of Company I from Lincoln County, McGuire led the 32nd Tennessee at Chickamauga, where he was wounded, and at Chattanooga and Nashville.

Lieutenant Colonel Christopher C. McKinney, 8th Tennessee Infantry. McKinney was the grandson of an Irish immigrant and was an attorney in Lewisburg, Tennessee. He led the 8th Tennessee at Chattanooga.

Colonel James A. McMurry, 34th Tennessee Infantry. The original lieutenant colonel of the 34th Tennessee, McMurry was killed at Chickamauga.

Major Joseph T. McReynolds, 37th Tennessee Infantry. Born in 1838 in Blount County, Tennessee, McReynolds was killed at Murfreesboro.

Colonel Rufus P. Neely, 4th Tennessee Infantry. This Irish-American officer was one of the early settlers of Hardeman County. Neely was a county court clerk, state legislator, and militia officer. After the war he was successful in the railroad business and constructed the Mississippi Central Railroad.

Colonel James F. Neill, 23rd Tennessee Infantry. Originally captain of Company E from Bedford County, Neill commanded the regiment at Shiloh, where he was wounded and was reassigned to staff duty.

Lieutenant Colonel William P. O'Neal, 32nd Tennessee Infantry. O'Neal was originally the captain of Company G from Belfast in Marshall County.

Colonel John G. O'Neill, 10th Tennessee Infantry. The popular captain of Company A from McEwen, O'Neill commanded the Sons of Erin sharpshooter detachment and led the depleted regiment at Missionary Ridge, Resaca, and Franklin. He was badly wounded at Resaca.

Major Samuel E. Shannon, 24th Tennessee Infantry. Born in Williamson County, Shannon was a farmer who commanded Company B at the start of the war. He led the 24th Tennessee at Murfreesboro and in the Atlanta campaign.

TEXAS

Brigadier General Matthew Duncan Ector. The grandson of an Irish immigrant, Ector was a veteran of the Mexican War and an attorney in Henderson, Texas. Commended for gallantry at Wilson's Creek and Pea Ridge, he was elected colonel of the 14th Texas Cavalry in May 1862 and was made brigadier general in September of that year, serving with distinction in the Army of Tennessee.

Colonel Clayton C. Gillespie, 25th Texas Cavalry. Gillespie organized this command, captured at Arkansas Post in January 1863 and later dismounted and assigned to the Texas brigade in Pat Cleburne's division.

Brigadier General Walter P. Lane. Born in Ireland, Lane settled in Texas and fought in both the Texas War for Independence in 1836 and the Mexican War of 1846–1848. He served in the Trans-Mississippi, commanding the 3rd Texas Cavalry at Wilson's Creek, Pea Ridge, and the Red River campaign. He was among the very last officers to be promoted to brigadier general in March 1865.

Brigadier General Ben McCulloch. The great-grandson of Irish immigrants, McCulloch was a veteran of the Texas War for Independence and the Mexican War. He led troops in the Trans-Mississippi and won an important victory at Wilson's Creek, but he died in action at Pea Ridge in March 1862.

Brigadier General Henry Eustace McCulloch. Ben McCulloch's brother, this Irish-American was a veteran of the Mexican War and a state legislator. He led the 1st Texas Mounted Rifles and was promoted to brigadier general in March 1862. He commanded troops in the Trans-Mississippi.

Major Matthew Nolan, 2nd Texas Cavalry. Ex-soldier, ex-Texas Ranger, and Sheriff of Nueces County, Irish orphan Nolan conducted operations against Federal forces near Corpus Christi. He was killed in December 1864 when he was ambushed in Corpus Christi by the stepsons of a Unionist collaborator.

Colonel James Reily, 4th Texas Cavalry. A former soldier and diplomat for the Republic of Texas, Reily failed in his mission to win Mexican support for the Confederacy. He was killed in action at Franklin, Louisiana, on April 14, 1863.

Lieutenant Colonel Denman W. Shannon, 5th Texas Cavalry. Originally captain of Co. C, from Grimes County, Shannon was promoted to lieutenant colonel in May 1863. He was captured at Fort Butler, Louisiana, in June 1863.

VIRGINIA

Brigadier General James Boggs. A County Down native, Boggs was a prominent planter in West Virginia before the war. He commanded the 18th Virginia Militia brigade. The 65-year-old Boggs died of illness in January 1862.

Major David B. Bridgford, 1st Virginia Infantry Battalion (Irish Battalion). The son of a British diplomat, Bridgford was a merchant in Richmond when the war began. As provost marshal for Stonewall Jackson, he did much to shape the Irish Battalion into the provost guard for the Army of Northern Virginia.

Brigadier General William Montague Browne. A native of County Mayo, Browne was a newspaper editor, diplomat, confidante of high ranking Confederate politicians, and (after the war) professor of history at the University of Georgia. He also served as a military aide to President Jefferson Davis and commanded the 1st Virginia Cavalry Battalion, a local defense force near Richmond.

Major John Dooley, 1st Virginia Infantry. An Irish immigrant and prominent Richmond businessman, Dooley was captain of the Montgomery Guard at the outbreak of the war and was promoted to major in November 1861.

Lieutenant Colonel Connally H. Lynch, 63rd Virginia Infantry. Lynch, a 32-year-old clerk from the mountains of southwestern Virginia, raised a company from Washington County in 1862 and eventually commanded the 63rd Virginia, one of a handful of Virginia units to serve with the Army of Tennessee, during the Atlanta campaign, at Franklin, and at Nashville.

Major General William Mahone. Born in Virginia of Irish ancestry, Mahone was the son of a tavern-keeper. A graduate of Virginia Military Institute, he was one of Lee's most capable commanders. After the war he built the Norfolk & Western rail line and was a U. S. Senator.

Brigadier General John McCausland. The son of Irish immigrants, McCausland was born in St. Louis. He graduated at the top of his class at Virginia Military Institute. He was promoted to brigadier general in May 1864, operating in the Shenandoah Valley and raiding into Maryland and Pennsylvania, where he put the town of Chambersburg to the torch in July 1864. McCausland lived in Europe and Mexico for two years after the war, then returned to his farm in West Virginia. He died in 1927 at the age of 91.

Lieutenant Colonel Joseph McGraw, Pegram's Virginia Artillery Battalion. An Irish immigrant and former teamster, McGraw rose to the command of Pegram's Battalion. He lost an arm at Spotsylvania yet insisted on returning to duty, commanding an artillery battalion at the end of the war at Appomattox.

Brigadier General Patrick T. Moore. Born in Ireland in 1821, Moore settled in Richmond, where he became a successful merchant and commanded the Montgomery Guard. He was colonel of the 1st Virginia at 1st Manassas, where he was badly wounded. Later Moore was as a volunteer aide to Joseph Johnston and commanded local defense forces in Richmond.

Colonel Charles T. O'Ferrall, 23rd Virginia Cavalry. Born in Frederick County in 1840, O'Ferrall earned a reputation as an aggressive cavalry officer and was wounded eight times during the war. He conducted operations in the Shenandoah Valley in 1864–1865. He was elected governor of Virginia in 1893.

Colonel Frederick G. Skinner, 1st Virginia Infantry. Born in Maryland, Skinner took over command of the 1st Virginia in July 1861. He was wounded at 2nd Manassas in August 1862.

Chapter Notes

Preface

1. Ella Lonn, *Foreigners in the Confederacy* (Chapel Hill: University of North Carolina Press, 1940), 228–229.
2. David Thomas Gleeson, *The Irish in the South, 1815–1877*, diss., Mississippi State University, 1997, 297; Lawrence J. McCaffrey, *The Irish Catholic Diaspora in America* (Washington, DC: Catholic University of America Press, 1997), 103; Kelly J. O'Grady, *Clear the Confederate Way!: The Irish in the Army of Northern Virginia* (Mason City, IA: Savas, 2000), xvii.

Prologue

1. Kelly J. O'Grady, *Clear the Confederate Way!: The Irish in the Army of Northern Virginia* (Mason City, IA: Savas, 2000), 50–59.
2. Lee A. Wallace, *1st Virginia Infantry* (Lynchburg, VA: H. E. Howard, Inc., 1985), 18.
3. Wallace, *1st Virginia Infantry*, 11.
4. O'Grady, *Clear the Confederate Way*, ix, 247–248; Phillip Thomas Tucker, *The South's Finest: The First Missouri Confederate Brigade from Pea Ridge to Vicksburg* (Shippensburg, PA: White Mane, 1993), 56–57; Ed Gleeson, *Rebel Sons of Erin: A Civil War Unit History of the Tenth Tennessee Infantry Regiment (Irish) Confederate States Volunteers* (Indianapolis: Guild Press of Indiana, 1993), xvii, 326.
5. O'Grady, *Clear the Confederate Way*, xviii.

Chapter 1

1. David Thomas Gleeson, *The Irish in the South, 1815–1877*, diss., Mississippi State University, 1997, 5–6.
2. Gleeson, *Irish in the South*, 5; Lawrence J. McCaffrey, *The Irish Catholic Diaspora in America* (Washington, DC: Catholic University of America Press, 1997), 63–64.
3. Gleeson, *Irish in the South*, 12–13; McCaffrey, *Irish Catholic Diaspora*, 64–65.
4. Gleeson, *Irish in the South*, 35, 54, 34; Earl F. Niehaus, *The Irish in New Orleans, 1800–1860* (Baton Rouge: Louisiana State University Press, 1965), 43–44.
5. Michael Glazier, ed., *The Encyclopedia of the Irish in America* (Notre Dame: University of Notre Dame Press, 1999), 357.

6. Niehaus, *Irish in New Orleans*, 44–49.
7. Niehaus, *Irish in New Orleans*, 48; David T. Gleeson, *The Mississippi Irish, 1700–1865*, masters thesis, Mississippi State University, 1993, 39.
8. Glazier, *Encyclopedia of the Irish*, 357–358; Gleeson, *Mississippi Irish*, 38; William Barnaby Faherty, *The St. Louis Irish: An Unmatched Celtic Community* (St. Louis: Missouri Historical Society Press, 2001), 54–55.
9. Fussell Chalker, "Irish Catholics in the Building of the Ocmulgee and Flint Railroad," *Georgia Historical Quarterly* 54 (1970): 507–516.
10. Gleeson, *Irish in the South*, 89.
11. Edward M. Shoemaker, *Strangers and Citizens: The Irish Immigrant Community of Savannah, 1837–1861*, diss., Emory University, 1990, 269–271.
12. Shoemaker, *Strangers and Citizens*, 269–272; Faherty, *St. Louis Irish*, 53–54.
13. Kathleen C. Berkeley, *"Like a Plague of Locusts": From an Antebellum Town to a New South City, Memphis, Tennessee, 1850–1880* (New York: Garland Publishing, Inc., 1991), 15; Niehaus, *Irish in New Orleans*, 37–38; Shoemaker, *Strangers and Citizens*, 272.
14. Niehaus, *Irish in New Orleans*, 39.
15. Gleeson, *Irish in the South*, 73.
16. Gleeson, *Irish in the South*, 72, 74; Niehaus, *Irish in New Orleans*, 40.
17. Gleeson, *Irish in the South*, 54; Dennis Clark, *Hibernia America: The Irish and Regional Cultures* (Westport, CT: Greenwood, 1986), 102; George E. Yater, *Two Hundred Years at the Falls of the Ohio: A History of Louisville and Jefferson County* (Louisville: Filson Club, 1987), 62.
18. Glazier, *Encyclopedia of the Irish*, 542; Gleeson, *Irish in the South*, 79; Shoemaker, *Strangers and Citizens*, 146.
19. Niehaus, *Irish in New Orleans*, 31, 46.
20. McCaffrey, *Irish Catholic Diaspora*, 66; Shoemaker, *Strangers and Citizens*, 17.
21. Niehaus, *Irish in New Orleans*, 117–118.
22. Niehaus, *Irish in New Orleans*, 115–116.
23. Theodore O'Hara obituary, *Confederate Veteran* 7 (1899): 202.
24. Shoemaker, *Strangers and Citizens*, 192–194; Herbert Weaver, "Foreigners in Ante-Bellum Savannah," *Georgia Historical Quarterly* 37 (1953): 7.
25. Niehaus, *Irish in New Orleans*, 22.
26. Gleeson, *Irish in the South*, 26–27.

27. Yater, *Two Hundred Years at the Falls*, 66; John E. Kleber, ed., *The Encyclopedia of Louisville* (Lexington: University Press of Kentucky, 2001), 97.

28. Faherty, *St. Louis Irish*, 66–67.

29. Niehaus, *Irish in New Orleans*, 88–91.

30. Gleeson, *Irish in the South*, 223–224.

31. Michael Damon Seigle, *Savannah's Own: The Irish Jasper Greens, 1842–1865*, masters thesis, Armstrong State College, Savannah, 1994, 25–26; Gleeson, *Irish in the South*, 224.

32. Gleeson, *Irish in the South*, 227.

33. Gleeson, *Irish in the South*, 268, 303; Niehaus, *Irish in New Orleans*, 157–158.

34. Howell and Elizabeth Purdue, *Pat Cleburne: Confederate General* (Tuscaloosa: Portals Press, 1977), 44–45.

35. Niehaus, *Irish in New Orleans*, 54–55; McCaffrey, *Irish Catholic Diaspora*, 74.

36. Gleeson, *Irish in the South*, 239.

37. Niehaus, *Irish in New Orleans*, 49–53.

38. D. Clayton James, *Antebellum Natchez* (Baton Rouge: LSU Press, 1988), 167–168.

39. Shoemaker, *Strangers and Citizens*, 197–201.

40. Joseph M. Hernon, Jr., "The Irish Nationalists and Southern Secession," *Civil War History* 12 (1966): 43–53.

41. Kelly J. O'Grady, *Clear the Confederate Way!: The Irish in the Army of Northern Virginia* (Mason City, IA: Savas Publishing Company, 2000), 24; Clark, *Hibernia America*, 103–104; Gleeson, *Irish in the South*, 263.

42. Gleeson, *Irish in the South*, 269.

43. Gleeson, *Irish in the South*, 270, 304–305.

44. Gleeson, *Irish in the South*, 268, 297; McCaffrey, *Irish Catholic Diaspora*, 103.

45. Purdue, *Pat Cleburne*, 36, 45.

46. O'Grady, *Clear the Confederate Way*, 279–280.

Chapter 2

1. *War of the Rebellion: A Compilation of the Official Records of the Union and Confederate Armies* (Washington, DC: Government Printing Office, 1880–1901) (hereafter cited as *OR*), Series I, Volume 30, Part IV, 594.

2. *OR* 52: II, 587, 589.

3. Kelly J. O'Grady, *Clear the Confederate Way!: The Irish in the Army of Northern Virginia* (Mason City, IA: Savas Publishing Company, 2000), 142–143, 248.

4. Ella Lonn, *Foreigners in the Confederacy* (Chapel Hill: University of North Carolina Press, 1940), 228–229; David Thomas Gleeson, *The Irish in the South, 1815–1877*, diss., Mississippi State University, 1997, 291.

5. O'Grady, *Clear the Confederate Way*, 247–248.

6. *OR* 16: I, 950; 30: II, 260; John Berrien Lindsley, *Military Annals of Tennessee: Confederate* v. 1 (Wilmington, NC: Broadfoot Publishing Co., 1995), 151; Ed Gleeson, *Rebel Sons of Erin: A Civil War Unit History of the Tenth Tennessee Infantry Regiment (Irish) Confederate States Volunteers* (Indianapolis: Guild Press of Indiana, 1993), xvii, 326;

7. Lonn, *Foreigners in the Confederacy*, 230; *OR* 3: 330–331; Lindsley, *Military Annals of Tennessee*, 74–75, 146.

8. L. G. Williams, "Hand to Hand Fight in the Army," *Confederate Veteran* 2 (1894): 228–229; J. E. Carruth, "Gallantry of General Rosecrans," *Confederate Veteran* 14 (1906): 514–515.

9. Gleeson, *Rebel Sons of Erin*, 18–19.

10. Lindsley, *Military Annals of Tennessee*, 150.

11. John McGrath, "In a Louisiana Regiment," *Southern Historical Society Papers* 31 (1903): 115–116.

12. Hilary A. Herbert, "History of the Eighth Alabama Volunteer Regiment, C. S. A.," *Alabama Historical Quarterly* 39 (1977): 113–114, 253.

13. Gleeson, *Rebel Sons of Erin*, xviii,15–16.

14. McGrath, "In a Louisiana Regiment," 105–106.

15. Lindsley, *Military Annals of Tennessee*, 149–150.

16. Gleeson, *Rebel Sons of Erin*, 226–228; "Bernard McCabe," *Confederate Veteran* 15 (1907): 422.

17. McGrath, "In a Louisiana Regiment," 104.

18. Terry L. Jones, *Lee's Tigers: The Louisiana Infantry in the Army of Northern Virginia* (Baton Rouge: LSU Press, 1987), 17–18, 230.

19. Larry J. Daniel, *Soldiering in the Army of Tennessee: A Portrait of Life in a Confederate Army* (Chapel Hill: University of North Carolina Press, 1991), 106.

20. *OR* 11: II, 571; O'Grady, *Clear the Confederate Way*, 79–85, 257.

21. Daniel, *Soldiering in the Army of Tennessee*, 18; Bell Irvin Wiley, *The Life of Johnny Reb: The Common Soldier of the Confederacy* (New York: Bobbs-Merrill, 1943), 40–42.

22. Gleeson, *Rebel Sons of Erin*, 19–20, 39–40.

23. Frank L. Richardson, "War As I Saw It, 1861–1865," *Louisiana Historical Quarterly* 6 (1923): 96–97

24. McGrath, "In a Louisiana Regiment," 106; Gleeson, *Rebel Sons of Erin*, 39–40, 152–153.

25. Lonn, *Foreigners in the Confederacy*, 447.

26. Irving A. Buck, *Cleburne and His Command* (Jackson, TN: McCowat-Mercer Press, 1959), 224–225; Stan C. Harley, "Gen. Pat Cleburne's Division of Sharpshooters," *Confederate Veteran* 7 (1899): 307.

Chapter 3

1. David Thomas Gleeson, *The Irish in the South, 1815–1877*, diss., Mississippi State University, 1997, 309–310.

2. Mary S. Hill Obituary, *Confederate Veteran* 10 (1902): 124.

3. Ed Gleeson, *Rebel Sons of Erin: A Civil War Unit History of the Tenth Tennessee Infantry Regiment (Irish) Confederate States Volunteers* (Indianapolis: Guild Press of Indiana, 1993), 3, 7, 11–12; Sarah McGavock Lindsley Obituary, *Confederate Veteran* 11 (1903): 368.

4. Letitia Austin Fraser Obituary, *Confederate Veteran* 32 (1924): 75.

5. Roger S. Durham, ed., *The Blues in Gray: The Civil War Journal of William Daniel Dixon and the Republican Blues Daybook* (Knoxville: University of Tennessee Press, 2000), 163, 165, 350.

6. Gleeson, *Irish in the South*, 318.

7. William Barnaby Faherty, *The St. Louis Irish: An Unmatched Celtic Community* (St. Louis: Missouri Historical Society Press, 2001), 77.

8. Phillip Thomas Tucker, *The South's Finest: The First Missouri Confederate Brigade from Pea Ridge to Vicksburg* (Shippensburg, PA: White Mane, 1993), 54.

9. Sean Michael O'Brien, *Mobile, 1865: Last Stand of the Confederacy* (Westport, CT: Praeger, 2001), 19–20, 24–25.

10. Michael Damon Seigle, *Savannah's Own: The Irish Jasper Greens, 1842–1865*, masters thesis, Armstrong State College, 1994, 45, 49–52, 71; Lillian Henderson, *Roster of the Confederate Soldiers of Georgia, 1861–1865*, Vol. 1 (Hapeville, GA: Longino and Porter), 1959), 115–131, 157–169.

11. Gleeson, *Irish in the South*, 305; Faherty, *St. Louis Irish*, 80

12. Gleeson, *Irish in the South,* 303–306.

13. John Brendan Flannery, *The Irish Texans* (San Antonio: University of Texas Institute of Texan Cultures, 1980), 62.

14. Gleeson, *Irish in the South,* 306–309; O'Brien, *Mobile,* 18.

15. Gleeson, *Irish in the South,* 322, 341; Kathleen C. Berkeley, *"Like a Plague of Locusts": From an Antebellum Town to a New South City, Memphis, Tennessee, 1850–1880* (New York: Garland Publishing, Inc., 1991), 100–101.

16. Gleeson, *Irish in the South,* 323–325.

17. James J. McGowan Obituary, *Confederate Veteran* 9 (1901): 126.

18. Willard E. Wight, "Letters of the Bishop of Savannah, 1861–1865," *Georgia Historical Quarterly* 42 (1958): 93–94, 99.

19. Edward M. Shoemaker, *Strangers and Citizens: The Irish Immigrant Community of Savannah, 1837–1861,* diss., Emory University, 1990, 209; James David Griffin, *Savannah, Georgia, During the Civil War,* diss., University of Georgia, 1963, 225, 235.

20. Faherty, *St. Louis Irish,* 81–82.

21. Larry J. Daniel, *Soldiering in the Army of Tennessee: A Portrait of Life in a Confederate Army* (Chapel Hill: University of North Carolina Press, 1991), 122.

22. Kelly J. O'Grady, *Clear the Confederate Way!: The Irish in the Army of Northern Virginia* (Mason City, IA: Savas Publishing Company, 2000), 26–27.

23. Joseph T. Durkin, ed., *Confederate Chaplain: A War Journal of Rev. James B. Sheeran, C. SS. R., 14th Louisiana, C. S. A.* (Milwaukee: Bruce Publishing Co., 1960), 4, 21, 128.

24. Gleeson, *Rebel Sons of Erin,* 276–277, 304.

25. Albert C. Danner, "Father Bannon's Secret Mission," *Confederate Veteran* 27 (1919): 180–181; Tucker, *South's Finest,* 10–11; Faherty, *St. Louis Irish,* 79–80.

Chapter 4

1. Terry L. Jones, *Lee's Tigers: The Louisiana Infantry in the Army of Northern Virginia* (Baton Rouge: LSU Press, 1987), 4–5.

2. Richard Taylor, *Destruction and Reconstruction: Personal Experiences of the Late War* (New York: 1879), 24; Ella Lonn, *Foreigners in the Confederacy* (Chapel Hill: University of North Carolina Press, 1940), 105.

3. Jones, *Lee's Tigers,* 51–53; Gary Schreckengost, "Confederate Zouaves at First Manassas," *America's Civil War* May 1999: 26 +.

4. *War of the Rebellion: A Compilation of the Official Records of the Union and Confederate Armies* (Washington, DC: Government Printing Office, 1880–1901) (hereafter cited as *OR*), Series I, Volume 2, 570.

5. Jones, *Lee's Tigers,* 54–55.

6. *OR* 2: 372.

7. James I. Robertson, Jr., *The Stonewall Brigade* (Baton Rouge: LSU Press, 1963), 13.

8. John W. Daniel, "A Charge at First Manassas," *Confederate Veteran* 39 (1931): 345, 358.

9. Robertson, *Stonewall Brigade,* 38–39.

10. *OR* 2: 394, 481–482.

11. Robertson, *Stonewall Brigade,* 41.

12. Daniel, "A Charge at First Manassas," 358.

13. *OR* 2: 570.

14. Robertson, *Stonewall Brigade,* 44.

15. *OR* 12: I, 384, 394, 396.

16. *OR* 12: I, 406–407; Kelly J. O'Grady, *Clear the*

Confederate Way!: The Irish in the Army of Northern Virginia* (Mason City, IA: Savas, 2000), 274, 287.

17. O'Grady, *Clear the Confederate* Way, 65; Taylor, *Destruction and Reconstruction,* 54, 68.

18. *OR* 12: I, 800.

19. *OR* 12: I, 780, 801.

20. Taylor, *Destruction and Reconstruction,* 68.

21. *OR* 12: I, 717, 783.

22. John D. Imboden, "Stonewall Jackson in the Shenandoah," in *Battles and Leaders of the Civil War,* Vol. 2, eds. Robert U. Johnson and Clarence C. Buel (New York: Castle Books, 1956), 296; Taylor, *Destruction and Reconstruction,* 76.

23. *OR* 12: I, 717.

Chapter 5

1. *Charleston Mercury* December 29, 1860.

2. *Charleston Daily Courier* September 12, 1861, September 17, 1861.

3. Edward McCrady, "The Boy Heroes of Cold Harbor," *Southern Historical Society Papers* 25 (1897): 234–239.

4. "Fine Marksman in Virginia Army," *Confederate Veteran* 24 (1916): 285.

5. Ella Lonn, *Foreigners in the Confederacy* (Chapel Hill: University of North Carolina Press, 1940), 96; Willis Brewer, *Alabama: Her History, Resources, War Record, and Public Men, From 1540 to 1872* (Montgomery, 1872), 600–602.

6. Thomas D. Cockrell and Michael B. Ballard, eds., *A Mississippi Rebel in the Army of Northern Virginia: The Civil War Memoirs of Private David Holt* (Baton Rouge: LSU Press, 1995), 82–83; David T. Gleeson, *The Mississippi Irish, 1700–1865,* masters thesis, Mississippi State University, 1993, 35–36.

7. Ada Christine Lightsey, *The Veteran's Story: The Story of the Jasper Grays, 16th Mississippi Regiment* (Meridian, MS, 1899), 1.

8. *War of the Rebellion: A Compilation of the Official Records of the Union and Confederate Armies* (Washington, DC: Government Printing Office, 1880–1901) (hereafter cited as *OR*), Series I, Volume 11, Part II, 836.

9. McCrady, "Boy Heroes," 234–239; "Fine Marksman," 285; *OR* 11: II, 382, 861–862.

10. *OR* 11: II, 982.

11. *OR* 11: II, 614–616, 975; Robert G. Evans, ed., *The Sixteenth Mississippi Infantry: Civil War Letters and Reminiscences* (Jackson: University Press of Mississippi, 2002), 85.

12. *OR* 11: II, 767–768.

13. *OR* 11: II, 327, 774.

14. *OR* 11: II, 774, 778, 980; Brewer, *Alabama,* 598–601.

15. Hilary A. Herbert, "History of the Eighth Alabama Volunteer Regiment, C. S. A.," *Alabama Historical Quarterly* 39 (1977): 64–66, 294–305.

16. *OR* 11: I, 569, 593; *OR* 11: II, 980.

17. *OR* 11: II, 569.

18. Brewer, *Alabama,* 601–602; *OR* 11: II, 980; Kelly J. O'Grady, *Clear the Confederate Way!: The Irish in the Army of Northern Virginia* (Mason City, IA: Savas, 2000), 74.

19. Daniel H. Hill, "McClellan's Change of Base and Malvern Hill," in *Battles and Leaders of the Civil War,* Vol. 2, eds. Robert U. Johnson and Clarence C. Buel (New York: Castle Books, 1956), 383–395.

20. Herbert, *Eighth Alabama,* 294–305.

21. "Paroles of the Army of Northern Virginia,"

Southern Historical Society Papers 15 (1887): 328–329; Lightsey, *The Veteran's Story*, 46.

22. James Armstrong and Varina D. Brown, "McGowan's Brigade at Spotsylvania," *Confederate Veteran* 33 (1925): 376–379.

Chapter 6

1. Earl F. Niehaus, *The Irish in New Orleans, 1800–1860* (Baton Rouge: Louisiana State University Press, 1965), 158, 161.

2. Terry L. Jones, *Lee's Tigers: The Louisiana Infantry in the Army of Northern Virginia* (Baton Rouge: LSU Press, 1987), 233–234.

3. Ella Lonn, *Foreigners in the Confederacy* (Chapel Hill: University of North Carolina Press, 1940), 497; Niehaus, *Irish in New Orleans*, 115–116; Kelly J. O'Grady, *Clear the Confederate Way!: The Irish in the Army of Northern Virginia* (Mason City, IA: Savas Publishing Company, 2000), 281–282.

4. Jones, *Lee's Tigers*, 236–237.

5. Richard Taylor, *Destruction and Reconstruction: Personal Experiences of the Late War* (New York: 1879), 47; Jones, *Lee's Tigers*, 238–239.

6. O'Grady, *Clear the Confederate Way*, 271, 280, 288.

7. Taylor, *Destruction and Reconstruction*, 47; Jones, *Lee's Tigers*, 240.

8. Jones, *Lee's Tigers*, 241.

9. *War of the Rebellion: A Compilation of the Official Records of the Union and Confederate Armies* (Washington, DC: Government Printing Office, 1880–1901) (hereafter cited as *OR*), Series I, Volume 12: Part II, 680, 681, 685–689.

10. *OR* 12: II, 646, 718; Allan C. Redwood, "Jackson's 'Foot Cavalry' at the Second Bull Run," in *Battles and Leaders of the Civil War*, Vol. 2, eds. Robert U. Johnson and Clarence C. Buel (New York: Castle Books, 1956), 535; O'Grady, *Clear the Confederate Way*, 288.

11. *OR* 12: II, 681–682, 684, 812.

12. *OR* 12: II, 668–669, 814; Redwood, "Jackson's 'Foot Cavalry,'" 535–536.

13. W. A. Taliaferro, "Jackon's Raid Around Pope," *Battles and Leaders*, Vol. 2, 508.

14. *OR* 19: I, 216, 811, 968, 974, 978–979; Jones, *Lee's Tigers*, 130; Stephen W. Sears, *Landscape Turned Red: The Battle of Antietam* (New York: Ticknor and Fields, 1983), 189–190.

15. Jones, *Lee's Tigers*, 131–132; Sears, *Landscape Turned Red*, 194–195; *OR* 19: I, 1015–1018.

16. John B. Gordon, *Reminiscences of the Civil War* (New York: Scribners, 1903), 84, 87.

17. Montgomery *Daily Post* September 24, 1861; Lonn, *Foreigners in the Confederacy*, 95–96; Montgomery Greys Retired Corps, *The Montgomery Greys Under Two Flags* (Montgomery, AL: The Corps, 1908), 7, 19; Willis Brewer, *Alabama: Her History, Resources, War Record, and Public Men, from 1540 to 1872* (Montgomery, 1872), 598–599.

18. Sears, *Landscape Turned Red*, 243–244.

19. *OR* 19: I, 814; Sears, *Landscape Turned Red*, 244.

20. Hilary A. Herbert, "History of the Eighth Alabama Volunteer Regiment, C. S. A.," *Alabama Historical Quarterly* 39 (1977): 77–79; *OR* 19: I, 812, 1056.

21. Sears, *Landscape Turned Red*, 245–246; Brewer, *Alabama*, 598–599; *OR* 19: I, 1037–1038.

22. Sears, *Landscape Turned Red*, 288–289; *OR* 19: I, 989, 991–992.

23. Sears, *Landscape Turned Red*, 296.

24. O'Grady, *Clear the Confederate Way*, 99–100.

Chapter 7

1. Kelly J. O'Grady, *Clear the Confederate Way!: The Irish in the Army of Northern Virginia* (Mason City, IA: Savas Publishing Company, 2000), 108–109, 249–250; *War of the Rebellion: A Compilation of the Official Records of the Union and Confederate Armies* (Washington, DC: Government Printing Office, 1880–1901) (hereafter cited as *OR*), Series I, Vol. 21, 560.

2. *OR* 21: 632, 657–659.

3. *OR* 21: 560, 632, 651–652.

4. *OR* 21: 632; O'Grady, *Clear the Confederate Way*, 112.

5. *OR* 21: 607–608.

6. "A Gallant Irishman at Fredericksburg," *Charleston Daily Courier* December 30, 1862; O'Grady, *Clear the Confederate Way*, 115, 125.

7. David P. Conyngham, *The Irish Brigade and Its Campaigns* (New York: Fordham University Press, 1994), 347–350.

8. Conyngham, *Irish Brigade*, 343; *OR* 21: 129, 243; "Gallant Irishman at Fredericksburg."

9. *OR* 21: 582, 584, 608.

10. O'Grady, *Clear the Confederate Way*, 143; Conyngham, *Irish Brigade*, xvi.

11. O'Grady, *Clear the Confederate Way*, 143–150.

Chapter 8

1. Joseph T. Durkin, ed., *John Dooley Confederate Soldier: His War Journal* (Ithaca, NY: Georgetown University Press, 1945), 102–105.

2. Durkin, *John Dooley*, 51, 89.

3. Kelly J. O'Grady, *Clear the Confederate Way!: The Irish in the Army of Northern Virginia* (Mason City, IA: Savas Publishing Company, 2000), 258–259, 288.

4. *War of the Rebellion: A Compilation of the Official Records of the Union and Confederate Armies* (Washington, DC: Government Printing Office, 1880–1901) (hereafter cited as *OR*), Series I, Volume 5, 977; James I. Robertson, Jr., *The Stonewall Brigade* (Baton Rouge: LSU Press, 1963), 174.

5. *OR* 25: I, 807, 951, 959–960, 978–979, 1053; O'Grady, *Clear the Confederate Way*, 156.

6. Robertson, *Stonewall Brigade*, 190, 193; *OR* 25: II, 840.

7. Terry L. Jones, *Lee's Tigers: The Louisiana Infantry in the Army of Northern Virginia* (Baton Rouge: LSU Press, 1987), 147–148, 155; *OR* 25: I, 903.

8. Jones, *Lee's Tigers*, 149–152.

9. *OR* 25: I, 854, 858–861, 873, 1056.

10. Jones, *Lee's Tigers*, 152–155.

11. Robert G. Evans, ed., *The Sixteenth Mississippi Infantry: Civil War Letters and Reminiscences* (Jackson: University Press of Mississippi, 2002), 154; Hilary A. Herbert, "History of the Eighth Alabama Volunteer Regiment, C. S. A.," *Alabama Historical Quarterly* 39 (1977): 108; O'Grady, *Clear the Confederate Way*, 155.

12. Jones, *Lee's Tigers*, 175–176; *OR* 27: I, 234, 722, 894; *OR* 27: II, 340, 446–447, 475, 480–482.

13. *OR* 27: II, 503–504, 506, 532; Blayney T. Walshe, "Louisianians in the Virginia Army," *Confederate Veteran* 6 (1898): 177.

14. Robertson, *Stonewall Brigade.* 203–206; *OR* 27: II, 341, 486, 504, 526–530.

15. Durkin, *John Dooley*, 101.

16. *OR* 27: I, 431; Durkin, *John Dooley*, 105–107; Lee A. Wallace, *1st Virginia Infantry* (Lynchburg, VA: H. E. Howard , Inc., 1985), 43; O'Grady, *Clear the Confederate Way*, 165.

17. Herbert, "Eighth Alabama," 115–118, 125; E. Porter Alexander, "The Great Charge and Artillery Fighting at Gettysburg," in *Battles and Leaders of the Civil War*, Vol. 3, eds. Robert U. Johnson and Clarence C. Buel (New York: Castle Books, 1956), 366; *OR* 27: I, 425; *OR* 27: II, 618–619, 775.

18. Wallace, *1st Virginia*, 43, 76.

19. Stephen W. Sears, *Gettysburg* (Boston: Houghton Mifflin, 2003), 498.

Chapter 9

1. Lee A. Wallace, *1st Virginia Infantry* (Lynchburg, VA: H. E. Howard , Inc., 1985), 76.

2. James Armstrong, "McGowan's Brigade at Spotsylvania," *Confederate Veteran* 33 (1925): 376–379.

3. Jeffry D. Wert, A *Brotherhood of Valor: The Common Soldiers of the Stonewall Brigade, C. S. A., and the Iron Brigade, U. S. A.* (New York: Simon and Schuster, 1999), 294–300.

4. Hilary A. Herbert, "History of the Eighth Alabama Volunteer Regiment, C. S. A.," *Alabama Historical Quarterly* 39 (1977): 140, 294- 305.

5. Robert G. Evans, ed., *The Sixteenth Mississippi Infantry: Civil War Letters and Reminiscences* (Jackson: University Press of Mississippi, 2002), 257, 262.

6. *War of the Rebellion: A Compilation of the Official Records of the Union and Confederate Armies* (Washington, DC: Government Printing Office, 1880–1901) (hereafter cited as *OR*), Series I, Volume 36, Part I, 1060, 1094.

7. P. W. Alexander, "Some Florida Heroes," *Confederate Veteran* 11 (1903): 363–365; *OR* 36: I, 1032.

8. *OR* 40: I, 812–813; Willis Brewer, *Alabama: Her History, Resources, War Record, and Public Men, From 1540 to 1872* (Montgomery, 1872), 694–695.

9. Herbert, "Eighth Alabama," 294–305.

10. Lillian Henderson, *Roster of the Confederate Soldiers of Georgia, 1861–1865.* Vol. 1 (Hapeville, GA: Longino and Porter, 1959), 705–710.

11. *OR* 42: I, 431.

12. Herbert, "Eighth Alabama," 149, 151, 294- 305.

13. Wert, *Brotherhood of Valor*, 309.

14. Noah Andre Trudeau, *The Last Citadel: Petersburg, Virginia, June 1864-April 1865* (Boston: Little, Brown and Company, 1991), 338.

15. J. E. Gaskell, "Last Engagement of Lee's Army," *Confederate Veteran* 29 (1921): 261–262; Trudeau, *The Last Citadel*, 388.

16. Herbert, "Eighth Alabama," 37, 188–189.

17. Montgomery Greys Retired Corps, *The Montgomery Greys Under Two Flags* (Montgomery, AL: The Corps, 1908), 8; Terry L. Jones, *Lee's Tigers: The Louisiana Infantry in the Army of Northern Virginia* (Baton Rouge: LSU Press, 1987), 227; Wert, *Brotherhood of Valor*, 311.

18. Kelly J. O'Grady, *Clear the Confederate Way!: The Irish in the Army of Northern Virginia* (Mason City, IA: Savas Publishing Company, 2000), 200; Joseph T. Durkin, ed., *John Dooley Confederate Soldier: His War Journal* (Ithaca, NY: Georgetown University Press, 1945), 208.

Chapter 10

1. J. A. Wheeler, "Cleburne's Brigade at Shiloh," *Confederate Veteran* 2 (1894): 13.

2. Larry J. Daniel, *Shiloh: The Battle That Changed the Civil War* (New York: Simon & Schuster, 1997), 163.

3. Mauriel Phillips Joslyn, ed., *A Meteor Shining Brightly: Essays on the Life and Career of Major General Patrick R. Cleburne* (Macon, GA: Mercer University Press, 2000), 50; Daniel, *Shiloh*, 191; John Berrien Lindsley, *Military Annals of Tennessee: Confederate* v. 1 (Wilmington, NC: Broadfoot Publishing Co., 1995), 173–175, 333–335.

4. Frank L. Richardson, "War As I Saw It," *Louisiana Historical Quarterly* 6 (1923): 99, 100; Daniel, *Shiloh*, 211.

5. Daniel, *Shiloh*, 211.

6. Daniel, *Shiloh*, 211–212; John McGrath, "In a Louisiana Regiment," *Southern Historical Society Papers* 31 (1903): 114.

7. Daniel, *Shiloh*, 213; *War of the Rebellion: A Compilation of the Official Records of the Union and Confederate Armies* (Washington, DC: Government Printing Office, 1880–1901) (hereafter cited as *OR*), Series I, Volume 10, Part I, 488.

8. William Preston Johnston, "Albert Sidney Johnston at Shiloh," in *Battles and Leaders of the Civil War*, Vol. 1, eds. Robert U. Johnson and Clarence C. Buel (New York: Castle Books, 1956), 564.

9. Phil Gottschalk, *In Deadly Earnest: The History of the First Missouri Brigade, CSA* (Columbia, MO: Missouri River Press, Inc., 1991), 88.

10. Gottschalk, *In Deadly Earnest*, 96.

11. Gottschalk, *In Deadly Earnest*, 96.

12. Daniel, *Shiloh*, 262; *OR* 10: I, 580–584.

13. Gottschalk, *In Deadly Earnest*, 97–100.

14. Daniel, *Shiloh*, 305.

Chapter 11

1. Kenneth W. Noe, *Perryville: This Grand Havoc of Battle* (Lexington: University Press of Kentucky, 2001), 230, 268–271.

2. *War of the Rebellion: A Compilation of the Official Records of the Union and Confederate Armies* (Washington, DC: Government Printing Office, 1880–1901) (hereafter cited as *OR*), Series I, Volume 16, Part I, 1123–1124.

3. John Berrien Lindsley, *Military Annals of Tennessee: Confederate* v. 1 (Wilmington, NC: Broadfoot Publishing Co., 1995), 147–148; *OR* 16: I, 1123–1124.

4. Mauriel Phillips Joslyn, ed., *A Meteor Shining Brightly: Essays on the Life and Career of Major General Patrick R. Cleburne* (Macon, GA: Mercer University Press, 2000), 55; *OR* 52: I, 51–52; *OR* 16: 1, 1127; Edmund O'Neill, Letter, *Confederate Veteran* 5 (1897): 420.

5. Lindsley, *Military Annals*, 150; *OR* 20: I, 844–848, 857, 871–873; Gilbert C. Kniffin, "The Battle of Stone's River," in *Battles and Leaders of the Civil War*, Vol. 3, eds. Robert U. Johnson and Clarence C. Buel (New York: Castle Books, 1956), 619.

6. *OR* 20: I, 845; G. A. Williams, "Blow Your Horn, Jake," *Confederate Veteran* 5 (1897): 220.

7. *OR* 20: I, 848, 850, 852, 860; Lindsley, *Military Annals*, 149.

8. *OR* 20: I, 678, 973.

9. Grady McWhiney, *Braxton Bragg and Confederate Defeat*, Vol. 1 (Tuscaloosa: University of Alabama

Press, 1991), 357; Dunbar Rowland, *Military History of Mississippi, 1803–1898* (Spartanburg, SC: Reprint Company Publishers, 1978), 589–590; Kniffin, "Battle of Stone's River," 626.

10. *OR* 20: I, 677, 756.

11. James Lee McDonough, *Stones River: Bloody Winter in Tennessee* (Knoxville: University of Tennessee Press, 1980), 141; *OR* 20: I, 795–802; McWhiney, *Braxton Bragg*, 361.

12. McDonough, *Stones River*, 148.

13. David Urquhart, "Bragg's Advance and Retreat," in *Battles and Leaders of the Civil War*, Vol. 3, eds. Robert U. Johnson and Clarence C. Buel (New York: Castle Books, 1956), 607.

14. McDonough, *Stones River*, 193, 202; Lindsley, *Military Annals*, 150; *OR* 20: I, 678.

15. McDonough, *Stones River*, 10, 230.

16. McWhiney, *Braxton Bragg*, 352, 354–355; McDonough, *Stones River*, 222–223.

Chapter 12

1. Kathleen C. Berkeley, *"Like a Plague of Locusts": From an Antebellum Town to a New South City, Memphis, Tennessee, 1850–1880* (New York: Garland Publishing, Inc., 1991), 15–16, 32–33, 61–62.

2. John Berrien Lindsley, *Military Annals of Tennessee: Confederate,* v. 1 (Wilmington, NC: Broadfoot Publishing Co., 1995), 74.

3. Howell and Elizabeth Purdue, *Pat Cleburne: Confederate General* (Tuscaloosa, AL: Portals Press, 1977), 113.

4. Purdue, *Pat Cleburne*, 113–114.

5. *War of the Rebellion: A Compilation of the Official Records of the Union and Confederate Armies* (Washington, DC: Government Printing Office, 1880–1901) (hereafter cited as *OR*), Series I, Volume 30, Part II, 263.

6. *OR* 30: I, 300; 30: II, 154, 158, 168, 170, 174, 176–180, 542; Peter Cozzens, *This Terrible Sound: The Battle of Chickamauga* (Chicago: University of Illinois Press, 1992), 266; Shelby Foote, *The Civil War: A Narrative: Fredericksburg to Meridian* (New York: Random House, 1986), 722.

7. *OR* 30: I, 368, and II, 221–226, 368.

8. *OR* 30: II, 155, 177, 180, 185.

9. *OR* 30: I, 448; II, 346–347.

10. Cozzens, *This Terrible Sound*, 435–436, 461–462; *OR* 30: II, 318–319, 321–327.

11. Gleeson, *Rebel Sons of Erin: A Civil War Unit History of the Tenth Tennessee Infantry Regiment (Irish) Confederate States Volunteers* (Indianapolis: Guild Press of Indiana, 1993), 238–239, 243, 246–247.

12. *OR* 30: II, 156, 177–181; Lindsley, *Military Annals,* 150.

13. Cozzens, *This Terrible Sound*, 534; *OR* 30: II, 158.

14. Willis Brewer, *Alabama: Her History, Resources, War Record, and Public Men from 1540 to 1872* (Montgomery, 1872), 502.

15. *OR* 31: II, 653, 747–752; Irving A. Buck, *Cleburne and His Command* (Jackson, TN: McCowat-Mercer Press, 1959), 169–170.

16. James Lee McDonough, *Chattanooga: A Death Grip on the Confederacy* (Knoxville: University of Tennessee Press, 1984), 172, 175, 181–185, 187–188.

17. Gleeson, *Rebel Sons of Erin*, 267–268; Lindsley, *Military Annals*, 503.

18. Lindsley, *Military Annals*, 790–794.

19. McDonough, *Chattanooga*, 202, 204.

20. *OR* 31: II, 743; Gleeson, *Rebel Sons of Erin*, 268, 272.

21. *OR* 31: II, 754–757; Mauriel Phillips Joslyn, ed., *A Meteor Shining Brightly: Essays on the Life and Career of Major General Patrick R. Cleburne* (Mercer University Press, 2000), 83; Buck, *Cleburne and His Command*, 182–185; *OR* 23: I, 591.

Chapter 13

1. Sam Watkins, "Snowball Battle at Dalton," *Confederate Veteran* 2 (1894): 204–205; Howell and Elizabeth Purdue, *Pat Cleburne: Confederate General* (Tuscaloosa: Portals Press, 1977), 176; Mark K. Christ, ed., *Getting Used to Being Shot At: The Spence Family Civil War Letters* (Fayetteville: University of Arkansas Press, 2002), 79; Larry J. Daniel, *Soldiering in the Army of Tennessee: A Portrait of Life in a Confederate Army* (Chapel Hill: University of North Carolina Press, 1991), 94.

2. *War of the Rebellion: A Compilation of the Official Records of the Union and Confederate Armies* (Washington, DC: Government Printing Office, 1880–1901) (hereafter cited as *OR*), Series I, Volume 31: III, 822–827, 883.

3. Daniel, *Soldiering in the Army of Tennessee*, 139; Purdue, *Pat Cleburne*, 171.

4. William Milner Kelly, "A History of the Thirtieth Alabama Volunteers," *Alabama Historical Quarterly* 9 (1947): 153, 155.

5. Ed Gleeson, *Rebel Sons of Erin: A Civil War Unit History of the Tenth Tennessee Infantry Regiment (Irish) Confederate States Volunteers* (Indianapolis: Guild Press of Indiana, 1993), 284–285.

6. Albert Castel, *Decision in the West: The Atlanta Campaign of 1864* (Lawrence, KS: University Press of Kansas, 1992), 216.

7. Gleeson, *Rebel Sons of Erin*, 285; *OR* 38: III, 859–863.

8. Castel, *Decision in the West*, 237–241.

9. Illene D. Thompson and Wilbur E. Thompson, *The 17th Alabama Infantry: A Regimental History and Roster* (Bowie, MD: Heritage Books, Inc., 2001), 85.

10. Castel, *Decision in the West*, 316; Christ, *Getting Used to Being Shot At*, 84.

11. Purdue, *Pat Cleburne*, 228; Mauriel Phillips Joslyn, ed., *A Meteor Shining Brightly: Essays on the Life and Career of Major General Patrick R. Cleburne* (Macon, GA: Mercer University Press, 2000), 120.

12. Irving A. Buck, *Cleburne and His Command* (Jackson, TN: McCowat-Mercer Press, 1959), 232–234; *OR* 38: III, 730, 746.

13. Roger S. Durham, ed., *The Blues in Gray: The Civil War Journal of William Daniel Dixon and the Republican Blues Daybook* (Knoxville: University of Tennessee Press, 2000), 223.

14. *OR* 38: III, 418–419, 450–451; Gleeson, *Rebel Sons of Erin*, 292–293.

15. *OR* 38: III, 474–482, 758–759.

16. Durham, *Blues in Gray*, 217; Michael Damon Seigle, *Savannah's Own: The Irish Jasper Greens, 1842–1865*, masters thesis, Armstrong State College, Savannah, 1994, 49–51.

17. Durham, *Blues in Gray*, 223–224.

18. John Berrien Lindsley, *Military Annals of Tennessee: Confederate*, vol. 1, (Wilmington, NC: Broadfoot Publishing Co., 1995), 151; Castel, *Decision in the West*, 398–399.

19. Buck, *Cleburne and His Command*, 235; Castel,

Decision in the West, 400–402; Purdue, *Pat Cleburne,* 215; *OR* 38: III, 545–546, 588, 594, 608–610, 737–739.

20. *OR* 38: III, 318–319, 545–546, 564–565, 581–582, 730, 747, 751.

21. *OR* 38: III, 581–582, 588, 594, 605–606, 731–732.

22. *OR* 38: III, 545–546, 581–582, 588, 594.

23. *OR* 38: III, 25–26, 179–180, 217–218, 223–224, 245–246, 787–788.

24. Castel, *Decision in the West,* 407–408; *OR* 38: III, 139–140.

25. *OR* 38: III, 754, 756; Seigle, *Savannah's Own,* 58.

26. *OR* 38: III, 26–27, 547, 565, 582–583, 739–741.

27. Lindsley, *Military Annals,* 151; Castel, *Decision in the West,* 412.

28. Castel, *Decision in the West,* 431, 434; *OR* 38: III, 856–858.

29. Gleeson, *Rebel Sons of Erin,* 294–300; *OR* 38: II, 705–707.

30. *OR* 38: III, 729, 742–743.

31. Durham, *Blues in Gray,* 225; *OR* 38: III, 758.

32. Gleeson, *Rebel Sons of Erin,* 304–305.

33. Durham, *Blues in Gray,* 234–235; Kelly, "History of the Thirtieth Alabama," 155, 157.

34. Phil Gottschalk, *In Deadly Earnest: The History of the First Missouri Brigade, CSA* (Columbia, MO: Missouri River Press, Inc., 1991), 398.

Chapter 14

1. Isaac N. Shannon, "Sharpshooters in Hood's Army," *Confederate Veteran* 15 (1907): 123–125; Howell and Elizabeth Purdue, *Pat Cleburne: Confederate General* (Tuscaloosa: Portals Press, 1977), 230.

2. James Lee McDonough and Thomas L. Connelly, *Five Tragic Hours: The Battle of Franklin* (Knoxville: University of Tennessee Press, 1983), 92; Joseph Boyce, "Missourians in Battle of Franklin," *Confederate Veteran* 24 (1916): 102.

3. Boyce, "Missourians," 102; Phil Gottschalk, *In Deadly Earnest: The History of the First Missouri Brigade, CSA* (Columbia, MO: Missouri River Press, Inc., 1991), 465.

4. W. A. Washburn, "Cleburne's Division at Franklin," *Confederate Veteran* 13 (1905): 27–28.

5. Henry Stone, "Repelling Hood's Invasion of Tennessee," in *Battles and Leaders of the Civil War,* Vol. 4, eds. Robert U. Johnson and Clarence C. Buel (New York: Castle Books, 1956), 451; McDonough and Connelly, *Five Tragic Hours,* 93, 105.

6. McDonough and Connelly, *Five Tragic Hours,* 109.

7. *War of the Rebellion: A Compilation of the Official Records of the Union and Confederate Armies* (Washington, DC: Government Printing Office, 1880–1901) (hereafter cited as *OR*), Series I, Volume 45, Part I, 270–271.

8. *OR* 45: I, 256; Washburn, "Cleburne's Division," 27–28; McDonough and Connelly, *Five Tragic Hours,* 113, 130; Stone, "Repelling Hood's Invasion," 452.

9. Tillman H. Stevens, "Other Side in Battle of Franklin," *Confederate Veteran* 11 (1903): 165–167; Purdue, *Pat Cleburne,* 252.

10. McDonough and Connelly, *Five Tragic Hours,* 133, 136; *OR* 45: I, 256, 334, 352–354; Washburn, "Cleburne's Division," 27–28.

11. McDonough and Connelly, *Five Tragic Hours,* 136–137, 160.

12. Mauriel Phillips Joslyn, ed., *A Meteor Shining Brightly: Essays on the Life and Career of Major General Patrick R. Cleburne* (Macon, GA: Mercer University Press, 2000), 152.

13. Joslyn, *A Meteor Shining Brightly,* 179; John Berrien Lindsley, *Military Annals of Tennessee: Confederate,* v. 1, (Wilmington, NC: Broadfoot Publishing Co., 1995), 151–152.

14. Purdue, *Pat Cleburne,* 253.

15. Boyce, "Missourians," 102.; Gottschalk, *In Deadly Earnest,* 465.

16. Boyce, "Missourians," 103.

17. Gottschalk, *In Deadly Earnest,* 467–468; Boyce, "Missourians," 102.

18. Boyce, "Missourians," 103.

19. Boyce, "Missourians," 103; Gottschalk, *In Deadly Earnest,* 484.

20. Gottschalk, *In Deadly Earnest,* 468.

21. Gottschalk, *In Deadly Earnest,* 477, 491; *OR* 45: I, 716.

22. Illene D. Thompson and Wilbur E. Thompson, *The 17th Alabama Infantry: A Regimental History and Roster* (Bowie, MD: Heritage Books, Inc., 2001), 108–109.

23. Ed Gleeson, *Rebel Sons of Erin: A Civil War Unit History of the Tenth Tennessee Infantry Regiment (Irish) Confederate States Volunteers* (Indianapolis: Guild Press of Indiana, 1993), 25, 34, 313–314, 338.

24. Gottschalk, *In Deadly Earnest,* 485; McDonough and Connelly, *Five Tragic Hours,* 150; *OR* 45: I, 687–688.

25. Joslyn, *A Meteor Shining Brightly,* 179.

26. Boyce, "Missourians," 103; James McNeilly, "Incidents at the Battle of Franklin," *Confederate Veteran* 26 (1918): 117–118; *OR* 45: I, 241.

27. McDonough and Connelly, *Five Tragic Hours,* 157.

28. Joslyn, *A Meteor Shining Brightly,* 180; Irving A. Buck, *Cleburne and His Command* (Jackson, TN: McCowat-Mercer Press, 1959), 61.

29. Joslyn, *A Meteor Shining Brightly,* 180; Buck, *Cleburne and His Command,* 62.

30. Joslyn, *A Meteor Shining Brightly,* 133.

31. McDonough and Connelly, *Five Tragic Hours,* 167; Boyce, "Missourians," 103.

32. William Milner Kelly, "History of the Thirtieth Alabama Volunteers," *Alabama Historical Quarterly* 9 (1947): 162–163.

33. Kelly, "Thirtieth Alabama," 167.

34. Lillian Henderson, *Roster of the Confederate Soldiers of Georgia, 1861–1865,* Vol. 1 (Hapeville, GA: Longino and Porter), 1959, 115–149, 157–169, 663–671.

35. Frank L. Richardson, "War As I Saw It," *Louisiana Historical Quarterly* 6 (1923): 236.

36. Lindsley, *Military Annals,* 153; Gleeson, *Rebel Sons of Erin,* 324–325.

Chapter 15

1. W. Chris Phelps, *Charlestonians in War: The Charleston Battalion* (Gretna, LA: Pelican, 2004), 48–50, 58–59.

2. *War of the Rebellion: A Compilation of the Official Records of the Union and Confederate Armies* (Washington, DC: Government Printing Office, 1880–1901) (hereafter cited as *OR*), Series I, Volume 14, 90, 97.

3. *OR* 28: I, 373, 406, 417–420, 543–544.

4. *OR* 28: I, 409.

5. *OR* 28: I, 724–727.

6. Edward M. Shoemaker, *Strangers and Citizens: The Irish Immigrant Community of Savannah, 1837–1861,* diss., Emory University, 1990, 180–181, 364; Michael Damon Seigle, *Savannah's Own: The Irish Jasper Greens,*

1842–1865, masters thesis, Armstrong State College, Savannah, 1994, 3–7, 25–26; David Thomas Gleeson, *The Irish in the South, 1815–1877*, diss., Mississippi State University, 1997, 224.

7. Kelly J. O'Grady, *Clear the Confederate Way!: The Irish in the Army of Northern Virginia* (Mason City, IA: Savas Publishing Company, 2000), 233.

8. O'Grady, *Clear the Confederate Way*, 284–285.

9. William Lamb, "The Defense of Fort Fisher," in *Battles and Leaders of the Civil War*, Vol. 4, eds. Robert U. Johnson and Clarence C. Buel (New York: Castle Books, 1956), 642–654.

10. *OR* 46: I, 435–436, 439–440.

11. James Reilly, "Return of Maj. James Reilly's Sword," *Confederate Veteran* 2 (1894): 119.

12. *OR* 46: II, 1187.

Chapter 16

1. Dean DeBolt, "Life on the Front as Reflected in Soldiers' Letters," *Gulf Coast Historical Review* 4 (Spring 1989): 31; *Augusta Daily Constitutionalist* October 15, 1861.

2. *War of the Rebellion: A Compilation of the Official Records of the Union and Confederate Armies* (Washington, DC: Government Printing Office, 1880–1901), Series I, Volume 6, 460–463; *Augusta Daily Constitutionalist* October 15, 1861.

3. Lillian Henderson, *Roster of the Confederate Soldiers of Georgia, 1861–1865*, Vol. 1 (Hapeville, GA: Longino and Porter, 1959), 663–671.

4. Edward Y. McMorries, *History of the 1st Alabama Volunteer Infantry, C. S. A.* (Montgomery: Brown Printing Co., 1904), 21, 25; DeBolt, "Life on the Front," 30.

5. *OR* 10: I, 502–504; Arthur W. Bergeron, *Guide to Louisiana Confederate Military Units* (Baton Rouge: Louisiana State University Press, 1989), 70.

6. Willis Brewer, *Alabama: Her History, Resources, War Record, and Public Men, From 1540 to 1872* (Montgomery, 1872), 589–590.

7. Augusta *Daily Constitutionalist* May 31, 1861; *OR* 30: II, 85–86; Henderson, *Roster*, 663–671.

8. *OR* 35: I, 337.

9. W. H. Andrews, *Footprints of a Regiment: A Recollection of the 1st Georgia Regulars, 1861–1865* (Atlanta: Longstreet Press, 1992), 20; *OR* 35: I, 333, 337.

10. Andrews, *Footprints of a Regiment*, 128; *OR* 35: I, 337.

11. *OR* 35: I, 333.

12. John Kent Folmar, ed., *From That Terrible Field: Civil War Letters of James M. Williams, Twenty-First Alabama Volunteers* (Tuscaloosa: University of Alabama Press, 1981), 26.

13. Brewer, *Alabama*, 650; Folmar, *From That Terrible Field*, 100.

14. Brewer, *Alabama*, 695.

15. Doris Rich, *Fort Morgan and the Battle of Mobile Bay* (Foley, AL: Underwood Printing, Co., 1986), 57.

16. Brewer, *Alabama*, 695; Folmar, *From That Terrible Field*, 179.

17. Christopher C. Andrews, *History of the Campaign of Mobile* (New York, 1867), 136.

18. Andrews, *History of the Campaign of Mobile*, 236–237.

19. Phil Gottschalk, *In Deadly Earnest: The History of the First Missouri Brigade, C. S. A.* (Columbia, MO: Missouri River Press, 1991), 512–513.

20. Phillip Thomas Tucker, "The First Missouri Confederate Brigade's Last Stand at Fort Blakeley on Mobile Bay," *Alabama Review* 52 (1989): 278, 280.

21. Tucker, "Last Stand," 284.

22. Sean Michael O'Brien, *Mobile, 1865: Last Stand of the Confederacy* (Westport, CT: Praeger, 2001), 185–203.

Chapter 17

1. Bruce Catton, *Never Call Retreat* (Garden City, NY: Doubleday & Co., 1965), 204.

2. *War of the Rebellion: A Compilation of the Official Records of the Union and Confederate Armies* (Washington, DC: Government Printing Office, 1880–1901) (hereafter cited as *OR*), Series I, Volume 24, Part II, 417.

3. William Barnaby Faherty, *The St. Louis Irish: An Unmatched Celtic Community* (St. Louis: Missouri Historical Society Press, 2001), 11–12, 53–56.

4. David Thomas Gleeson, *The Irish in the South, 1815–1877*, diss., Mississippi State University, 1997, 272–273, 281.

5. Faherty, *St. Louis Irish*, 71–74.

6. *OR* 38: III, 919; Phillip Thomas Tucker, *The South's Finest: The First Missouri Confederate Brigade from Pea Ridge to Vicksburg* (Shippensburg, PA: White Mane, 1993), 56, 57, 69, 87, 94.

7. Phillip Thomas Tucker, *Westerners in Gray: The Men and Missions of the Elite Fifth Missouri Infantry Regiment* (Jefferson, NC: McFarland & Co., 1995), 21, 27.

8. Tucker, *South's Finest*, 94–95; *OR* 24: I, 575.

9. Tucker, *South's Finest*, 98, 99, 103.

10. *OR* 24: I, 738–742.

11. Pat Griffin Obituary, *Confederate Veteran* 29 (1921): 269; Pat Griffin, "The Famous Tenth Tennessee," *Confederate Veteran* 13 (1905): 553–560.

12. *OR* 24: II, 110–111; Tucker, *Westerners in Gray*, 181, 193.

13. Ulysses S. Grant, "The Vicksburg Campaign," in *Battles and Leaders of the Civil War*. Vol. 3, eds. Robert U. Johnson and Clarence C. Buel (New York: Castle Books, 1956), 510; *OR* 24: II, 112.

14. *OR* 24: I, 275.

15. Tucker, *Westerners in Gray*, 231.

16. *OR* 24: II, 415–416; Tucker, *Westerners in Gray*, 235–238.

17. *OR* 24: II, 441–417; Tucker, *Westerners in Gray*, 250.

Chapter 18

1. David Thomas Gleeson, *The Irish in the South, 1815–1877*, diss., Mississippi State University, 1997, 35, 56; John Brendan Flannery, *The Irish Texans* (San Antonio: University of Texas Institute of Texan Cultures, 1980), 28, 59, 99, 107, 110.

2. Phillip Thomas Tucker, *The Final Fury: Palmito Ranch, the Last Battle of the Civil War* (Mechanicsburg, PA: Stackpole, 2001), 22; *War of the Rebellion: A Compilation of the Official Records of the Union and Confederate Armies* (Washington, DC: Government Printing Office, 1880–1901) (hereafter cited as *OR*), Series I, Volume 9: 515.

3. *OR* 15: 395.

4. *OR* 9: 514, 516–517, 525.

5. Flannery, *Irish Texans*, 99–101.

6. John A. Drummond, "The Battle of Sabine Pass," *Confederate Veteran* 25 (1917): 364–365; *OR* 26: I, 297, 311–312.

7. *OR* 26: I, 304, 312.

8. *OR* 9: 623.

9. *OR* 34: I, 638–639.

10. Richard Taylor, *Destruction and Reconstruction: Personal Experiences of the Late War* (New York: 1879), 162.

11. *OR* 34: I, 618.

12. Alvin M. Josephy, Jr., *The Civil War in the American West* (New York: Alfred A. Knopf, 1991), 208.

13. Ella Lonn, *Foreigners in the Confederacy* (Chapel Hill: University of North Carolina Press, 1940), 500; *OR* 53: 651, 661–662; Tucker, *Final Fury*, 20–22.

14. Tucker, *Final Fury*, 32–33.

15. Tucker, *Final Fury*, 72–75, 151–152, 157–158.

Epilogue

1. Dennis Clark, *Hibernia America: The Irish and Regional Cultures* (Westport, CT: Greenwood, 1986), 105; David Thomas Gleeson, *The Irish in the South,*

1815–1877, diss., Mississippi State University, 1997, 334, 361.

2. Michael Glazier, ed., *The Encyclopedia of the Irish in America* (Notre Dame: University of Notre Dame Press, 1999), 543; Clark, *Hibernia America*, 106; Gleeson, *Irish in the South*, 334.

3. Clark, *Hibernia America*, 106; Glazier, *Encyclopedia of the Irish in America*, 36.

4. Gleeson, *Irish in the South*, 342; Kathleen C. Berkeley, *"Like a Plague of Locusts": From an Antebellum Town to a New South City, Memphis, Tennessee, 1850–1880* (New York: Garland Publishing, Inc., 1991), 124.

5. Glazier, *Encyclopedia of the Irish in America*, 893.

6. Gleeson, *Irish in the South*, 130–131, 340.

7. Glazier. *Encyclopedia of the Irish in America*, 544, 819, 836, 893.

8. John Berrien Lindsley, *Military Annals of Tennessee: Confederate,* Vol. 1 (Wilmington, NC: Broadfoot Publishing Co., 1995), 153.

Works Cited

Alexander, P. W. "Some Florida Heroes." *Confederate Veteran* 11 (1903): 363–365.

Andrews, Christopher C. *History of the Campaign of Mobile*. New York: 1867.

Andrews, W. H. *Footprints of a Regiment: A Recollection of the 1st Georgia Regulars, 1861–1865*. Atlanta: Longstreet, 1992.

Armstrong, James, and Varina D. Brown. "McGowan's Brigade at Spotsylvania." *Confederate Veteran* 33 (1925): 376–379.

Augusta Daily Constitutionalist.

Bergeron, Arthur W. *Guide to Louisiana Confederate Military Units*. Baton Rouge: Louisiana State University Press, 1989.

Berkeley, Kathleen C. *"Like a Plague of Locusts": From an Antebellum Town to a New South City, Memphis, Tennessee, 1850–1880*. New York: Garland, 1991.

Boyce, Joseph. "Missourians in Battle of Franklin." *Confederate Veteran* 24 (1916): 101–104.

Brewer, Willis. *Alabama: Her History, Resources, War Record, and Public Men, from 1540 to 1872*. Montgomery: 1872.

Buck, Irving A. *Cleburne and His Command*. Jackson, TN: McCowat-Mercer, 1959.

Carruth, J. E. "Gallantry of General Rosecrans." *Confederate Veteran* 14 (1906): 514–515.

Castel, Albert. *Decision in the West: The Atlanta Campaign of 1864*. Lawrence, KS: University Press of Kansas, 1992.

Catton, Bruce. *Never Call Retreat*. Garden City, NY: Doubleday, 1965.

Chalker, Fussell. "Irish Catholics in the Building of the Ocmulgee and Flint Railroad." *Georgia Historical Quarterly* 54 (1970): 507–516.

Charleston Daily Courier.

Charleston Mercury.

Christ, Mark K., ed. *Getting Used to Being Shot At: The Spence Family Civil War Letters*. Fayetteville: University of Arkansas Press, 2002.

Clark, Dennis. *Hibernia America: The Irish and Regional Cultures*. Westport, CT: Greenwood, 1986.

Cockrell, Thomas D., and Michael B. Ballard, eds. *A Mississippi Rebel in the Army of Northern Virginia: The Civil War Memoirs of Private David Holt*. Baton Rouge: Louisiana State University Press, 1995.

Conyngham, David P. *The Irish Brigade and Its Campaigns*. New York: Fordham University Press, 1994.

Cozzens, Peter. *This Terrible Sound: The Battle of Chickamauga*. Chicago: University of Illinois Press, 1992.

Daniel, John W. "A Charge at First Manassas." *Confederate Veteran* 39 (1931): 345, 358.

Daniel, Larry J. *Shiloh: The Battle That Changed the Civil War*. New York: Simon & Schuster, 1997.

_____. *Soldiering in the Army of Tennessee: A Portrait of Life in a Confederate Army*. Chapel Hill: University of North Carolina Press, 1991.

Danner, Albert C. "Father Bannon's Secret Mission." *Confederate Veteran* 27 (1919): 180–181.

DeBolt, Dean. "Life on the Front as Reflected in Soldiers' Letters." *Gulf Coast Historical Review* 4 (Spring 1989): 26–37.

Drummond, John A. "The Battle of Sabine Pass." *Confederate Veteran* 25 (1917): 364–365.

Durham, Roger S., ed. *The Blues in Gray: The Civil War Journal of William Daniel Dixon and the Republican Blues Daybook*. Knoxville: University of Tennessee Press, 2000.

Durkin, Joseph T., ed. *Confederate Chaplain: A War Journal of Rev. James B. Sheeran, C. SS. R., 14th Louisiana, C. S. A*. Milwaukee: Bruce, 1960.

_____. *John Dooley Confederate Soldier: His War Journal*. Washington, D.C.: Georgetown University Press, 1945.

Evans, Robert G., ed. *The Sixteenth Mississippi*

Infantry: Civil War Letters and Reminiscences. Jackson: University Press of Mississippi, 2002.

Faherty, William Barnaby. *The St. Louis Irish: An Unmatched Celtic Community.* St. Louis: Missouri Historical Society Press, 2001.

"Fine Marksman in Virginia Army." *Confederate Veteran* 24 (1916): 285.

Flannery, John Brendan. *The Irish Texans.* San Antonio: University of Texas Institute of Texan Cultures, 1980.

Folmar, John Kent, ed. *From That Terrible Field: Civil War Letters of James M. Williams, Twenty-First Alabama Volunteers.* Tuscaloosa: University of Alabama Press, 1981.

Foote, Shelby. *The Civil War: A Narrative: Fredericksburg to Meridian.* New York: Random House, 1986.

Fraser, Letitia Austin. Obituary. *Confederate Veteran* 32 (1924): 75.

Gaskell, J. E. "Last Engagement of Lee's Army." *Confederate Veteran* 29 (1921): 261–262.

Glazier, Michael, ed. *The Encyclopedia of the Irish in America.* Notre Dame: University of Notre Dame Press, 1999.

Gleeson, David Thomas. *The Irish in the South, 1815–1877.* Ph.D. diss., Mississippi State University, 1997.

_____. *The Mississippi Irish, 1700–1865.* M.A. thesis, Mississippi State University, 1993.

Gleeson, Ed. *Rebel Sons of Erin: A Civil War Unit History of the Tenth Tennessee Infantry Regiment (Irish) Confederate States Volunteers.* Indianapolis: Guild Press of Indiana, 1993.

Gordon, John B. *Reminiscences of the Civil War.* New York: Scribners, 1903.

Gottschalk, Phil. *In Deadly Earnest: The History of the First Missouri Brigade, C. S. A.* Columbia, MO: Missouri River Press, 1991.

Griffin, James David. *Savannah, Georgia, During the Civil War.* Ph.D. diss., University of Georgia, 1963.

Griffin, Pat. "The Famous Tenth Tennessee." *Confederate Veteran* 13 (1905): 553–560.

_____. Obituary. *Confederate Veteran* 29 (1921): 269.

Harley, Stan C. "Gen. Pat Cleburne's Division of Sharpshooters." *Confederate Veteran* 7 (1899): 307.

Henderson, Lillian. *Roster of the Confederate Soldiers of Georgia, 1861–1865.* Vol. 1. Hapeville, GA: Longino and Porter, 1959.

Herbert, Hilary A. "History of the Eighth Alabama Volunteer Regiment, C. S. A." *Alabama Historical Quarterly* 39 (1977).

Hernon, Joseph M., Jr. "The Irish Nationalists and Southern Secession." *Civil War History* 12 (1966): 43–53.

Hill, Mary S. Obituary. *Confederate Veteran* 10 (1902): 124.

James, D. Clayton. *Antebellum Natchez.* Baton Rouge: Louisiana State University Press, 1988.

Johnson, Robert U., and Clarence C. Buel, eds. *Battles and Leaders of the Civil War.* 4 vols. New York: Castle Books, 1956.

Jones, Terry L. *Lee's Tigers: The Louisiana Infantry in the Army of Northern Virginia.* Baton Rouge: Louisiana State University Press, 1987.

Josephy, Alvin M., Jr. *The Civil War in the American West.* New York: Alfred A. Knopf, 1991.

Joslyn, Mauriel Phillips, ed. *A Meteor Shining Brightly: Essays on the Life and Career of Major General Patrick R. Cleburne.* Macon, GA: Mercer University Press, 2000.

Kelly, William Milner. "A History of the Thirtieth Alabama Volunteers." *Alabama Historical Quarterly* 9 (1947): 115–167.

Kleber, John E., ed. *The Encyclopedia of Louisville.* Lexington: University Press of Kentucky, 2001.

Lightsey, Ada Christine. *The Veteran's Story: The Story of the Jasper Grays, 16th Mississippi Regiment.* Meridian, MS: 1899.

Lindsley, John Berrien. *Military Annals of Tennessee: Confederate.* 2 vols. Wilmington, NC: Broadfoot, 1995.

Lindsley, Sarah McGavock. Obituary. *Confederate Veteran* 11 (1903): 368.

Lonn, Ella. *Foreigners in the Confederacy.* Chapel Hill: University of North Carolina Press, 1940.

McCabe, Bernard. Obituary. *Confederate Veteran* 15 (1907): 422.

McCaffrey, Lawrence J. *The Irish Catholic Diaspora in America.* Washington, DC: Catholic University of America Press, 1997.

McCrady, Edward. "The Boy Heroes of Cold Harbor." *Southern Historical Society Papers* 25 (1897): 234–239.

McDonough, James Lee. *Chattanooga: A Death Grip on the Confederacy.* Knoxville: University of Tennessee Press, 1984.

_____. *Stones River: Bloody Winter in Tennessee.* Knoxville: University of Tennessee Press, 1980.

_____, and Thomas L. Connelly. *Five Tragic Hours: The Battle of Franklin.* Knoxville: University of Tennessee Press, 1983.

McGowan, James J. Obituary. *Confederate Veteran* 9 (1901): 126.

McGrath, John. "In a Louisiana Regiment." *Southern Historical Society Papers* 31 (1903): 103–120.

McMorries, Edward Y. *History of the 1st Alabama Volunteer Infantry, C. S. A.* Montgomery: Brown Printing, 1904.

McNeilly, James. "Incidents at the Battle of Franklin." *Confederate Veteran* 26 (1918): 117–118.

McWhiney, Grady. *Braxton Bragg and Confederate Defeat.* Vol. 1. Tuscaloosa: University of Alabama Press, 1991.

Montgomery Daily Post.

Montgomery Greys Retired Corps. *The Mont-*

gomery Greys Under Two Flags. Montgomery: The Corps, 1908.

Niehaus, Earl F. *The Irish in New Orleans, 1800–1860*. Baton Rouge: Louisiana State University Press, 1965.

Noe, Kenneth W. *Perryville: This Grand Havoc of Battle*. Lexington: University Press of Kentucky, 2001.

O'Brien, Sean Michael. *Mobile, 1865: Last Stand of the Confederacy*. Westport, CT: Praeger, 2001.

O'Grady, Kelly J. *Clear the Confederate Way!: The Irish in the Army of Northern Virginia*. Mason City, IA: Savas, 2000.

O'Hara, Theodore. Obituary. *Confederate Veteran* 7 (1899): 202.

O'Neill, Edmund. Letter, *Confederate Veteran 5 (1897)*: 420.

"Paroles of the Army of Northern Virginia." *Southern Historical Society Papers* 15 (1887).

Phelps, W. Chris. *Charlestonians in War: The Charleston Battalion*. Gretna, LA: Pelican, 2004.

Purdue, Howell, and Elizabeth Purdue. *Pat Cleburne: Confederate General*. Tuscaloosa, AL: Portals, 1977.

Reilly, James. "Return of Maj. James Reilly's Sword." *Confederate Veteran* 2 (1894): 119.

Rich, Doris. *Fort Morgan and the Battle of Mobile Bay*. Foley, AL: Underwood Printing, 1986.

Richardson, Frank L. "War As I Saw It 1861–1865." *Louisiana Historical Quarterly* 6 (1923): 86–106.

Robertson, James I., Jr. *The Stonewall Brigade*. Baton Rouge: Louisiana State University Press, 1963.

Rowland, Dunbar. *Military History of Mississippi, 1803–1898*. Spartanburg, SC: Reprint Company Publishers, 1978.

Schreckengost, Gary. "Confederate Zouaves at First Manassas." *America's Civil War* May 1999: 26+.

Sears, Stephen W. *Landscape Turned Red: The Battle of Antietam*. New York: Ticknor and Fields, 1983.

Seigle, Michael Damon. *Savannah's Own: The Irish Jasper Greens, 1842–1865*. M.A. thesis, Armstrong State College, Savannah, 1994.

Shannon, Isaac N. "Sharpshooters in Hood's Army." *Confederate Veteran* 15 (1907): 123–125.

Shoemaker, Edward M. *Strangers and Citizens: The Irish Immigrant Community of Savannah, 1837–1861*. Ph.S. diss., Emory University, 1990.

Stevens, Tillman H. "Other Side in Battle of Franklin." *Confederate Veteran* 11 (1903): 165–167.

Taylor, Richard. *Destruction and Reconstruction: Personal Experiences of the Late War*. New York, 1879.

Thompson, Illene D., and Wilbur E. Thompson. *The Seventeenth Alabama Infantry: A Regimental History and Roster*. Bowie, MD: Heritage, 2001.

Trudeau, Noah Andre. *The Last Citadel: Petersburg, Virginia, June 1864–April 1865*. Boston: Little, Brown, 1991.

Tucker, Phillip Thomas. *The Final Fury: Palmito Ranch, the Last Battle of the Civil War*. Mechanicsburg, PA: Stackpole, 2001.

_____. "The First Missouri Confederate Brigade's Last Stand at Fort Blakeley on Mobile Bay." *Alabama Review* 52 (1989): 270–291.

_____. *The South's Finest: The First Missouri Confederate Brigade from Pea Ridge to Vicksburg*. Shippensburg, PA: White Mane, 1993.

_____. *Westerners in Gray: The Men and Missions of the Elite Fifth Missouri Infantry Regiment*. Jefferson, NC: McFarland, 1995.

Wallace, Lee A. *1st Virginia Infantry*. Lynchburg, VA: H. E. Howard, 1985.

Walshe, Blayney T. "Louisianians in the Virginia Army." *Confederate Veteran* 6 (1898): 177.

War of the Rebellion: A Compilation of the Official Records of the Union and Confederate Armies. Washington, DC: Government Printing Office, 1880–1901.

Washburn, W. A. "Cleburne's Division at Franklin." *Confederate Veteran* 13 (1905): 27–28.

Watkins, Sam. "Snowball Battle at Dalton." *Confederate Veteran* 2 (1894): 204–205.

Weaver, Herbert. "Foreigners in Ante-Bellum Savannah." *Georgia Historical Quarterly* 37 (1953): 1–17.

Wert, Jeffry D. A *Brotherhood of Valor: The Common Soldiers of the Stonewall Brigade, C. S. A., and the Iron Brigade, U. S. A*. New York: Simon and Schuster, 1999.

Wheeler, J. A. "Cleburne's Brigade at Shiloh." *Confederate Veteran* 2 (1894): 13.

Wight, Willard E. "Letters of the Bishop of Savannah, 1861–1865." *Georgia Historical Quarterly* 42 (1958): 93–106.

Wiley, Bell Irvin. *The Life of Johnny Reb: The Common Soldier of the Confederacy*. New York: Bobbs-Merrill, 1943.

Williams, G. A. "Blow Your Horn, Jake." *Confederate Veteran* 5 (1897): 220.

Williams, L. G. "Hand to Hand Fight in the Army." *Confederate Veteran* 2 (1894): 228–229.

Yater, George E. *Two Hundred Years at the Falls of the Ohio: A History of Louisville and Jefferson County*. Louisville: Filson Club, 1987.

Index

Numbers in *bold italics* indicate photographs or illustrations.

251